The Limerick Compendium

The Editor and Publishers wish to acknowledge the
generous financial assistance of Mr Joseph O'Donoghue,
without whom this Compendium could not have been
published in its present form.

Publishers' Note

Jim Kemmy died as this book was about to go to press.
He had been ill but his death was not expected.
He will be mourned by all who knew him.
He was an exceptional man. Even rarer than that,
he was a truly good man.

THE LIMERICK COMPENDIUM

Edited by Jim Kemmy

Gill & Macmillan

Gill & Macmillan Ltd
Goldenbridge
Dublin 8
with associated companies throughout the world
© Introduction and selection, Jim Kemmy 1997
Copyright in the stories and poems is that of the individual authors and publishers
0 7171 2673 0
Design by Graham Thew Design
Print origination by Carrigboy Typesetting Services
Printed by ColourBooks Ltd, Dublin

This book is typeset in Goudy 10/12 point

A catalogue record for this book is available from the British Library.

5 4 3 2 1

Contents

Six: Sport

Seven: History

Eight: The Stage

Nine: The City

Preface

Literature in Limerick has a long history. The writings of its Gaelic poets, before and after the seventeenth-century sieges, have been well documented. But it is not generally known that one of its earliest known histories was written in verse more than 300 years ago. In a rare undertaking, embracing literature and history, an unknown versifier wrote a chronological account of Limerick's past in rhyming couplets. This work became known as the Davis Manuscript. We know little about the work and its author. The manuscript came into the possession of a Robert Davis and has never been printed in its entirety. The work chronicles a series of important local events and some of the people involved. An early extract tells of the laying of the foundation of the Tholsel (City Hall) in 1449 and how the building was later converted into a jail where prisoners being denied bail were kept.

> This year the foundation of the Tholsel's laid,
> Where justice in those days was well displayed;
> The use diverted, now 'tis the common jail,
> Where men do lie, not wanting crimes — but bail.

On 18 February 1667 a violent storm broke and a spring tide, which did not ebb for fourteen hours, rose to the level of the Courthouse in Quay Lane, forced up one of the arches of Baal's Bridge, overflowed shops and houses, carried away buildings and quantities of corn, levelled the banks of the river and wrecked several ships. The sequel to this freak flood was thus noted in what Maurice Lenihan airily called 'the homely doggerel' of the manuscript:

> A drought excessive came, it was so great,
> The Shannon from the city did retreat;
> The Mayor and many more upon dry ground,
> Outside the walls, on foot, did walk around.

We owe a debt of gratitude to the unknown seventeenth-century versifier who wrote this history. The simple but lively lines have not only preserved a series of events and dates which would otherwise have perished from memory, but they also contain a variety of critical, humorous and favourable comments on these happenings.

Limerick's printers did not emerge until the second half of the seventeenth century. An entry in the Limerick Corporation Book for the year 1680 reads as follows: 'Samuel Terry certified by Mr Reid to have been his apprentice for seven years, and had well and truly served his time, admitted to the freedom of this city.' This is the earliest documented record of a printer having served his apprenticeship in the city.

The entry also shows that Mr Reid, the master printer, must have been in business in Limerick from at least 1673. Samuel Terry went on to become a fully fledged printer in his own right, and printed a number of books at his premises on Baal's Bridge. During the Williamite campaign in Ireland, a perambulating press was in operation and many proclamations and bulletins were issued. This press was used in Limerick, during the siege of 1690, for the printing of the translation of a Latin poem by an Irish Capuchin priest.

The eighteenth century saw the flowering of many more printers in Limerick, including Andrew Welsh, John Ferrar, John Cherry, Andrew Watson and William Goggin. Many hundreds of books bearing the Limerick imprint were published in the city in this period. County Limerick had two paper mills, at Annacotty and Ballyclough, in the same century. Joseph Sexton opened his first mill in 1749 and, in the same year, *Biggs's Military History of Europe* was printed in Limerick on paper 'made by Joseph Sexton'. Many more paper works operated in the city and county in the following century. *The Limerick Chronicle* was founded in 1766 and is the oldest surviving newspaper in the Irish Republic. Further Limerick printers emerged in the nineteenth century. The firm of McKern, founded in 1807, is the city's oldest operating printing company. In 1811, McKern's published the book, *An Account of the Siege of Limerick, from the landing of King William*.

Thus over the centuries, poets, historians, novelists and journalists have written about Limerick and its people. Many of their publications have, of course, been published outside the city, mainly in Dublin, London and New York. Given this rich store of literature, the publication of a comprehensive anthology of Limerick writing was long overdue. Indeed, every centre of population should have an updated literary collection in each generation. The work of compiling such a collection provides an opportunity to collect the best of out-of-print and not easily available literature, the bulk of which is not worth reprinting.

When it comes to the selection of this material Michael Hartnett has provided some useful guidelines and cautionary advice for the unwary:

> The making of an anthology is an important, laborious and thankless task. The editor can approach it in many ways: the historical line can be followed, regardless of quality; a personal — and therefore eccentric — choice can be made; affection for friends (and friends' friends) can overawe the judgment; and the geographical limits implied in its title can be treated with some flexibility. The editor must consider the work of the old, however decrepit, and of the young, however undisciplined, and the question of exclusion sometimes comes to be more worrying than that of inclusion: the luminary of today may be the footnote of tomorrow and vice versa.

The poet and critic W.H. Auden has also written on the inevitable conflicts between taste and personal judgment.

The anthologist must first of all do his homework and read and reread. . . . Secondly he must recognise the difference between taste and his judgment and be loyal to both. . . . In matters of artistic taste and judgment, we are all the children of our age, but we should not and need not be its slaves. Each of us must be loyal to his own taste, though always ready to enlarge it; for this very reason, we must rid ourselves of all prejudices, for a prejudice is always created by our social milieu without our conscious consent and frequently blinds us to what our real tastes are.

In compiling this work I hope I have managed to steer clear of some, at least, of these pitfalls and that I have done literary justice to my native place.

Last year, Frank McCourt's *Angela's Ashes* burst on the literary firmament like a bombshell. The memoir of the writer's Limerick childhood received immediate critical acclaim and quickly became an international bestseller, putting Limerick on the map of world literature. I am fortunate to have been able to include two extracts from the Pulitzer Prize-winning book in this collection.

Jim Kemmy
August 1997

Acknowledgments

I wish to thank the following people who have assisted me in compiling this anthology: Tony Bromell, Peadar Cremin, John Curtin, Tom Donovan, Desmond FitzGerald, Knight of Glin, Patsy Kelly, Paddy McGarvey, Tadhg Moloney, Ann Mulqueen, Joe Neiland, Ronan O'Brien, Margaret O'Donoghue, Mary O'Mara and Sean Spellissy, Stephen O'Shea, Fergus Quinlivan, Mainchín Seoighe and Chick Donohoe (New York).

I also wish to express my gratitude to Gerard Lyne and Eugene Hogan, the National Library of Ireland, Dolores Doyle, Brendan Martin, Eileen McMahon, Deirdre O'Dea, Ann Culhane and all the other members of the staff of Limerick City Library, Tony Storan and other members of the staff of Limerick County Library, Larry Walsh, Curator, Limerick City Museum, and Kay McGuinness, Chairperson, Limerick 800 Committee, and Bob Kelly, Limerick Civic Trust, for their generous responses to all my requests for information.

The Shannon
(Translation Brendan Kennelly)

Shannon,
How you smile at me
As you still your voice
Westwards towards the sea.

Brooding from Sliabh Iarann,
God's fluent work,
You speed through Lough Ree
And Lough Derg.

Over Doonass Rapids
You can't be held in check
Yet you have learned to linger
Gracing west from Limerick.

Strong at our borders
You move
Past all our dwellings
Like a vigorous legend of love.

The Boyne is noble, and the Laune,
And the Suca, but the good books
That are as old as rivers
Say
That you, O Shannon,
Are nobler than they.

From *Ireland of the Welcomes*, Vol. 40, No. 3, May–June 1991

ONE

RELIGION

The Franciscans
J.F. O'Donnell

Here we have not a suitable opportunity to dwell upon the courage, constancy and activity of the Franciscans, under the most disheartening circumstances, in ministering to the Irish people the blessings of religion, the consolations of piety, and the example of humility, self-sacrifice, and final perseverance. . . .

It only remains to be added that they possess, at present, thirteen houses among us. Some of these are romantically situated under the ivied shade of the edifices reared by their predecessors in the olden times. Wherever they exist their benefit is experienced, especially where wanted most, among the humbler classes, exposed to the double misfortune of ignorance and temptation. The spirit of St Francis in its pristine lustre still survives in the humble brotherhood, his virtues still manifest themselves in theirs; and so, as the Church ever wills it, she manifests her holiness in that of the saint and his faithful representatives. . . .

When a lad, it afforded me an ever fresh, if subdued, delight, to wander through the roofless and deserted cloisters of the Franciscan convents and oratories, whose venerable remains stud the broad fields, and cast their shadows over the legend-haunted rivers of Munster. With their story, at the time, I was but vaguely and remotely acquainted, but I at least knew that those ruins were the monuments of an Order which had rendered Ireland noble and abiding service in evil and calamitous days. Years, and perhaps distance, served only to deepen the impressions which I experienced whilst meditating amid the desolate beauty of Adare, or finding some reliable traces of the great Franciscan house which, according to local tradition, once dominated the Limerick flank of Thomond-bridge. Later on, the Rev. C.P. Meehan's scholarly and delightful book, *The Franciscan Monasteries*, came upon me like a revelation, and lighted up those grey chancels and slender arcades, not only with the cold illumination of fact, but with the warmer light of pathos and imagination as well.

From the *Introduction to Memories of the Irish Franciscans*, James Duffy, 1871

The Reformation
Mainchín Seoighe

In the last days before the Reformation the general decadence that was so evident in the Church all over Europe found many parallels in Ireland. Abuses were numerous amongst clergy and laity.

The Reformation Parliament (1529–1536) had given the Reformation the sanction of law in England; it was the Dublin Parliament (1536–37) that gave it legal sanction in Ireland. Both parliaments passed the Act of Supremacy recognising Henry VIII as head of the Church in his domains. John Quin, a former Dominican friar of Kilmallock, had been appointed Bishop of Limerick in 1524. Shortly afterwards he took unto himself a concubine, an action that surely indicates the laxity then obtaining within the Church, and the need for genuine reform. Dr Quin was still Bishop of Limerick when Henry VIII broke with Rome.

In 1538, the Viceroy, Lord Grey, visited Limerick, summoned the Mayor and Corporation, and had them sworn according to the Act of Supremacy to renounce the 'usurped authority' of the Pope. It is unlikely that they realised the full impact of what they swore. Bishop Quin was then sent for, and he, too, took the Oath of Supremacy. That done, he was ordered to call his clergy together and administer the Oath to them. A number of parishes in the diocese were without pastors, and King Henry, in his new role as head of the Church, made the appointments required to fill the vacancies — Thady O Mulrian, canon of Emly, to the rectorship of Croom; William Casey (future Protestant Bishop) to the vicarage of St Nicholas, Adare; William Kelly to the vicarage of St Munchins; and Thady Boe to the rectorship of Effin. Despite the fact, however, that Bishop Quin had taken the Oath of Supremacy and rejected the authority of the Pope, there was little change in the external rites of religion in his diocese; Mass was still celebrated in the churches, and the sacraments administered. Many people in the city still gave their allegiance to the King, but were not prepared to change their religion.

Henry VIII died in 1547, and Edward VI came to the throne. He introduced far greater and more fundamental changes than Henry had done, abolishing the Mass, and having parliament pass a law denying the Real Presence in the Blessed Eucharist. St Leger, the Lord-Deputy, was given the task of introducing these radical changes in Ireland. He had copies of the *Book of Common Prayer* sent to Limerick city, but these Bishop Quin — whom St Leger described as old and blind — objected to. Shortly afterwards the Bishop was pressurised into resigning the bishopric, and the King appointed William Casey as his successor. Canon Begley (*Diocese of Limerick*, Vol. 2, p. 165) says of Bishop Casey: 'During his short term of office many clergymen were appointed to benefices, who were not only schismatic but heretical.' He banned the use of the crucifix, which Bishop Quin had tolerated, and ordered the parish clergy to rebuild the chancels of their churches to facilitate the requirements of the new service which had replaced the Mass. Despite all this, the Reformation made very little real progress in Limerick.

From *The Pope in Limerick*, edited by Rev. John Fleming, Diocesan Offices, Limerick, 1980

Persecuting the Quakers
A Letter From Thomas Herbert

To Colonel Ingoldsby

Sir, — The Council being credibly informed that there are at present in the city of Limerick divers persons, commonly called Quakers, who have repaired thither out of England and other places, making it their practice to wander up and down, seducing divers honest people, neglecting and impoverishing their families, troubling the public peace of the nation, disturbing the congregations of sober Christians in the worship of God, and with railing accusations aspersing and discouraging divers of the godly ministers of the gospel in their faithful labours, and thereby bringing into contempt the ordinances of God, and encouraging evil-minded persons to looseness and profaneness: — Out of a due sense whereof, their Lordships have commanded me to signify unto you their dislike of such pernicious practices, and that they do (from good grounds) apprehend, that persons committing such misdemeanours do (under colour of such their wild carriage and proceedings) advance some designs which may be of dangerous consequence to the public good and safety, if not seasonably looked into and prevented; and do, therefore, desire you to inquire into the truth thereof, and to take speedy and effectual course that such persons as are come thither upon that account be excluded the garrison, and not permitted to return or reside there. And if any of the inhabitants profess themselves such, and shall at any time disturb the congregations when assembled for the service and worship of God, or otherwise break the public peace, you are then to secure such persons, and take care they be proceeded with according to due course of law in such cases provided, having due regard to preserve (by all good ways and means) the good government of that place, and timely to discountenance and suppress all disorders.

From *Limerick; Its History and Antiquities, Ecclesiastical, Civil and Military, from the Earliest Ages,* by Maurice Lenihan, Hodges, Smith and Co., 1866

The Curse of Saint Munchin
Michael Hogan

The workmen employed in the building of the ancient church of Saint Munchin were one day striving to raise a very heavy block of stone to a certain part of the work. The saint who, at that time, was standing by, called on some of the citizens to help the men to put the stone in its desired position. These, having refused to lend their aid, the saint appealed to some strangers who were passing, who readily lent their assistance, whereupon St Munchin fervently thanked them and prayed that the strangers may always prosper in Limerick and the natives be unfortunate and unsuccessful. This story has been well confirmed from time to time by the fact of affairs turning out as the saint devoutly wished. (Michael Hogan, *The Story of Shawn-a-Scoob*, 1886)

When Saint Munchin was building his church —
Sure he was the first that began one —
With its steeple, and windows, and porch,
Looking down on the waves of the Shannon.
The good saint in temper was rank,
Such a stock of devotion he'd got in;
But he kept no account at the bank,
So his workmen were working for nothing;
Sure 'twas well to get something to do.

Yet he kept a few masons on hire —
They were not free masons I'll warrant,
But true ones, who'd toss up a spire,
Or fling a bridge over a torrent.
In those times good builders were few,
By reason their guild was diminished;
Because they had nothing to do,
For all the round towers were just finished,
And mortar and stones were damn scarce.

There was a large quoin stone one day,
To be rolled to the top of the building;
And the saint always took his own way
With his stonework, and painting, and gilding;
So he called on his neighbours to come,
And give help where 'twas instantly needed;
But they all stared as if they were dumb,
And his call or his cry was not heeded,
For they were too lazy to hear him.

'Oh, ye worthless and weak herd of rogues!'
Roared the saint, in a wild fit of passion;
'Ye are graceless and lazy *caubogues* —
May ye never leave off ye're bad fashion!
And I solemnly pray!' says the saint,
With his hands and eyes raised in aversion;
'May ye're trade, like an ould woman, faint,

And ye're commerce become an abortion,
To smother ye all with *meyah*!

May ye always want something to wear,
And always want something to buy it;
And always have nothing to share,
And always have ways to supply it!
And may every pound of ye're bread
Have the flavour of sawdust and clinkers;
While ye gang, like poor gipsies, to bed,
And get up in the morning, like tinkers,
With fleas dancing round ye, like goats.

And the devil will send ye a pest,
In shape of a Chief Corporation;
Who from striking big rates will not rest,
Till they murdher ye dead with taxation.
No other good works will they do,
But robbery, ruction, and jobbery;
Pandemonium can't show such a crew
For base, brutal bombast and snobbery,
To damn ye're unfortunate town.

And ye'll feast on each other's bad luck,
With the sweetest of sweet animosity,
And ye'll never be out of the muck
Of poverty, pride and pomposity.
And ye'll love one another, like sharks,
When they meet in the depths of the ocean;
While ye act to ye're neighbours, like Turks,
In the beautiful garb of devotion,
Ye sly, creeping, low-cowering clods!

And ye're harbours shall lose their big ships,
Till ye're state shall be laughed at, for pity.
And the beer that ye'll raise to your lips,
Shall be brewed far away from your city.
For your breweries, and marts, and trade-halls,
Will run dry, like an ould, empty puncheon;
When ye look at their bare, shivering walls,
Ye'll remember the curse of Saint Munchin,
While ye flock to the poorhouse, like crows.

And the poorhouse will clench ye're amounts
Of felicity, to the last fraction;
Where ye'll swallow the shortest accounts,
By the science of double subtraction.
Troth, 'tis there ye will get the right taste
Of sublime Christian civilisation;
And, if ye don't die in great haste,
Ye'll get a foredose of salvation —
Black docks and the devil to eat!'

He was just in the heat of his curse,
When some Danes and Norwegians were passing;
He hailed them for better or worse,
And to each one he pumped a good glass in.
He asked them to help up the stone;
And he found them obliging, good people;
For they never would let it alone,
Till they tumbled it up on the steeple,
And would roll it up to the clouds.

Saint Munchin was pleased with the job,
And he laughed with devout satisfaction;
Then he gave every stranger a bob
Along with his best benediction.
'May the strangers henceforward!' he cried,
'In Limerick fast prosper and flourish;
While, like the bad froth of the tide,
The natives will dwindle and perish,
With plenty of nothing to do!'

Thus, from that day to this, 'tis well known
How strangers in Limerick are thriving;
While the natives all backward are thrown,
Or headlong to ruin are driving!
Och, troth, 'twas a very droll stone,
To cause them so bitter a luncheon;
Filched, fleeced, starved, and stripped to the bone,
By the course of the blessed Saint Munchin;
And 'tis every day growing worse.

But he hadn't all things his own way,
For, in spite of his good, holy doings,
The Danes came from Denmark, one day,

And they tumbled his church into ruins;
And Brian Boru leathered their race,
For molesting such fine, pious people;
Then the Protestants took the saint's place,
And soon built up another big steeple;
But devil a curse did they give.

From *The Old Limerick Journal*, No. 2, March 1980

A Bloody Mission
M. Collet

It was at the solicitation of Innocent X that St Vincent sent missionaries into Ireland. As the circumstances of the times rendered this succour more necessary than ever, the saint, without delay, sent eight of his priests, some of whom, on their arrival, laboured in the diocese of Limerick, the others in that of Cashel. The people of the country, who pined in ignorance, were made acquainted with the obligations which Christianity imposes upon its professors. They were invested with that spirit of strength which breaks the chains of sin, and teaches us to die for the faith in the time of persecution. The change of heart was so general and so sudden, that the bishops of Ireland could scarcely believe it. The nuncio whom the Pope had still in that kingdom, congratulated those truly apostolical men on their zeal. The parish priests and other ecclesiastics, who were always the first to follow the exercises of the missionaries, seized so well their manner of catechising and instructing, that they preserved in their parishes the fervour of which those worthy priests had laid the foundation. Never was fervour more necessary both for pastors and people. Oliver Cromwell, after having planned and executed the impious scheme which brought the King of England to the block, taught Ireland, which had proclaimed the Prince of Wales under the name of James II, that his will was not to be opposed with impunity. Although the Catholics were not the only ones who detested the enormous crime of Cromwell, they had a greater share than any other persons in the misfortunes of the royalists. But there was not a single one of the pastors where the mission had been made, who abandoned his flock. All without exception remained, until banishment or a violent death separated them. It is known that one of the most fervent of those worthy pastors, after having made his annual confession to a missionary who was lodged in a poor hut at the foot of a mountain, was the night afterwards taken and massacred by heretical soldiers, whilst administering the sacraments to the sick. His glorious death crowned a most innocent life. For a long time he had desired to shed his blood for the faith and for charity; God thought him worthy of it, and his prayers were heard.

As the flames of persecution spread more and more throughout Hibernia, and it was no longer possible to make missions there, Vincent of Paul, who was informed of it, gave orders to five of his priests to recross the sea; and to the other three, to remain at Limerick. The Bishop proposed to them to make a mission in that city. The undertaking was pretty considerable. Limerick had then 20,000 communicants, because a number of Catholic villagers had taken refuge in it. But of what are not three priests capable, when, assembled in the name of the Lord, they can calculate upon his being in the midst of them? Sustained by his grace, and encouraged by the prelate who placed himself at their head, these gentlemen announced judgment and mercy. The spirit of dread and compunction was at first insinuated amongst the people. Each one thought seriously of his conscience; and of 20,000 persons capable of profiting by the mission, not one failed to make a general confession. People who had grown old in sin, gave marks of true conversion; and a numerous people was seen in a situation to serve as a model of the most exact penance.

Such holy dispositions could not have been manifested at a more proper time. Contagion soon reached Limerick; and in a little time it was so violent, that it carried off nearly 8,000 persons. Of this number was the brother of the Bishop, who had exposed himself with the missionaries, and like them, in consoling the sick and supplying their necessities. It was admirable to behold the patience, or rather the peace with which this afflicted people received the scourge with which God visited them. They died contented, 'because,' said they, 'the Lord has sent us angels who have reconciled us to him'. The pious Bishop of Limerick, who, as a good father, knew better than any one else how to appreciate such holy dispositions, could not contain his tears. 'Alas!' said he a hundred times, 'had Mr Vincent done for the glory of God only the good which he has done for these poor people, he ought to think himself happy.'

To the horrors of the contagion succeeded those of war. Ireton, the son-in-law of Cromwell, besieged Limerick, and at the end of four or five months became master of it. The army of the parliamentarians, inflated with their success which, however, it owed to famine, naturally stained its victory: it made it a point of religion to do so. Many of the inhabitants were put to death, precisely because they preferred the ancient faith of the Roman Church to the new faith of the English tyrant. Four of the principal citizens were of this number, at whose head was Thomas Strich, an alderman of the city. These brave men went to the place of execution, like warriors to a triumph. Before execution, they harangued the people according to the custom of the country; but they did it in so moving a manner, that the heretics themselves were melted to tears. They declared in the face of heaven and earth, that they died for the faith; and by that glorious acknowledgment they taught the Catholics who were present, that there was no death or torment that should separate them from the religion of their fathers.

Of the three missionaries who had remained in Ireland, only two returned to Paris, after having passed, at Limerick, through all the terrors of pestilence and war.

The third finished his career there; the others disguised themselves and escaped as they could. One of them retired to his own country with the grand vicar of Cashel. The other found in the mountains a pious woman who concealed him for two months. A brother who waited on them was less fortunate, or rather more so. The heretics, having discovered his retreat, massacred him under the eyes of his mother. They broke his head, after having cut off his feet and hands, an inhuman and barbarous treatment, which taught the priests what they would have to expect, should they be seized.

These missionaries laboured in Ireland nearly six years; and with the exception of some help given them by the Duchess of Aiguillon, it was the house of St Lazarus, which, through the inexhaustible charity of its superior, supported the rest of the expense. Vincent, although reduced to extremity, did not regret it. More than 80,000 general confessions, and other innumerable advantages, were ample indemnification for him. We should have been acquainted with much more, had his humility permitted it.

From *Life of St Vincent of Paul, Founder of the Congregation of the Mission and of the Sisters of Charity*, James Duffy, 1846

Fr O'Grady Finds a Lodging-House
John Harley

The priest of our parish (Ballingarry), the Rev. Gilbert James O'Grady, who was a relation of my aunt's, and constantly at her house, and also related to the late Chief Baron of Ireland, was a most excellent and worthy character, highly respected and esteemed by people of all ranks and persuasions. Having been summoned to Dublin, where the Parliament was then sitting, as a witness on a contested election, and having a great aversion to stop at inns or hotels, he expressed his anxiety to one or two of his young country friends who travelled with him, never having been in the metropolis himself, to get into some snug, quiet lodging, where he might be free from interruption or noise. The young wags, who knew Dublin well, immediately volunteered to procure one for him, and on their arrival placed him in that highly fashionable and select lodging-house, kept by Mrs B____s, in Trinity Street, a house well known and much frequented in those days. The poor priest was greatly pleased with the attention paid him by the lady of the house and her inmates, and, being fatigued by his long journey, he retired to rest at an early hour, highly gratified with the selection his friends had made, and the reception he had met with.

On the following morning, having risen at an early hour, as was his usual custom, he stood at the street-door in his slippers to breathe the pure fresh air, and sharpen his appetite for his morning's repast. He had not been many minutes in this situation, when some of his acquaintances from the County Limerick happened to pass, whom he saluted in the most friendly manner, utterly unconscious of the injury his moral character momentarily sustained in their eyes, and of the unpleasant reflections his being seen on such familiar terms in such a house, naturally gave rise to.

Several persons had already passed him, contented with barely returning his salute with apparent respect, when one gentleman, more thoughtful than the rest, and very probably placing a greater degree of reliance on the virtue and innocence of his worthy pastor, at once addressed him, and asked him, with seeming unconcern, how he happened to lodge in that house, and how long he had been an inmate of it. 'It was,' said the poor old man, 'at the recommendation of one or two young friends, who travelled with me yesterday, that I came here. I have been in it of course but one night, but I can truly say that kinder or more polite attention I have never received from any family, than I last night experienced from the lady of the house and her charming and interesting daughters.' 'Good Heavens!' exclaimed the gentleman, 'Do you know, Father O'Grady, where you are? Can you be aware that you are in a house universally noted for its infamy? Quit it instantly, sir, or your character is lost for ever.' He then explained to him the nature of Mrs B____'s establishment, and very kindly offered to conduct him to more reputable lodgings. It is almost unnecessary for me to add, that he immediately left the house, and was so exceedingly indignant at the treatment he had received, that the authors of this ill-timed trick were obliged to keep out of his way for several months afterwards.

From *The Veteran, or Forty Years in the British Service*, Vol. 1, Henry Colburn, 1838

The Vicar of Bruff
Dawson Massy

Bruff sorely tried the faith and energy of its new vicar at his first visit. He arrived on a glorious summer's day, but the spacious old church repelled him by its dilapidated and desolate appearance. The cobwebs and dust of ages seemed to have overspread it; and broken panes of glass in every window suggested that malice had conspired with neglect in effecting so dismal a ruin. Tommy Mee, the little sexton, heightened the gloom by naming successively the former owners of the pews, and attributing their desertion to emigration, or 'to being reformed to Mass'; or to intermarriage with Romanists 'under the priest's thumb' — which, with a self-complacent grin, he described as his own case — or to the 'impossibility of now collecting Church-rates in Bruff'. . . .

John Riggs, the old clerk, did not much mend the matter, by detailing his recollections of the previous five vicars; and by specifying particularly, with a searching look, the intimacy which subsisted between them and the Romish priests in the parish, especially in the case of one called Luther, who had shared one house with the priest, and eventually one grave! Then, with a sly glance over his spectacles, he remarked, 'I suppose that things will get a change now that, by all accounts, Bishop Jebb has sent us a parson Calvin, but my wife and children are under the priest's thumb already.' As the words passed his lips Godfrey espied the rude bust of a cherub, in the cornice of the ceiling over the reading-desk. He quietly called for a ladder and hammer, and deliberately smashed off its hideous head, saying: 'The Scriptures call idols lies, and I am sure there never was a greater lie than this, for it resembles nothing in the heavens above, or in the earth beneath. I hope that my destroying this papistical figure will show you all, that your new and true Protestant vicar is no admirer of images in churches.' That act was of considerable service to him in a controversy which he held many years after with a Romish tradesman, who triumphantly referred to that very figure as a proof that Protestants used images in their worship! The tale of its destruction silenced the disputant, and the result was, his frequent presence with his family in Bruff church.

The Vicarage house was a poor half-finished cottage on a rising ground, having a beautiful view of the distant Galtee Mountains; of a picturesque range of hills; of the ruins of Bulgaden Hall, a fine baronial seat of the Carbery family; and of a shining river at the foot of the lawn, rejoicing in the poetical title of the Morning Star. The glebe was so bare of tree or shrub that it was exposed to every blast; and, though it paid the high rent of three guineas per acre, it was so badly fenced, that in winter a large portion of it was flooded, and in summer it was a mere commonage for the neighbours' cattle. His first tour through the parish was also discouraging. The land, a part of the Golden Vein, though it absolutely teemed with fertility, was crowded with wretched hovels; and the river, which in England or in Scotland would have rivalled the fabled Pactolus in the gold which might be obtained from its water-power, flowed on wastefully and unobservedly amongst rocks which had been undisturbed since the Deluge. The densely populated town was composed of small shops and cabins. On the Limerick side was an extensive fairgreen, all dotted with stagnant pools and holes, and flanked by a great staring Romish chapel on the one hand, and its twin brother a court-house on the other. In every direction you could see unmistakable signs of excessive pauperism. Groups of strange beggars, on their way to or from Cork, or Kerry, or Limerick city, mingled with the local mendicants, and oddly contrasted with them, in the parti-coloured blue and grey of the tattered clothing peculiar to their native counties, and in the varieties of accent or 'brogue', which added to the strange effect of their whimsical appearance. The motley multitude pursued the retiring steps of the 'New Parson' with urgent entreaties to pity 'your own, ould widow', or 'the dark (blind) man', or 'the poor cripple', or 'the father of five small children down in the fever, and unable to keep breath in their bodies'; all vehemently declaring that they were '*wake* with hunger, glory be to the Vargin!' and backing up their petitions with vociferous prayers — 'May the heavens be your bed!' 'May the Man above never turn the deaf ear to you!' — till he had expended his last penny, and good humouredly turned his pockets inside out, to convince them that further importunity would be fruitless. Then it was amusing to hear the volatile people chaffing with one another, with characteristic fun and freedom, upon the personal appearance of him, whom they had so recently loaded with respectful epithets. A great, gaunt virago, Mary Gammel, a tinker's wife, who ruled the Bruff beggars with as despotic a sway as that of a gipsy queen, and who boasted that her curse never went from her in vain, clapped her arms a-kimbo and stopped further criticism by a loud 'Hem!' which displayed the strength of her powerful lungs, adding in a tone which admitted of no controversy, 'Glory be to the Vargin, I had a sounder nurse that this pale-faced gintleman! But look at his open little hand, and his kind smile! He'll be a power better to us that the ould parson that's gone with his hard, griping fist and his cowld eye — although he was so thick with the priest!'

His visit to the dispensary was also disheartening. Dr Raleigh, a one-armed old half-pay surgeon who conducted it, although a Romanist, was greatly disliked, and his doleful description of the apathy of the subscribers, and of the insolence of the patients, backed by 'strange oaths', asseverating his own activity and skill, showed that there also reform was sorely needed. He next bent his way to an outlet of the town called Palatine Road, in search of the industrious and respectable Protestants who bear the name of Palatines, as descendants from the Germans who, in the days of Queen Anne, resigned dear Fatherland in the Palatinate for 'freedom to worship God', and who settled in different parts of Ireland, especially at Adare, Rathkeale, and Kilfinnane, where they yet exist, an interesting and valuable part of the Protestant population. Traces still remained to indicate that their neat cottages and pretty gardens had once crowned 'The Hill of Bruff'. The Palatines had all emigrated, except old Adam Bovanizer, who was jeeringly called by the Romish rabble 'the King of the Jews'. So small was their knowledge of the Bible that they fancied his outlandish name was scriptural! Still the brave fellow maintained his Protestant spirit, and was admired by the mob as he shouldered his rusty old musket which had done the state good service in '98, and fiercely tapped the trigger when asked 'by what license he carried arms'. Out of the three Protestant cottagers residing in the Palatine Road, two had long since intermarried with Romanists, and their wives and children were 'under the priest's thumb'.

It is enough to say of the Protestant gentry then resident in the neighbourhood, that they hailed the Romish priest as a familiar friend; and that in some houses there was an apartment called, in honour of his repeated visits, 'the priest's room'. As the natural result of this intimacy, one very respectable family had already lapsed into popery. Indeed, according to the astute policy of the Court of Rome, this priest was exactly adapted to the place. His smooth, oily manners and insinuating address, his electioneering powers and racy wit, secured his welcome at the tables of the rich; while his singular skill in ruling and in pleasing the mob, made him a perfect dictator amongst the poor. It would be hard to meet a priest who had such a complete command of countenance, and so thoroughly knew his own strength. His fine intellectual forehead, the bland smile which was ever playing over his handsome face, and his plausible mien, created a strong persuasion of his placability; but to a close observer he occasionally exhibited a keen, sly, fox-like aspect that bespoke him a dangerous adversary to the new vicar. 'He could run with the hare, or hunt with the hounds, as best might serve his turn.'

From *The Faithful Shepherd: Memoir of Godfrey Massy, B.A., with Sketches of his Times*, Hamilton and Co., 1870

A Spiritual Trip
Tom Steele

There is power and magic in the ruined battlements. And when I stand in the ancient cathedral of Limerick and listen to the choir and organ; when I hear the chant of the High Mass and ringing of the Mass bell, and view the incense ascending from the altar in one of their convent chapels; when I wander through the garden of the Holy Sisterhood of St Clare and view their figures gliding among the Gothic ruins, or when I stand within the sanctuary of their convent chapel; when I sit upon a gloomy evening, and listen to the sullen sough of the wind among the dark elms over my head, and the rushing flood of the Shannon that sweeps at its basement, and hear the roar of the bugles, the beat of the drum and 'the voice of the trumpet' within the court of the castle — I become inspired by a feeling, solemn and mournful, different from that of which I am susceptible in any other place in the world, but not very unlike that with which, upon the shore of the solitary lake where he reposes, I hear the wind whisper at night in the grass around the grave of my father, whom I have never seen.

From *Practical Suggestions for the Improvement of the Navigation of the Shannon*, Sherwood Gilbert, 1828

Celebrating O'Connell's Victory in Shanagolden

The news of O'Connell's glorious victory at Clare reached the Shanagolden vicinity early on Sunday evening. Preparations were immediately commenced to commemorate this memorable event. Early on the Monday morning, the light-hearted peasantry of the surrounding country were seen flocking in all directions towards the parish chapel, where after the holy sacrifice was offered, an appeal was made by the Very Rev. Dean McNamara, P.P., Kilmoylan, to the people to observe an inviolable fidelity to their religion and their country. A feeling not to be described was produced by this admirable appeal. Immediately afterwards the whole multitude divided into four distinct groups which called to as many cemeteries in the vicinity where, over the tombs of their fathers, they embraced each other and swore on the sacred turf an eternal friendship and mutual oblivion of all past injuries.

At the approach of evening the multitude was seen moving towards the hills, the whole line of which from Knockpatrick to Shanid Castle presented a continuous sheet of flame. Every spot, every eminence on this lofty range was crowned with a pyramid of fire. Two lofty trees with transverse beams in the form of a cross and covered in convenient places with pitch and tar were placed one on each of the great landmarks already mentioned and on the given signal set on fire. The effect was sublime and imposing to a high degree. The innumerable bonfires on the inter-mediate hills presented a bold and magnificent panorama, curving through a space of five miles, which coupled with the occasion called forth a grand exhibition of national feeling and filled the mind with the greatest devotion to and love of country. During the whole day the chapel bell chimed merrily and at night the people illuminated their houses. Two days and nights were dedicated to the cele-bration of this great festival of Irish liberty and both passed over without anything to disturb the happy tranquillity of this joyous scene.

From the *Limerick Evening Post* and *Clare Sentinel*, 11 July 1828

The Legend of the Bells
Anonymous

> Soft shades foretold the coming of the night,
> Yet goldenly on Shannon's emerald shores
> As charmed, or fallen asleep, the sunset light
> Still lingered — or as there sweet day
> Had dropped her mantle, ere she took flight.
> Up Shannon's tide a boat slow held its way;
> All silent bent the boatmen to their oars,
> For at their feet a dying stranger lay;
> In broken accents of a foreign tongue
> He breathed fond names and murmured words of prayer;
> And yearningly, his wasted arms outflung,
> Grasped viewless hands and kissed the empty air.
> Sudden, upon the breeze came floating down
> The sound of vesper bells from Limerick Town;
> So sweet 'twould seem the holiest of chimes,

Stored up new notes amid its silent times,
Some wandering melodies from heavenly climes,
Or gathered music from the summer hours,
As bees draw sweets from tributary flowers;
Peal followed peal, till all the air around
Trembled in waves of undulating sound.
The dying stranger, where he gasping lay,
Heard the sweet chime and knew it ringing nigh;
Quick from his side the phantoms fled away
And the lost soul-light kindled in his eye!
His cold hands reaching towards the shadowy shore;
'Madonna, thanks!' he cried, 'I hear the bells once more' —
And then he died.

From the *Labour Party National Conference Magazine*, April 1997

The Limerick Papal Brigade
Maurice Lenihan

A movement of surpassing interest and importance went on during the greater portion of this year (1860), which marked the deep sympathy of the Catholic hierarchy,
clergy, and people, with Pope Pius IX, who had been suffering at the hands of the
King of Italy and the Emperor of the French. Meetings were held throughout Ireland
to sustain the Pope; but nowhere was there more enthusiasm in the cause than in
Limerick, where not only large sums were contributed to the papal exchequer, but
where many brave young fellows volunteered for enlistment in the Irish Papal Brigade,
which was formed in Rome, and which distinguished itself in many hard-fought fields
in Italy, viz. Perugia, Spoletto, Castel Fidardo, and Ancona. The government sought
to prevent this enlistment, but young men enrolled themselves rapidly notwithstanding; and as detachments of the recruits left the Limerick station by train, *en route*
to their destination, they were loudly applauded for their chivalrous resolution. The
Right Rev. Dr Ryan presided, on 5 June, at a meeting in St John's old chapel, at
which resolutions expressive of active and warm sympathy with the Pope were
adopted, and a subscription list to aid his Holiness was opened. The city of Limerick
contributed more largely than any other in Ireland in men and money, towards the
cause. On 17 October, a solemn requiem High Mass was celebrated in St Michael's
church for the repose of the souls of the soldiers of the Irish Brigade who were slain
in Italy, and their companions-in-arms; and on the return home of the surviving
brigadiers, on the conclusion of the Italian war, an ovation awaited them in

Limerick, whilst on 3 December a grand banquet was given to them at the Theatre. Limerick diocese contributed a sum of £6,000 towards the papal exchequer this year.

From *Limerick; Its History and Antiquities, Ecclesiastical, Civil and Military, from the Earliest Ages*, Hodges, Smith and Co., 1866

The Castlemahon Pattern
Richard Baptist O'Brien

Wagons filled with straw and bearing invalids, or cars more comfortably furnished with feather beds, and carrying some ancient woman telling her beads; old men and young, decrepit from age or from accident, and moving slowly on their crutches, while the eye suddenly uplifted and the spasmodic contraction of the lip denoted weariness or pain; young girls 'dressed for the day', with laughing eyes and happy smile going to 'make their rounds' for some old parent at home, or some lonely and helpless friend — for the dead it may be, or for the sick; and children in their mothers' arms, that wondered with their great large eyes at the gathering so novel to them — all pursued their way along the road. Occasionally some ill-mannered and unaccommodating horse would deliberately turn from the wall side and make himself a perpendicular across the narrow way, to the great discomfiture of the inactive and the absorbedly devout, but raising an innocent laugh among the youthful, whose 'bad manners to you for a horse!' hardly saved them from the rebuke of venerable hairs. Sometimes, too, an itinerant piper was, on a nearer approach to the fountain, found in a snug nook, puffing out his claim to the religious dole of the visitors, and an iron-lunged 'boccagh' made the valleys ring with his wants and prayers, and his blessings when charity ministered to his need. And now we approach the entrance to the holy well. . . . On the day of the events which we chronicle — and let it be understood that we write a true history — faith and hope had brought more than ordinary confluence to the well. Within the precincts of the sacred place were gathered a strange assemblage of almost every class, and outside, as we have already intimated, a large number had collected to gratify curiosity, to amuse themselves, or to beg. . . .

There were present old and young, binding themselves by the 'communion of saints', with the dead and the distant; or in filial or parental piety, praying for blessing upon fathers, mothers or offspring. The crippled and the blind, too, lay by the well . . . as did the afflicted by the mysterious lake of Judea; but, far from having 'none to let them down into the waters', fond friendship, full of faith, lifted its hands to heaven in their behalf and cried 'Our Father' for their restoration.

From *Life of Dean O'Brien* by M.J. Egan, M.H. Gill and Son Ltd, 1949

The Burial of Aubrey de Vere
John P. Gunning

In his later years the memory and hearing of the bard became somewhat impaired but his physical health was perfect. During these years he lived in comparative retirement at Curragh Chase. Every Sunday morning, however, he attended divine service at the Catholic parish church at Adare, which is about five miles from his ancestral home. For many years his tall and graceful figure was never missed from the performance of this act of religious duty; and the people of the locality today speak of his absence from amongst them in the light of a personal affliction. His habit on those Sunday mornings was to arrive about half an hour before the time appointed for the celebration of Mass. This half-hour, as well as a half-hour after divine service, the poet spent at the presbytery with Very Rev. Dean Flanagan, chatting and talking about theology, current topics, and other matters which might incidentally arise in the course of conversation. On these occasions he was, as the amiable and courteous Dean remarked to the present writer, always entertaining, never dull, never in a hurry to leave off, and 'thoroughly instructed in Catholic faith and dogma'. Needless to say the venerable Dean enjoyed Mr de Vere's friendship for close on forty years. But the years were stealing on, and the shadows of age were gradually deepening round the bard. On 19 January of the present year, the poet was missed from his usual place in the church. He was taken ill a few days before, and the doctor (Dr Thomas Hayes), a life-long friend, was unable to further prolong a life which was fast ebbing away. The last sacraments of his Church were administered to him by Father Fitzgerald, and Mr de Vere, in the fullness of age, passed calmly and peacefully away early in the morning of 21 January. Indeed so peaceful and serene was the close of his life that it looked as if the Angel of Death came noiselessly on tiptoe, and, with kindly look, called away the gentle spirit to the unknown land, where the material has no place, where the jarring discords of earth-life are not heard.

On the 24th, all that was mortal of the poet was laid to rest in the cemetery attached to the Protestant church at Askeaton. A short time before ten o'clock in the morning the remains were encased in a coffin of old Irish oak, surmounted by a cross of the same material and with simple brass mountings, were removed from Curragh Chase by a party of the tenantry, who attended in large numbers, and placed in the hearse in waiting.

The following inscription engraved on the plate and cut in the shape of a heart was on the coffin:

AUBREY F. DE VERE
DIED TUESDAY, JANUARY 21, 1902.
AGED 88 YEARS.

Numerous wreaths, some of very ornamental design, sent by friends and relatives, were laid on the coffin.

The morning of the poet's interment was bitterly cold; and to make matters worse the funeral cortège had to walk or proceed a distance of five miles in carriages in a blinding snow and hail storm. Notwithstanding the inclemency of the weather, the funeral was a representative one. With the Protestant and the Catholic, the parson and the priest, were the representatives of the noble houses of Dunraven, Inchiquin, Monteagle, Clarina and Emly: all anxious not only to pay the last tribute of respect to the memory of a friend whose family for centuries have been knit in the closest bonds of sympathy and kindliness with the peasantry dependent on them and living under them as tenants, but to the poet whose genius has enriched English literature, and whose patriotism and Catholicity have burned brightly in the resplendent flame of his muse. Much sympathy was felt for the deceased's brother, Sir Stephen de Vere, the present baronet and the last surviving male representative of the family, who, in his 90th year, was unable to be present.

At noon the funeral procession quietly wended its way into Askeaton. Snow lay thickly on the ground; the old mills in the district were capped with white: a wintry scene was indeed visible everywhere. In accordance with an express wish of the poet, the remains were not laid to rest in the family vault, but in a new-made grave to the left of the passage leading into the church. The bard did not want the 'sounding brass or the tinkling cymbal' of vault or 'storied urn or animated bust' to mark his last resting-place or proclaim the greatness of his name or the immortality of his fame. The simplicity and humility so characteristic of him during life should also be preserved in his tomb.

That new-made grave, too, was in view of the historic ruins of Desmond Castle and Banqueting Hall, Askeaton Abbey, and the mountains of Knockpatrick. . . . No more fitting resting-place could then be found for him who has woven into song those ruined fanes, and thrown an immortal, poetic charm round the old mills, the ruined castle and the historic abbey.

From *Aubrey de Vere: A Memoir*, Guy & Co. Ltd, 1902

The Trials and Tribulations of Dr Long
Michael J.F. McCarthy

The Convent of the Good Shepherd in Clare Street, of which we shall hear more in the present chapter, is an immense institution, containing 78 admitted nuns and novices; an asylum with 100 selected, poor, Limerick Magdalens; an 'industrial' school with 109 derelict little girls, for whose support the state pays £1,637 7s. 1d.

per annum; a reformatory containing 27 criminal little girls, for whom the state pays £661 14s. 11d., or £24 10s. 2d. per child per annum; and an 'Angels' Home' for the girls discharged from the 'industrial' school when out of employment! What a factory! That is the manufacture to which the Catholics of Limerick can point as *their* contribution, under the guidance of their priests, to the prosperity of the city! . . .

Those who have read this work so far are aware that the sacerdotal establishment in every county in Ireland, except two or three counties in Ulster, is far stronger than the services of the imperial and local governments; and it is so in Limerick. It may be fairly laid down, that wherever the imperial or local authorities find themselves at variance with the priests, the authorities always yield gracefully, or acknowledge themselves beaten and precipitately retreat. They can venture to contest a position with the Irish members of parliament, the landlords, or any organisation or class of lay-folk; but they always defer to the priests' superior power, which is now established beyond doubt by the official returns.

A Limerick Redemptorist priest happened to be prowling and scowling about the corner of Thomas Street, in the holy city of the violated treaty, on a fine September forenoon in 1898, and he saw a woman coming out of a doctor's house, a Catholic woman, a poor Catholic woman . . . he stopped her and probed the suspicious matter to the bottom; and he learned that a young doctor, possessing the highest medical qualifications, but associated with the Irish Church Missions in Dublin, had given the woman free medical advice; and that he was in the habit of speaking to his patients about — Christ! . . . Let us hear from the Redemptorist what he did on that memorable occasion.

The doctor's door was open, and the Redemptorist actually walked in. Several poor Catholic people, men and women, were inside. 'There were eleven or twelve women, and three or four men present', says the Redemptorist.

'I said,' he tells us, 'there are Catholics here present, and if so they should clear out at once!'

'How dare you come into my house!' exclaimed the doctor, rushing out from his consulting room.

'There is the door open and I walked in,' replied the Redemptorist sternly, knowing his own power; 'I understand that some of these people are Catholics, and they must leave this house.'

'Get out of this at once,' said the doctor.

'Just you try and put me out,' said the Redemptorist, trailing his robe on the floor.

The Redemptorist adds: 'I walked to the steps' — from which I infer that the doctor looked muscular — 'and some of the women went out. The doctor banged the door. Some of the Catholics were inside then.'

Then the Redemptorist seized the doctor's knocker, and, in his own words, 'knocked at the door, and kept knocking'. A crowd collected and a scene of disturbance followed; and the Redemptorist, representing the ecclesiastical arm in

Limerick, desisted for that day, triumphant and uninterrupted by the inferior secular arm.

From October 1897 to October 1898 the number of different individuals who had voluntarily attended the mission doctor's consulting room is stated at 3,458 — poor, neglected Roman Catholics almost entirely; and, even in the year following the ban of the Redemptorist, the number is given as 3,000, which shows how sadly in need of medical assistance, and how unaverse to hear the truth about Christ, poor lay Catholics are!

On Sunday morning Limerick Catholics were warned from all the pulpits to boycott the doctor. The Redemptorist himself harangued his Confraternity of the Holy Family and told them, in the course of a long sermon, that 'these inhuman creatures, who gloated in the sufferings of those whom they called obstinate and incorrigible papists, were the representatives of those who, in a former age, burned, hanged, outraged, and robbed their unfortunate fellow-countrymen. There are, yes, here in this city of Limerick, there are men and — God save the mark! — women, too, who, if they could set up outside this church their gallows and triangle, would drag us from our homes, and scourge, burn, and hang us without mercy. . . . Men of the confraternity, stand up on your feet, raise up your hands and say after me — "I protest, in the sight of God against the attack which has been made by the bigots of Limerick upon our religion. I promise never to attend myself, and to prevent all whom I can from attending this sŏuper dispensary."' . . .

A great deal of unChristian conduct followed these events. The house of a Limerick man who was said to have become a Protestant was attacked in the small hours of the morning, his windows were broken, and he and his family had to escape by the back door — first from the house and afterwards from Limerick!

The imperial authorities dared not interfere, as it was a religious case. If the crime had been connected with land or trade, they could have intervened.

The doctor, in the year 1901, received an order from a Dublin court of justice empowering him to receive in loco parentis the custody of a little girl then confined in Clare Street Convent, Limerick. And he went to that great emporium, accompanied by some policemen and asked for the child; but the nuns contemptuously refused to give her up. The Redemptorist again addressed his 'Holy Family', telling them that Dr Long, 'that pious fraud of Thomas Street, the law-breaker, has gone down to Clare Street Convent, to those unprotected holy ladies, and has grossly insulted them, guarded by Government officers, and we are to stand by and witness this without interfering. Our blood is up. I will not be answerable for the peace of the city, nor for the actions of the women of Clare Street.' And he stings his male audience by saying of the women: 'One of them is worth the whole of you, and I leave that pious fraud of Thomas Street in their hands!'

The women of Limerick have long been notorious; hence the Redemptorist's appeal . . . when he finds that the men do not respond to his incitements. The women now began to pelt not only Dr Long, but Mrs Long, in the streets with flour and stones.

The Redemptorist's objection to the interference of 'Government officers' in such purely ecclesiastical matters produced the desired effect. The magistrates, presided over by a stipendiary, unanimously dismissed a charge brought by the police against the ringleaders of one of those mobs who pelted the doctor and his wife.

Dr Long summoned a priest for having used threatening language to him in presence of an excited crowd when he was attending a Protestant patient. The priest stated that he had acted 'in discharge of his duty as a priest, knowing Dr Long to be a proselytiser, and thinking he would interfere with the Catholic people of the house'. Recognising that it was an ecclesiastical case, the magistrates at once dismissed the summons. . . .

Dr Long's friends had appealed to the county inspector of constabulary to protect him, but the inspector could do nothing except to threaten, in a letter dated 29 February 1901, 'to place restrictions upon his [Dr Long's] movements through the city'. The police felt equal to restraining Dr Long, but to restrain the vastly superior sacerdotal army was beyond the power of the constabulary. . . .

The licensed car-drivers of Limerick then systematically refused to drive Dr Long and his wife. The young doctor appealed to the Corporation to put the bye-laws into force and punish the drivers, either by fine or deprivation of licence, for refusing to ply for hire on being tendered their fare. But the Corporation declined to interfere or give any relief. Their doing so would have been an interference with the ecclesiastical authorities, and they had not the courage to enter upon so perilous a path. Then the Corporation sued Dr Long, before the magistrates, for obstructing the public thoroughfare by asking the car-men to drive him and by getting on their cars, in the hope that they would move on, and thereby collecting crowds. But the magistrates dismissed the case. They were not prepared to bring their court into collision with the sacerdotal organisation either!

From *Priests and People in Ireland*, Hodder and Stoughton, 1902

Limerick Bells
Richard Ross-Lewin

> Sweet bells of St Mary's,
> Sweet bells of old time,
> On green banks of Shannon
> Why silent your chime?
> Break forth into music
> O'er valleys so fair.
> By lonely Knockfierna

And groves of Adare.
Awake the far echoes,
Ringmoylan's fair dells,
Shall hark to the sound of
Old Limerick bells.

Wake Cratloe's far highlands
And mountains of Clare
Beyond Ardnacrusha
Thy notes shall repair;
The voices of Shannon
Shall join with each chime,
Rolling on to the ocean
In music sublime,
Till mountain and valley,
In unison swells,
In the clang and the peal of
Old Limerick bells.

May clamour and passion
Be hushed as you toll,
Melodious and cadent,
Our bosoms control.
Let all who love Erin
In harmony join,
No longer discordant,
By Shannon and Boyne.
Then haply the future
Of happiness tells,
To all who shall list to
Old Limerick's bells

From *Poems by a County of Clare West Briton*, George McKern & Sons Ltd, 1907

The Bruff Scandal
Michael J.F. McCarthy

The controversy between Bishop O'Dwyer of Limerick and the Bruff Christian
Brothers, as well as the whole attitude of the clergy towards that Order, could not

be adequately dealt with in this book; but we may lift a corner of the curtain. It appears the Christian Brothers at Bruff had the privilege of what is called 'reservation of the Blessed Sacrament' in the oratory of their residence. Dr O'Dwyer discovered this, and, as he says, 'stopped the reservation'. The Christian Brothers appealed to Rome, but the Bishop's decision, as Dr O'Dwyer triumphantly tells us, was upheld. His next step, as he himself tells us, was to prevent the Brothers from hearing Mass in the nuns' convent chapel at Bruff. It appears Bishop O'Dwyer visited the convent himself, and found 'a nun and a Christian Brother' arranging the altar in preparation for the Mass which was about to be celebrated. He made inquiries, and discovered 'that the Christian Brothers heard Mass daily, and frequently answered Mass in the nuns' chapel, *which was situated in the centre of the house, and that there was no separation whatever between them and the nuns and the young lady boarders*. . . . All of which was most improper . . . and must cease. . . . And he decreed that the Christian Brothers could not continue to hear Mass in the convent.' Against this decree, and, I should say, still more so, against the insinuation it conveyed, the Brothers also appealed to Rome; but Dr O'Dwyer's 'decision was upheld'. Whereupon, and consequent upon other proceedings, the Superior-General very naturally withdrew the Brothers from Bruff, to the indignation of the inhabitants, who freely vented their displeasure on Bishop O'Dwyer.

From *Five Years in Ireland 1895–1900*, Hodges, Figgis & Co. Ltd, 1902

Fr John Creagh
William Packer

'How my hands trembled the first time I opened the tabernacle and touched Our Lord in person. May it always tremble. . . .' Such is one expression that the writer recalls from a retreat given at Manly College about the year 1933. 'Daddy', as we called the grey-headed Father John, was regarded by some students as screwy, but he certainly portrayed and conveyed a strong faith in the Eucharistic presence.

He was born at Thomondgate, Limerick, on 19 August 1870. Education for the priesthood and the Redemptorist calling was obtained at the CSSR House in Limerick, at Bishop Eton and Teignmouth Order Houses in England. Profession was pronounced on 15 October 1888, and ordination conferred on 1 September 1895. First years appear to have been employed as a teacher at Teignmouth and at Clonard in Belfast. In the early 1900s he was engaged in parochial and missionary duties in Limerick. Highlights of his stay in that city was his successful directorship of the Holy Family Confraternity, and his involvement in trouble with the city's Jews whom he was alleged to have attacked. In 1905 or earlier he was posted to the

Philippines where through a feverish zeal he suffered a nervous breakdown. So in poor shape he came for a year to Waratah, NSW, recovered his zeal and balance, and went to Wellington, NZ. There his missionary activity became a household word. Returning to Australia he was appointed Rector of the Perth House, remaining at the post from 1914 to 1916. Next came Creagh's appointment as Vicar-Apostolic of the Kimberleys.

Taking up the movements from there we find him listed as acting parish priest of Bunbury from 1923 to 1925. Then came an overseas visit and holiday. From 1926 to 1930 he was stationed at Pennant Hills. Next station was Waratah and it was there that he suffered a paralytic stroke. But an eventual recovery meant more active years of preaching missions and retreats both in Waratah and in Wellington, NZ. And there the chapter of 76 years and a golden jubilee of priesthood closes. He died on 24 January 1947, at Lewisham Hospital, Wellington, and was interred at Karori.

From *Footprints*, October 1978; reprinted in *The Old Limerick Journal*, No. 23, Spring 1988

Memories of a Catholic Education
Kate O'Brien

Reverend Mother was not just English; she was late Victorian upper-class English almost one might have said (but wrongly) to the point of caricature. Unfortunately in appearance she suggested Queen Victoria in miniature.

She was aquiline and neatly rotund and very small. And her eyes, surprisingly blue when you got a straight look from them, were not protuberant like the Queen's but hooded; a bird's eyes. She was in her quiet way an almost fanatical instructor in behaviour, or deportment, on the obligation in a lady to move quietly, to hold her back straight, to open and close doors correctly, and to sit still. She aimed to teach us total outer command of our bodies; yet in the twelve years in which I watched her with respectful attention and grew most affectionately interested in her, I never saw her in command of her little claw hands.

She was a tiny and disconcerting pillar of control and reserve; yet those ugly little hands were never still. Except, conceivably, when she slept. I hope they rested then. But when she prayed they fidgeted and fought together while all the rest of her was statue-still.

Over the long view one has seen how absurd it was that that little Englishwoman, that one especially, should have been in charge of the education of Irish girls of the Catholic middle class in the years so quickly leading up to 1916. Indeed, quite early in the century a Dublin weekly called *The Leader* which seems to have been more socially than nationalistically avant-garde, in an article assaulting the absurdities of education in Ireland, called out Laurel Hill Convent by name and accused it of educating Irish girls to be suitable wives for bank managers and British colonial governors.

If this charge was brought to Reverend Mother's attention — and almost certainly it was — she might have winced about the bank managers, as they would have been a very low social target; but that we should be made fit to partner British colonial governors — that, by all means, she would have accepted as fair description of the product she aimed at.

I left Laurel Hill and said goodbye to Reverend Mother in June 1916. No more than 90 per cent of my fellow countrymen and I understood the curious event of Easter Week. And for Reverend Mother certainly it was no more than another sad little piece of Irish foolishness.

For her, who was to die very soon, the climactic date had been August 1914; she had to weep and pray for the sons and brothers of many of her dear daughters, boys fallen at Mons, Ypres and Gallipoli. And she had indeed kept us all busy knitting mufflers for Munster Fusiliers.

This little nun had a very hard role in the Ireland of my childhood. She was cold, nervous, inexpressive and non-intellectual. She was hide-bound English; her father, uncles, nephews were lawyers, doctors, judges. Yorkshire bred and Stonyhurst men. But she had grown up in London, off Park Lane. She held to all the clap-trap standards that went with the 'season' and Church Parade and shopping, with your maid, in Bond Street; and Her Majesty's Court and all that lot. She did not exactly talk of these social fixtures. . . . No, it was simply that in Reverend Mother's 'politeness lessons', which took place on the evenings of Monday and Thursday, this background and its standards had to come through. . . .

She was, from an Irish viewpoint, unprepossessing. She had no charm; she took no interest at all in the Gaelic Revival, which was deeply infecting a few of the more intelligent of her nuns; she resented the visits to these nuns of Limerick's very intelligent and arrogant bishop, Edward Thomas O'Dwyer.

These two were indeed in dramatic terms well met. The Bishop of Limerick had no authority over this French foundation of Laurel Hill; all that was required of the community was courtesy and general conformity, which indeed were not withheld. But the Bishop had a habit of authority, and he took a very great interest in the Latin and the Irish teaching of certain excellent nuns in Laurel Hill, whom he visited with regularity. And he regarded himself as an authority on trees, and on roses.

So when he did occasionally meet Reverend Mother, as he paced the grounds, talking in Latin with Mother Thecla or Mother Lelia, he always had kind advice to give to this little Englishwoman about the roses, or about the trees.

He was a very handsome aristocratic-looking man, Edward Thomas. Very deaf, with the piercing, tiring voice of a deaf man. He used to yell at Reverend Mother that she must cut down the elm trees that shaded the Visitors' Walk. It was clear from her courteous acknowledgments of these shouts, clear even to him, that she would never do so.

The Gaelic Revival was sweeping in, and three or four of her most gifted teaching nuns — led by Mother Lelia Ferguson, the chief Latinist — were insisting on the study of Irish. Without any sympathy for the movement, this cold little English-woman allowed them evening classes and all the books they wanted and allowed them to receive teaching and directions from such cranks as Douglas Hyde and Lord Ashbourne. (It is admissibly arguable that she was influenced — if puzzled — by the fact that these gentlemen belonged to the ascendancy class; as indeed did the two or three nuns of her community who were pursuing this new study.) . . . I know, because I was one of its addicts, under the brilliant teaching of Mother Lelia, how frequently Reverend Mother reflected in wonder and distaste, about the revivalist passion.

She used to ask me about it: 'Do you like this language?'

'Very much. I find. It's very difficult — but so is Latin.'

'Ah yes. But Latin is important.'

I think she was remarkably wise and considerate, as a passive authority, in a climate of thought which she could not enter. But then, she did not enter the climate of thought. From outside them, I think she watched with an attention of sensibility which only those could measure whose confidence, in distress, she would force. She forced mine, as I suppose she knew she could, after twelve years of love. And she forgave me then for all this after-life, which has been an insult to her simple ideals.

I told her a lie on that day when she forced me to speak about my non-belief and my private sins; and she accepted my lie and said she expected it and went on talking as if I had not uttered it. She never smiled; she said none of the bright things that one came to read later from English Catholics. She spoke, I think, in grief — and I was not able to help her. And she knew that.

I was never to see her again after that painful conversation under the elms of the Visitors' Walk. After twelve years I was going out from her house an unbeliever — my silly lie had been of no avail.

During Lent or Advent, we usually gave up sugar in our tea or coffee. Reverend Mother always breakfasted in our refectory, at the Table of Honour. That was, if you like, High Table. It was on a dais and the Senior Honours people sat there.

Let me recall, as I pass, what I owe to that refectory. It carried on its walls a complete series of really beautiful colour prints of the Raphael cartoons. Twelve years' day-in, day-out association with those reproductions, hung at eye-level and for a child to stare when she was in despair about finishing the fish-pie on her plate — that was an accidental soaked-in experience for which I am far more grateful than for all the Piranesis of the playrooms.

But pardon the aside — I was recalling breakfast with Reverend Mother. She sat always at the centre of the table, under the ugly engraving of the very boring Mother Foundress. And sometimes when we came in from Mass she was in her place before us. Grace was said — and then I or Marie Baggott, or whoever was directly opposite her began to pour the coffee. And ah, that coffee! Not for nothing were the lay sisters in the kitchen still French! I can smell it now as we came half-fainting from Mass!

Well, in Lent or Advent there was in our general intention no sugar. But often, if Reverend Mother was there before us, you found when you drank your coffee that there was sugar at the bottom of the cup. So you protested, delightedly. And she used to say in her cold little voice that the Holy Ghost had told her that we needed, she thought, some sugar for just that day. . . .

Mother Lelia and her younger sister, Mother Sabina, were Fergusons. I believe that they were nieces of Sir Samuel Ferguson, the distinguished scholar-pupil. Their father was a judge. They had been brought up in intellectual circles; but were very intelligent, and the elder of them, Mother Lelia, was a natural and vivid intellectual.

They two and Mother Maria (who was a ffrench with her two small f's and Mother Thecla, who was a Patterson) were all, although near-aristocrats, what the Americans call cradle Catholics. That means that none of them owed their cultivated minds to England, although their families took their comfortable status in Ireland, no doubt, from their acceptance by the Castle and the Viceroy. But in my hindsight now — I did not notice political moods or gradings in my youth — every one of those four nuns stands out as her own kind of rebel — anarchists all four, I'd say. And each of them, on her own grounds, entirely contemptuous of English rule in Ireland.

This, because Reverend Mother was a controlled and just and eccentric governor, did not make difficulties for these four unusual nuns. Yet, characteristically and anarchistically no one of the four liked that Englishwoman. I would swear that no one of them, mature and witty women, understood her or admired her as I did, a mere child.

Note: Kate O'Brien did not complete the autobiography fragment from which this article is taken.

From The Stony Thursday Book, No. 7, edited by John Liddy, 1977.

Saint Mary's Bells
Alfred Perceval Graves

How many a time in Cratloe's dells
I list your chime, St Mary's bells
And hearing, seem to find unfold
As in a dream, the legend old,
Which tells of one with master hand,
Who of silver spun your magic bland.

That from yon tower, at the holy hour,
Around us swells, St Mary's bells.

Again I view your founder sail
The ocean blue for Inisfail;
Again I hark the breakers' roar
About his bark on Shannon shore;
Till, in heaven-sent calm to the hope forlorn,
Your angel psalm o'er the ocean borne
Rings on his ear with rapture clear,
And with tears he tells his own sweet bells.

From the *Labour Party Conference Magazine*, April 1997

Fr Creagh in the Kimberleys
S.J. Boland

The north-west corner of Australia is a lonely country, the last region of the continent to yield to settlement. Even the Aboriginal people who were there when the Europeans came, were fiercely independent, protecting their traditional hunting grounds against all newcomers, black or white. But the Kimberleys were coveted by the 'cattle kings' in the closing decades of the last century, and they moved in to occupy their vast holdings reckoned by the thousands of square miles. To this wild region, sparsely inhabited, hot for most of the year with the thermometer soaring as high as 120 Fahrenheit, with its immense, scarcely explored distances, came Father John Creagh, the Limerick-born Redemptorist.

Fr Creagh was 46 years old at the time and had been a Redemptorist since 1895. He was a flamboyant character, a persuasive preacher, quick-tempered, sympathetic, of more than ordinary ability, but impetuous; and he just loved a fight. He had gained some measure of notoriety when he was Director of the Holy Family Confraternity in Limerick; he had been one of the founders of the Philippine missions; and he had come to the Kimberleys from New Zealand.

His responsibilities extended along the six or seven hundred miles of coastline from Broome to Wyndham and eastward until all traces of habitation were lost in the Dead Heart of the continent. . . .

But nobody had warned him about Broome. It was a teeming pearling port with an incredibly cosmopolitan population — Japanese, Chinese, Filipino, Malay, as well as the ever-present Aborigines and a confused European hotch-potch. John Creagh came to them in 1916 and for the seven years he was in the Kimberleys he could rarely get away from Broome. It was an untamed community, and he saw it in all its moods, from the 'lay-up' in the cyclone season when the luggers were beached in Roebuck Bay and the crews fretted in the steamy heat and clouds of mosquitoes, always on the lookout for a chance to even the score for grievances only half-remembered, to those equally turbulent days when the discovery of the pearl of great price was celebrated in ways other than those described in the Gospel. . . .

There were grim moments, of course; and few reveal the true character of the man more clearly than the Jackie Parks case. Parks was a drover who, finding an Aboriginal stockboy sneaking off and leaving the team short, fired a charge of buckshot at his legs. The boy was killed, and Jackie Parks was charged with murder. A violent outcry in Broome demanded that he be hanged.

That was not good enough for John Creagh. He made one of his rare visits to Perth to give evidence at the trial. He was able to show that it had long been the practice of drovers to punish any misdemeanour in the team with the familiar charge of birdshot. His evidence swayed the Perth court to change the charge of murder to one of manslaughter, for which Jackie Parks went to prison. The evidence and the publicity it gained in the papers had the further good effect of putting an abrupt end to much of the ill treatment of the Aboriginal stockboys. Even those who had been loudest in condemning him for his part in the trial, in the end came to recognise him as a man of justice and humanity.

From *Apostolicum*, Melbourne, July 1980; reprinted in *The Old Limerick Journal*, No. 23, Spring 1988

Aunt Fan
Kate O'Brien

This Presentation Order that she joined — an early nineteenth-century foundation — had a hard rule. Until quite recently, it was absolutely enclosed — meaning that the postulant entered the house outside of which she would never step again, and in whose garden she would be buried; with some measure of the old contemplative rigours and office readings the nuns of Presentation had to combine hard, realistic teaching of the children of the poor. Large crowded schools, great classes of very poor and in Aunt Fan's young days very dirty and wild children, boys and girls, had to be dealt with daily, against a background of prayer, austerity and silence.

The convent in Limerick had a curious charm. It was set down — probably there first — to the north of the railway station, and encircled by small nineteenth-century streets that were orderly and respectable when the convent was young, but have gone down in the world. But the house where the nuns live is a large, late Georgian merchant's-mansion type — not embellished or beautiful, but plain and spacious;

it is completely walled in from the town, and its gardens are long and quiet, and run in three parallel divisions — visitor's garden, cloister garden, and kitchen garden — from the convent proper to the great schools and playgrounds where the nuns work all day. . . .

When Fan was a child in Kilfinane she was not expected to live long; she was the 'delicate' one, and neighbours thought, and said, 'They'll never raise her. If the creature get to fourteen years it'll be a wonder.' Thus, great and anxious care was spent on her by her parents, by her loving young sisters, by the family doctor, and by specialists in Cork. Among the Little Women she was Beth; but unlike Beth she did not die. She made fourteen, against the betting; and lived for seventy-three more years as an indomitable and vigorous invalid. A warning, if you like, that it is wise to take very great care of children.

I suppose it was 'consumption', as they called tuberculosis, that was mainly feared for the small Fan; and indeed she may have manifested symptoms — her brother was to die of it in his thirties, hurrying it on with alcoholism. She was almost certainly anaemic; also highly nervous, excitable and easily distressed. She was to be all of the last three as and when she pleased throughout her life.

It was sad and ironic for her, the delicate 'pet', that her sisters had to leave her so long on the bleak shore alone. For fifty years she had to do with just remembering Katty, and telling us about her; and for more than a quarter of a century she had no sisters at all. . . .

She was in her sixties now, and still had a long way to go; but not, naturally, at a hard pace, or under any pressure, for she was by now the convent pet and its invalid queen; with the years she was to become its doyenne, a golden jubilarian, and the oldest member of the community.

But suddenly in the 1930s she witnessed a revolutionary change in the Presentation rule. From its foundation the Order was an absolutely enclosed one. This enclosure within what was now a near-slum combined with hard work in hot and overcrowded classrooms made for much ill health among the younger nuns, and for some nervous breaks. So the Bishop of Limerick ordained that for one month of the summer vacation the community should withdraw to some house in the country or by the sea, waiving entirely for that one month their rule of cloister.

There was consternation at first in the community room, and some weeping and heart-searching in the cells. Fear entered many of these locked-away breasts. . . .

The young nuns rallied from their first shock, and soon found themselves delighted, exhilarated by the prospect of seeing again the sea and fields and roads and houses — all that they had by no means forgotten. . . .

Aunt Fan listened to them all with the benevolence which now in age was making her so much a favourite with the younger nuns.

When they began to cut out bathing costumes for themselves — huge affairs from vast rolls of black cloth — she was at first shocked, but then began to take an interest in the strange labour. . . .

Well, to cut a long story, the 1st of August came, and my sister Nance with her little son drove to the Presentation Convent in the morning, to see this really historic exodus. And there, ready before all the others, alone and beautifully stowed in comfort in the best seat in the leading charabanc sat Fan. Smiling like a seraph, irradiating the happiness of a child.

And for the remaining twenty summers of her life, she was a demon of zest for the summer holiday. Though of course she never swam, or made herself a bathing suit. She was content to direct the younger nuns from the rocky shore.

She was very gentle in old age. . . . We all kept in touch with her over the years — we all were very fond of her — and it was fun when one returned to Limerick to go and sit for many hours with her in the same unchanged parlour, and to try to eat the terrific lunch that she would have commanded. And I recall a story against me in relation to one such return-of-the-native visit. It seems that at the date lipstick, already a commonplace in London, had not yet reached Limerick, and I visited Fan in my best suit, and in general I hope suitably groomed. Well, she made no comment — admired my clothes, I imagine, for she always loved to discuss what one wore, and she seemed to find me in satisfactory order in general. . . .

But — the minute I left her, she wrote in despair to my sister Nance, with whom I was staying — an exclamatory, frightened letter about poor Kitty's painted mouth! And what on earth had come over the child? What would her darling mother have said? And what was to be done about it?

When my first novel, *Without My Cloak*, came out, she wanted very much to read it. Nance explained to her that it was not reading for nuns, and that it would only upset and puzzle her. But still she fretted. So my kind sister took a copy, went through it and pinned certain pages together at several points.

'Now, Fan,' she said, 'if you don't move the pins you ought to be all right.'

And Fan did not move the pins, and she was all right.

From *Presentation Parlour*, William Heinemann Ltd, 1963

Hands off Sunday!

Referring to Sunday special trains calling at Rathkeale (Co. Limerick) station at an early hour, the Rev. Monsignor O'Donnell P.P., V.G., preaching at Rathkeale church yesterday, said that last summer it was shocking to see the number of young men who deliberately lost Mass in order to amuse themselves at sports and matches.

He did not say that these persons were from Rathkeale parish, but, wherever they came from, it was deplorable to see so many of them going on the verge of denying their faith and giving a bad example to youths who witnessed and were aware of the heinousness of their conduct.

It was surprising that the railway authorities did not time Sunday pleasure trains so as to allow people to hear Mass before rushing to the railway station. Many of the shareholders if consulted, he felt sure, would be decidedly opposed to making profit by means of inducing young men to lose Mass on Sunday.

'In some places where people are considered to have less religion than the people of our country, the great matches are held on Saturday. In those places the understanding seems to be, "Hands off Sunday." Such a motto might be desirable here', concluded Monsignor O'Donnell.

From *The Irish Times*, 21 March 1927

Crossing the Iron Bridge
Michael Hartnett

My dear brethren, boys and girls, today is a glorious day! Here we have a hundred lambs of our flock, the cream of the town, about to receive the Body and Blood of Christ, about to become Children of God, and to enter into a miraculous union with Jesus. . . .

> Into the cobweb-coloured light,
> my arms in white rosettes,
> I walked up Maiden Street
> across the Iron Bridge
> to seek my Christ.

It will be a wonderful moment when the very Body and Blood of Our Lord Jesus Christ is placed upon your tongues — what joy there will be in Heaven! So many valuable little souls safely into the fold! Look behind the altar! There will be angels there, ascending and descending, singing songs of joy. . . .

> Into the incense-coloured light,
> my arms in white rosettes,
> I walked the marbled floor
> apast parental eyes
> to seek my Christ.

Christ will be standing there in all his glory, his Virgin Mother will smile and there will be a great singing in Heaven. . . .

Under the gilded candle-light,
my arms in white rosettes,
my mouth enclosed my God,
I waited at the rail
to find my Christ.

There will be the glow of God in your veins, your souls will be at one with Heaven:
if you were to die today, angels would open the gates of paradise, and with great
rejoicing bear you in. . . .

Back to the human-hampered light,
my arms in white rosettes,
I walked: my faith was dead.
Instead of glory on my tongue
there was the taste of bread.

From *Selected Poems*, New Writers' Press, 1970; *Collected Poems*, The Gallery Press, forthcoming

The Knights
Evelyn Bolster

I am fully aware of the Order's low profile. I have heard the Knights described as job-
traffickers, opportunists, 'Catholic' Masons and hot-gospellers, and I have received
my share of anonymous letters about their 'underhand and damaging activities'. . . .
   Oddly enough, relations between Knights of Saint Columbanus and the Ancient
Order of Hibernians have never been more than peripheral. . . .
   At the same time, when the Hibernians decided in 1957 to close their Irish Club
in Limerick it was to the Knights that they made an offer which was substantially
lower than sums offered to themselves by other societies. Somehow or other, the
Limerick Councils of the Knights of Saint Columbanus were plagued by difficulties
— internal as well as external — relating to their cheaply purchased club premises,
and it was from Limerick that some of the most severe indictments of the Order
came. (These indictments have been conveyed to me personally by way of innuendo
and through anonymous letters. I have dealt with the matter of anonymous letters
in the Introduction, and as for charges made orally, none of my informants was
willing to corroborate or substantiate his accusations, thus leaving me with no
other option but to ignore them.)

From *The Knights of Saint Columbanus*, Gill and Macmillan, 1979

The Lord Taketh Away
Michael Hartnett

In virgin cloisters from fourteen
It was taught as the only life:
Before the body made its moves
The best wife was the spiritual wife.

They preached the convent was the bar
Between the wanted and the wild
And poured their holy lies upon
The immaculate logic of this child

For her I wrote impotent songs,
Transparent and slight as tears,
And offered her mortal happiness
For some unspecified years.

Because for her death was
The consequence of a kiss,
While Christ, as ghostly husband,
Offered immortal bliss.

I fought, that devious lessons
Might somehow be undone,
But the odds were three to one:
Father and Son and Holy Ghost.
I had no chance against such a host.

From *Selected Poems*, New Writers' Press, 1970; *Collected Poems*, The Gallery Press, forthcoming

On the Trail of a Jewish Princess
Frank McCourt

So what was I doing prowling at dusk in a Jewish graveyard two miles beyond
Limerick, the city where I was reared? And why, without a smidgen of Hebrew in
my head, was I searching for the grave of a Jewish princess when I could be down
at the Hurler's Cross pub knocking back a pint of stout or a glass of whiskey and

warming my bones before a turf fire? It was a scene devised by the sisters Brontë:
dim violet sky, black scudding clouds, full moon, shy since her rape, evening star a-
twinkle, traffic light for the recent dead, a dog howling from a distant hill, the wind
screaming an answer through tormented trees, gaunt headstones, rearing out of the
ground, rigid as the stance of Jeremiah. The day before I had sat in the train from
Dublin drinking beer, watching the countryside slip by, thinking of a Limerick
childhood.

'Do you see that shop,' my mother used to say, 'that was a Jewish sweet shop. We
used to run up there when we were small and we'd press our noses against the window.
The oul' woman would come out an' scream at us "Vot ye vont?" and we'd yell
back, "We vont noddings" an' she'd scream again, "Vell take your snotty nose away
from my window", an' we'd run off up the street laughin' over her accent.' That was
Collooney Street, the street of Jews. Further up was the house that once was a
synagogue. With only one Jewish family left in the city there is no need now for a
synagogue Why did they leave? . . . It was years before I discovered why in the
42nd Street Library in New York. . . . I remembered last spring's fuss when the
Mayor of Limerick, Steve Coughlan, tossed off an anti-Semitic remark. He said the
Jews deserved what they got in 1904, and when the storm broke around him the air
was charged with wrath and indignation. . . .

Across the street from the Limerick railway station I had a pint of stout in Charlie
St George's pub. An old man told me about the Jewish cemetery in Kilmurry out
the Dublin Road. 'And do you know what?' he said. 'No,' I said, 'what?' 'There's a
Jewish princess buried abroad in that same graveyard.' My God! A Jewish princess
buried near Limerick. . . . 'They have a little house in the graveyard where they do
wash the bodies.' . . .

A friend drove me out to Kilmurry where I asked about the cemetery in the local
pub. The barman said yes, go across the road and up the path. . . . Oh yes, there was
a princess up there all right, a Russian, the last one to be buried there. . . . To get
to the cemetery I had to climb through a gap in the hedge where cows wandered. I
pushed open the door of the little wash-house. On the wall in the dim light a stone
tablet in Hebrew said nothing to me. The floor was covered with straw and cow
dung. . . . Was I going mad? Whether it was the full moon or the drink or a simple
obsession I had to find that princess before I returned to New York. . . . Here was
an inscription, partly in English:

Maurice L. Morrison
Died February 23, 1930, 569

No sign of a princess, not in English anyway. With the light almost gone words
were hard to make out and I had to step carefully around cow droppings. . . .

In Memory of Zlato Maissel
Died 5th Nieson 5666 aged 65

Alas, poor Zlato. It's a long way to Lithuania — or wherever you came from. As I peered at the words the wind rose to a banshee shriek. . . . The door of the little house banged shut . . . it was a priest, a Redemptorist, who incited the people . . . calling the Jews bloodsuckers, parasites, Christ-killers, Shylocks. . . . The Jews gradually left Limerick, though Zlato, by the looks of it, stayed on to die in a strange year, 5666.

Still no sign of a royal grave. I talked to the other graves: told them I was sorry for their troubles but I was after a princess and would settle for nothing else. What in God's name, I wondered, would bring Jews from the ghettos of Europe — Poland, Germany, Lithuania, Russia — to this part of the world, Limerick on the Shannon? Why would they come to a land deserted even by its own people? After wandering for thousands of years and millions of miles they came to rest in Kilmurry in the County of Limerick. . . .

On the way back to Limerick my friend told me if I wanted to track down the story of the princess I should talk to Eddie Donnelly who knows all the gossip going back fifty years. 'Take it with a grain of salt,' he said. 'Eddie gets carried away and what he doesn't know he'll invent.' I stopped at Eddie's meat shop and asked him if he knew anything about a Polish or Russian Jewish princess buried in Kilmurry. ''Course I do but she wasn't Polish and she wasn't Russian. She was a Romanian and she shot herself.' 'But I heard she died at sea.' 'Nodatall, nodatall. She shot herself above in the Crescent Hotel.' . . . Could he tell me more about the princess? When did she die? 'During the war,' he said. ''Twas all kept quiet because the Irish papers usen't to report suicides in those days. But I'll tell you what you'll do. Go up an' see Christy Bannon . . . and buy him a drink . . . an' he'll tell you all you want to know about the princess. You'll find him at the White House bar.'

I should not have gone to the White House bar. There was a plane to catch at Shannon and I knew Christy was a man of many words and endless theories. When I asked him about the princess there was that groping look on his face of a storyteller oiling his muse and I realised I'd need not a grain but a sack of salt. 'Of course I heard of her. Sure wasn't it all in the papers.' 'Eddie said it wasn't.' 'Never mind Eddie. If he knew so much he wouldn't be sending you to me.' I told him how the old man in Charlie St George's said the princess was Polish. . . . 'What the bloody hell do they know about it in Charlie St George's? . . . That princess was a German an' that's all there is to it.' Christy persuaded me to have another pint before I went to the airport and treated me to a talk on Jewish burial customs. The Jews are buried standing up. But what about the horizontal mounds? Never mind the bloody horizontal mounds. They're put there to fool the rest of us because on the last day the Jews won't have to be struggling off their backs like the Christians. They'll be ready to run and off the mark like a flash, first in line at the throne of God Almighty so that they'll catch him in a good mood before he's worn out and cranky from judging the whole human race. I said I had to go, I'd miss the plane. 'Let me tell you one more thing before you run off to America. If you open a Jewish grave, you'll find they have plenty of money grasped in their fists so they can bribe St Peter at the gates, for isn't he one of their own when all's said an' done? But believe you me if the day ever comes that I'm down an' out you'll find me abroad in Kilmurry with a shovel. A pound note is as good to me as it is to St Peter.'

I had to go. I had to go. I rushed out, got a taxi and arrived at Shannon, just in time to miss the plane. And all because of a dead Jewish princess — Polish, Russian, Romanian, German — who may never have lived in the first place.

From *The Village Voice*, 2 September 1971

Remembering Elsa Reininger
Des Ryan

Elsa Reininger was born in 1882 in Neulistritz, Bohemia, then a Czech province of the Austro-Hungarian empire. She married Berish Hofler (also spelled in a variety of other ways), a Polish citizen who had acquired Greek nationality. The couple, both Jews, settled in Vienna. In 1938, the Hoflers were forced to flee Austria from Hitler's persecution, leaving property and money behind them. They came to Limerick where their daughter, Margaret Kaitcher, lived at 74 Wolfe Tone Street, Berish arriving in early September with the sum of £440 and his wife a month later. They stayed, as paying guests, with another Jewish family named Tobin, at 18 Newenham Street. Elsa suffered from depression and often spoke to Mrs Tobin about Hitler and the money she had lost on the fall of Austria. On Thursday, 27 October 1938, she booked into the Hotel Crescent, 87 O'Connell Street, for the second time in two days, having earlier written a number of letters, sending one to Germany with instructions to have her income tax paid. Between 6.45 p.m. and 11.45 p.m. she shot herself in the head and died. She was aged 56. On the following Sunday, 30 October, she was buried in the presence of her husband, her daughter, her son-in-law, Gaskel Kaitcher, and the last serving Rabbi of Limerick, Simon Gewurtz, who is also buried in the cemetery. An inquest was held at Barrington's Hospital on the next day and the jury brought in a verdict of suicide while of unsound mind. Almost sixty years after her lonely death, Elsa Reininger lies forgotten in an unmarked grave in the Limerick Jewish cemetery at Kilmurry.

From a manuscript in the possession of the Editor

Confraternity Campaign
John Liddy

Sermonising to a hushed congregation
Of God-fearing men
On the dangers of close dancing,
Evil literature and cinema necking,

The Spiritual Director
Declared from his pulpit
That young people were being
Deliberately provocative,

Outrageously suggestive
On the dance-floors of the City,
That 20% of Limerick's population
Had read *Lady Chatterly's Lover*

And would burn in hell for it,
That picture-houses were
Dens of iniquity
Because of inadequate supervision.

Vigilante patrols were formed
To separate passionate dancers,
Scrutinise publication lists,
Root out courting couples

With flash-lamps.
That was nineteen-sixty-three
And things have changed since then,
The Spiritual Director

Quit the priesthood,
Leaving behind
A diminishing congregation
Of disillusioned men.

From the *Limerick Socialist*, Vol. 7, No. 4, April 1978

A Limerick Homily
Pope John Paul II

Here in Limerick, I am in a largely rural area and many of you are people of the land. I feel at home with you as I did with the rural and mountain people of my native Poland, and I repeat here to you what I told them: Love the land; love the work of the fields for it keeps you close to God, the Creator, in a special way.

To those who have gone to the cities, here or abroad, I say: keep in contact with your roots in the soil of Ireland, with your families and your culture. Keep true to the faith, to the prayers and the values you learned here; and pass on that heritage to your children, for it is rich and good.

To all I say, revere and protect your family and your family life, for the family is the primary field of Christian action for the Irish laity, the place where your 'royal priesthood' is chiefly exercised. . . .

Your homes should always remain homes of prayer. As I leave today this island which is so dear to my heart, this land and its people which is such a consolation and strength to the Pope, may I express a wish: that every home in Ireland may remain, or may begin again to be a home of daily family prayer. That you would promise me to do this would be the greatest gift you could give me as I leave your hospitable shores.

I know that your Bishops are preparing a pastoral programme designed to encourage greater sharing by parents in the religious education of their children under the motto 'handing on the faith in the home'. I am confident that you will all join in this programme with enthusiasm and generosity. To hand on to your children the faith you received from your parents is your first duty and your greatest privilege as parents. The home should be the first school of religion, as it must be the first school of prayer. The great spiritual influence of Ireland in the history of the world was due in great degree to the religion of the homes of Ireland, for here is where evangelisation begins, here is where vocations are nurtured. I appeal therefore to Irish parents to continue fostering vocations to the priesthood and the religious life in their homes, among their sons and daughters. It was, for generations, the greatest desire of every Irish parent to have a son a priest or religious, to have a daughter consecrated to God. May it continue to be your desire and your prayer. May increased opportunities for boys and girls never lessen your esteem for the privilege of having a son or daughter of yours selected by Christ and called by him to give up all things and follow him.

From *The Pope in Limerick*, edited by Rev. John Fleming, Diocesan Offices, Limerick, 1980

Dr Jeremiah Newman
Kenneth Griffith

Through a friend it was arranged that I should meet a Roman Catholic priest who was close to the men who had fought with the Irish Republican Army, under Michael Collins's leadership. The priest was introduced to me without much explanation, as Monsignor Jerry Newman. Now, I knew nothing about 'ranks' in the Roman Catholic hierarchy and for whatever reason I was a little overchallenging in my exchanges with this Christian Irishman; my language was not the best. But Jerry Newman rode it with ease. He took me out to a very good supper at the seaside, just outside of Dublin. We had a drop to drink and I decided that he was a very good chap.

At the end of the evening Jerry said to me: 'We ought to continue our discussion tomorrow. If you are free, come and have a bit of lunch where I live, and I'll have a close friend of Mick Collins there to meet you. I live at a teaching college.' He gave me directions on how to get to Maynooth, and added: 'But anyone here in Dublin will tell you.'

I had imagined one of those lonely priests — like a captain on a ship at sea — perhaps with a dour housekeeper, and I actually imagined my new friend preparing a bit of something personally over a gas ring. But as my car drove into a great Gothic complex, which is the very centre of Roman Catholic power in all of Ireland, I began rapidly to readjust my expectation. At the central entrance of the main building I enquired of the man supervising that post: 'Where do I find Monsignor Jerry (I think I should have said Jeremiah) Newman? I have an appointment with him.'

'He's waiting for you, sir', and I was whisked upstairs.

Jeremiah Newman stood in his fine atmospheric apartment with a gentle-faced man, surmounted with a mass of white hair.

'Hello, Kenneth. This is Sean Kavanagh who was a close friend of Michael Collins and he is most anxious to help you in any way he can.'

Sean Kavanagh was to become a close friend of mine and now that he is gone — like all of the Old Patriots — I miss him very much. He was a fighting agent for Collins and a train-raider.

Jerry said: 'We must go; I mustn't keep my colleagues waiting', and we chased after him down the stairs. He stalked ahead of us like a virile white rabbit and suddenly we were in a vast dining-room with very lengthy refectory tables stretching away, and as we entered the massed priests rose.

Monsignor Jeremiah's ritual was brief and peremptory; I sat on one side of him, Sean on the other. The food and the wine were first class. The very last time I spoke to my chum was in the city of Limerick, where he reigned as Bishop. And so I was well launched into the best of republican circles.

From *The Fool's Pardon: The Autobiography of Kenneth Griffith*, Little, Brown and Co., 1994

TWO

THE GARRISON

A Glenstal Romance
Mark Tierney

Standish O'Grady took up residence at once, and was still living at Cappercullen House in 1772, when his daughter, Mary, married Henry-Thomas, Lord Stavordale, son and heir of the first Earl of Ilchester. There is quite a romance attached to this marriage, which was also responsible for the christening of one of the oaks in the deerpark of Glenstal as the 'Ilchester Oak'.

According to the story, Lord Stavordale, a young lieutenant, was posted with his regiment to Limerick city. In the course of his social rounds he met Mary Grady of Cappercullen, and the young couple fell in love at first sight. For months they continued to meet at parties and dances, while Stavordale lost no opportunity to ride out to Cappercullen to visit Mary. It soon became obvious to Capt. Grady that the young lieutenant was not suffering from a mere infatuation, but rather that he was pressing his suit seriously with a view to marrying Mary. He therefore made up his mind to take action, believing that the Earl of Ilchester would never allow his son and heir to marry the daughter of a poor and unknown Irish squire. Capt. Grady wrote at once to the Earl, saying that he had learnt that young Stavordale had got into some kind of scrape, and it would be as well to have him removed from Limerick. The Earl acted on his advice, and the young lieutenant was sent elsewhere. His visits to Cappercullen ceased and poor Mary had to pine her heart out as she walked the woods alone. In fact, the separation from her lover soon caused Mary to languish and she became quite ill. But her father, though he loved his daughter dearly, could find no solution to her predicament.

One day, about three months after Lord Stavordale had left Limerick, Capt. Grady received a letter from the Earl of Ilchester, saying that a friend of his, a certain Colonel Prendergast, would be passing through Limerick in a few days, and he had asked the Colonel to call to thank him personally for the way he had acted in connection with Stavordale. Col Prendergast duly arrived at Cappercullen and was received by Capt. Grady, who insisted that he stay there for a few days. After seeing Mary and noticing how pale and unhappy she looked, Prendergast decided to take the subject up with his host. He suggested that the girl should be sent to a warmer climate for a rest. But Capt. Grady, who knew all the time the cause of his daughter's depression, decided to take his guest into his confidence and tell him the whole story. He explained that Mary had only begun to fail when she was separated from her lover, and that the young man in question was none other than Lord Stavordale. He then told how he had acted in writing to the Earl of Ilchester, feeling that the latter would never allow his son to marry her. At that moment, Col Prendergast, who was in fact no less a person than the Earl of Ilchester, turned to Capt. Grady and said: 'I am the Earl of Ilchester, sir, and I could think of no one more suitable for my son to marry than she. I have walked and talked with her, these past few days, and have already come to love her as my future daughter-in-law.'

And so it turned out that Mary Grady married Lord Stavordale. On the left of the front avenue leading up to Glenstal Abbey, there is an old oak tree, called the 'Ilchester Oak'. Tradition has it that the couple used to swing from one of its branches.

From *Glenstal Abbey: A Historical Guide*, Glenstal Abbey Publications, 1990

Taking the Shilling
John Harley

A regiment was raised in the County Limerick by Sir Vere Hunt, Bart. Nearly all the officers who joined him in the undertaking, many of whom I knew very well, were, although men of high respectability, much reduced in circumstances, and labouring under pecuniary embarrassments. The sentries, therefore, at the barrack-gate had strict orders not to admit any person in coloured clothes, lest they should be visited by a limb of the law. And, when the recruits once entered, they were never allowed to go out until they were sent on foreign service. An old acquaintance of mine, Morgan O'Dwyer, a captain in the regiment, and as good a fellow as ever lived, being considerably in debt in Limerick, kept close quarters within the barrack-gates at the Curragh, where the regiment then lay. One of those ingenious fellows called a sheriff's bailiff, of the name of Hartigan, from Limerick, devised a curious stratagem. Having procured a soldier's old coat, he obtained admission, and immediately arrested poor O'Dwyer. Although completely taken by surprise, O'Dwyer did not lose his self-possession, but observed to the bailiff that he was not at all displeased with him for doing his duty. 'And as proof of it,' said he, 'here is a shilling, get whiskey at the canteen, and I will then accompany you wherever you wish.' When Hartigan had sufficiently refreshed himself, he returned for the captain, in order to escort him to prison, when, to his astonishment, he was handed over by O'Dwyer to the sergeant-major, as having been enlisted by the shilling he had given him. Nor had O'Dwyer any other alternative, as he would have been ultimately ruined had he gone to prison.

Hartigan was immediately conducted to the orderly-room, where he was measured, and his name entered upon the muster-roll and regimental books; and, when he exclaimed that he did not want to be a soldier, and on his knees entreated to be let out again, he was frightened into silence by being told, that if he continued to annoy them, he would be put into the black hole and severely punished for mutiny. He was then fitted by the master tailor with regimentals, and had a stiff leather stock clasped about his neck; and was finally handed over to the strict, old drill-sergeant, to be instructed in the manual and platoon exercises. I dined at the mess on the day this singular scene occurred, and saw the unfortunate bailiff led in with the other recruits to be shown to the colonel; and was, I must confess, very much amused with his stiff appearance, with the broad leather stock and the rueful expression of his countenance. He made one or two efforts to complain, but was instantly stopped by the drill-sergeant with the usual threat of the black hole and mutiny.

From that day to the day of his embarkation, he was regularly drilled and exercised from six o'clock in the morning until nine, then from ten till two, when the recruits dined, and again from three until eight o'clock at night. He embarked with his regiment for the West Indies, but, fortunately for him, the transport he was in, encountering a storm, was blown into the Bristol Channel, and, in consequence of the injury the vessel received, the detachment was obliged to land. On his arrival at Bristol, he made application to the mayor to be released, stating his situation and the manner of his detention. The mayor was not a little surprised, and very probably amused, at the recital of his adventure, but thought it prudent to take no further notice of it than ordering his immediate discharge, which was instantly complied with. When he obtained his liberty, he lost not a moment in bidding adieu for ever to a military life, and, crossing over to Waterford, he walked from thence to Limerick in his red coat, relating to his friends his campaign, and declaring his determination never to enter a barrack again to arrest an officer.

From *The Veteran, or Forty Years in the British Service*, Henry Colburn, 1838

A Limerick Letter
Sir Arthur Wellesley*

To Brigadier-General Lee, at Limerick
Cork, 7 July 1808

My Dear Sir, — According to the desire which you expressed in the conversation, which I had with you at Lord Harrington's on Wednesday, I proceed to give you my opinion on the nature and circumstances of the command which you are about to exercise in the County of Limerick. In the first place I must point out to you, that the situation of a general officer commanding in a district in Ireland, is very much of the nature of a deputy-governor of a county or a province. He becomes necessarily charged with the preservation of the peace of the district placed under his command; and the Government must confide in his reports and opinions, for the adoption of many measures relating solely to the civil administration of the country. From these circumstances it is obvious, that it is the duty of every general officer to make

* Arthur Wellesley, who later became the Duke of Wellington, wrote this letter on his departure for the Peninsula in 1808.

himself acquainted with the local circumstances of his district, and with the characters of the different individuals residing within it, in order that he may decide for himself according to the best of his judgment and information, and that he may not be misled by others.

This duty will be still more obvious, by a consideration of certain circumstances which exist in nearly all parts of Ireland. It frequently happens that disturbances exist only in a very small degree, and probably only partially, and that the civil power is fully adequate to get the better of them. At the same time the desire to let a building to Government for a barrack — the desire to have troops in the county, either on account of the increased consumption of the necessaries of life, or because of the increased security which they would give to that particular part of the country — would occasion a general rise in the value and rent of land, which probably at that moment might be out of lease, — or in some instances the desire to have the yeomen called out on permanent duty — occasions a representation that the disturbances are much more serious than the facts would warrant. Upon these occasions letter after letter is written to the commanding officer and to the Government; the same fact is repeated through many different channels; and the result of an enquiry is, generally, that the outrage complained of, is by no means of the nature or of the extent which has been stated. The obvious remedy for this evil, and that which is generally resorted to, is to call for informations on oath of the transactions which are complained of. But this remedy is not certain, for it frequently happens that the informations on oath are equally false with the original representations. The general officer then has no remedy, excepting by his acquaintance and communication with the magistrates and gentlemen of the county to acquire a knowledge of characters, and to become acquainted with all the circumstances which occur.

It frequently happens that the people who do commit outrages and disturbances have reason to complain; but in my opinion that is not a subject for the consideration of a general officer. He must aid in the preservation of the peace of the county, and in the support of the law: and he who breaks the law must be considered in the wrong, whatever may have been the nature of the provocation he may have received.

It is possible that grievances may exist in the County of Limerick; provisions may be too dear, or too high a rent may be demanded for land, and there may be no poor-laws, and the magistrates may not do their duty as they ought by the poor. But these circumstances afford no reason why the general officer should not give the military aid he may have at his command to preserve the peace, to repress disturbance, and to bring those to justice who may have been guilty of a violation of the law.

In respect of the gentlemen of the county in which you are posted, I recommend you to attend particularly to the Lord Chief Baron O'Grady; you will find him well informed of the transactions in the County of Limerick, and well acquainted with the characters, and disposed to assist your judgment. I also recommend to your attention Mr Dickson, the late High Sheriff of the County, and Colonel Vereker, the member for the City of Limerick. There may be, and certainly are, other gentlemen in the County of Limerick on whose information you may depend. But I have requested Mr Trail, through whom I send this letter, to apprise you confidentially of the names of those whom you ought to consult. Believe me, etc.

From *Limerick; Its History, Ecclesiastical, Civil, and Military, from the Earliest Ages*, by Maurice Lenihan, Hodges, Smith and Co., 1866

The Capture of John Scanlan
Aubrey de Vere

A young man of gentle birth fell in love with a beautiful and virtuous peasant girl, married her secretly, got tired of her, and drowned her in the Shannon. For a considerable time it was impossible to arrest the murderer: his capture was described to me by a near relative of mine, the magistrate who arrested him. He had received secret information, and led a body of police to the house of the murderer's parents at a late hour of the night. Apparently there had been a dinner party in that house, for on the door being opened after a slight delay, he was received in the hall by its mistress, a tall and stately lady in black velvet dress. She addressed him with quiet scorn, informed him that her house was a hospitable one, had been favoured by many guests, but none resembling those who had come at that unusual hour to visit it; that she knew his errand; that her son had not been in that house for many weeks; but that he was welcome to search for him as he pleased.

They searched the house in vain; they next searched the offices. When on the point of returning, one of the party remarked a ladder within the stable the top of which leaned against a small door in the wall. The policemen refused to mount it, for they said that if the murderer was hid on the premises he must be behind that door, and would certainly stab the first to enter. The magistrate mounted. The search was again in vain and all had descended from the loft except the last policeman, who, as he approached the door, carelessly prodded with his bayonet the straw with which the floor was covered. A loud scream rang out from it and the murderer leaped up. He had been grazed, not wounded, and if he had held his peace must have escaped. His scream was almost immediately re-echoed by a distant one louder and more piercing. It came from one who knew her son's voice well. The magistrate told me that the most terrible thing he had ever witnessed was the contrast between that mother's stately bearing at first and the piteous abjectness of her later appeals as, on her knees, she implored him to spare her son.

The guilt was conclusively proved, and the murderer was sentenced to be hanged; but in those times justice was not always impartially administered, and the peasantry were certain that a gentleman would never be hanged. He requested that he should be taken to the place of execution in a carriage, but his crime had excited universal abhorrence and none of the livery stables in Limerick would supply one. A vehicle was procured from a distance on the morning of the execution, and the unhappy man entered it. On the middle of the bridge that spans a small arm of the Shannon, the horses stopped, and no efforts could induce them to go further. The crowds were more certain than ever that somehow there would be an escape; a gentleman could not be hanged. The horses plunged more and more furiously but would not advance. The murderer fell into an agony of terror. He exclaimed 'Let me out and I will walk.' He walked to the place of execution, and was hanged.

From *Aubrey de Vere: A Memoir*, John P. Gunning, Guy & Co. Ltd, 1902

A Military Station, 1848
William S. Balch

Crossing the bridge into the 'English Town', the hue became, if possible, still darker, as the evidences of *moral* depravity thickened on all sides. This added to the picture colourings of disgrace and wretchedness which transcend all attempts at description — most appalling and repulsive exhibitions of vice, in which soldiers from the barracks acted prominent parts.

Crossing another Limerick bridge, we passed one of the military stations, when still stronger marks of vice and infamy were to be seen. Under the best regulations, a large share of iniquity clusters about such large establishments. But here it seemed to revel without restraint. From this place flows the blighting influence which leaves such palpable traces of crime and moral pollution upon both men and women, young in years, but, it is feared, already old in vice and deep in depravity. Who ever searched minutely, the *full* history of large bodies of men, closely packed in barracks or monastery, without finding traces of depravity which have festered into the rottenest crimes; sometimes kept secret for a time, but afterward divulged? . . .

We visited this morning, one of the barracks, occupying a large fort on the high ground in the eastern part of the city. We bolted in unasked, and looked at the comfortable quarters of the soldiers. English statesmen are wise in one thing, keeping strong the right arm of their power. The soldiers are well fed, and well paid, and have an easy time of it. None of the common people fare half so well. They are a sort of indigent nobility, furnished with red coats, glazed caps, and good rations at the public charge, and required to exercise barely enough to digest their food. And the ranks of an army are well suited to the hereditary gradations so indispensable in the working of British institutions. There is no motive for a soldier to desert unless in a foreign land; it would be folly to forsake his beef, and bread, and whiskey, which come to him with perfect regularity, and at no cost, to seek a precarious livelihood on a patch of ground he might hire at an enormous rent, but could never own. His instinct makes him loyal, and natural rights and political and social wrongs do not trouble him. It is food and raiment, and a place to sleep, that concerns him most, and so he becomes mechanically valorous, when occasion requires.

Some three or four thousand of these minions of power, are now stored in the four barracks in this city, and thirty thousand more in different parts of the kingdom. Fresh troops are constantly arriving from England and Scotland. . . .

Two or three squads were going through a course of artillery drill. They were tall, noble looking fellows; and as they strutted through the evolutions around their brass pieces, pretending to put in cartridges and ram them down, prime, elevate, take aim, fire off and swob out, all at the direction of little slim lads, in cloth caps, who swaggered about, flourishing rattan canes, like Broadway dandies, a feeling of pity and disgust was awakened, to think that the best energies of these 'noble' young men were to be prostituted to the base purpose of learning how to kill their fellow men scientifically — by rule and by 'law and order', and subject to the command of her Royal Majesty.

From *Ireland, as I saw it*, New York, 1850

Come, Listen to the Band!

On Sunday evening last the members of what is known as the Boherbuoy Temperance Band proceeded from their rooms in Edward Street, followed by a large crowd of idlers, male and female, and played through the streets in defiance of police regulations.

As they reached the head of the Crescent, gaining an accession of strength on the way, they were followed by a strong force of Constabulary who — in obedience to a recent proclamation of the Magistrates against such processions — put an end to the tuneful display by seizing the instruments, which they carried off to William Street barrack, followed by the crowd, who, not content with groaning the Sub-Inspector and his men, resorted to stone-throwing.

The Head Constable's shako was cut by a blow of a stone, another constable received a blow of one over the eye which cut him, and several others received them on the back and other parts of the body, happily without injury to their persons.

The Constabulary retaliated by charging the mob, several of whom were arrested and conveyed to the barracks.

From *The Limerick Chronicle*, 22 March 1870

The Siege of Clampett's Bow*
Thomas Stanley Tracey

Oh! murdher, blood and thunder
Are the muses dead, I wonder?
Those fine old ancient maidens
That once lit the poet's glow.
Are our bards all gone to blazes?
That none will sing the praises
Of the city of the sieges
And the Siege of Clampett's Bow.

There's many a fight and ruction
That causes more destruction
But was ever one more striking?
The never a one I know,
Except that siege more glorious
When Limerick was victorious
And when women fought for Sarsfield
And Ireland long ago.

You may boast of all the glories
Won by Russians, Turks and Tories,
In Plevna, Afghanistan and on later
Fields you know,
And the Zulus may surprise you,
But Garryowen defies you,
For such a siege you'll never see
Than that of Clampett's Bow.

Shure the neighbourhood of John St
Is immortalised by one street,
Where our heroes on Chalk Sunday
Marched forth to meet the foe,
When the baton-wielding pol-ice
Were routed holus-bolus,
With stones and broken bottles
By the boys of Clampett's Bow.

* This incident took place on Chalk Sunday, 2 March 1879, in a narrow laneway off John Street called
  Clampett's Bow (now Mitchel Street).

Upon the battle's border
The friends of law and order,
Kept modestly retiring when
The boys began to throw,
But soon tremendous chargins
Knocked down our boys and vargins,
And roused the mortal vengeance
Of the men of Clampett's Bow.

'Twas the grandest of all shindies,
When they barred the door and windies,
And let fly their hail like missiles
On the beleaguered down below.
You may talk of pioneering
And 'civil' engineering,
But Vanban himself must yield
The palm to the boys of Clampett's Bow.

We are told that many a Zulu
That fought at Isandula
Put a dead man on his head-piece
To ward the coming blow,
So each peeler stout and able
On his noddle placed a table,
Which afforded no protection from
The stones of Clampett's Bow.
Then hurrah for drink and fightin'
And the sprees we take delight in,
And the good ole times when constables
Were rare as summer snow,
With John Jam-e-son to feed us
And the Clampett boys to lead us,
We'll never want such laurels
As we won at Clampett's Bow.

From *The Old Limerick Journal*, No. 1, December 1979

A Militia Departure

On yesterday at 10 o'clock the fifth Battalion of the Royal Munster Fusiliers (County Limerick Militia) assembled at the Strand Barracks for embodiment. Nearly 600 of the 650 comprising the full strength of the Battalion turned up in response to the notice. From 10 o'clock large crowds of relatives, chiefly women, thronged the Strand in the neighbourhood of the barracks, to bid farewell to the men, who were carefully kept within.

Sometimes a man would come to the gate with a bundle of clothes to hand to his wife, but no further was he allowed to come, and as soon as the message was delivered, he was rudely shoved back. About six o'clock, the time fixed for the departure of the men, the crowd became so large as to be unmanageable, and a large force of police under District-Inspector Hetseed came to reinforce the small number of constables under Sgt Lloyd, who were on duty at the gate. Nearly an hour elapsed, and there was no appearance of the men. A few baggage vans came out and drove in the city direction, but this was a ruse on the part of the authorities, because it was intended from the first that the militia should entrain at Long Pavement, to avoid any scene at the station.

Shortly before seven the gates of the barrack were thrown open, and the staff brass band marched out at the head of the regiment, with the fife and drum band immediately behind. The men marched as far as the Treaty Stone — the word 'march' is used advisedly — surrounded by female relatives. The disorder was something disgraceful. At the Treaty Stone portion of the police escort went off towards the Long Pavement, but the fife and drum band wheeled suddenly to the right and marched over Thomond Bridge contrary to all orders. The officers fumed and stormed to no purpose. The men had their way and marched through Mary-Street and John-Street taking the most circuitous route they could to the station. Fully fifty per cent were drunk, and the spectacle was most disorderly.

At the station large crowds received the warriors, who, with considerable difficulty, were entrained for Salisbury Plain for training. The corps may be in training for six months, but there is a feeling that foreign service may be their portion after that. The Regiment is in command of Colonel Massey-Westropp, and the other officers are Major and Hon. Lieutenant Colonel Glosier, Major W.G. Gubbins, Captain the Earl of Limerick, Captain Leiland, and D'Esterre, Lieutenant-Hampson, Cotter, Hall, Fitzgerald, Fitzmaurice and Warburton, with Captain and Adjutant A.C. Maxwell and Quarter-Master J.C. Crumpe.

From the *Limerick Leader*, 11 May 1900

A Limerick Haunting
Robert Graves

Hauntings, whether in waking life or dream, are emotionally so powerful, yet can be so seldom ascribed to any exterior agency, that they are now by common consent allotted to the morbid pathologist for investigation — not, as once, to the priest or augur. A number of hauntings 'yield to treatment', as the saying is.

There are also occasional hauntings which most psychologists would tend to dismiss as fantasies, or as symbols of some inner conflict; but which, however grotesque, deserve to be accepted at their face value and placed in the correct historical context. Let me describe a persistent haunting from my own case-history. I am glad to say that it did not originate in a ghost-ridden childhood and is therefore easier to assess, though I cannot claim to have been in good mental or physical health at the time; on the contrary, I was suffering from vivid nightmares and hallucinations of the First World War, in which I had just fought. Shells used to burst on my bed at night, by day I would throw myself flat on my face if a car backfired, and every rose garden smelt terrifyingly of phosgene gas. However, I felt a good deal better now that the war seemed to be over: an armistice had been signed, and the Germans were not expected to renew the struggle.

January 1919 found me back with the Royal Welch Fusilier reserve battalion at Limerick; where twenty years before my grandfather had been the last Bishop of the Established Protestant Church of Ireland. Limerick, a firm stronghold of Sinn Féin, King George Street had become O'Connell Street, and when our soldiers took a stroll out of barracks they never went singly and were recommended to carry entrenching-tool handles in answer to the local shillelaghs. This return as a foreign enemy to the city with which my family had been connected for over two hundred years would have been far more painful but for old Reilly, an antique dealer, who lived near the newly renamed Sarsfield Bridge. Reilly remembered my father and three of my uncles, and gave me fine oratorical accounts of my Aunt Augusta Caroline's prowess in the hunting field, and of the tremendous scenes at my grandfather's wake — at which his colleague, the Catholic Bishop, had made attendance compulsory in tribute to his eminence as a Gaelic scholar and archaeologist. I bought several things from Reilly: Irish silver, prints, and a century-old pair of white, elbow-length Limerick gloves, left by the last of the Misses Rafferty and so finely made (from chicken-skin, he told me) that they folded into a brass-hinged walnut shell.

The shop smelt of dry rot and mice, but I would have gone there to chat more often, had it not been for a nightmarish picture hanging in the shop entrance: a male portrait brightly painted on glass. The sitter's age was indeterminate, his skin glossy-white, his eyes Mongolian, their look imbecile; he had two crooked dog-teeth, a narrow chin, and a billy-cock hat squashed low over his forehead. To add to the horror, some humorist had provided the creature with a duddeen pipe, painted on the front of the glass, from which a wisp of smoke was curling. Reilly said that the picture had come from the heirs of a potato-famine emigrant, returned at last with a bag of dollars to die comfortably of drink in his native city. Why this face haunted and frightened me so much I could not explain; but it used to recur in my imagination for years, especially when I had fever. I told myself that if I ever saw a midnight ghost — as opposed to midday ghosts, which had been common enough phenomena during the later, neurasthenic stages of the war, and less frightening than pathetic — it would look exactly like that.

From *Encounter*, July 1955

The Battle for Kilmallock
John McCann

Kilmallock RIC Barracks was a stoutly built erection, fortified by the addition of slotted steel shutters. Its normal complement was twenty men and it held a good store of rifles, grenades and ammunition. When Commandant Seán Forde led some sixty-odd Limerick and East Clare Volunteers to take the barracks, on the night of 27 May 1920, he knew that the task would not be an easy one. He expected that the attack would be a sustained affair and had seen to it that approach by road or rail from any direction would not be possible.

Overlooking the barracks, which was a low, block structure, were comparatively high buildings. These houses were occupied by thirty riflemen, while forty volunteers armed with shotguns acted as outposts. Clery's Hotel, facing the barracks, dominated, being as high again as the RIC post. From Clery's the main attack would be directed, each unit to act upon flash-lamp signals from Seán Forde, who was posted on a roof-top only ten yards south-west of the barrack gable.

At half past eleven the men were ready. Everything had worked well, the RIC seemingly having no knowledge of what was afoot. All was quiet. Then Forde's torch flashed three times in the darkness and from the surrounding houses the merry crack of many rifles sounded, to the accompaniment of bursting bombs. In quick succession Forde hurled three 56 lb weights through the roof, which were followed by numerous bottles of petrol and bombs.

The RIC were now at their posts, twenty-eight of them returning round after round. Above their heads the bombs burst and the petrol bottles came hurtling in. Still there was no sign of fire. In these circumstances a huge paraffin-oil distributing car was brought into service. Daringly, the men drove it quite close to the barracks and with a hose connection poured many gallons through the breach in the roof. Even with that it was a considerable period before the roof took fire, and in quick time the height of the flames made it appear that surrender by the garrison would be only a matter of minutes. But no, the RIC men stuck to their guns, and, after two hours, when the Volunteer leader had signalled the cease-fire, their answer to Forde's question was: 'No Surrender.'

With the barracks burning fiercely, the RIC still continued to keep up a hot reply of rifle grenades, firing aimlessly through the dense fog of foul-smelling smoke that enveloped the town. One hour — two hours — three hours! They were still holding out. Again the question: 'Do you surrender?' and again the answer: 'Never.'

Somewhere a cock is heard crowing as day breaks, clearly revealing an almost gutted building. Higher the flames lick momentarily as the roof collapses, followed by terrific explosions in quick succession as the stores of grenades and bombs catch on.

Still no sign of capitulation from the gallant defenders, who have retired to a fortified little outhouse at the rear. Six hours of continuous fighting in a raging furnace finds them indomitable. The Volunteers renew the attack upon the outhouse. Their ammunition is fast running out. In broad daylight now the danger of reinforcements arriving is imminent. These RIC men will die rather than surrender. 'Let them live' is the decision of the Volunteer leader, as he signals a parting volley by way of goodbye to a heroic company.

From *War by the Irish*, The Kerryman Ltd, 1946

The Limerick Night Police
(Not to be Sung in Public Houses!)

This ancient corps, though hoary, allow me to remark,
Does deeds of 'derring' glory, but does them in the dark,
Can boast a few flat-runners and steeplechasers four —
If anyone could wake them from the County Club hall-door!
Some constables wear whiskers, and one Jim Barry's hat,
None suffers from insomnia — you can bet your boots on that!
And though weighed down with helmet, top-coat and pretty pole,
They seldom miss a trick on their nocturnal stroll.

* * *

Perhaps some drunken stranger should chance to cross a beat,
To arms, our brave defender! 'To arms?' Oh, no — to feet!
He knows how to surrender, but 'Fog-a-boll-a'? No!
For his heart disease is dangerous, his corns a holy show.

A stray-way mule or mud-cart he'll wallop to the pound,
No sleep for that locality while whacks and kicks resound,
'Tis here he lays on varnish and paints his masterpiece,
Joe Lynch's Irish heirlooms, the Limerick Night Police.

When playboys, young and older, take a turn 'on the loose',
Our nervous night protector is subject to abuse . . .
'Oh, kick and bate me, gentlemen. My pockets? As you please',
Not often are they empty with the Limerick Night Police.

*   *   *

Yes, Limerick, you are beautiful, and Garryowen you're blest,
With Corporators dutiful, high rates and all the rest,
Take care! Some day the Shannon — a word from Dan McNeice —
Might clear ye to Ballycannon, on top of yeer Night Police!

From *The Bottom Dog*, Vol. 2, No. 48, 1 November 1918

The Caherguillamore House-Dance
Patrick Lynch

On St Stephen's Night, 1920, the moon shone brightly on the highways and byways of east Limerick. On the byways, from the four points of the compass, young men and women made their way through the valleys and across the hillsides. All were gay with the festive spirit and eager for the enjoyment of a night of music, song and dance. In normal times, the St Stephen's night dance in any part of rural Ireland would be looked forward to with pleasurable anticipation after the three weeks of Advent. But 1920 was not a normal year. During the six months before Christmas, the armed struggle for independence in east Limerick, as elsewhere throughout the country, had been gaining in momentum. Men from every town-land were on their keeping among their 'friendly allies, the hills'. In every town and in many of the villages there were recently reinforced garrisons of regular British troops, RIC and Black and Tans. Members of the active service units visited relatives or friends infrequently and always swiftly and silently. Those were days and nights when men carried their lives in their hands. Occasions for dancing and jollification were few and far between.

So it was, then, that during the days of Christmas, eyes of brown and eyes of blue shone brightly under tossing tresses of auburn, raven or flaxen hair, and many a blush suffused already rosy cheeks as the word of mouth was passed from farmhouse to cottage around the town of Bruff that there was to be a dance on St Stephen's night. Rumour had it that the dance was to be held at Herbertstown, but rumour has ever been a lying jade. On this occasion, however, she was being used as a decoy. The dance, surely, was to be held — but not, as had been given out — at Herbertstown which was some miles away from the real location.

Caherguillamore House, the great rambling mansion of the Viscounts O'Grady, the kinsfolk of Lord Fermoy, was where the fiddlers and accordion players would set impatient Irish feet tapping in the high-ceilinged ballroom where the mincing steps of the ladies of the ascendancy were wont to trip to the gentle measure of the minuet. The reigning Viscount had gone from Caherguillamore in a retreat to climes that were deemed safe from the smoking muzzles of the rifles that were the harrying forces of the Crown on most of the roadways of Munster. Amidst its deep woodlands the big mansion presented its shuttered windows to deserted parks and avenues.

Day in and day out the only evidence of life at Caherguillamore was provided by the caretaker, Tom O'Donoghue, and his family, and by the occasional visits of supervision from the Honourable Mrs Baring, wife of Colonel Baring, Master of the Foxhounds, who lived at Knockbarton mansion some distance away. Mrs Baring was the daughter of Lord Fermoy and was to inherit the mansion and its surrounding estate.

To the great house, too, from time to time, came Paddy O'Donoghue, the caretaker's son. Paddy was a member of the Bruff Battalion of the Volunteers and it was through his co-operation and that of his father that Caherguillamore House had been selected for the dance. The selection had been made by the members of the Bruff Battalion and the function was being held to raise funds for the purchase of arms to equip the Battalion Flying Column. The decision to form battalion columns as distinct from the brigade columns, had been taken in a number of districts including Bruff.

Having spread the rumour that the dance was to take place at Herbertstown, the organisers went ahead with their programme for Caherguillamore. Approximately 300 were expected to attend and as the charge for admission was to be four shillings it was decided to give a free supper to the dancers. For this purpose a number of sheep were obtained and slaughtered, and willing women helpers attended to the cooking and other catering arrangements. Practically at the eleventh hour, word was again passed through the countryside giving notice of the change of venue. And in the bright moonlight the lads and lasses converged on Caherguillamore House, remote amidst its guardian trees and well off the main road.

Scouts had been posted on the surrounding roads although any kind of enemy action was deemed remote — as remote, indeed, as the very situation of Caherguillamore itself.

Inside the house the dance went on. Young men and women took the floor gaily oblivious of the hundreds of British troops, RIC and Black and Tans who were just then moving on foot along the roadways leading from Limerick city towards Bruff. In snake-like dark columns they moved between the tall hedges, under the moon, marching mile after mile because travelling by lorries would give warning of their approach in the stillness of the night. Despite all the precautions, including the spreading of the rumour about the Herbertstown venue, the enemy had got word that most of the much-wanted Volunteer leaders and column members would be at Caherguillamore that night. Neither for the first nor the last time the British grapevine of information was proving its effectiveness. But if the troops and the RIC and the Tans marched without their customary transport, they did not leave the lorries behind. The operation was so well timed and co-ordinated that the lorries were following up — sufficiently far to the rear to eliminate the danger of warning noises, but not too far to be brought readily to the fore at the crucial moment.

Caherguillamore was approximately 13 miles from the city and most of the distance was covered on foot. A surprise attack was intended and a surprise it proved to be.

The witching hour of midnight came and went and some of the dancers were sitting down to supper when word was passed from the scouts that all was not well. . . . Suddenly, the near-midnight stillness was shattered by volleys of rifle fire. A hail of bullets thudded into the walls of Caherguillamore House and poured through the wooden shutters and windows. Glass smashed and fell with terrifying noise as Verey Lights whizzed, zoomed and burst over the shrubbery and the trees. Volley after volley crashed out from the unseen military, police and Tans who were on every side. Inside the great ballroom young girls shrieked in fright and sought refuge in the arms of their dancing escorts. Round after round of .303 was fired in through the windows. Again and again the blunderbuss-nosed Verey Light pistols sent up high arcs of light to illumine the dread scene with a bizarre and even a nightmare effect . . . hell seemed to break loose with renewed frenzy. . . .

Recovering from the initial shock, the Volunteers in the house reacted rapidly in efforts to try to protect the scores of girls and to organise some kind of a defence once all realised simultaneously that they were being subjected to a large-scale attack. But it was useless. Taking full advantage of the well-mounted element of surprise, and acting in accordance with a carefully prepared plan, the attackers closed swiftly on the house and burst through the front and rear doors and even through the windows. The cold steel of fixed bayonets and the brass of their rifle butts gleamed in the lamplight as they charged in on the 150 young men and more than 90 young women running hither and thither in the ballroom and adjoining corridors of the house.

Brutality ran rampant and naked at Caherguillamore that night. Bayonet and rifle butt were used with abandon on young men who showed signs of resistance or of anxiety to protect the screaming young girls who clung to them in terror. The girls were torn from their companions who were, in many instances, knocked down by blows of rifles on the face or the back of the head. Some were savagely stabbed with bayonets intended for trench warfare and not for use on defenceless and mostly unarmed youths on the floor of a ballroom. Many of the boys at the dance had no connection with the Volunteers except, perhaps, the most tenuous link of family relationship or the general sympathy to be found among all peoples in occupied countries for freedom fighters. . . . There was, apparently, to be no escape from Caherguillamore House. So thoroughly were the plans laid that it was intended to use the hounds to track down any Volunteers who might succeed in getting out of the ring of steel thrown around the grounds. . . . Back at Caherguillamore the girls were roughly herded up the wide stairway to rooms where they were searched by women searchers who had been brought out expressly from Limerick for the job. . . . The girls heard clearly the cries and moans of the young men who were being bay-oneted, batoned and beaten with rifle-butts as they were marshalled into the huge kitchen on the ground floor.

The Commander of the attacking forces, Colonel Wilkinson, decided to carry out interrogations in the ballroom for the purpose of endeavouring to identify Volunteer leaders and others who were 'on the run'. As each man was ordered to proceed, in turn, from the kitchen to the ballroom, he had to run the gauntlet of two long lines of RIC, Black and Tans and regular military. And as he tried to make his way between the lines of green-blue, khaki and black, he was beaten on the body, the head, and the limbs with the rifle-butts of those on his left who struck from the front and those on the right who struck from the back.

Young men fell to the floor of the passageway, crying out in extreme pain, as rifle-butts thudded into their bodies and heads. From the floor they were forced to rise again and stagger and stumble onwards as heavy hob-nailed boots kicked them in the ribs and stomach. Moans and shrieks rang through the corridors of the great house and in the upstairs rooms the young women sank to their knees to recite the Rosary. . . . One young Volunteer officer spat out most of his teeth which had been broken by a blow from a rifle-butt and then stumbled beneath further buffeting to the place where Colonel Wilkinson and his brother British officers were conducting their 'interrogation'. He was James Maloney who was later to become Commandant of the Bruff Battalion. Another blow knocked him to his knees and Sergeant Honan of the Royal Irish Constabulary placed the butt of his loaded rifle on the floor and said to Maloney: 'Did you ever look down the barrel of a loaded gun?' Maloney was compelled to place his eye to the muzzle of the loaded weapon whilst the sadistic sergeant of the RIC placed his own finger on the trigger. But even in the midst of brutality the gallantry of some fighting men asserts itself in extraordinary ways. As the sergeant of the Royal Irish Constabulary forced the Volunteer officer to place his eye to the muzzle of the loaded rifle, a Black and Tan, who was standing beside him, violently kicked the stock of the weapon from the police sergeant's hands and barked 'Stop that! Do you want to blow the man's head off.'

During the initial stages of the attack some of the Black and Tans had come up to and fired on Volunteer sentries who returned their fire. In this exchange of shots one of the Tans was killed. He was Constable Alfred C. Hogsden, of London, who had joined the Black and Tans only seven weeks before. Prior to that he had spent fifteen years in the British Navy. The death of one of their number, despite the fact that several Volunteers had been killed, was like a match to a powder keg when the Tans and RIC learned of it. Once again they wreaked savage and spiteful revenge on the 120 young men cornered in the kitchen and ground-floor passageway leading to the ballroom.

In a bout of particularly destructive vandalism, these allegedly disciplined police and military tore and smashed the banisters from the big staircase and, using the pieces of timber as clubs, they bludgeoned the defenceless men.

All through the night, the girls imprisoned in the rooms upstairs prayed as they listened to the curses and swears and beatings that went on on the floor below. Not until ten o'clock on the following morning were these young women released. By that time the dead Volunteers had been taken to Limerick in a lorry whilst the others, some of them very severely wounded and all with blood-smeared and unbandaged faces and heads, were loaded into other lorries and taken in convoy to Limerick where they were imprisoned at the New Barracks (now Sarsfield Barracks). The citizens of the Shannon-side city who witnessed their passage, in the lorries, along the streets never forgot the awful procession of vehicles bearing over 100 blood-stained and obviously suffering young men.

Military, RIC, and Black and Tans took part in the attack on Caherguillamore, and the RIC personnel from the Limerick city police stations were reinforced by the garrisons from Bruff, Fedamore, Croom and Pallasgreen.

The five Volunteers who were killed in the encounter were: Martin Conway, the company captain, and the Vice-Commandant of the Third Battalion of the East Limerick Brigade; Daniel Sheehan, of Caherguillamore; Harry Wade, of Cahernorrey, Ballyneety; John Quinlan, of Grange Lower, Bruff, a lieutenant of the local Company; and Ned Moloney, of Grange. . . .

At the New Barracks the prisoners spent the night of 27 December lying on the floor of an old church into which they had been kicked on their arrival. On the morning of the 28th they were taken out into the barrack yard and subjected to further interrogation — this time in the presence of members of the RIC, from a number of the rural areas, who had been brought in to assist in the identification of 'wanted' men.

Dr Michael O'Brien, the column medical officer, and Paddy O'Donoghue, the son of the caretaker at Caherguillamore, were singled out for very special attention and, after prolonged interrogation, were taken to another part of the barracks and again savagely beaten. Another who was given an added beating apparently in an effort to break his will and extract information from him, was Tom O'Brien, of Holy Cross, Bruff. But the beatings failed in their purpose. Subsequently, all the prisoners were transferred to the Limerick jail and were court-martialled before a tribunal presided over by Major-General Eastwood. Many were given sentences of ten years' imprisonment and were sent to prisons in Portsmouth and Dartmoor. Others received lighter sentences — in some cases of as little as six months. Those were sent to the convict prison and military post on Spike Island in Cork Harbour. A number of those sentenced were not members of the Volunteer movement, but had merely been present at the dance. All were held until the general amnesty following the signing of the Treaty.

From *Limerick's Fighting Story*, edited by J.M. MacCarthy, Anvil Books, 1966

The Black and Tans
P.J. Ryan

The Black and Tans usually acted in an intelligent manner — to cause the maximum of terror with the minimum of effort. One arch of Annacotty Bridge, near the city, was blown up to prevent the movement of British forces across the Mulcair river. The following morning the Tans arrived at the local creamery where the farmers were delivering milk. They collected all the men within a mile of the place and compelled them to tear down nearby stone walls and fill in the broken arch with stones and rubble. When at the end of the day, when the work was finished and the bridge made usable again, the labourers were dismissed with gunfire and ashplants. Annacotty Bridge was not blown up again until July 1922 when the Tans had left the country.

While the military in the four barracks were content to blow up houses with explosives, they always acted in an orderly manner. They first removed the tenants from the selected house and the nearby houses, before placing the explosive in the best engineering manner, and up went the house and its contents. In this manner four houses were demolished in Limerick city. On the other hand, the Tans loved a blazing fire. When given a box of matches and a tin of petrol by their officer, they needed no further instructions. They burned down four houses deliberately and two more by accident. The Tans were not concerned whether the tenants remained in the building or not.

From 'The Fourth Siege of Limerick', *Limerick Socialist*, Vol. 4, No. 10, October 1975

Ancestral Voices
James Liddy

Voice of Mother:
Limerick was full of them in the old days, marching to the different churches, the redcoats, each regiment going along, pipers and flags. On Sunday afternoons the

officers used to sit in a club in the house where the Augustinians live now near their church. I can remember Armistice Day, you could hear the roar of the crown on O'Connell Street, even though we were living out on Corbally. Dan went in and waved the Union Jack with the rest of them, he was spanked when he came back. Once he went in and bought something in Roche's Stores and brought it back wrapped in a Union Jack bag. My mother made him return it.

Voice of Father:

I remember the three days' rioting after the visit of Carson. He spoke in the Crescent by the statue of O'Connell. No Protestants would stay for three days afterwards; the Protestant shops were all looted and burnt, the Bishop was chased over the fields of St Mary's. There were terrible baton charges down Catherine Street outside the house, you could hear the screams inside. Sometimes I used to run with the crowd, or I'd pull my friends out of it and take them into the kitchen and make pancakes.

Voice of Mother:

We lived out in Avondale, in Corbally, beside the O'Malleys, the father was the crown solicitor for Limerick. That was the last house in Limerick to fly the Union Jack.

Voice of Father:

The Civil War was much worse in Limerick than what went before. There were snipers on the roofs for days. Andy Killeen was on the Republican side, he was holed up for two days with one of his friends who'd been shot.

Voice of Mother:

I saw the Civil War in three places. We were in Kilkee and went to Carrigaholt for a picnic. We walked along the headland beyond the castle. We came upon a sniper with his gun facing the Shannon. He told us to get lost. We lived in Earlsfort Terrace, in one of the first houses built in Dublin as apartments. Mother and I used to hear the shooting every night along the Grand Canal. The Brennans, you know, took over Limerick, they were all generals and colonels afterwards. They were friends of mother's and great boys. During the fighting in Limerick they went into Roche's Stores and ordered uniforms for the Free State troops; when asked about payment, they took out their guns. Once Dan and I went to Bodenstown for the Wolfe Tone celebration. We stopped by our men on the way back. Colonel Brennan took out his gun. We passed through. He was the first captain of the Dáil guard.

From *On the Counterscarp: Limerick Writing 1961–1991*, edited by Anthony O'Brien, Ciaran O'Driscoll, Jo Slade, Mark Whelan, Salmon Publishing, 1991

THREE

LAND AND LABOUR

The Silversmiths of Limerick
Douglas Bennett

It is impossible to say when the working of precious metals first took place in County Limerick, but from archaeological evidence goldsmiths certainly plied their trade there about 700 B.C., as shown by the magnificent gold gorgets found in parts of what is now that county.

The earliest dated piece of silver is probably the Askeaton Chalice, inscribed *Ex Do Simo Eaton Armr Par Askeaton Anno 1663*. The little Eglish paten, however, has an inscription on the base with '1559' in Tudor lettering and also *Ye church of Eglish 1775*. The paten is in typical sixteenth-century style but it also bears the mark 'GM' (for George Moore, flourishing 1748–84). The later inscription is poorly done and Moore may merely have had the paten in for repair and stuck his mark on it.

A fair quantity of silver was manufactured in Limerick from the mid-seventeenth century until about 1820, by which time the Act of Union had dealt a hard blow to craftsmen generally in Ireland.

From 1637, under Royal Charter of Charles I, all silver was required to be sent to Dublin for testing and hall-marking. The charter made no provision for any marks on Irish silver other than the harp crowned and the maker's mark. The first entries for Limerick plate sent to Dublin occur in 1711, and the Dublin Assay Office records show parcels varying from 3 lb to 20 lb in weight being sent up by Limerick silversmiths. Although all articles manufactured in Limerick should have been sent to Dublin, because of distance and travelling difficulties (added to the likelihood of theft by highwaymen), very little Limerick silver actually found its way to Dublin for marking. This makes provincial silver all the more interesting.

The charter of 1637 was so complete that no further Act of Parliament was necessary until 1729. In that year an Act (3 George II Chapter 3) imposed a duty of 6d. an ounce on all gold or silver wares manufactured in and imported into Ireland on and after 25 March 1730. This produced the further complication that silver not sent to Dublin for assaying was being sold without the tax being paid, thus creating a revenue offence.

During the seventeenth century the marks on Limerick silver consisted of the maker's mark, a castle gate and a star. It has been suggested that the latter marks derive from the middle of the century when Sir Geoffrey Galway added a fourth armorial tablet to the fifteenth-century tomb of Edmund Galway in St Mary's Cathedral. This fourth quartering, depicting Baal's Bridge, had been granted to John de Burgo of Galway in 1361 or 1364 for his spirited defence of that bridge. It shows the bridge with four arches guarded at each end by a castle, and the mark has two mullets above the bridge and one beneath it. Sir Geoffrey, whose house stood at the corner of Quay Lane and Nicholas Street, was Mayor of Limerick in 1652 and an extremely influential citizen. It may be that the silversmiths adapted their mark from part of his arms, or it could be a variant on the arms of the city itself, a gateway between two towers. Many seventeenth-century pieces exist with these marks, e.g. the Askeaton Chalice already mentioned and the Ennis Chalice. An early eighteenth-century toll stamp belonging to the Tholsel Court also has the castle gate with supporting towers.

Like those of Cork, the Limerick silversmiths seem to have adopted the Sterling mark about 1710, and for most of the eighteenth and nineteenth centuries their products bear the word Sterling and a maker's mark, often struck twice. One curious mark used by three Limerick silversmiths was a punch resembling the crowned harp punch used in Dublin, but with the maker's initials replacing the strings of the harp. The initials 'IS' (John Strit), 'GH' (George Halloran) and 'PW' (Philip Walsh) have been found on this mark. Another interesting mark used by four Limerick silversmiths in the middle of the eighteenth century was a lion rampant between the maker's initials. This is known with the initials 'CB' (Collins Brehon), 'IB' (Jonathan Buck or Jonas Bull), 'II' (Joseph Johns) and 'SI' (Samuel Johns). Occasionally a punch of a fleur-de-lis appears with the maker's initials, dating from about 1780 until after 1800. This was the period of bright-cut engraving, and many Limerick spoons bear the motif of a fleur-de-lis or of Prince of Wales feathers, these not being in general use elsewhere.

The city of Limerick had a total of fifteen corporations, consisting of smiths, carpenters, weavers, shoemakers, tailors, saddlers, masons, bakers, coopers, surgeon-barbers, butchers, tobacconists, tallow chandlers, hatters and brewers, the goldsmiths being part of the corporation of smiths. In 1769 Ferrar's *Directory* shows Richard Bennis as master and Samuel Johns and Thomas Carr as wardens of the smiths.

Admission to the Freedom of the City was by right or by grace or, in certain cases, by purchase. This last category applied mainly to tradesmen and was controlled by the 'New Rules' of Charles II. Admission by right could be obtained under one of three conditions: (1) Birth, i.e. being born the firstborn of a freeman, being over 21 years of age and resident in the city; (2) Marriage, i.e. being married to the daughter of a freeman, being over 21 and resident in the city; (3) Apprenticeship, or service, i.e. having served a seven year apprenticeship to any merchant or tradesman who was himself free of the city. In this case it was necessary to prove that the claimant's master was free and that he had served seven years to him in the city. This seven years' training resulted in a high standard of craftsmanship in all crafts, including that of the silversmith.

The 1783 Act of Parliament was obeyed by several people connected with the trade in Limerick, who complied with the order and entered their names in the register at Goldsmith's Hall, Dublin. Where the word 'registered' appears in the biographical notes, it means he registered in Dublin under this Act.

Since no date-letter appears on either Limerick or Cork silver, biographical information concerning the actual silversmiths is of considerable value, more especially their dates of death. Hitherto little information has been available concerning the

Limerick silversmiths and indeed many of them are difficult to trace. The following notes have been assembled mainly from newspapers, Church of Ireland registers and the Registry of Deeds. Most of the silversmiths lack a known date of birth, hence the importance of the more easily found marriage date: as a rough guide, a silversmith was probably aged between 25 and 35 when married.

From *Collecting Irish Silver 1637–1900*, Souvenir Press, 1984

Limerick Lace
Ada K. Longfield

Limerick, which gave its name to the lace, was the second oldest of the nineteenth-century centres and the industry owed its inception there to commercial rather than philanthropic enterprise. Mr Charles Walker, a native of Oxfordshire, having married the daughter of a lace manufacturer, abandoned his studies for the Church and conceived the idea of setting up a lace-making industry in the city of Limerick. In 1829 he brought over twenty-four girls from England as teachers, and thus arose the centre which gave so much employment for many years.

Limerick, like Carrickmacross, is not a true lace in the rigidly technical sense of the term, but it is more conveniently generally classed as a lace, rather than as embroidery. There are two varieties — tambour and run work. The former is so named from the fact that the frame on which the net is stretched for working somewhat resembles a drum-head or tambourine. Nottingham machine net is usually employed, and through the meshes floss or cotton thread is drawn by a special hooked tambour needle resembling a crochet needle, in order to form the design, which is copied from a paper pattern placed before the worker. Actually tambour work originated in the East where it is still much done, especially for coloured embroideries on cloth. It was practically unknown in Europe until about 1750, when it began to be made in Saxony and Switzerland, but the art did not reach England till about 1820.

Run lace is of a lighter character, the pattern being formed on the net with a fine thread which is darned, or run in with a point needle like a darning needle. Thus it is a descendant of the sixteenth and seventeenth-century darning on meshed grounds or lacis, and originated in France with the Broderies de Luneville. It was also made in Nottinghamshire when machine net made the work easy and is still called by some, 'Nottingham lace', although the patterns were usually derived from Lille lace designs. Limerick run lace is very similar to the nineteenth-century Nottingham run lace and to the Broderies de Luneville. The distinction between tambour and run work, however, is not so marked in many Irish productions because the two techniques are often utilised in the same piece. This helps to give the better Limerick lace — where the design is good — a light and graceful effect. The heavier tambour stitch gives a clear outline, while run work makes a dainty filling, especially when enriched with a variety of ornamental point stitches.

The later history of the Limerick industry was similar to that of many others in Ireland. It was very successful during Mr Walker's lifetime and found a large market in Great Britain — first through a lace house in London, and after 1834 through a traveller who went round taking orders in England, Scotland and Ireland. But after Mr Walker's death in 1842 many of his first workers returned to England and there was no proper supervision, so that the old designs deteriorated from inferior copying and there was no stimulus to create new and suitable ones. Consequently by about 1870 Limerick lace fell into disrepute and only cheap goods of poor quality were produced. The industry was saved from complete decay by the nuns of the Convent of the Good Shepherd, and after 1888 a revival took place when Mrs Vere O'Brien established and maintained a Limerick lace training school. This school partly owed its inception to Mr Alan Cole, who gave a lecture at the Limerick Chamber of Commerce in September 1888, and the painful contrast between the older and the then contemporary lace was illustrated by photographs and a loan collection. (Mr James Brenan, R.H.A., of the Crawford Municipal School of Art, Cork, and afterwards Headmaster of the Metropolitan School of Art, Dublin, gave able assistance to Mr Cole in improving the lace industry especially throughout the South of Ireland.) As a result of these activities, centres for making Limerick lace increased — mainly as with Carrickmacross, through classes attached to convents, such as that of the Sisters of Mercy at Kinsale, Co. Cork. More important still, the standard of design was raised, for the centres were put in touch with special art classes at the Schools of Art in Dublin and Cork, so that the studios could keep in connection with the workrooms and thus secure co-operation in the adaptation of patterns and their execution. Further help was rendered by the Art Industries Exhibition established in connection with the Horse Show by the Royal Dublin Society in 1887 (most unfortunately discontinued about 1923) since it not only provided an incentive for good work, but was also instrumental in disposing of the products of Limerick and other lace centres.

It should be added that for a brief period in the nineteenth century appliqué and guipure were also made at Limerick. The former was probably introduced by Lady de Vere and usually consisted of cambric applied to net — as in Carrickmacross — but in some few pieces net was applied to net with a beautifully light effect. The guipure was like that made at the Carrickmacross Schools.

From *Catalogue to the Collection of Lace*, National Museum of Ireland

O Holy Liberty
Michael Hogan

'Tis night; Earth's wrapt in a celestial swoon
As o'er the welkin glides the young May moon
Whose soft beams quiver on proud Shannon's tide
Sweet as the smiles of a fair blushing bride.
Oh! how I love to look upon thy face,
Sweet moon, so full of purity and grace,
And watch thy silver light in shimmering showers
Fall soft and sweetly on yon crumbling towers,
Whose massive heights and moss-enamelled walls
Defied the thunder of King Billy's balls,
When lovely maidens, sweet and pure as light,
To save their city joined the frantic fight,
And mid huge carnage and despairing screech
Beat back the Saxon from the blazing breach;
While street and alley, strewn with shot and shell,
Grew red and ruddy as the hearth of hell.
Yes, lovely maidens, fiery sons and sires —
Their hearts aflame with freedom's holy fires —
Rushed to the fierce and terrific attack
And beat the plunderers of Ireland back!
Yes, maidens, widows, hoary sires and wives
On freedom's altar sacrificed their lives,
Faced the fell foeman in a solid throng
And made huge havoc in the ranks of wrong!
O holy Liberty, benign and bright!
O glorious goddess of majestic might!
When shall thy flaming banner be unfurled
To wave triumphant o'er a warless world?
When shall thy scythe, with sweepings sharp and sure,
Mow down the villains who oppress the poor?
When shall all hypocrites and tyrants fly
Before the glance of thy indignant eye?
When, when shall despots fade like foam and froth
Before the cyclones of thy rage and wrath?
When shall oppression and class greed decay
And peace with justice linked all nations sway?
Alas! such blessings sacred and sublime
Lie buried deep yet in the womb of Time.

But come they will despite the gilded knaves.
Who'd have all mankind live the life of slaves.

From *Continuation of Poetical Satire on the Limerick Corporation and Other Sordid Citizens* by Oliver Twist, Bard of the Brand (Michael Hogan) *circa* 1875

Little Famines
Mary Carbery

Father said, 'I have known of poor people, five and six in the family, sleeping in a one-roomed cabin so small that none could lie flat on his back for want of room, but each one must lie on his side. And in another hovel where the floor space was already occupied, a beggar asking for shelter was given "the length and breadth of herself" under the table. There was no other place.' . . .

'I don't care to speak of miseries,' father went on, 'but I can never forget the efforts my mother made to keep life in the families who lived on the farm and worked for her, and yet not rob her children of food. Farmers like ourselves had cows and hens and a little corn and oats, so there was no fear of starvation for us, but we should have been ashamed to eat more than was strictly necessary when children all round us were famished. Often a labourer was so weak that the spade would fall from his hand and when he stooped to pick it up, as likely as not he would fall beside it. The worst time of the year was when the potatoes were finished and the new crop not ready for digging. Those were called the meal-months, when there was nothing to eat but stir-about made from siftings of flour more than half bran. And then, at times, after the months of dreadful hunger, disease came in the potatoes, or the crop failed entirely. . . .'

Father's voice grew husky and went out for a time.

'There was a potato famine in the winter of 1821–22, when I was a little fellow. The roads then were cumbered with people making for Bruff and Limerick to beg for charity, old folk, desperate men without work, mothers with long trails of half-naked children. . . .

I daresay you have seen a ewe lying dead in a field and her day-old lamb butting and tugging at her? So I have seen little children patting and pulling at their mother to wake her, and she lying by the roadside, dead. . . .

I was quite a little fellow when the first of the IC (Irish Constabulary) came to Limerick. They made the country safer. We were safer too, because my mother decided to take in a Poor Scholar. He had a room in the yard, and a gun to frighten vagabonds, but he never had to use it.'

From *The Farm by Lough Gur: The Story of Mary Fogarty (Sissy O'Brien)*, Longmans, Green and Co., 1937

A Tale of Woe
Michael Hogan

Once more, I had to throw off my 'singing robes', and turn to hard material labour to support myself and Nannie. Again I found employment at Russell's, but this time it was at Lock Mills. And I toiled from six o'clock in the morning until one at night at the rate of eight shillings per week, with an additional nine pence for every half-night I wished to remain at work.

Ah those were cruel hard times for incessant labour and small pay. There was a remorseless old fellow who acted as manager and clerk of this establishment, and he knew no mercy or consideration for working men. The harder he worked them the more delighted he was. I have often known him to make one man do the work of two.

He tried the same trick with myself, but I rebelled — and told others to rebel against his tyrannical imposition. This led to my final dismissal from the degrading, cruel slave market of Lock Mills. . . .

Between Newtown Pery and Lock Mills I worked out sixteen years of the primest time of my life, and I left the employ as poor as if I had never earned a penny. . . .

In the summer of 1862 I got myself into a quagmire of trouble about loan money which I had secured to oblige a neighbour. The sum was left unpaid by the borrower, and the lender — a hungry, pettyfogging vampire — let loose the helldogs of the law at my throat. The day and the scene is yet before my eyes, when two gallows-looking bailiffs came into Valhalla to distrain me. They appeared like the procurors of Antichrist. They carried out all my little things on the side of the street, while Nannie was crying bitterly, and I was standing outside the door mutely looking on.

I saw the stalwart amazons of Nicholas Street gathering into a silent mass, like a thunder cloud. I saw the spirit of battle kindling in their crimson faces, while the ominous throng grew denser; but no more signal was made until the bailiffs commenced to lift the things on to the car.

Then a sudden angry yell resounded through the street, and a charging brigade of war-goddesses fell like a hurricane on the amazed bailiffs. They were knocked down — they were kicked like footballs — leaped upon — dragged like dead dogs through the sinks, and in less than two minutes one would think them more like shapeless masses of mud and blood than anything resembling human form. And while the conflict was raging another section of the brigade was employed at rescuing my chattels by running away with them to places of safety. But I certainly felt delighted at the novel display of feminine faith and valour so boldly exhibited in my interest on that day.

The car which the sons of Antichrist — those bailiffs brought to carry away my effects — was smashed into smithereens, and the unfortunate bailiffs themselves were no better. They were rescued from total destruction by the police, and carried bruised, battered and bleeding to Barrington's Hospital. With grateful courtesy I warmly thanked those war-like women for their work of love, and I need hardly say that a bailiff never troubled me again in the same quarter.

But I was brought before the chairman of the Quarter Sessions for hounding a mob on the officers of the law, thereby getting them assaulted and battered in the discharge of their duty. The magnanimous John O'Donnell, Sol., one of the brave rebels of '48, ably defended me, without fee or reward, and actually got the whole case — loan money and all — dismissed. . . .

My mother thought of a new plot of torment and humiliation to my goaded and perplexed heart. She brought a basket of periwinkles along with some shell-delisk to the other side of the street, nearly opposite my door, and there she sat to vend her beggarly merchandise. The shabbiest pauper that ever strayed from a poorhouse looked a queen in comparison to her. She had attired herself in a babel of old rags that were actually confusing each other as they fluttered around her wretched form. They appeared like a mass of ivy leaves on an old wall quivering and shaking in the wind. I knew she had no other object in rigging herself thus, and coming there, than to shame and scandalise me. What could I do? I couldn't use force to remove her; neither could I employ the law to do it. Kileely Glebe House was at that time untenanted, and there at the lawn wicket she located herself on neutral premises, and no one had authority to turn her away.

I was almost sure the cold weather would finally expel her, but in this speculation I was deceived. For two years she occupied that bleak position, and never quitted it for even an hour up to the very moment I left my cottage, to return to it no more. Then she gave up her miserable occupation, well satisfied and in high glee. During those two provoking years she left no device untried to outrage my patience. She tried to prevent many persons from dealing in my shop, under the threatened penalty of her avenging curse. She slandered, belied and denounced me to everyone that passed by. The bad neighbours exulted at her unnatural villainy and used to bring her scraps of food, by way of alms, just to taunt and humiliate me. To avoid looking at these disgusting scenes I often ran into the city and remained away all day. . . .

I bore it with a silent immovable resolution. I waited for the advocacy of Time, the alleviator of all injuries and evils.

From *Memoirs* by Michael Hogan, the *Limerick Weekly Echo*, 26 February 1972

Wild Geese
Tim Lehane

Cacklecalling,
Wild geese
In sudden aerial flurry,
Windspreads swishing,
Climb away in skeins
On old flyways,
Through cloud spaces,
In skywastes. . . .

Out from our city, once,
With their drums thrum — thrumming,
With their flags flap-fluttering,
Marched the ranks of Sarsfield's men
Flocking to France and thundering battles,
These 'Wild Geese' left — all remember them. . . .

Others have left,
Have gone unnoticed,
Have left without
Flurry or swish or drum,
Have gone in their thousands,
Have quietly departed,
Have taken wing,
Unmourned, unsung;
No ancient callings,
No martial urges,
Have forced their flight
Towards other lands;
But their feeding-ground,
Being grey and barren,
Promised little
To their willing hands;
One-way tickets
In empty wallets . . .
Heavy cases . . .
Leaden speech . . .
Their migration
Is only echoed

When sea birds scream
By a wave-washed beach. . . .

From *The Old Limerick Journal*, No. 23, Spring 1988

The Spalpeens
Mary Carbery

My father, who was born in 1816, farmed about 200 acres of land, rented from Count de Salis. He gave constant employment to a number of men and women, some of whom lived in the four cottages on the farm. There was a potato garden for each cottage, also a goat. The labourers were paid a shilling a day, which was three-pence more than the wages usually given in the neighbourhood. Their wives and daughters helped with the milking of our fifty beautiful cows, under the supervision of the head dairywoman, whose wages were £30 a year. Extra men, called *spalpeens*, coming usually from Kerry and Cork, were hired for the potato-digging in October. My father's head man, Dick Dooley, used to go to Bruff on a Sunday in late September — if the ground was dry enough then for digging — and after Mass he inspected and engaged the required number of *spalpeens* who were waiting in the street to be hired by the highest bidder. The same *spalpeens* came year after year to our farm: quiet and unobtrusive they were, grateful to my father for giving them work and to my mother for providing abundant nourishing food. . . .

Our farm was like a little colony, self-contained, where everyone worked hard and all were contented and happy. Besides the fields, the farmhouse and its good out-buildings, there was a quarry, a kiln for burning lime, a sandpit, a turf bog and the productive eel-weir. Eels were sent direct to Limerick market or taken by Meggy-the-Eels who came from Bruff to buy 'the take', which she peddled from house to house in the little town. Everything we ate and drank came from the farm except tea and coffee and J.J. (John Jameson's whiskey), which was kept for visitors and for medicine. We lived by a strict routine, a necessity on a farm if it is to prosper, and all the indoor work took place in the two dairies and the large stone-paved kitchen which was about twenty-eight feet square and well-lighted by a large window overlooking the lake. On the opposite wall was the great hearth, the light and glory of the house, where a huge fire of turf, wood and coke burnt all day and smouldered all night, to be roused before dawn into flame by a few strokes of the well-built bellows. On the third wall hung a fine array of brass and copper saucepans with the old mincer on a bracket next to the great dresser, gay with willow-pattern plates, with dishes of various shapes and colours and here and there a jug. In the lower part of the dresser, instead of cupboards was a long coop in which were sitting hens; it seems to me now that they sat there perpetually except when two geese took their place in early spring. A third goose and many more hens were put to sit in the barn, while the gander, our terror, patrolled the yard, refusing to leave it till his proud wives returned to him, leading their lovely goslings, small moving balls of yellow fluff. It was ear-splitting to hear the gander's welcome to his mates when they came from the nesting.

In the centre of the kitchen was a long oak table at which the ploughman and farmboys had their meals, sitting on forms. For breakfast they had maizemeal stir-about with plenty of milk, sometimes potatoes; in later years home-made bread was added. Dinner was at 12.30, consisting of milk, potatoes and 'dip' (a make-up of gravy and bread); bacon was given twice a week, but later on every day. The men's tea was taken out to them at four o'clock, with bread and butter in great slices. The maids had the same food, but at a different time, and for supper at 7.30 break and milk, hot or cold, or porridge with plenty of sweet milk. On this simple fair maids and men throve; they were all healthy, hearty and good-tempered.

Opening out of the kitchen was a passage leading to the front door, our parents' bedroom and the little room where after our four o'clock dinner we sat to read or sew or learn our lessons. Upstairs were the spare room and two other bedrooms for ourselves and the maids, besides a storeroom where mother kept her dovetailed chest, books, linen, spinning wheels and many other things. The farmboys had a room in the yard, fitted with good beds and chairs; except for meals and prayers they were not allowed inside the house, nor was any sort of friendship allowed between them and the maids, who were ever under the watchful eye of 'the misthress'. . . .

All the maids worked hard, following the example of 'the misthress', and except for short runs to their homes now and again they had little respite from labour, nor did they expect it. I remember once seeing a number of girls and boys dancing at the cross-roads on a summer Sunday, but this diversion was strictly forbidden by priests and parents, who had a great dread of young people falling in love. Archbishop Croke was the first, as far as I know, to encourage football, hurling and other games for boys and young men; no entertainment was considered necessary for girls. But for the matchmaker there would have been no marriages. . . .

In those days young girls had nothing to look forward to but a loveless marriage, hard work, poverty, a large family and often a husband who drank. Small wonder that when they could they escaped to America. One of our maids, Nancy Brian, Con the ploughman's sister, a fair, tall girl of 17, gentle and childlike, left us to go to her relations in New York; she never reached them, and in spite of every effort made to trace her she was never heard of again. There was consternation in many little homes when time went on and nothing more was learnt of Nancy Brian. Mothers tried to keep their daughters in Ireland. The matchmakers backed them up and hastened to arrange marriages; even with this professional help there was many a slip 'twixt the cup and the lip. . . .

This was the farm routine. All hands rose at 4.30 a.m., the fire was blown up until it blazed, turf and coke were piled on and an immense iron pot of water suspended from a crane was moved by a lever to hang directly over the flames to boil for the feeding of the calves. Outside, one of the boys lit a furnace in the yard over which was a boiler for more hot water. This was set close to the pump.

At 7 a.m., when the milking was over, my mother came from her room to receive the milk in the upper or lower dairy according to the season: the lower one, which was reached from the upper by stone steps, was cooler and used in summer. On the stone shelves were rows of flat earthen and glass pans; all was spotlessly clean and fragrant, in fact visitors who came to Lough Gur seldom left without visiting 'Mrs O'Brien's show dairy'. Here entered in a long file, the head dairy-woman and her maids, carrying milk pails on their heads; lowering them carefully, they poured the milk through strainers into huge lead cisterns where the cream for butter-making was to rise, the remainder being strained into flat pans on the shelves. A lovely, homely sight: rich, ivory milk, golden cream — all to be hand skimmed — firm 1 lb pats of perfectly made butter ready to be sent off to special customers in Dublin and London; other great pats for home consumption — we children did not spare it — and the bulk of the butter in firkins, each containing 70 lb, set aside for the butter buyer to take to market.

At nine we had our breakfast: two boiled duck eggs every day for our father, a hen's egg for mother; for us children stir-about, home-made bread, and butter and milk.

Breakfast for all was over by 9.30 when we children set off across the hills to school. The men had gone to the fields, the women dispersed — some to feeding numerous turkeys, geese, hens, ducks, others to wash the dairy and scrub and scald pails, pans, strainers and churns; one to do housework and another to prepare the men's midday meal and perhaps set a great batch of dough to rise in the warmth of the hearth while the brick oven was being heated by burning bundles of furze and sticks. Our dinner was at four o'clock. The evening milking was from five to seven. The morning routine of straining and scalding was repeated. Milking was something of a mystery to us children, as our father forbade us to enter the byres, but from the outside we heard the rhythmical swish of milk falling into pails and the dairymaids singing or crooning, each to her cow. . . .

At seven o'clock we sat down for a happy time round the table in the little room, a bright, shaded reading lamp in the middle, and while the rest sewed, one of us or our mother read aloud books suited to our years, such as *Little Women*, which we loved and knew almost by heart, *The Wide, Wide World*, which made us weep over the griefs of pious Ellen Montgomery and shocked us with the irreligion of her Aunt Fortune, *Scottish Chiefs*, *Masterman Ready*, *Robinson Crusoe*, and many other children's books.

My father meanwhile sat contentedly with his pipe in an uncomfortable armchair, reading the paper and sipping a glass of fresh spring water. He was very abstemious and had nothing but this between his four o'clock dinner and breakfast next day.

All hands were called to say the Rosary at 9 p.m., mother giving it out, the rest responding. She ended with a fine generous prayer beginning thus: 'Bless, O Lord, the repose we are about to take, so that by renewing our bodily strength we may be better able to serve Thee.' The prayer was for those in authority over us, for the poor, sick and sorrowful, for unbelievers and for the dead. One of the farmboys was always the last to answer the call to prayers; my father reproved him, saying, 'It's for only ten minutes, Mike, ten minutes given to Almighty God.' 'Faix, sir,' Mike replied, 'they are the longest ten minutes of the day.'

At 9.30 the long day's work was over.

From *The Farm by Lough Gur: The Story of Mary Fogarty (Sissy O'Brien)*, Longmans, Green and Co., 1937

Tim Costello
Michael Hogan

This is the grave* of Tim Costello,
Who lived and died a right good fellow;
From his boyhood to his life's end,
He was the poor man's faithful friend.
He fawned before no purse-proud clod,
He feared none but the living God;
And never did he do to others,
But what was right to do to brothers.
He loved green Ireland's mountains bold,
Her verdant vales and abbeys old;
He loved her music, song and story,
He wept for her departed glory.
And often did I hear him pray,
That God would end her spoilers' sway;
To men like him may peace be given,
In this world and in heaven. Amen.

* This verse is carved on the tombstone of Tim Costello, who died near Glin in 1873, at the age of 85, and is buried in Kilfergus graveyard.

Michael Joyce: Shannon Pilot and MP
Brian Donnelly

Without doubt, the most remarkable Shannon pilot was Michael Joyce, square-rigger, alderman, Member of Parliament, Mayor of Limerick and President of the

United Kingdom Pilots' Association. He was born on 4 September 1851, at Merchants' Quay in Limerick city, and educated by the Christian Brothers in their schools at Bridge Street, Pery Square, and later at Sexton Street.

At the age of 14, Joyce joined the barque *Red Gauntlet* on his first voyage. During his subsequent career at sea, he was shipwrecked four times, losing all he possessed on each occasion. In November 1869, he joined the *Herald* at Limerick on a voyage to carry coals from Cardiff to Rio de Janeiro. About 150 miles west of the Bay of Biscay, the ship encountered a hurricane and began to take water. The crew of an Italian barque, sinking in the vicinity, were drowned within sight of the *Herald*, and Joyce and some of his companions were eventually saved by a French brig. He had another narrow escape from death while serving on a sailing boat carrying a cargo of timber across the Atlantic. The vessel capsized during a gale and Joyce and the rest of the crew clung to the waterlogged derelict for five days without food or water until picked up by another boat. He was twice wrecked in the North Sea, once when his ship was blown ashore by a storm and on another occasion when his vessel went aground due to the removal of all buoys and light-ships during the Franco-Prussian War. Joyce was later to recount that as he was so unfortunate at sea his family used to insist that he stay as close to home as possible!

In the early 1870s, Joyce returned to Limerick to serve his apprenticeship as a river pilot, and on Friday, 8 March 1878, presented himself to the Pilot Committee of Limerick Harbour Commissioners for examination as a candidate for a pilot's licence.

The committee noted that he was 26 years of age, had been five years at sea, had made several foreign voyages and had enrolment in the Naval Reserve. He was judged particularly suitable to be granted a licence and thus join the ranks of the Limerick pilots bringing ships up the river to the city from Cain's Island, and piloting them down the river to Scattery Island and even as far as Loop Head.

Henceforth, he played an active part in local nationalist and social affairs. He was one of the founders of the old Sarsfield Branch of the National League in Limerick. Joyce occupied the chair at the founding of Garryowen Rugby Football Club, and played in the first fifteen for both Garryowen and Limerick County.

The local Government Act of 1898 widened the franchise for local elections and caused an upheaval in local politics. The first municipal election after the Act, in January 1899, saw mass participation on a level unequalled in local elections prior to that date. Joyce contested this election as a Labour candidate for Custom House Ward, pledged to a democratic programme. He headed the poll in his ward, and the Labour interest was to secure a majority of eight men in the new Corporation, which was hailed by the *Limerick Leader* as a 'People's Parliament' and an epoch in Limerick's municipal history.

In the general election in the following year, he went forward as a candidate for the Irish Parliamentary Party. When the results of the election became known, Joyce, with his '. . . hardy, weather-beaten countenance, with the bluff hearty manner which characterises the sailor man the world over . . .' was found to have won an overwhelming majority over his unionist opponent, winning by 2,521 votes to 474.

Many years later, 'Quidnunc' of *The Irish Times* recounted Joyce's entry into the House of Commons when '. . . Mr Joyce commended himself to the tender mercies of the suave Speaker Gully of those days and asked him to guide him through "the shoals and quicksands of parliamentary procedure", a touch which was greatly relished and loudly applauded. Mr Joyce was soon dubbed "the Pilot of the House" and became immensely popular. . . .'

For most of the following two decades, Joyce served as an alderman of the Corporation; on two occasions he was mayor of Limerick, as well as being a member of parliament for the city. He played an active role as a member of the Limerick Harbour Board and of its Pilotage Committee.

Joyce became active in the United Kingdom Pilots' Association (founded 1884), and together with the President of the Association, George Cawley, led a deputation to see Winston Churchill, which resulted in an order being signed for a departmental committee on pilotage to begin work in 1909. Joyce was a member of the Marine Advisory Committee of the Board of Trade and gave evidence during its twenty-five sittings between November 1909 and April 1910 on the state of pilotage on the Shannon. The crowning effect of the committee's work was the Pilotage Act of 1913, which was a considerable advance on previous legislation, particularly in respect to freedom from illegal pilotage, a restriction of the issue of pilotage certificates, and better representations of pilotage committees. When Commander Cawley died in 1910, Joyce succeeded him as President of the UK Pilots' Association.

The Great War heralded the end of Joyce's political career, as well as that of other notable local supporters of the Irish Parliamentary Party. The year, 1914, had seen the false dawn of the Home Rule Act eclipsed by the outbreak of war.

It was a time of personal tragedy for Joyce, with the premature death of his second eldest son, Joseph. His eldest son, Richard, had emigrated to America, and later fought in France with the 165th United States Regiment. Joyce once again experienced the trauma of shipwreck when, as a passenger to Holyhead on his way to attend to his parliamentary duties at Westminster, he was aboard the SS *Leinster* when she was torpedoed near the Kish lightship, a month before the end of the Great War, with the loss of 500 lives. Joyce was later praised for his coolheadedness and assistance to his fellow-passengers.

The approach of the general election at the end of that year saw the Irish Parliamentary Party in disarray as a result of the rise of Sinn Féin. Joyce, by then 67 years old, intended to contest the city seat with the Sinn Féin candidate, P. Colivet. His election meeting on 25 November 1918 was, however, disrupted by Sinn Féin elements, and Joyce decided to stand down to save the city from turmoil.

Joyce's term as Harbour Commissioner ran for another year. His retirement from the Harbour Board in January 1920 was a cause of universal regret. He retired as

President of the United Kingdom Pilots' Association in 1923. He had been well liked and highly respected in that office.

Joyce maintained his interest in cultural and social affairs over the next two decades. He was Chairman of the Michael Hogan (Bard of Thomond) Memorial Committee which erected a cross over the Bard's grave in May 1933. He had known Hogan well and was able to confirm that a portrait painted by Dermod O'Brien for the committee 'was a living picture'.

T.P. O'Connor introduced Joyce to Mark Twain as 'the Shannon Pilot to the Mississippi Pilot'. He also met John McCormack, Ada Rehan, the famous Limerick-born Shakespearean actress, Eva O'Connor, the Australian soprano and, of course, all the leading parliamentarians of his day. Limerick could hardly have had a better ambassador.

Michael Joyce died at his home, The Moorings, O'Connell Avenue, on 9 January 1941, in his ninetieth year.

From *The Old Limerick Journal*, No. 27, 1990.

When the Pig-Buyer was King
Jim Kemmy

The story of the rise and decline of Limerick's pig-buyers has never been documented. Only residual memories of their halcyon days now linger on. These memories mainly find expression in humorous tales about some of their more unusual exploits. Many of the pig-buying families — the Reids, Crowes, O'Connors, O'Donovans and Sheahans — came from the terraces of one-storey houses below the present St Mary's Catholic church. The suitability of the long, narrow yards of these houses for pig-rearing may have been a factor in the decision of so many of these families to take up residence in Athlunkard Street.

Up to the end of the Second World War many people in the working-class areas of Limerick kept pigs in their back yards. A bucket of potato skins and other slops delivered to the pig owners would invariably yield ½d. or 1d. and often earned the price of the 'pictures' for enterprising children. The urban-bred pigs were sold to the pig-buyers, who in turn sold them to the bacon factories at a handy profit. The buyers acted as middlemen and bought most of the pigs from farmers in the rural hinterland.

The prosperity of the pig-buyers is now only a legend, but their social pretensions, in relation to the merchants and professional people in the city, always remained suitably modest. They preferred to be big fish in a small pond. The pig-buyers greatly contributed to the fame achieved by the Garryowen Rugby Football Club; many of their names are scattered closely through the club's Munster Cup-winning teams, and Paddy and Tom Reid went on to gain international honours.

When they escaped from the business of buying and selling pigs, the buyers were a pleasure-loving lot. Their fondness for grand opera, musical comedy and Victorian parlour songs shows that they frequented the old Theatre Royal. They also helped to make Kilkee the popular seaside resort that it is today. West Clare was one big pig-market for the buyers, so they knew and liked the district well enough to spend the whole summer (the off-season in the pig-buying business) there. They lodged mostly on Albert Road (now O'Curry Street) and in the houses around the Market Square. (The elegant Regency terraces on the West End were the preserve of the Limerick merchant princes, the social seaweed curtain being the Royal Marine Hotel.)

But with the elimination of the role of the pig-buyers — mainly brought about through the agency of the Pigs and Bacon Commission — their affluence dwindled away; many took up other occupations and some died in relatively poor circumstances. But colourful stories about their business and social activities continue to live on in Limerick folklore. Who has not heard the tale of the pig-buyer who requested that the wheels be taken from under a cart so that he could make a closer inspection of the precious pigs?

From the *Limerick Socialist*, Vol. 4, No. 1, January 1975

The Knocklong and Bruree Soviets
Emmet O'Connor

The occupation of thirteen Limerick creameries in 1920 was a more political affair. The plants were part of the extensive complex owned by the Cleeve Company, whose workers had fought a hard and only partially successful fight for a wage rise the previous year. On that occasion sabotage had been used. Now, plans were laid to seize the plants and run them as a going concern. Led by John Dowling and John McGrath, two Socialist Party of Ireland members, and Jack Hedley, an English communist, all of whom now worked as ITGWU officials, a council of action was formed. On 16 May the creameries were occupied. A red flag was hoisted over the central factory at Knocklong and a banner displayed which read 'We Make Butter Not Profits. Knocklong Creamery Soviet'. Normal milk supplies to the plants were maintained and butter was sold under the soviet's brand. On 22 May, the premises were returned to Cleeve's after demands on wages and conditions had been met. The episode inspired a less successful occupation by creamery maids at the Tipperary town Cleeve's factory in July.

The Knocklong soviet, as the occupations at Cleeve's came to be called, was the first to provoke widespread interest in Labour circles and illustrates the way in which developments in Ireland were making sense of international events.

The soviet declared by Cleeve's employees at Bruree was similar to those at Arigna and Knocklong. It originated in a wage dispute and followed the same pattern of occupation and relinquishment in return for a financial settlement. The slogans and style of Bruree were akin to those of Knocklong. A red flag was hoisted over the premises and inside the mill's retail shop a poster announced 'Bruree mills and bakery are now the property of the workers. . . . It is hoped to reduce prices and do away with profiteering within a day. By order of the workers.' The soviet lasted from 25 August to 3 September and was an outstanding financial success. . . . On balance, 1922 had not been a good year for commercial interests and employer dissatisfaction with the trend of events found its most coherent and most legitimate expression in political participation. . . . The Limerick Farmers' Association threatened to withhold rates unless a firm line was taken against soviets and discipline imposed on local authority employees who were assisting the 'red flaggers'. . . . The last soviet to be declared was in Limerick where striking printers seized their newspaper's offices to publish their own paper, the *Limerick Herald*.

From *Syndicalism in Ireland 1917–1923*, Cork University Press, 1988

Requiem for Paddie O'Reilly
Desmond O'Grady

I just read, in a Boston newspaper:
Paddie O'Reilly, native of Limerick City,
Ireland, died Thanksgiving after an accident.
His remains may be seen in Tamburro's Funeral
Parlour, Watertown, Massachusetts. Tomorrow,
a Requiem Mass in Gaelic will be celebrated
by the Rev. Fr John Kelleher at 9.30 a.m.
in St Michael's Parish Church.

The story begins on the shores of the Atlantic
in the rain, the ruin, the bogs and stony fields.
It continues with the cheapest steerage
across the Atlantic and concludes with a widow,
a small boy and a funeral in Watertown, Mass.

When all's said and done,
anywhere's the same for dying:
There, where wild heather perfumes

the stones after rain; here,
where pollution permeates everything.
It's all the one — whether a body becomes a stone,
industrial waste, snow or shamrocked fresh air.
It's not the dying that's full of sorrow,
here rather than there.

Requiem aeternam Paddie O'Reilly
among the coloured plastic flowers
in Tamburro's Funeral Parlour.
All the hovels of Ireland
hold their huddled hour,
hide their hearts.
A second-class funeral,
fifty dollars. *Libera me*
Domine de morte aeterna.

The seacrow circles your western seaboard.
Dies irae. What's soaked in sorrow
never dies. *Dies illa;* here rather
than there, without glory.

Your ancestors inspired their times with adventure.
No wake for you in Tamburro's Funeral Parlour —
you were waked elsewhere, with whiskey and weapons
and the tragic colours of terror.

Paddie O'Reilly died for no visionary madness.
His kind of Irishman dies anonymously,
far from Ireland where whiskey bottles spill blood.

Paddie O'Reilly. He's dead. *Libera me Domine.*
He came from green fields, the wide world his country.
He founded no city, gave his name to no sea. He died
alone, for a few dollars counted in dimes.
Requiem aeternam. Those who can afford to die
only on weekends — the week's work done — come to say
their goodbyes: Irish, Arabs, Italians, Greeks.
That's their history: Ireland, Poland, Italy, Spain . . .

Tamburro's Funeral Parlour, Watertown, Massachusetts —
and a few lines in a Boston newspaper.

From the *Limerick Socialist*, Vol. 6, No. 5, May 1977

Farmers' 'Boys'
Roger Moran

Some of the farmers treated their workmen, or as they were called, 'farmers' boys' — their age didn't matter, they were all 'farmers' boys' — in the same category as the sheepdogs.

It must surely be a source of wonder to people with a knowledge of the time, that a variety of the biblical plagues was not visited on the farming community in retaliation for the blackguarding and ill treatment they meted out to 'servant boys' and 'servant girls'.

They hired out in this region, usually for eleven months, at the January fair in Newcastle West. From early morning, they would gather in the square of this west Limerick town, from all over the county, and as far afield as Cork and north Kerry. There, they would shelter along the walls of the buildings, and the farmers examined them as if they were beasts of the field, feeling the girls' bodies through their clothing, to ascertain if they had the physique suitable for slaving on the land. These girls would not hire out merely for housework, but indeed for all types of farmwork.

They rarely slept in the farmhouse proper. Usually, some shed in the yard was touched up for this purpose, probably the barn, and there, on a makeshift bed, or beds, they would sleep. Lest one might think that this was a glorious opportunity for sexual encounters, the amount of work these people were obliged to perform left very little energy for any other type of performance. They would not be allowed to sit at table during mealtimes with other members of the family. They took their meals in the back kitchen. If they were lucky, they had a table for this purpose; usually the meal was eaten off a box. . . .

The workman continued living in the barn as before, until his health could no longer withstand the cold and damp of the rat-hole, and he was of no more use to the farmer. He was taken for the first and only motorcar ride of his life, his destination, the Home in Newcastle West. He lived there . . . and when he died he was laid to rest in the Paupers' Plot. He had plenty of company, as most of the older farmers' boys of the area went the same road; the younger ones escaped to England.

From *The Wildfowler: A Tale of the Shannon Estuary*, The Blackstaff Press, 1982

A 'Day Out' in Foynes
Liam O'Donnell

On one occasion I was involved with a servant boy who lost his job for not return-ing to his work on a Sunday evening and, God help them, there was no union or farmworkers' body to protect them in those days. It happened as a result of an outing to Foynes in County Limerick where the seaplane, the Yankee Clipper, was to land. At the time this was all the local news and strange to us. People from all around the district were thrilled with excitement to hear of this great wonder when word got around that the Yankee Clipper would be at Foynes on the Sunday afternoon. So a few of us decided to go and see it. It was the month of July in the late thirties, a busy time of the year for farmers. We had in our company a few servant boys who were game for anything. It was a long journey, about 32 miles, so with our jobs done and the milk delivered to the creamery we got early Mass, had a quick breakfast and mounted our bicycles.

We set off on our journey and in our own right we were lords of the road, happy as Larry, with a few extra bob in our pockets. We were like the mountain lark, free as the air, as if we owned the whole world. It was non-stop until we got to Foynes, where there was quite a big crowd of people there who had travelled long and short journeys. They had come cycling, walking, travelling by ass-cart, horse-trap and quite a few sidecars which were very popular for transport among the well-to-do who could afford them.

When we arrived we heard to our disappointment that the Clipper would not be arriving until Monday. We took it in our stride and accepted the news in good faith; of course we had no other choice. A few of us who could afford it decided to stay on for the day and make the best of a bad lot. The servant boys who had to return for the evening's milking couldn't wait but one wild lad decided he'd chance his arm and wait on for the evening. He said he'd come up with some good excuse.

We fooled around for the day. There were plenty of amusements although we had little money. We did, however, have something to eat as there were plenty of eating-houses as we called them. Restaurants were not heard of in those times. You'd get plenty of tea, bread and butter and maybe a bun for a shilling and sixpence. That kept you happy for the day with maybe the odd bottle of lemonade. On win-dows of eating-houses there were notices written with white paint: tea and ham 2s. 6d. — out of our reach so we were thankful for small mercies. For us it was a great day's enjoyment and we decided to stay on for a few hours in the evening as the day was beautiful with a good long bright evening. Later we heard that there was a carnival in Adare which was approximately 12 miles from Foynes, so it didn't take much persuasion to get us moving. It was partly on our way home — maybe a little bit out of the way. There was also a dance there that night which could go on until the small hours of the morning. Money now was at the end of the trimmings; still with fire in our blood we were raring to go. So having hit the road again we arrived at the carnival late in the evening. It was fairly crowded with every type of amusements and tents erected about the grounds for refreshments with a huge one for the dancing. . . .

We thoroughly enjoyed ourselves at a great night's dancing. We struck for home about 2 a.m. having about 18 miles to cover over bad roads and we were not as fresh now returning as we were when we started out on Sunday morning. The long hard day had taken its toll on us. The night was fine and summery with the beautiful fragrance of new-mown hay everywhere.

From *The Days of the Servant Boy*, Mercier Press, 1997

Rural Cage
From: The Person Nox Agonistes
Michael Hartnett

Every rural cage has prisoners,
every small hill-sheltered townland,
every whitewashed tourist'd village
holds a heart that cannot speak out,
lives a life of angered murmurs.
Over eleven pints of Guinness,
over fifty bitter Woodbines,
we have talked about our futures:
we have found no quick solution.

If one is lax in adoration,
still the priests have satisfaction
by our appearance every Sunday.
If to small tyrant employers
we bring the benefit of Unions
we are unemployed eccentrics.

If what we love is all corruption,
we must sacrifice our reason,
we must sit here in this townland
talking always of the future,
finding out no quick solutions,

over eleven pints of Guinness,
over fifty bitter Woodbines.

From *Selected Poems*, New Writers' Press, 1970; *Collected Poems*, The Gallery Press, forthcoming

Hay-Making in Bracile
James Kennedy

When I think back to the period in summer we called 'the hay' I have no difficulty in recalling it in vivid detail. I'm sure that it is because I disliked it with an intensity I've never encountered in myself for anything else — animal, vegetable or mineral.

I shiver when I recall the despondency I felt, at 12, looking down the length of a swath (mispronounced 'swart' by all of us for some reason) of drying hay maybe two hundred yards long which had to be turned with a fork and in tune with three or four grown men who could go left-hand underneath on the way down and right-hand underneath on the way back. I had only one way of turning hay — left hand underneath — so I had to set backwards on the return. Then I always seemed to get the bum fork, the one with the worn prongs and a handle made out of a piece of ash which my father always kept in the loft and which although rasped down was a bit rough and knobby.

When the hay was heavy and 'scrammely' (knitted together) — not nearly as bad in my time as half a generation earlier when one meadow was a water meadow — I'd hear the sergeant-major's voice of my father urging, 'Shake it out well! Don't leave any holes. Get the green bits on top to dry out.'

I often left the green bits lying where they were so I could keep up. As well as turning it we rowed it, cocked it and piked it with the fork and every year I got plenty of blisters and no sympathy.

The hay was a period of panic and tension. Our house became obsessed with it mainly because of my father. Normally he was a sort of ancient Greek to us in temperament — he liked to stop and talk, to philosophise, to drag out a job until tomorrow. But during the hay he reverted to being a barbarian.

Freedom was curtailed. A new discipline which we never experienced for the rest of the year was imposed. We weren't allowed to betray any form of indifference — and that discipline was imposed on my mother and sisters, too.

One day while waiting at home for the weather to shake up I picked up a book to continue reading where I left off the night before. Pop had gone up to the quarry to view the Clare Hills and the Galtees to work out a weather forecast. He and our neighbour, Billy Gleeson, used to do short-range predictions quite accurately. When he came into the kitchen and saw me reading a book he said to the family in general: 'Look at that bloody fella reading a book — in the middle of the hay!' and his voice rose at the bit after the dash.

'The hay is wet,' I said, 'and it's in the meadow, not here in the kitchen.'

'That's not the point!' he growled. 'You should be thinking about it.'

That summed up his attitude. It was only afterwards when I grew up that I understood why.

In our small-farm economics there was nothing as important as the hay. It generated trepidation about what could happen. The worst was that it would rain for two months, the hay would rot, and in the winter we'd have nothing to feed the cows. The best was that we would get the hay up in spite of the friction and the panic and still be on speaking terms.

I am sure too that the panic about hay related to the size of the holding. The smaller the farm the more tension. The loss of one cow to a small farmer was a major blow. To a well-to-do farmer a loss or two could be sustained. The small farmer like my father or Bill Byrane, a quarter-mile up the road, treated his cows with the reverence of a Hindu for his Brahmin bulls. The hay had to be the best. It was even then supplemented with cabbage leaves and turnips. In the fields, *geosadáns* were pulled and ditches kept trimmed to keep pasturage at its maximum. At the first sign of rushes clogged drains were opened and freed.

These things come back to me now because, although I'm in a different business, the same loyalty to an industry is necessary, the same pride in one's handiwork is demanded, the same meticulous attention to the important details of life and work. The same basic aim: to survive the year, and not owe anyone anything.

There was drudgery then about hay-making. When I go down to Pallas during the summer I still get the same feeling in a meadow I used to have forty years ago even though the machinery is there now to make hay-making a job for robots. It was the feeling then of being a small cog in a big machine. One had no control over breakfast, dinner or supper. It was the same sort of discipline I came across later in a monastery. The river flowed enticingly along one end of the meadow but we were not allowed to flirt with it until the hay was finished. I have the impression that, every year, the hay dragged on and on and on.

From *The People Who Drank Water from the River*, Poolbeg Press, 1991

Remembering Harry Craig
Jim Kemmy

When H.A.L. (Harry) Craig, the Limerick-born writer, died in Rome last month at the age of 57, his passing went unnoticed in the local press. Craig himself would hardly have expected otherwise. He spent the first two decades of his life in Clarina, Co. Limerick, before going to Dublin to study at Trinity College. He showed an early interest in literature and became assistant editor of *The Bell* magazine in the 1940s. He also had a deep interest in the trade union movement and spent much of his time in organising rural workers.

In an appreciation, published in *The Irish Times* on 1 November 1978, a friend of Craig, who signed himself 'R.B.', wrote about this time in the writer's life:

> His letters of that period speak of his grief at the poverty of Ireland. He travelled around the country addressing meetings in connection with the Workers' Union of Ireland, often hungry himself, sharing the life of the rural workers, whom he was trying to organise with a view to improving their lot. He would cycle many miles in order to speak at several meetings in a day. 'The only way to speak', he said 'is out of your heart.' He had no use for charity as such: he wished to reform the existing order of things so that everyone would have enough. He experienced in himself a conflict between his love of material justice and his love of literature, his indignation on behalf of society and his love of poetry. . . .

Craig wrote a good deal for *The Bell* until it ceased publication in 1954 and proved to be a lively literary and social critic. He later went to London and scripted many outstanding programmes for the BBC. The last years of his life were spent in Rome where he worked as a film script-writer. During these years he became a friend of the poet Desmond O'Grady, who was then teaching in Italy. . . .

Craig's death coincided with the publication of a new book, *The Best from the Bell*. It is disappointing that the editor of this work has apparently gone for the 'big' literary names rather than include some of the more rewarding contributions of other less well-known writers. As a result of this policy, Harry Craig's writing is not included.

A final salute to Craig was published in *Hibernia* on 8 November. The poem, *30 October, 1978*, was written by his old *Bell* colleague, Lochlinn MacGlynn. It is a fitting tribute to a talented and warm-hearted Limerickman, who deserves to be remembered in his native place:

> This morning no letters delivered.
> It is a freedom-day
> Called the new Bank Holiday . . .
> Only one more October day
> On the other side of tonight;
> Then it will be November
> But here in the cemetery
> Of Mount Jerome
> It is bright noon.

The sky is Italian.
A summer day has come back
With Harry Craig.

Remembering
Harry Craig in a hurry . . .
Chuckling . . .
Then suddenly serious
Remembering
He should be somewhere else:
His crusade for the farm-workers
Who had only a few friends then . . .
I like to think
That some old worker
Going home from the fields
With the ghosts of October
Will remember Harry Craig.

From the *Limerick Socialist*, No. 11, Vol. 7, November 1978

FOUR

PEOPLE

Dr Thomas Arthur (1593–1675)
J.B. Lyons

Destined to become the most sought-after doctor in the Ireland of his day, Thomas Arthur was born in Limerick on 24 November 1593 into a staunchly Catholic family that had given a number of mayors and bishops to his native city. The first of the Irish line came to the country with the Normans in 1171 and obtained a gift of lands at Emly a few years later. A descendant, John Arthur, a substantial property owner in Limerick city, was elected to the office of mayor in 1274.

Thomas was the son of William Arthur and his wife Anastace Rice. Nothing is known of his boyhood and early schooling but the 'Arthur MS.' now in the British Library contains his diary, fee-book and other papers which afford a glimpse of his university period and enable us to visualise his professional career in unusual detail. Extracts from the manuscript with translations from the Latin were published by Maurice Lenihan in the *Journal of the Kilkenny Archaeological Society* in 1867. Professor J.D.H. Widdess, the doyen of Irish medical historians, has given a more recent account of Arthur and his manuscript in the *Irish Journal of Medical Science*.

He studied arts at the University of Bordeaux and took a master's degree. . . . This was in May 1619 and without delay he embarked on practice. What he lacked in experience was compensated for by energy, eagerness and, what was more important in the eyes of prospective patients in Limerick (then a city with a population of less than 11,000), a fresh acquaintance with the latest cures from the great city of Paris and elsewhere. . . .

A testimony of his expectation of success was his decision in that year to build a great 'stone house in Mongret Street, in the south suburb of the city of Limerick' which despite its early beginning, Lenihan tells us, was 'scarcely finished when Ireton was thundering at the gates'. Meanwhile, Thomas Arthur was to achieve a national rather than local acceptance. . . .

The most rigid sectarian barrier can be breached by an effective therapist, but, nevertheless, it was a remarkable tribute to Thomas Arthur that he should be called to treat Archbishop Ussher in 1625. . . . The nature neither of Dr Ussher's ailment nor of his physician's cure is known but Dr Arthur remained with the prelate during a period of convalescence on Lambay Island, then owned by the Ussher family, and received the munificent fee of £51.

Passing on to Dublin in June, Thomas Arthur found himself famous and a focus of attention. He was sought out by those to whom formerly 'I had been hateful on account of the Catholic religion'. He was entertained by the Viceroy and other noblemen. The former, Viscount Falkland, put him at his ease, extracted from him an account of the Archbishop's illness and where the royal doctors had been wrong. Impressed and satisfied the Viceroy invited Arthur to be his personal physician and doctor to the Viceregal household.

Returning to Limerick he resumed practice and the fee-book continues to include names of distinguished or notorious persons, William Greatrakes, George Devenish of Castle Devenish, Co. Westmeath, Stephen Sexton, Sir Henry Titchborne and Sir Charles Coote.

Demands for his presence in Dublin were so frequent that in 1630 he transferred his residence there. Meanwhile, investments in real estate had kept pace with his increasing professional reputation and eventually proved the more remunerative. Medical fees for 1630–31 were £145 13s. 6d. while income from rents, mortgages and loans amounted to £462 16s. 6d. . . . .

Dr Arthur's practice flourished in Dublin and his fee-book includes the names of many of the Ussher family, Daniel Molyneaux, Sir James Ware, Thomas Lutterell of Lutterellstown, the Countess of Fingall and Rory O'Moore. The fact that he treated O'Moore in the same week as many Establishment figures caused Lenihan to remark that while adhering to his religious convictions, 'his knowledge of men and manners kept him clear of politics, and enabled him to make friends on both sides'. In July 1633 he treated Sir Basil Brooke of Ulster who was troubled by a urethral inflammation and discharge.

Despite his popularity and standing with all factions Thomas Arthur was ill-at-ease in Dublin after the commencement of the insurrection of 1641 and in December he returned to Limerick, a Catholic stronghold. He was still there in 1651 when the city was besieged by the Parliamentary army commanded by Ireton, Oliver Cromwell's son-in-law.

Dr Arthur's medical skills must have been invaluable and he has recorded his attendance on Dominick FitzDavid Rice whose wounds necessitated amputation of a leg and Dr Credanus whose hands were lacerated and tendons severed by a shell. Lenihan in his *History of Limerick* describes the dreadful conditions. 'The plague was raging in the city. In every street the wild wail of sorrow was heard over the stark corpses of the victims of famine and the black sickness, which the want of air, the stench, and the awful circumstances of the place had caused.'

When eventually the city wall was breached and the East gate delivered up, Dr Arthur's services, in the best tradition of his profession, were soon available to his foes many of whom were victims of scurvy, *cholera morbus*, wounds and pestilence. . . . Thomas Arthur's geniality is evident in his reply to Dr Abraham Yarner's dinner invitation, regretting that he cannot join Yarner and Dr Fennell for 'the plunder of a fat goose' and enclosing verses to be read at the dinner, purporting to be written by the goose, seeking mercy and requesting that a cock, the bird sacred to Aesculapius should be substituted. Arthur concluded his letter: 'May you live, thrive, eat, drink and enjoy yourselves.' Widdess claims that this is the earliest surviving reference to a medical dinner in Dublin and suggests that Drs Arthur, Fennell and Yarner may have been co-founders with John Stearne and Sir William Petty of the Fraternity of Physicians.

Lenihan referred to Arthur's library which Widdess, knowledgeable in biblio-graphy, analysed in more detail: 'Only the wealthy in Arthur's time would have possessed such a library as he had.'

There were 315 items of which 152 were medical. Naturally there were books by Hippocrates and Galen, then still relevant to medical practice, and volumes by Renaissance authors such as Jean Fernel of Paris and the eminent surgeons da Vigo and Guy de Chauliac. On botany, pharmacy and *materia medica*, Widdess tells us, 'He had the best authors of the time, and his special interest in chemical medicines is reflected in his possession of works on chemistry and alchemy. The occult writers Lully and Porta are also included.'

The non-medical books included works on logic, philosophy, religion, ancient history and architecture. He included many classical authors but while fluent in Latin probably had little Greek.

Thomas Arthur who seems to have retired from practice in 1666 may have been twice married for in a codicil to his will on 2 January 1675 he refers to 'my now wife Christian'. He had three daughters, two of whom, Mary and Anastace, pre-deceased him. In 1641 Mary, the eldest daughter, married Bartholomew Stackpoole of Limerick, whom Dr Arthur supported at the Inns of Court, London, during the betrothal period. Dymphna married her second cousin, John Arthur of Galway, and brought him a dowry of £1,000. The youngest daughter also married an Arthur.

Dr Arthur's disappointment at having no sons was mitigated by the birth of two sons to John and Dymphna Arthur but unfortunately his daughter and son-in-law quarrelled with him almost losing a fortune, for the indignant old man wrote a will which disinherited Dymphna and her offspring. Fortunately common-sense and the entreaty of his wife prevailed and in the codicil his grandson William (or in the event of William having no male issue, his younger brother, Thomas) was left the estate. Dr Arthur died in January 1675.

From *Brief Lives of Irish Doctors*, Blackwater Press, 1978

Dáibhí Ó Bruadair
Michael Hartnett

It is not rare for a poet to be obsessed with the work and mind of another poet. The obsession can express itself in many ways — scorn (which is often public), awe before a massive superiority (which is always private), and love (which can become a bore to readers who do not share the obsession). I have been obsessed by the work and mind of Dáibhí Ó Bruadair and, though I certainly loved them and him, my obsession usually expressed itself in frustration. And it has done so since 1954, when I was 13.

Like many Irish children I was reared on a diet of folktale, republicanism and mediocre ballads. I knew some Gaelic but it was merely another school subject, not a key to another culture. But in 1954, a friend, Seán Brouder, told me of Ó Bruadair. He recited some verses which he translated for me. He claimed that the poet had been born in my own town (Newcastle West, Co. Limerick) and had lived most of his life in my own county, and further, that he was buried in Monagay churchyard, not far from Newcastle West. I was enthralled. I knew what poets looked like from their portraits in library books, so I invented my own picture of Ó Bruadair. The following year I wrote and published my first poem — in English.

A man in his sixties and a boy of 13 discussing, in a decrepit country town, the life and work of a poet who had been dead for over 250 years, a poet of an extinct society whose works were not published in his lifetime and which were now available only in distant city libraries: this event, I later saw, profoundly illustrated the obstinacy of the Irish mind, its constant connection with the past. Even though I did not read a word of Ó Bruadair's until the late 'fifties, he had become for me the symbol of what I wanted to be. But when I read him, in some school anthology of Gaelic verse, I was shocked. I could not understand him! It seemed a gnarled, concertina'd kind of Gaelic, written for a distant and savage people. I went for consolation to the more accessible fields of Hopkins, Yeats and Eliot. I continued to read simpler Gaelic poetry, most of it written in the two centuries before Ó Bruadair's death. Why was my hero so unapproachable? How could an old man quote him with so much reverence and fluency? I determined in 1962 not to let him escape me, to unravel his language and to restore him as my idol. I still have not done so to my satisfaction.

The name Ó Bruadair (Brouder, Broderick) has been found in west Limerick since the ninth century: it is possibly of Danish origin. The poet Dáibhí was born about 1623. As is the case with most Gaelic poets our information on him is scant, but a number of details can be gleaned from his poetry. One of my dreams vanished when I read that it was unlikely that he had been born in Newcastle West but more probably in the barony of Barrymore in east Cork. My addiction to his work, however, did not vanish, and at least I found that he had lived most of his life in County Limerick, where his main patrons were the Fitzgeralds of Springfield (Gort na Tiobraid), near Broadford, and the Burkes of Cahirmoyle. Patronage was still deemed essential to a poet's survival: there were no publishers, no royalties, no grants; there were gifts, hospitality, cattle, horses, clothing and, sometimes, gold. But the Gaelic poet was no mere pensioner.

Ó Bruadair was a recorder of his race's history and because of his place of birth two great local Norman-Irish families, the Fitzgeralds and the Burkes, became the symbols of that race for him. Indeed he did not write for the contemporary Burkes and Fitzgeralds, but for all of them who had ever existed and who ever would exist.

Living as he did throughout almost all of Ireland's most tragic century, he was also deeply immersed in the affairs of his time. . . .

After 1690 Ó Bruadair's life assumed a pattern that was to become sadly common-place among poets in the next few years: the *file*, the professional poet, the dignified chronicler of his race, gave way to a ragged, horny-handed itinerant, muttering under his breath. Although Ó Bruadair's predicament was not unique, he felt, like many poets of his time, that he was the sole survivor, the last receptacle of Gaelic culture, and that his death would be the end for all. He was right, in a way. His death, and the death of the culture he stood for, was not a total annihilation: the eighteenth century was perhaps the most active time ever known for the production of poetry: but it was the *people*, rather than the professional poets, who began to sing; the poetry came out of cabins rather than castles. Ó Bruadair would have hated it. He would have looked down his nose at the sometimes flaccid extravagances of the Munster poets of the 1740s. But there had been a change of priorities: their purpose was to save a language, not a culture. Culture, as Ó Bruadair understood it, was gone. The style of poetry had already changed in his time: he wrote no songs but the poets of the eighteenth century seemed to write little else.

Ó Bruadair died, with his culture, in 1698. . . . It was always customary for Irish poets to write laments for their fellows. Ó Bruadair was famous in his lifetime, but there is no lament in Gaelic extant that mentions his death: this fact reflects the breakdown, the chaos of the 1690s.

Ó Bruadair, who wrote for his race, had a fierce and deep contempt for the lower-class Irish, the peasants, the little shop-keepers, the 'hucksters'. But this attitude was common among the professional Gaelic poets and even persisted right up to the 1740s. When I came to discover him for myself this aristocratic *hauteur* was something I disliked. Almost all my illusions were vanishing — but I was making the mistake of judging him by mid-twentieth-century liberal standards — I had to reconsider his real position with his own society. He was 'anti-Irish' though he wrote in Gaelic: he was anti-clerical, though he was a Catholic — witness his satire on two priests. He upheld and was upheld by what was left of the aristocracy of his time. He lived in an Ireland where for centuries the Holy Trinity was not so much Father, Son and Holy Ghost as prince, prelate and poet. The prince, to Ó Bruadair, had to have an impeccable pedigree, had to be a cultured man and a generous one: he was the living symbol of Ireland. . . .

Ó Bruadair could be funny, obscene and anguished. He had immense dignity and immense bitterness. If he is anti-democratic it is because he confused survival with betrayal. He was concerned with culture.

From Ó *Bruadair: Translations from the Irish*, The Gallery Press, 1985

The Maigue Poets
Eleanor Hull

The group of bards whom we have now to consider recalls us again to those local bardic assemblies which endeavoured in the eighteenth century to keep alive by friendly rivalry the composition of Gaelic poetry and the interest in the Irish tongue and the history and antiquities of the country. On the death of Seán Claragh MacDonnell, in 1754, his friend, John O'Tuomy, succeeded him as chief of these assemblies, and became the acknowledged head of Munster poetry during his lifetime.

He was born at Croom in County Limerick, in 1706, or a couple of years later, and during his residence there he made the little town, which stands on the eastern bank of the river Maigue, an intellectual centre for the surrounding district. He kept an inn at Croom during the earlier years of his married life, afterwards moving into Limerick, where he seems to have died in 1775. During MacDonnell's lifetime the bardic assemblies had been usually held half-yearly either at Charleville or Bruree, and in the open air. But under O'Tuomy's presidency they met at his tavern in Croom, a village which earned for itself the title of Croom 'an t-súghachais' (the merry), no doubt on account of the gatherings of these witty and pleasant companies of bardic associates. O'Tuomy was himself commonly known as 'an ghrinn' (the jovial). A certain mock solemnity was attached to these assemblies, the 'warrants' issued being couched in the terms of English law, and officers called sheriffs being appointed to conduct the proceedings. But though they may have done something to preserve an interest in the composition and recitation of Irish verse, the results attained are not to be taken too seriously. They did not tend to the production of poems of a high level, and the mutual recriminations in verse into which the output of the assemblies often degenerated are unworthy of any sort of immortality.

Many of O'Tuomy's own poems are, however, exceptionally melodious. Such songs as 'A chuirte na h-éigre, éipig ruar,' or his aisling 'Im aonar real ag pódardheacht' are delightful; but he was, like most of his contemporaries, unequal in his work. He seems to have been a man of some education and respected both for his ability and wit and for the solid qualities of his character. Probably it was owing to his generosity to his fellow-bards that he fell into poverty and was forced for a time to accept a position as steward on the farm of a gentleman residing in Limerick. He seems in any case to have been in straitened circumstances at the time of his removal to that city. He is buried at Croom within sound of the waters of the river Maigue, whose charms are so often celebrated in the poems of this group of writers.

Among the bards who gathered around O'Tuomy the best known is Andrew McGrath, called the 'Mangaire Súgach' (Jolly Pedlar), not because he actually followed the trade of peddling, but from his roving and thriftless life.

Though closely associated with O'Tuomy in the bardic assemblies, and often taking advantage of his bounty, he was a man of very different character. Reckless, hot-tempered and dissolute, he was never long able to keep steady to his profession of schoolmaster, and even so good a friend as O'Tuomy suffered under the lash of his caustic wit. The dates of his birth and death are unknown, but he survived O'Tuomy, on whose death he, like several other of their companions, wrote an elegy. He was, however, an old man before O'Tuomy died, and probably did not long survive him. At one time, driven to any expedient by want, he thought to gain employment by a pretended conversion to Protestantism, but he was as little welcome in the Church to which he offered himself as he had been in his own. Denounced by his own priest and rejected by the Protestant rector of Croom, he took advantage of the occasion to write a humorous poem complaining of his outcast position. Wild as he was, and rakish in character as are several of his pieces, McGrath had a true gift of song. Several exquisite compositions are from his hand. Of these one of the most touching is his 'Slán le Máigh', bidding farewell to the river which flowed through his native district, to which O'Tuomy wrote a reply; and the hardly less graceful love song, 'Cé fada mé le haep an traoghail'. A vigorous and forcible poem is his political 'Duan na raoipre' (Song of Freedom), beginning, 'Is fada mé I g-cumhagan tnút le téapnamh', which seems to have been composed in the earlier period of the Seven Years' War (1756–63), an appeal in favour of the exiled Stuarts and calling for vengeance on their enemies. Among his remaining songs are two other Jacobite poems, satires, drinking songs and amatory pieces. There are also a number of pieces written in the form of questions and replies with O'Tuomy. In several of their songs, these writers adopted the Irish ornament of binding the stanzas together by making the new verse begin with the same word as that which ended the verse before it.

Among the minor poets who gathered round MacDonnell and O'Tuomy, one of the best was William O'Heffernan, called William Dall or 'the Blind', a native of Shronehill, Co. Tipperary. He was born sightless, and wandered about the county subsisting on bounty. He often contended in the bardic sessions of the Maigue. . . .

More remarkable than any of these poets is the religious writer Tadhg Gaedhealach O'Sullivan whose devotional poems were familiar in every home in Munster so long as the Irish language was the natural vehicle of speech between man and man. They had the unusual good fortune to be printed in Limerick during O'Sullivan's lifetime, and so widely were they used and appreciated that they passed through several editions in the early years of the nineteenth century. Tadhg is believed to have died in 1795.

From *A Text Book of Irish Literature*, Part II, M.H. Gill and Son Ltd, 1908

The Knight of Glin, John Fraunceis FitzGerald
J. Anthony Gaughan

The Knight of Glin, John Fraunceis FitzGerald, enjoyed a very full social life which in the years following his marriage could be described as rather hectic. Moreover, in his unique way he enjoyed socialising with his tenants as much as with those who belonged to his own class. . . .

John Fraunceis regularly hunted with the County Limerick foxhounds and prior to 1820 was master of the hunt in west Limerick.

The knight was also very much involved in the social life associated with the Shannon. In his thirty ton cutter, Rienvella, which carried a number of guns, he attended the various regattas on the river. And when, from time to time, important elements of the British fleet anchored at Tarbert he accepted the hospitality of the highest ranking officer and reciprocated in kind.

If John Fraunceis was untypical of his class in many ways there was one way in which he was typical, namely his eccentricity. He was eccentric in his appearance, his manners and in almost everything he did. Allied to this, he was most temperamental, suffering from alternating moods of hilarity and moroseness. When relations between them had reached their nadir, Father Daniel O'Sullivan nicknamed the knight, *Seán Gruama* (Grim-faced John).

Another nickname given to the knight — this time by the people — was *ridire na mBan* (the knight of the women). This was even more appropriate. His weakness for the fair sex was a byword. His long-suffering wife, Bridgetta (daughter of Reverend Joseph Eyre, of Westerham, Kent), whom he married in July 1812, had to share his favours with quite a few other women. When Mrs FitzGerald had exhausted all other means of reforming her errant husband she pestered the parish priest with accounts of her husband's misconduct. She impressed upon him his duty to deal with those members of his flock who were 'sinning' with her husband. Eventually Bridgetta, who was described by Reverend Richard FitzGerald as 'one of the loveliest of her sex' and as one who suffered 'many painful trials', resigned herself to the situation. Although sorely tried, she remained in Glin Castle until John Fraunceis died in 1854. Then she transferred to the Villa, a dower house of the Knights of Glin and now the Catholic parochial house. In 1866 she moved into Cahara House and remained there until her death in 1876. (Considering her family background — her father was a clergyman and her five sisters married men of the cloth — she presided over a curious *ménage à trois* at Cahara House. Her second son, Edmund Urmston McLeod, a ne'er do well, resided with her and raised two illegitimate families, the first with Mary Culhane and the second with Nora (Norry) Enright. From time to time, probably when Edmund's domestic arrangements tested her beyond endurance, she took refuge for periods in the Villa with one or other of her sisters from England.)

It was inevitable that the parish priest would not indefinitely turn a blind eye on what Archdeacon Begley later quaintly described as 'the oriental proclivities of his aristocratic neighbour'. Because of the grave scandal in the parish caused by the Knight's amorous exploits, Father O'Sullivan, who was known to be remarkably strict in such matters, became more and more forthright in his condemnations, both public and private, of the Knight's extra-marital activities. Conversely, John Fraunceis became a more and more strident critic of the manner in which the parish priest was caring for his flock. He alleged that Father O'Sullivan was not properly recording baptisms and that on occasion had even failed to assist the

dying. Such was the Knight's influence that in 1826 Father O'Sullivan was con-
strained to appear before an enquiry into these matters. The enquiry was held at
Newcastle West and the Knight attended to swear the witnesses.

The confrontation between the Knight and the parish priest was given national
prominence because of a case involving Mary Wright. She was from Tarbert whence
she had been brought to Glin by the Knight and installed in a cottage in the demesne
as a 'kept woman'. She bore a child and it was publicly known that he was its
father. In fact, the child was named Catherine FitzGerald. The parish priest remon-
strated with Miss Wright privately and appealed to her to return home. Failing this,
he 'publicly named her from the altar' in the most intemperate terms. As a result,
she became a Protestant. After her change of faith Father O'Sullivan excom-
municated her and, it seems, incited his parishioners to 'cut her off from food and
turf'. Prompted by John Fraunceis, she responded by bringing an action of slander
against the parish priest. The Knight, who financed her action, was High-Sheriff
of Limerick at that time. As such he summoned the jury and ensured that only those
who would give a judgment against the priest were empanelled. The case, which was
heard on 25 July 1831, attracted a great deal of attention because of the circumstances
surrounding it. The Knight appeared as a witness summoned by Father O'Sullivan
but every question as to the financing of Miss Wright's case or the Knight's knowledge
of, or relationship with, the plaintiff was disallowed. The judge, Baron Foster, charged
the jury and left the case in their hands. After a short deliberation, the jury brought
in a verdict for Miss Wright for 40 shillings (£2) and costs. Such was the rage of the
people at the verdict that the jury had to be protected from a crowd which had
gathered to hear the result of the case. For the Knight it was a Pyrrhic victory because
Father O'Sullivan returned to Glin justified in the eyes of the people and thereafter
wielded extraordinary influence in the area.

There was a tragic postscript to the story, in that subsequently the body of Mary
Wright was found floating in the Shannon, after a boat carrying pigs to Limerick
in which she was travelling capsized in rough waters. All on board, including the
pigs, were drowned. . . .

Soon after Mary Wright had disappeared from the scene the Knight installed a
new mistress, named Peig Devine, in her place. A native of County Galway, she
was petite and was soon nicknamed the *caillichín* (the little hag). 'The Lodge' in
which she resided was near the Catholic church at Glin. . . .

In 1842, Father O'Sullivan, then aged 82, resigned and went to reside with
friends at Granagh, Ballingarry. During most of his time at Glin his relations with
the Knight had been tempestuous. As Thomas F. Culhane wrote: 'Neither the
priest nor the Knight believed in turning the other cheek.' However, they were
reconciled in 1844 when they met at the baptism of a son of Tim Costello, who was
later to become the sculptor, engraver and poet. (Also present at this happy event
was the local schoolmaster, Michael Stackpoole, who celebrated the occasion by
giving the first ever rendering of his poem 'The humours of Glin'.) From that time
onwards the priest and the Knight were on good terms — both, no doubt, having

mellowed somewhat. And when Father O'Sullivan died on 24 August 1850 the Knight insisted on being a pall-bearer at the funeral. . . .

Always a just, perhaps it would be more accurate to say, an indulgent landlord, John Fraunceis's qualities in this regard were well known. The *Freeman's Journal* of 17 February 1816 carried the following excerpt from the *Limerick Evening Post*:

> Rents. In addition to the reductions which have taken place in the county, we feel great pleasure in recording the liberal and patriotic conduct of the knight of Glin, who has abated 25% on all lands taken within these last five or six years on his estates. This highly respected character lives in the midst of his tenantry, he spends his fortune amongst them, and on every occasion they find in him a kind friend and a benevolent protector.

John Fraunceis first won the appreciation of his tenants by his practical concern for them in 1822. According to a survey by Richard Griffith in June of that year, Glin was one of the districts in County Limerick wherein 'the distress has reached its greatest height'. This meant that 'the proportion of the people wanting food amounts to one and a quarter in two'. Later, John Fraunceis was deeply affected by the Great Famine. His care and concern for his tenants during those tragic years was remembered for a long time. After the famine years he became more and more pre-occupied with the affairs of his estate, and, as his obituary in *The Limerick Chronicle* of 26 April 1854 stated: '. . . the influence of his position and his personal exertions were ever directed to relieve the wants of the poor'. . . .

In spite of his flagrant sexual misconduct and the law-suit which he was instrumental in bringing against Father O'Sullivan, John Fraunceis retained a good deal of his original popularity because of his undoubted concern for his tenants. Also, of course, his promiscuity was not unique at that time. A few members of his class in the district, who exhibited none of his good qualities, insisted on the *ius primae noctis*, that is, that the daughter of a tenant had to spend the night before her wedding in bed with her father's landlord. Moreover, there were quite a few illegitimate children in the district about whom it was euphemistically said: '*Thánadar le teas na gréine*' (They came with the heat of the sun).

John Fraunceis was a highly charged person whom one either hated or loved. The first of these reactions is to be found in a ballad which was used in the Limerick election of 1830 by opponents of the faction which, in the run-up to the election, promised to appoint him high sheriff. According to the Knight he intervened in the election 'in consequence of the interference of the priests and particularly the intemperate address of that notorious agitator Father [Michael] Fitzgerald [PP, Askeaton]'. Father Fitzgerald, who, in a letter to the press, 'viciously' attacked landlords in general and 'the bigoted, persecuting and merciless Massys' in particular, was at that time condemning as unconstitutional the extreme pressure being put by landlords on their tenants to vote in their interests. The supporters of what could be termed the tenants' candidate, Lieutenant Colonel Standish O'Grady, responded to the Knight's statement with a lampoon which was slyly introduced as follows: 'The fidelity of the picture has been recognised by all who have known the original, but there is still a question as to the strength of the colouring.' Three of the verses read:

> His vices have made, and still make him so poor,
> That bailiff or creditor is ne'er from his door.
> And deep tho' in debt, yet he's deeper in sin,
> That lecherous, treacherous knight of the Glin.

> This hoary old sinner, this profligate rare,
> Who gloats o'er the ruin of the virtuous and fair;
> In gambling and drinking and wenching delights
> And in these doth spend both his days and his nights.

> Yet there is the man who's heard to declare
> 'Gainst O'Grady he'll vote if the priests interfere.
> But the priests and O'Grady do not care a pin
> For the beggarly, profligate, knight of the Glin!

The opposite reaction surfaces in Michael Stackpool's 'In praise of Glin' (1826):

> There, on the margin of a stately wood,
> With ancient oaks coeval with flood,
> Stands the proud castle of our present knight,
> Whose sterling virtue I would fain indite.
> Unlike our absentees, who now devour
> the vitals of our country — crush her power,
> Relentless spend, enormous wealth they draw
> From ruined tenants whom they never saw,
> Nor even know, unless their rent-roll tells
> How much a tenant owes or where he dwells,
> . . .
> No, no, he spends his wealth among the poor,
> Dispensing happiness from door to door. . . .

John Fraunceis died of cholera on 25 April 1854 after only a few hours' illness. He contracted the disease while carrying out his duties at the Poorhouse. (It was later said ironically that he was the only gentleman from Glin district to have caught it.) He had been prolific to the end. A daughter, named Frances, was born to him and Johanna McCarthy on 6 October 1852. A son, named Daniel, was born to him and Mary Murry on 11 February 1853, and another son, named John, was born to him and Catherine Fitzgerald on 24 October 1853.

From *The Knights of Glin: A Geraldine Family*, Kingdom Books, 1978

John F. O'Donnell
William Colopy

A cloud above my destiny, and anguish in my soul!
I saw the waste of waters between us foaming roll;
I saw the dear old 'City of Sieges' fade away.
Like evening's cloud-built battlements that melt at close of day.

But hope still hovered o'er me, her spirit was divine;
I knew thy heart and faith would live, responsive beat to mine;
I knew the place of battles would still preserve its name —
Thy youthful genius there to guard, the temple of its fame.

When Sarsfield died at Landen, thy star of glory fell.
From Luma's 'Stone of Treaty' pale Freedom sighed farewell;
And in her fane, oh! friend of youth, a lyre she left to thee.
Inspired to sing the deeds, the names, and glories of the free.

Long may'st thou live to sing their deeds, thy city's hope and pride.
Strength, eloquence, and fire, and truth in thy wild song allied;
Leaving a tale of dimless fame to other bards to tell —
Friend of my soul, across the waves, I breathe this fond farewell.

From the *Limerick Reporter*, September 1854

Kennedy, the Piper
Mary Carbery

Three times in the year came Kennedy, the piper, or, as my mother called him,
Kennedy the musician, for he was no mere noise-maker but an artist to the tips of
his delicate expressive hands. He was lank and lean, clean-shaven, and wore the cast-
off clothes of a priest. He came in at the door with a gentle greeting, 'God save all
here', bowing low to my mother and going over to his place, the piper's corner, beside
the hearth, where with a hot ember he lighted his clay pipe and with another bow
went out to smoke in the yard, for in those days of courtesy and refinement no one
would smoke indoors, whether in cabin or castle, without the invitation of the
master of the house and the approval of the mistress.

The coming of Mick Kennedy gave untold joy. At the end of the day's work, the
farmboys washed at the pump in the yard, put on their Sunday clothes and their

well-polished shoes, while the maids discarded their aprons, replaited their shining hair, tied fresh collars and ribbons round their necks and came happily into the kitchen to meet the shy, self-conscious young men. Then the piper came forth from the chimney corner to the two chairs set ready for him, and sitting carefully down he arranged the bundle containing the pipes on his knee while he tied a leather strap to the second chair on which to rest them, perhaps also to save his threadbare trousers. He then very delicately removed several wrappings, stopping to look up with a smile when an impatient boy or girl tapped heel and toe on the stone floor to hasten him, or when we children in the doorway of the little room wriggled and squeaked with excitement. The last wrapping was a red silk handkerchief from which the bright pipes emerged; they were adjusted and after a few preliminary wails a stately quadrille started the dance, to be followed by reels, jigs, sometimes a hornpipe, and winding up with, 'Sir Roger de Coverley'. Round dances were never seen at that time.

Kennedy would play any tune called for except one, the 'Fox-Chase', and when in the middle of the evening we children were put up by the maids to ask him for it, he would turn a deaf ear, the reason being that this tune needed re-adjustment of the pipes. Nor would he listen until after my mother had gone to a cupboard for a glass of J.J. (John Jameson's whiskey) which she gave him with a smile, bidding him rest awhile. Then the panting dancers seized piggins of milk, standing at the open door to drink as they cooled in the evening air, giggling and joking but ever mindful of the near presence of 'the masther' and 'the misthress', those watchful guardians of their manners and morals.

Fresh wails from the pipes announced the wished-for 'Fox-Chase' and with clapping of hands and stamping of feet the dance went on.

Another musician was Mr Regan, a short, fat, bald little man who was a fine violinist. He played Purcell, Mozart, Schubert, even Bach, and was the 'Opener of the Door' into a new world for us children.

From *The Farm by Lough Gur: The Story of Mary Fogarty (Sissy O'Brien)*, Longmans, Green and Co., 1937

The Death of Martin Cherry
Jim Kemmy

On 12 August 1880, *The Limerick Chronicle* carried the following report of an incident in faraway Australia:

The Kelly gang of bushrangers, notwithstanding their extraordinary career of murder and rapine, and who for so long defied the efforts of the police to capture them, were run to earth on 27 June, at Jones's Hotel, Glenrowan, a town on the north-eastern line of railway, about 136 miles from Melbourne. . . . Among those who lost their lives in the fray, was a man named Martin Cherry, who it appears hails from Limerick city, and has been a considerable number of years in this colony.

The same edition of The Limerick Chronicle also contained a further and longer account of how Cherry was killed, 'during the destruction of the infamous band of outlaws who, under the leadership of Edward Kelly, for nearly two years had been the scourge of Victoria'. This account included a report from the Melbourne Argus of 20 June 1880:

> In the outhouse or kitchen, immediately behind the main building, Martin Cherry, who was one of the prisoners made by the gang, and who was so severely wounded that he could not leave the house when the other prisoners left, was found still living, but in 'articulo mortis' from wounds in the groin. He was promptly removed a short distance from the burning hotel, and laid on the ground, when Father Gibney administered to him the Last Sacrament. Cherry was insensible, and barely alive. He had evidently suffered much during the day, and death released him from his sufferings within half an hour from the time when he was removed from the hotel. It was fortunate that he was not buried alive. Cherry, who was unmarried, was an old resident of the district, and was employed as a platelayer, and resided about a mile from Glenrowan. He was born in Limerick, Ireland, and was 60 years old. He is said by all who knew him to have been a quiet, harmless man, and much regret was expressed at his death. He seems to have been shot by the attacking force, of course unintentionally.

. . .

The date of Martin Cherry's departure for Australia is not known, and little information is available on his life. . . . He worked as a goldminer before he became a railway worker, and he lived near Glenrowan. He was one of three innocent people killed in the final shoot-out between the Kelly gang and the police, some of whom were Irish. Indeed, it could be said that, like hundreds of thousands of other immigrants in Australia, he would never have been heard of again except for the sensational siege and the terrible circumstances of his death. . . .

The police, under the command of Superintendent Francis Hare, surrounded the hotel and began to fire at will. They were to be augmented with reinforcements as the siege continued. Among the early casualties were Hare and Ned Kelly, who were both wounded. John Jones, the young son of the owner of the hotel, was shot in the abdomen. His mother, Ann Jones, frantically appealed for help in carrying him to a bed. Martin Cherry responded, and said to the man near him: 'Come on, lad, we'll carry him in.' The boy later died in hospital. Despite their best efforts to avoid being hit by lying on the floor and hiding behind all available cover, three of the prisoners were killed by the police and some more were wounded. The police also shot the bushrangers' four horses to cut off escape.

Under cover of darkness, the wounded Ned Kelly slipped out of the hotel into the surrounding bush and was later captured. Between 5 a.m. and 6 a.m. on Monday morning, the besieged bushrangers suffered a further blow when Joe Byrne was killed. Some time later in the morning, Martin Cherry was shot in the groin. He had been sitting on the floor with two other men, protected, they thought, by bags of oats. . . .

At about 3 p.m., a policeman set fire to the inn. When the building was fully ablaze, Dean Matthew Gibney, a Catholic clergyman from Perth . . . walked up to the front door . . . stepped aside . . . and found the dead bodies of Joe Byrne, Dan Kelly and Steve Hart.

Martin Cherry had been so severely injured that he had been unable to leave the hotel with the other prisoners. Dean Gibney was joined by the police and they found Cherry's insensible body in an outhouse behind the main building. He was barely alive and had suffered a great deal during the day. He was removed from the building and laid on the ground outside, where Dean Gibney administered the last sacraments. Gibney later testified:

> Cherry became unconscious on being carried out of the little back house where he lay. He made no statement. His mate told me Cherry was shot by the police.

The Melbourne *Herald* commented on the circumstances of Martin Cherry's death:

> In all conscience Ned Kelly's crimes are more than sufficient for one wretch to bear without being charged with another infamous and cold-blooded act, which he did not commit. There is no doubt that Cherry's death was caused by the reckless firing of the police. All accounts agree that after Ned Kelly left the hotel he never got back, and Cherry was undoubtedly alive when Ned Kelly left.

Martin Cherry's death evoked deep feelings of sadness in the Glenrowan community. By all accounts he had been a quiet, law-abiding man. According to J.J. Kenneally in his book, *The Inner History of the Kelly Gang*, Cherry's body was handed over to his sister by Superintendent John Sadleir.

On Wednesday, 30 April 1880, Cherry's corpse was brought by train, with the wounded Ned Kelly and dead Joe Byrne, to the town of Benalla. He was buried in a quiet ceremony in a corner of Benalla cemetery, a short distance from where the yellow clay covers the bones of Joe Byrne.

No inquest on the cause of the death of Cherry, or of any of the other people who were killed at the Glenrowan Inn, was ever held. Instead, a magistrate's inquiry, conducted by Robert McBean, JP, was hastily arranged. . . .

Superintendent Sadleir wrote a deliberately misleading police report on the death of Cherry. He stated:

> It was known at this time that Martin Cherry was lying wounded in a detached building, shot by Ned Kelly early in the day, as it has since been ascertained, because he would not hold aside one of the window blinds; arrangements were made to rescue him before the flames could approach him. This was subsequently done.

In response to press and public criticism of the conduct of the police during the Kelly search and shoot-out, on 7 March 1881, the Berry government appointed a Royal Commission to inquire into the affair.

Superintendent Sadleir gave evidence on oath to the commission on 14 April 1881. When asked about the magistrate's finding, and confronted by sworn testimony on the death of Martin Cherry, he was forced to reply: 'Shot by the police in the execution of their duty.'

These terse words may serve as an epitaph for the seven people who lost their lives in the Siege of Glenrowan, but they offered little consolation to their relatives, particularly those of the innocent people who were gunned down. And criticism of the conduct of the police 'in the execution of their duty' during the Kelly hunt has continued to reverberate through Australian history to this day.

From *The Old Limerick Journal*, No. 27, Autumn 1990

Nicholas Flood Davin
Pierre Berton

As the railway towns began to prosper, the parochial jealousies that were a feature of Canadian life from Vancouver Island to the Maritimes blossomed out on the prairies. A bitter three-cornered battle, fought largely in the newspapers, took place all that year and the next between Winnipeg, Moose Jaw, and Regina. The argument, ostensibly, was over the choice of Regina as capital, but it was really over real estate. The Winnipeg *Times* charged that the new capital was nothing but a few tents and shacks, that the water was anything but pure and wholesome, and that the accommodations were terrible. The *Sun* said the capital should be moved — why, the CPR [Canadian Pacific Railway] was so ashamed of it, the trains went through only in the dark of night! The Moose Jaw *News* declared that Regina was 'dead beyond the hope of resurrection'.

Fortunately Regina had acquired a champion in the person of Nicholas Flood Davin, one of the most distinguished journalists in Canada. Davin had come to

Regina the previous fall for a visit at the invitation of W.B. Scarth of the North-West Land Company, who had brought a private carload of prominent Canadians to look over the new city, no doubt in an attempt to nullify the bad press publicity. . . . In Regina, Davin met a delegation of leading citizens who pleaded with him to start a newspaper in their city. He told them that he could not afford to start 'a paltry concern'. It might be a small paper, but it would have to contain the latest news 'and would I hoped be something of a power'. To launch such a journal, Davin said, would certainly entail an initial loss of $5,000.

'We'll give you a bonus of $5,000', somebody exclaimed.

Davin, looking about him at the huddle of tents and timber houses, only laughed. Nevertheless, he agreed to meet them that evening at a dinner in the Royal Hotel. There, to his astonishment, they voted him the $5,000 he asked for, subscribing $2,700 in cash on the spot and promising the remainder within a few days. Davin, cane in hand, took a long walk out on to the prairie to think about it. He was a creature of impulse, a romantic who lived for the day; his contempt for money — he spent it as swiftly as he made it and existed for most of his life on the cliff-edge of penury — was equalled by his love of good food, fine wine, comely women, and high adventure. He had been wounded at the siege of Montmorency while covering the Franco-Prussian War and injured so badly while riding to hounds in England that he had come to Canada in 1872 on sick leave, never to return home. His life appeared to be a series of accidental encounters. Here he was, a barrister, politician, and international journalist used to the sophistication of London and Paris, suddenly transported to the rawest of frontiers, trudging about on the open plains on a chill November night, pondering a journalistic future in a one-horse prairie town. He could not resist it; he succumbed. Regina had its champion.

A Kilfinane, Co. Limerick Irishman, Davin was a commanding presence, almost six feet tall with a massive head, entirely bald save for a sandy fringe about the ears. At 40, he was a bachelor with a long record of romances and flirtations. His dress, like his personal life, was unconventional, but his professional reputation in a variety of fields was enviable. As a journalist he had worked for the London *Standard*, *The Irish Times*, and the *Pall Mall Gazette*; he had been literary critic for the *Globe* of Toronto and editorial writer for the *Mail*. He had read law at the Middle Temple and had been called to the bar in both London and Ontario. His defence of the murderer of George Brown, the *Globe*'s publisher, had increased his reputation ('one of the most masterly appeals for human life that has ever been heard in a Toronto courtroom'), even though his client was later hanged. He was an author of note (*The Irishman in Canada*), a poet of distinction, an unsuccessful candidate for office, a friend of Sir John A. Macdonald, a master of six languages, and one of the best impromptu orators in the country. Regina had got him cheap. So great was the enthusiasm over the catch that, as a sweetener, Scarth and some others threw in an additional $5,000 worth of choice lots.

Several names were suggested for Davin's newspaper — the Shaganappi, the Blizzard, the Scalper, the Buffalo. He chose to call it the *Leader*, for he intended to make it the leading publication in the North West and in this ambition he was eminently successful. With his bonus money he set out to purchase the best possible equipment and was able to boast in the first issue that 'in truth, so much money was never before sunk in a newspaper enterprise in a place the size of Regina. Nor ever before were such complete fonts of type and so able a staff combined to furnish a paper for a town six months old.'

Once established in the editor's chair, Davin struck back at Regina's critics. . . . When he ran out of prose, Davin turned to poetry to hit at Regina's detractors. . . .

For all of the railway construction period, the Mounted Police were locked in a battle of wits with the whiskey peddlers. Every device that human guile could invent was used to smuggle liquor into the North West and to keep it hidden from official eyes. . . .

Under the prohibition laws the Mounted Police in the North West Territories could legally enter and search any premises at any hour of the day or night. This 'detestable duty' did not add to the popularity of the force. The constables themselves indulged, on occasion, in some private bootlegging. . . .

Sometimes, however, the search was more intensive, as Nicholas Flood Davin discovered. Davin had been attacking the Mounted Police vigorously in the *Leader*, especially Superintendent W.M. Herchmer. He had the ill luck to be on the same train as Herchmer on 4 August 1884, when a constable came through on a routine liquor check at Moosomin. Davin had a small flask of whiskey lying on the seat behind him. The constable pounced. Normally, the practice was to order the offender to pour the liquor out and leave it at that, but Davin got special treatment. He was charged and hauled into court in Regina, where the magistrate was none other than Herchmer himself.

Davin the journalist gave way to Davin the lawyer. Appearing in his own defence, he charged that Herchmer was interpreting the liquor Act in a narrow and capricious manner for personal reasons. In an impassioned address, he declared that he had never imported liquor into the Territories, that he never carried it, and that he was being trapped 'into appearing as to be a lawbreaker'. His eloquence was of no avail; he was fined $50 and $15.50 costs. . . .

Davin was probably more embarrassed at being publicly found with liquor than he was by being arrested, since, in his newspaper, he had been a strong temperance advocate. Most frontier editors were hard drinkers, but because temperance was as popular a cause in the eighties as pollution was ninety years later, the majority publicly embraced it. Everybody, indeed, seemed to pay lip-service to the principle, including the worst topers. Davin himself thrived on whiskey. Before preparing a speech it was his habit to lock himself in his room with a shelf of books and a full bottle. The more the wine flowed, the greater became his powers of improvisation. At one well-lubricated banquet in eastern Canada, he was called upon to speak every half-hour or so, as the glasses were filled and refilled, and did so, in several languages, until four o'clock in the morning. Though he paid public homage to prohibition, he did not go so far as to approve the spilling of confiscated liquor on the ground, an accepted practice which must have caused many an inward shudder.

From *The Last Spike: The Great Railway 1881–1885*, McClelland and Stewart Ltd, 1971

Hessy*
Charlotte Grace O'Brien

Good-night, little Hessy, good-night curly head,
Your eyes are still watching me round,
Though I've tucked you in tight and I've shaded the light,
And there goes the supper-bell's sound.

Good-night, little Hessy; you've spent the long day
In joy and in brightness and fun;
With your sweet Irish brogue, you dear little rogue,
My foolish soft heart you have won.

When I wanted to kiss you, my own little child,
You'd race away quickly from me,
And hide your sweet face in some corner-like place,
Peeping over your shoulder in glee.

Your neck is so fair, and so soft, and so round,
Your eyes are so shaded and quaint,
And the sunbeams they gloss your hair's ruddy toss,
Like the halo around some old saint.

Good-night, little Hessy; God bless you, sweet child,
And keep you your parents' delight;
Now rest you must take, till the morning shall break,
Good-night, little Hessy; good-night.

* Charlotte Grace O'Brien's nephew

From *Lyrics*, Kegan Paul, 1886

Some Limerick Writers
Michael Hartnett

The work of writers such as Kate O'Brien in prose and Desmond O'Grady in poetry made the modern reputation of Limerick as a possible literary place. The county, looked at in part by Sean O'Faolain, had been in the main neglected since the days of Aubrey de Vere and Gerald Griffin; so I would propose that while Kate O'Brien and Desmond O'Grady were the first modern writers to lodge the idea of a Limerick literature as a whole, both were *émigrés*. But however cosmopolitan they became, they never dropped their Limerick mantles: the reputations of such writers as Gerard Ryan who remained at home, were in the main local. And side-by-side with the growth of this building of a Limerick-blooded literature, with less flamboyance but not with less hope or less talent, the Irish language was being fostered by writers like Art Ó Conghaile and Criostóir Ó Floinn, who rekindled in the public the notion of a modern Gaelic literature of Limerick origins.

Dáibhí Ó Bruadair (d. 1698) was the first major poet to deal with Limerick people and history and though a Corkman, his literary life was spent in the county. In the mid-1700s the Croom poets, under the leadership of Seán Ó Tuama and Aindrias Mac Craith, unleashed a flood of song-verse of varying quality: Mac Craith's 'Slán is Céad' is one of the finest of Irish songs. In the appendix to his *Éigse na Máighe* (Oifig an tSoláthair 1952) Risteárd Ó Foghludha lists some forty-two 'poets and scholars' in the Limerick of the eighteenth and nineteenth centuries, among them Standish Hugh O'Grady and Eoghan Ó Caomhánaigh, who as I have read, wrote in Newcastle West another fine song, 'Táimse im codladh is ná dúistear mé'. Worth noting also is that fine religious poet Tadhg Gaelach Ó Súilleabháin from the parish of Kileedy; his *Pious Miscellany* (1802) must have been one of the first published books of verse from such a source. Many of the forty-two 'poets and scholars' were dabblers in verse, if not in scholarship: but out of the county in those years there was one 'might-have-been' Limerick writer. When Peter Mangan left Shanagolden about 1790 he bequeathed his son James Clarence to a Dublin destiny. . . .

Seán Ó Tuama (d. 1775), Aindrias Mac Craith (d. 1793) and Fr Liam Inglis (d. 1778), all Limerick poets, occasionally wrote poems in the metre which is now known as the 'limerick'. Many books credit Edward Lear with the invention of this form; but his *Book of Nonsense* did not appear until 1846, after he had been on a visit to Ireland and after James Clarence Mangan had published some translations of Seán Ó Tuama's 'limericks'.

From the Introduction to *On the Counterscarp: Limerick Writing 1961–1991*, Salmon Publishing, 1991

Sophie Peirce
Robert J. Cussen

Dr George Peirce of Newcastle West was as good a doctor as his father and he added considerably to the practice, not to mention his many appointments. He married twice, first to Thomasina D'Arcy Evans of Knockaderry and, secondly, to Henrietta Georgina Hewson of Ballybunion. He had eight children, one boy and seven girls, by the first marriage and none by the second. Of the eight children, the eldest was John (otherwise Jackie).

Dr George may have been an excellent doctor but he was an abysmal father. His first wife died in 1889 and, after that, he tried for several years to rear the children himself. . . .

His only son, Jackie, was a holy terror, full of pranks and devilment, and he had no authority whatever over him. Jackie was the heir to the lands of Knockaderry, the property of his maternal grandfather, Thomas D'Arcy Evans (Old Tom Evans as he was called). He spent much of his time with Old Tom, who had a drink problem and was poor company for the young man. Eventually, his father, in an attempt to civilise him, got him into the Provincial Bank and he was appointed to the Kilrush branch in County Clare. He wasn't long in the bank when the most extraordinary things began to happen there.

The Kilrush bank called in the police to investigate one of Peirce's appalling pranks and the police put their finger on him. He didn't like the intrusion of the police so he arranged a trap to baffle them and to make them look foolish in the eyes of the Kilrush people. After bank hours he used to go down to the pier and fool around there in a most suspicious way, looking here and there, and dodging every time he saw a policeman. This got on the policemen's nerves and they commenced shadowing him. Then, one evening, sure that he was being followed by a police-man, he went to the pier with a timber-shaped contraption on his back — for all the world like a coffin. When he reached the pier, he placed the contraption into a boat and rowed out into the centre of the wide Shannon River. By this time, all the police in Kilrush were centred on the pier with field-glasses directed at Jackie and his boat. The next thing they saw was Peirce tumbling the contraption into the water. When he came back to the pier they put him under arrest and rowed down river, bringing the contraption back to the town. Then they took him and the contraption to the police barrack, opened it and found only stones and timber shavings inside. All Kilrush was delighted at the occurrence. . . .

When he came home he once again spent most of his time with his maternal grandfather, Old Tom Evans, out in Knockaderry House and its broad acres. Now, having a clear hand, he behaved like a jester and kept the Knockaderry people full of talk and enjoyment about his antics. Eventually, on the death of his grandfather, he succeeded to Knockaderry House and farm. He lived alone in the house and found he couldn't keep up with the work, so he put an advertisement for a house-keeper in the local papers. A woman named Kate Teresa Doolan from Kerry answered the advertisement. She was a fine, upstanding woman of 34 or 35 years and had no difficulty in getting the job. Things went well in Knockaderry at the beginning but Peirce was a difficult man and was not on the best of terms with a lot of his neighbours and was jealous if she mingled with them.

There was an extensive farmer, named William Power, living next to the house and lands at Knockaderry and they were black out with each other. Jackie got the notion that Power was courting Miss Doolan, his housekeeper, and he went around slandering him. Power brought an action to recover damages laid at £1,000 for alleged slander and libel. Peirce defended the case, denied the slander and libel, and pleaded that if the words were written or published the occasion was a privileged one. The action was held in the High Court, Dublin, on Monday, 22 April 1895.

Peirce lost the action and had to pay a considerable sum of money to Power and, in addition, he had to pay all the costs — his own and Power's. It broke him and he was soon dodging debts, sheriffs and the devil-knows-what. At the height of all this trouble he married Miss Doolan on 29 May 1895 in the Dublin Registry Office.

A girl was born to the couple on 10 November 1896 and christened Sophie Catherine Peirce. Shortly after the birth of the child, Teresa Peirce was found dead in Knockaderry House and there was no trace of her husband or the child. Jackie went on the run but was arrested and charged with the murder of his wife. He was found to be insane and was put in a mental institution where he spent the rest of his life. Dr George Peirce took charge of the infant Sophie and brought her to his home in Newcastle West, where she was reared and looked after by her aunts. She went to St Margaret's Hall School, Dublin, where she later became a student in the College of Science and got a degree there in the early 1920s.

Shortly after the First World War, she met and fell in love with an English Army man named Elliott Lynn, who was home on vacation from East Africa and visiting friends in Ireland. They were married and she threw everything to the winds and went to East Africa. Here, in her happiness, she turned poet and wrote many verses for the press. But the happiness did not last and the marriage broke up. She published her poems in England in 1925. Here is her farewell to Elliott Lynn:

Divorce

We built a house with kisses,
And we pull it down with tears,
The mortar of our happy hopes
Could not withstand the years.

We lit our hearth with laughter,
    And danced beside its pyre;
Its ashes scatter to the winds,
    And cold its sacred fire.

We dreamed of little children,
    How children's voices thrill,
Their wistful voices haunt me yet,
    Unborn and shapeless still.

He wooed me in the courts of love
    And now that love must die;
We wrangle in the courts of men
    The courts that break the tie.

It's like a bunch of lilies
    You draggle in the slime,
The love we lost — and only fears
    Are with us all the time.

She got involved in athletics in England and on 6 August 1923 she set up a world record for the high jump at a height of 4'11". She was also British javelin champion in 1923. She became Vice-President of the Women's Amateur Athletics Association and an advocate for athletics for women and girls — so much so that in 1925 she wrote a book on the subject.

Returning by plane in May 1925 from Prague, where she had been attending an Olympic Conference and had delivered a paper on women's athletics, she was sitting beside an RAF man called Reid and, expressing an interest in flying, he promised to help her learn to fly. She joined the London Light Aeroplane Club immediately, being its first woman member, and had her first flight in August 1925. She showed an immediate aptitude for flying and proceeded to involve herself in competitive flying. Over the next few years she broke many records and her solo flight from Cape Town to London (a distance of 10,000 miles) brought her world acclaim. She also held the world altitude record for light planes, and was the first woman to make a parachute jump in April 1926.

She married a wealthy English industrialist, Sir James Heath, about this time but the marriage also ended in lawsuits and notoriety, Sir James commenting, 'My wife has flown away in the clouds.' She went to live in the United States in 1928 and continued her success as an aviator, through flying demonstrations and giving lectures. In August 1929 she was involved in an air crash in Cleveland in which she suffered severe head injuries and, though she seemed to make an excellent recovery and flew again, she was never quite the same person and seems to have suffered a personality change.

She married for the third time, a black aviator named Reggie Williams, and they both continued to give flying exhibitions on both sides of the Atlantic. However, she became increasingly unstable and developed a drink problem. Her last years were sad ones. In May 1934, she was fatally injured in a fall down the stairs of a tram-car in London.

She ended her life on a characteristic note, typical of her late father. Sophie — about to die — arranged that her remains be cremated and the ashes taken by aeroplane over the Square in Newcastle West, Co. Limerick. The plane was to arrive at 12 noon and the ashes were to be scattered over the ground adjoining the houses in the south-western side of the Square. At that time, this side was made up of:

(a) Peirce's house, where Sophie lived for many years. The Newcastle West branch of Allied Irish Bank now stands on this site.
(b) The house of Captain Richbel Curling (Agent of the Earl of Devon's Limerick lands). There had been a deep hatred between Sophie and Richbel.
(c) The chapel of the Church of Ireland, enclosed by a stone wall facing on to the Square. It was the captain's habit to walk out at noon every day into the Square and place his back up against the church wall to take in the view.

The aeroplane passed over and the captain — as usual backed up against the church wall — couldn't escape inhaling the ashes. It kept him coughing on the spot for a considerable time. When he heard what it was all about his dislike for Sophie grew more and more. For years thereafter, when the March winds raised the dust along the Square, the captain, at his usual stance, used to salute passers-by, saying: 'There's that Peirce lady at it again; will I ever be clear of her?'

There was no answer. Peirce's house is gone. The intrepid Sophie has passed on. The captain and the chapel are no more. All are now gone except the March winds. *Sic transit gloria mundi.*

From *The Annual Observer*, Newcastle West Historical Society, June 1983

My Five Aunts
Kate O'Brien

I had five aunts. So had my brothers and sisters, the same five in name and place. But my five aunts are not theirs any more than theirs are mine. All nine of us had each his own five aunts, in as much or as little as we possessed, observed or remembered them. Were there then forty-five aunts? Maybe. But they lived, conventionally and unassumingly, behind five names and five faces.

On the one hand, there were mother's three sisters — Aunt Mary, Aunt Fan and Aunt Annie, all younger than mother. On the other, there was father's only sister whose name was Anne, but who was known to us by her married surname as Aunt Hickey. She was twenty years older than father. And there was the wife of father's quite old brother, Uncle Mick. Her name also was Anne, so she was called Auntie Mick — a kind of pet name which did not become her at all.

These aunts with, in a few cases, accompanying uncles made a constant and lively background to our youth — as aunts and uncles do. But as our mother died when all nine of us were very young — running from fifteen years to nine months — our father, and we with him, became more than is usual dependent upon the five — for authority, fun, advice or affection. And we would have been a lost and queer bundle of orphans without them. Anyway, they were there.

They created impressions. They made from five to forty-five different sorts of dents in the surface of family life. They were, in their contrasted natures, all as emotional as we were — some of them were as distressible. They were an anxious lot on the whole, I think; and they took us very seriously. Poor Katty's children. They took us on, to help Tom — our father, and they found or decided — found, I think they would insist, that they loved us. We found in our turn that we loved some of them. And one of us thinks that perhaps through a long labyrinth of remembrance, and family feeling and plain curiosity, she has arrived at loving them — in an elderly fashion. Perhaps somewhat in the way in which Auntie Mick, she flatters herself, loved her.

Love aside — and who is to define it in relation to the long-dead, the memory-and-wish-invented? — I have reflected sometimes in my later years on the personalities and lives of these aunts. It interests me to observe that whereas they all came out of the same mould — their fathers having been hard-beaten peasants of the desperate 'forties who had survived to reach the refuge of a town, then courageously to earn their way on to the foothills of the middle class, they, the daughters, having received only such minimum convent education as could not now be called education, and being all five steeped, but steeped, in Roman Catholicism, of which the conventions and period-bigotries were as unquestionable to them as the rules — were indeed one and the same thing, for my aunts were not theologians — as I began to say, it interests me to recall that they were individuals, to a woman. They were personalities — each with emphasis, even on occasion with clangour and commotion. Sisters-in-law they might be, with interests the same and entangled; and sisters emotionally, even hysterically attached; five of them, reading the same few books, attending similar missions, holding more or less the same political views, all agreed that a certain few things and ideas and ways of life were right, and that a thousand others, not to be mentioned if possible, were totally wrong and abominable — yet these five were separated and different from each other in all that gave them identification of soul as ash tree is from birch, or blue eye from brown.

My recollections are not pure. Time and myself have worked upon my aunts for me, and the portraits I have sketched are perhaps not portraits even in the freest,

most expressionist sense, for anyone but me. And even for me, they are not repres-
entational or within sight of being photographic. The time is too long; I peer through
half-shut eyes from very far away, and the knowingness of adult life cannot help but
throw in accents and shadows which the child who knew these women could not
have perceived. I must suppose.

Santayana, in his memoirs, ponders the relationship between what the child saw
and what he, the man, remembers — and in one place says: 'From that coachman's
box my young mind saw nothing but the aesthetics of mechanism; yet my unconscious psyche kept a better watch, and I can now evoke images of impressions that
meant nothing to me then but that had subtler significance.' I would say something
similar of how my own long-ago seeing relates to my recalling of what I saw. And I
think that my unconscious psyche was an active sprite.

Nevertheless, these portrait sketches, done *con amore* and to refresh and amuse
myself, are the unaided work of an elderly woman. I have been earnest to avoid
picturesque foreground presentation of that 'touching small figure' which most 'I'
narrators of family chronicles and humours become. I have had to intervene in my
youthful guise more often than I find satisfactory, because these women existed for
me and gave me my long memories of them simply as my aunts and through their
relationship with me. But my attempt now, as a kind of response to all they gave
and tried to give — some of them anyway — to the person they saw in me, is to try
to re-create them free and in themselves — to try to detach them, if I possibly can,
from the states of emotion, fuss, exasperation and temerity in which their concern
for us obscured, or half-distorted them.

I have a nephew who when he was a child and schoolboy had, all to himself,
seven bona fide aunts. Their number has thinned by now. He is an only child and
when he first went to boarding-school he found the ways and ideas of boys in herds
somewhat surprising. When his mother visited him early in his first time he said
this:

'The boys here are often very peculiar, mamma. Last night a lot of us were
talking, and they all kept making fun of their aunts and people! They said they
hated their aunts!'

'And what did you say?'

'Oh, I said that I couldn't agree with them at all! I told them that I love my
aunts!'

From *Presentation Parlour*, William Heinemann Ltd, 1963

Brendan Bracken at St John's Hospital
Dr John F. Devane

The children patients at St John's Hospital always amused me. I liked their unin-hibited chat on things that interested them, and when I had obtained their confidence, after the first few days of discomfort in hospital had passed, I used to enjoy sitting on the edges of their beds and quizzing them about various things.

Brendan Bracken, a lad from County Tipperary, was referred to me at St John's from Mungret College where he was at school. He was an intelligent little chap with a very inquisitive mind. During his convalescence he wandered all over the hospital chatting with everybody, and even into the theatre wanting to know the why and the wherefore of all the gadgets — sometimes to the annoyance of poor Mother Ambrose, the overworked Matron-Theatre Sister-Administrator of the hospital. She often said to me, 'For goodness sake, take that little lad with you on some of your country calls and keep him out of mischief's way.' I did so on many occasions, and enjoyed his amusing chat and interesting comments during those long journeys.

On one occasion I had a call to County Kerry and took young Bracken with me. The patient lived in a farmhouse at the end of a bohreen off the main road. I left the car on the road in charge of Brendan. After we had seen the patient the family doctor and I returned to the main road accompanied by the patient's husband, who courteously came with us, and whilst I was having a few last words with the doctor and the husband about the patient, and perhaps trying my best to look the part of the heavy consultant, I was completely debunked by my little friend Brendan popping his head out the window of the car and shouting to me in a loud voice: 'Hi, doctor, how much did they give you?' I was hard put to keep from laughing but I enjoyed the anticlimax enormously. It was perhaps a forecast of his subsequent success in financial matters.

Soon after leaving St John's he went to Australia, but he returned to England later, and succeeded in being admitted to the well-known English public school, Sedbergh. How the red-haired Irish boy got in there so quickly is a mystery, because Sedbergh had a long waiting list. Perhaps he captivated the headmaster with his intelligence and his ready wit, and literally talked his way into the school.

He had no influential friends in England but, before he was 29, he had been elected a Member of Parliament (Conservative) for Paddington, and had become a director on the boards of several important companies — all before he had reached the age of 30! . . .

His financial success was no less brilliant than his social and political career. At an early stage he became a very close personal friend of Winston Churchill. . . . Wherever Churchill went Brendan went, so much so that he was known as 'Churchill's Shadow'.

During the Second World War he became in turn Private Secretary to the Prime Minister, Member of the Privy Council, Minister of Information, and finally, First Lord of the Admiralty. . . .

Brendan Bracken never married. He occasionally wrote to me during his years of success and always referred to the happy days at St John's and our pleasant drives through the country. More than once he asked me to go and stay with him at his house in the West End of London; but somehow I didn't feel inclined to do so. I felt I would have enjoyed his company more in the days when he shouted at me on that road in Kerry — 'Hi, doctor, how much did they give you?'

From A History of St John's Hospital, Limerick, printed privately, 1970

Memories of an Influential Uncle
Desmond O'Grady

'Ah, my dear children, why do you look at me like this?'
EURIPIDES: Medea

'. . . and yet one word makes all those difficulties disappear.'
SOPHOCLES: Oedipus at Colonus

I

In a crow black suit you'd confuse for a beggar's, grey hair combed
straight flat across his head,
he stands in the door of his condemned house, bronzed
fists in his coat pockets, spit grey eyes
no brighter, no bigger than nailheads. In his forehead
a small dent from the shaft of a backing cart when a child.
Away over the rooftops and pigeon-coops, the spire of St John's
Cathedral. Straight in front, his slum
inheritance — his mother's empire. Over his head
the three floors of the old house that bred
the lot of them, still furnished, its harm
done. Forty years of dust on the sheet-covered forms.
Up in the rat looted attic, black sea trunks still standing half open,
packed with the wardrobe he wore on those Indian
cruises after his mother's death and her will.
Not a penny has seen daylight since. He remained alone:

his position with contemporaries always the blind side of form, playing rare
and wise in his silences — a kind of hostility.
He was tight with money, superstitious, secretive, cold
as a herring when driving a bargain, honest as salt.
He feared his God, but distrusted his clergy.
He returned unchanged from his cruises and never again went anywhere.

II

But for me as a child, in that long toyless night of the War, his presence
was brightly Homeric. While Hitler's huns
converged on the Channel and Goering came nightly to hammer
down Coventry, I sat by the fire while he told me of other
times and their heroes: the mad Black and Tans
or Cuchulainn, O'Neill, Dan O'Connell, or Niall of the Nine Hostages,
the Children of Lir or the Wooing of Emer, the Salmon of Knowledge
or the story of Deirdre, the Coming of Patrick,
the Three Sons of Uisneach, the Return of Ossian or death
of Cuchulainn, the Danes and the Normans, Hogan the Poet
of Thomond or the ballad The Blacksmith of Limerick,
the Civil War that divided the family, my grandfather's plunge
to ruin and death from his drinking, my grandmother's curse on his sons'
children. He distrusted success and any characteristic
trait of a questionable ancestor. His greatest hate
was proud independence in youth, or any sign that might
lead to it; frequently warning individualistic
action from pride could only end badly — and cited relations.

III

In the natural, if unbalanced, struggle between generations we form
an unworded, life-long alliance of forces:
the older delivering oracles, the younger interpreting —
simply at first, but with more complicated, harrowing
subtlety later, till the final phase is
compulsive dedication to living these oracles through to their dénouement.
So that time after time, down the long black night of our northern winter,
he would lead me helpless to that dark ledge
of the heart's land's-end (where the soul's black sea, like an epileptic,
works out its ceaseless agony far below, and the frantic
seabirds scream and wheel at their scourge)
and he'd show me a vision of the flawed man's torment in ultimate failure.

But now that the adult eye has its own perspective, and human
fear and the heart their own reservation,
I dimly see through the dark significance his presence
held then for the trusting child — oracular in the province
of his native caution, his mystery and notion
that the sins of our ancestors inevitably fall on the lives of our own.

We all sail sightlessly out to our own self-wreckage, and years
later, in far away cities, when the lean
north wind is loping the streets like a grey famished animal
hunting for something to claw and devour, when maternal
need casts a shadow like a crime on the town,
when fathers are dead at the hands of departed children and laws
that achieve their own order give us marriage and offspring, we live out the word
of our ancestors' warning irrevocably, and consummate
our own private ruin — for the dead slay the living in turn.

And is there then no escaping? Is our final salvation
human love's condemnation to failure in spite
of the will to choice and to action, and the will to negate the absurd?
Whatever the consequence, to attempt the impossible, step off the ledge
of restrictive inheritance — this is not failure;
but failing to act for fear of the failure in consequence . . .
The heart's obligation to the soul's vision and sense
of the self — its satisfaction; our
degree of decision given chosen action; this alone is our judge.

Vale

Now, a far lost cry from the coast of my origins, my final rest is
at last by this ancient equestrian statue.
I blindly face west to what's now my uncle's kingdom.
My lone daughter's image surrounds me. Who needs a tomb
once terms are made with love's reasons? Who
is not his own instrument blindly seeking his known final peace, his Colonus?

From *The Dark Edge of Europe*, MacGibbon & Kee, 1967

John Hunt at Lough Gur
Frank Mitchell

In the early 1940s I decided that I would have to take archaeology more seriously, and I enrolled as an occasional student in University College, Dublin, where I attended Seán Ó Ríordáin's lectures. . . .

During the later part of the war my wife was away in England teaching in a boys' prep school, and I was relatively foot-loose. Seán and I had also become friends, and I asked if I could join his excavation programme at Lough Gur, where over a period of many years he carried out a series of very important digs. Unfortunately he died prematurely before all the work was published, but this has now appeared after Eoin Grogan and George Eogan did an enormous amount of work piecing together Seán's detailed drawings and notes.

We dossed down in an old schoolhouse, where Seán's only contribution to the house-keeping was to wake us up as he went out to the pump in the yard where he filled the porridge-saucepan. He put it on the stove and went back to his ablutions. After some time I noticed that a man of about my years, or a little older, was also taking part in the excavations; he was John Hunt, and we became friendly. I of course didn't know that he was a very distinguished medievalist, but I enjoyed his company.

John and his wife, Putzel, had recently come to Ireland, and had chosen the Limerick area, as John had family connections with the county. Being of German origin, Putzel found life in wartime England at times trying, and they had set up in a small farmhouse on the edge of the lake, which they gradually enlarged and transformed. Putzel had a flair for interior decoration, and John could direct tradesmen without the intermediary of an architect, and the house quickly changed out of all recognition.

Our friendship developed, and after a time Putzel suggested that I would be more comfortable lodging with them, with twenty-four-hour hot water assured, rather than continuing to survive in the schoolhouse. This I was very glad to do, and on subsequent visits I always lodged with them. It took some time for it to dawn on me that they were both medievalists of world-wide reputation, who had spent many years dealing in medieval antiquities, as well as objects from other periods. Like Somerset Maugham, John had started life as a medical student in London, but drifted into constant attendance in sale rooms. Putzel was the daughter of a museum director, and had been brought up surrounded by art. John was one of Sotheby's chief cataloguers, and together they had bought many things for Sir John Burrell; these are now to be seen in his museum outside Glasgow.

Thus it was in the Hunt home in Lough Gur that my interest in, and knowledge of, medieval and other antiquities was born, and I shall always be grateful to them for that awakening. Not only was I surrounded by beautiful objects, but I was encouraged to handle them, and also to browse through their wonderful library of art books. The knowledge I gained there was to be turned to special advantage many years later, when I became involved in the organisation of an exhibition of Irish art treasures, including the Book of Kells, in the United States. I would never have undertaken the preparation of the catalogue without this grounding in medieval material from John and Putzel.

After some years at Lough Gur the Hunts moved to Dublin, but John's attachment to the Limerick area continued. They secured the establishment of the Craggaunowen Centre, 5 km south-east of Quin, where John supervised the construction of a crannog and a rath; there was a small castle on the site, and this the Hunts furnished with some of their medieval collection. John's collection of prehistoric Irish material was lodged in Limerick University. Towards the end of his life, with the assistance of Peter Harbison, John published a comprehensive two-volume survey of Irish medieval carving. In Trinity College his name was on the list of those proposed to receive honorary degrees, but he unfortunately died before the formalities were completed.

At Lough Gur I was once more in familiar karstic limestone country, as the lake was surrounded by limestone slopes with a thin soil cover. A limestone knoll, Knockadoon, stood on one side of the lake, which formed a horseshoe around it. Thus the area, with the knoll surrounded by fertile slopes, and the lake with abundant fish and wildfowl, was obviously most attractive to early inhabitants, particularly in the Neolithic period.

There was a tremendous scatter of prehistoric debris; at one site which we excavated, a house of seventeenth-century age, with a floor of beaten earth, yielded an Elizabethan brooch, and when the mud walls were demolished, pieces of Neolithic pottery which had been embedded in the mud fell out of them. As in the typical Irish farm until very recently, the Neolithic farmhouse had a manure-heap near by, and as earthenware vessels got broken, the pieces were thrown into the manure, to be later spread on the fields. When earth was later gathered to build the house-wall, pieces of pottery were also collected.

John fitted me out with a crude raft made by lashing oil drums together, and from this I made a boring in one of the arms of the lake. There was a considerable depth of deposit, which reached right down into the late-glacial period, and also recorded was a splendid development of Neolithic agriculture. Unfortunately the lake had been partly drained in the nineteenth century, and when the water-level fell, and exposed the marginal muds, these were rapidly re-washed by rain out into the basin to accumulate once more. Thus the upper layers of the muds I brought up were contaminated by pollen in secondary position, and I could not carry the record up to the present day, as I had hoped to do.

Another boring was made in the lake in 1986 by a Swedish worker, Liz Ahlmgren. She was armed with a new line of approach, unheard of when I made my boring. Iron, an element with high magnetic response, is very common in the earth's crust. Nearly all soils have some content of iron, and this content can be detected by magnetometers. Whenever the plant cover on the soils on the slopes round Lough

Gur was broken by tillage, some of the soil, carrying magnetic iron particles with it, was washed into the lake, to be incorporated in the mud.

When the columns of undisturbed mud taken up by the borer are laid out along a laboratory bench, a sensitive magnetometer can be passed along the line of mud. The instrument will pick out the layers of mud that have a content of inwashed soil. This record can then be compared with the pollen counts, where it will be found that richness in pollen of weeds associated with cultivation will coincide with layers of higher magnetism. Under ideal conditions the layers of mud doubly associated with agriculture can then be dated by radiocarbon determination. All this detail is reported by this new investigation.

The prehistoric peoples who had lived round the lake had lost many objects in the shallow lake margins, and as the muds were washed away a large collection of material, including some very fine Bronze Age objects, came to light. Some of this material reached the National Museum, including a splendid shield of beaten bronze, fabricated, perhaps, about 700 B.C.

In late-glacial times, 10,000 years ago, long before the arrival of humans, the area was also attractive to animal life. Remains of the giant deer are commonly found in the vicinity, and one small cave near the lake, the Red Cellar Cave, produced the bones of Arctic lemming and Arctic fox. The cave had later been used by a bear as a hibernating den, but after the bear had dug itself into the underlying deposit, it expired during the course of its winter sleep. When the cave was excavated the bear skeleton was found, surrounded by and embedded in bones from a much earlier period. I looked without success for scratch-marks on the cave walls where the bear might have sharpened his claws; John Jackson did find scratch-marks in a Sligo cave where there was a bear skeleton, again probably from an animal that died during hibernation. It is not known when the bear became extinct in Ireland; at Dalkey Island, David Liversage discovered bear canine teeth in association with Neolithic material, but the Irish language has no native word for bear, using instead a loan-word from Latin; it may have disappeared from Ireland before the beginning of the Christian era. We proceed on from Lough Gur and cross the Shannon at Limerick.

Parteen

Just before it passes through Limerick, the Shannon makes an enormous loop to the north, and at the tip of the horseshoe, about 5 km north of the city, is the village of Parteen. Here in pre-Shannon Scheme days one of the sons of William Smith O'Brien, Donough O'Brien, built himself a house overlooking the river and a picturesque ruined weir, popularly known as King John's Weir, as it is thought to go back to the thirteenth century.

The house was of a very individual style; the main part, which faced the river, could be likened to a hay-barn because it was a long rectangular structure with a curved roof; the drawing-room was here, with a splendid bow window looking straight down the river. At either end there were wings, that at the east housing the bedrooms, and that at the west the kitchen and other smaller rooms. When the Shannon Scheme was being developed in the twenties, the house narrowly escaped demolition, because the tailrace from the power-house upstream at Ardnacrusha passed within a few yards of it. Thus the house which until then stood on the banks of the Shannon now found itself at the tip of a peninsula between the river and the tailrace.

Donough O'Brien left the house to his niece, Lucy Gwynn. Lucy Gwynn was a sister of Edward Gwynn, a don in, and later Provost of Trinity College, and Edward's children, who included my wife, also a Lucy, enjoyed many happy childhood holidays at Parteen. After our marriage, my wife brought me to the house, and I made good friends with her aunt, Lucy Gwynn. When returning from Lough Gur, I would stop off for a few days with her. The house had been built by an educated man, who had in some way imparted a very special atmosphere or flavour to it.

Donough O'Brien had been very interested in natural history and antiquities, and many distinguished workers in those fields had frequented the house. W.J. Knowles, a distinguished antiquary, was frequently there, and also his sister, Matilda Knowles, who was a distinguished botanist with a special interest in lichens. Matilda, or Matty as she was generally known, worked in the herbarium in the National Museum for many years, and when I first began to visit the herbarium in the early thirties, Miss Knowles, an elderly lady with an ear-trumpet, was occasionally to be seen, sitting at a microscope, examining some lichens in detail.

I cannot be certain that Praeger ever visited the house, but I think it more than likely that he must have done so. At one stage he was very keen on promoting joint meetings of the various field clubs dotted round Ireland; Donough O'Brien was a leading member of the Limerick club which certainly acted as host on more than one occasion, and it would have been at such a meeting that Praeger would have had an opportunity to visit.

The tradition of education was strong in the Gwynn family, and the aura of the house continued uninterrupted during Lucy Gwynn's occupation of it. The library, in addition to books and journals on natural history and antiquities, also contained the full range of nineteenth-century novels that sat naturally in such surroundings. During my stays at Parteen I took to reading these to my great profit. Up to that point my acquaintance with English literature had been based on a somewhat pot-boiling book, *Masters of English Literature*, compiled by Lucy's elder brother, Stephen, author and Nationalist Member of Parliament. This had been the material on which I was prepared for my school examinations.

I read the novels avidly. I read all the Brontës, all the Trollopes, and much of George Eliot, though I got stuck in *Daniel Deronda*, and I did not get any great distance with Meredith. Thus my visits to Limerick in the early forties proved very fruitful for my further development; with the Hunts I widened my horizons; with Lucy Gwynn they deepened rather than widened.

From *The way that I followed: a naturalist's journey around Ireland*, Country House, 1990

'Wires'
Thomas Ryan

I remember this extraordinary person with a vividness his appearance deserves. He was quite exceptional. Anyone in contact with Mars, as he was reported to be, was outside the range of the conventional small town madman. Then his reputation as 'an educated man' gave him a further distinction. . . .

Anyhow, this man was distinctive in his dress. It wasn't that it was extravagant or archaic: it was largely original. He was a walking powerhouse. As clerks used to carry biros, pencils and fountain pens to dazzle the bedazzled, so did he display a collection of batteries, lead aprons, and wires and wires galore.

He was held together — 'connected' as it were — with wires! They ran from the batteries he supported on his head under an enormous distended cap to a small electrical factory he wore on his chest and from the bound bundles of 'Ever Readys' on the carriers — he had two, over front and rear wheels — and from another enormous one suspended from the bar of the frame to his person. Very sensibly, he wheeled the bicycle — at least I never saw him mount the machine. Anyway, the tires were flat. The poor man was as dark as a Hottentot. He was covered from head to toe with dirty black grease. Whether this was to conduct the Martian rays with superior efficacy, or to protect himself from injurious leaks, I do not know: I only know that he looked abominably black and smelled like a dirty engine.

Wires was the spontaneous nickname given to him soon after his first arresting appearances on the streets of Limerick. He was reputed to speak in an Oxford accent, a confirmation of the story that he was an Englishman, a gentleman, an officer and, we suspected, a Protestant. . . .

The clothing of Wires deteriorated badly over the years until he was reduced to wearing a girdle or skirt of window blinds material. It gave him a Robinson Crusoe look which, with the wired-up bike, was most wonderful to behold. Wires had a room in 'The Soldiers' Home' in Hartstonge Street. Boys boasted of having peeped in to see a veritable Ardnacrusha: wires, hawsers, bubbling cauldrons, 'like Frankenstein had', and books all over the place. Truly an unusual person. He was quite harmless: worse, he was unresponsive and gave no reaction, verbal or otherwise, to a 'rise'. . . . Wires was reputed to be well-to-do. It was said he had a British Army pension which he regularly collected. As he did not beg or seek alms at religious houses, his solvency was, no doubt, somewhat exaggerated; but the story of an educated man shell-shocked into lunacy seemed a likely one.

At some stage during the war years he was no longer about. Someone said he was dead.

From the *Limerick Socialist*, Vol. 7, No. 4, April 1978

Dr Richard Hayes (1882–1958)
J.B. Lyons

On an afternoon in June 1906 two young Limerick men, John Devane and Richard Hayes, house-surgeons at the Mater Misericordiae Hospital, strolled aimlessly from Eccles Street to Grafton Street where they happened to see in a travel agent's window an advertisement for a cheap excursion to Paris. They went there and enjoyed themselves but for Hayes it was a fateful occasion — he returned a franco-phile which, combining with a *furor scholasticus*, led to a lifetime's research into Irish links with France.

Devane, less productive in a literary sense, later wrote a history of St John's Hospital, Limerick; his brother, Dr James Devane, was the author of *The Isle of Destiny*. John Devane, F.R.C.S.I., had a busy surgical practice in Limerick city but in 1916 he managed to come to Dublin for Easter and on Easter Sunday he took his fiancée to Lusk, Co. Dublin, where Dick Hayes was dispensary doctor. They chatted and reminisced. Hayes showed them his garden and gave them tea and in the evening the lovers left him with no inkling that next day as Commander of the Fingal Battalion he would be embroiled in the Easter Rebellion.

Richard Hayes soon relinquished his command to Thomas Ashe in order to tend the wounded, friend and foe alike. General Richard Mulcahy has left this description of an unmilitary soldier:

> In a rushed moment of contact-making in the first lull of the fighting at Rath Cross I met him, erect, alert, absorbed in thought, his revolver aimless in his hand. I broke his thought by a word — 'You'll want these' — to give him his satchel of medical supplies picked up some yards away. Later after four hours fighting on a road margined with death and pain and anguish he tended the wounded.

His capital sentence for participation in the battle of Ashbourne was commuted to twenty years' penal servitude. He was incarcerated first in Dartmoor, to be trans-ferred to the Isle of Wight some months later and moved in December to Lewes Jail. He was released in a general amnesty in 1917.

When Dr Hayes was appointed medical officer to Earl Street dispensary the Local Government Board refused to sanction the appointment and his salary was withheld from 1916 to 1920 when, on the election of a Sinn Féin Board of Guardians, he received what was owing to him. Meanwhile he was re-arrested in 1918 and sent to Reading Jail; while imprisoned there he was elected MP for East Limerick.

He also represented Limerick in the Dáil; he participated in the Treaty debate and voted for it: 'I am voting for the Treaty and I am also supporting its adoption. . . .' He saw it as a compromise 'the culmination of a whole series of compromises'; he believed that were it not for the oath contained in it ninety-nine per cent of the Dáil would accept it as a compromise at least. . . .

The political arena had little attraction for him. Just as he had lacked the instincts of a combatant soldier he had no flair for the cut-and-thrust of parliamentary debate. He seldom spoke in the Dáil and resigned his seat in 1924 to devote himself to his medical practice and historical scholarship.

A native of Bruree, Co. Limerick, where he was born in 1882, Richard Francis Hayes was the son of a local schoolteacher, Richard Hayes, and his wife Margaret Ruddle. Having obtained secondary schooling in Rathkeale he became a student of the Catholic University Medical School and took the diplomas Licentiate of the Royal College of Physicians in Ireland and Licentiate of the Royal College of Surgeons in Ireland in 1905. After being house-surgeon at the Mater Hospital he was resident medical officer in Galway Central Hospital and an external assistant at the Coombe Lying-in Hospital before his appointment as dispensary medical officer in Lusk from where he moved later to Earl Street dispensary and finally to Donny-brook Number Two dispensary, living during the tenure of those appointments at Lusk House, Thomond House, South Circular Road and at Guildford Road, Sandymount. . . .

Richard Hayes's own first literary compilation, a pamphlet on anatomical terms and names of diseases in Irish, was published in 1905 but the works which earned him fame were the fruit of many years of historical research at home and abroad. When the National University of Ireland awarded him its Historical Research Prize in 1934 the *Catholic Bulletin* described him as 'also well known to his friends as a most systematic worker in undeveloped areas of modern Irish history'. . . .

Frank O'Connor was impressed by Dr Hayes's clinical ability. His diagnostic perception could sometimes seem uncanny. O'Connor showed him a letter from AE (George Russell) in which the poet said he was ill and that a London doctor had diagnosed colitis. 'I am very sorry to say that is not colitis', Hayes said, and events were to prove him right. 'That is cancer.'

The demands on his time were irregular and unpredictable. Despite those calls to which priority must be given he published several books incorporating original research. It has been said that he was made Film Censor in 1944 to enable him to pursue his avocation more freely, but by then his major works were completed. Besides, as his predecessor James Montgomery said, the job was no 'sinecure'. It entailed viewing two full-length films daily, as well as trailers, the re-showings of cut versions and other items.

He was the author of *Ireland and Irishmen in the French Revolution* (1932) which was translated into Irish in 1933; *Irish Swordsmen of France* (1934); *The Last Invasion of Ireland* (1937) and *Old Irish Links with France* (1940).

He also compiled a *Biographical Dictionary of Irishmen in France* and wrote many articles for periodicals such as *Studies* and the *Dublin Magazine*. From the latter, rather than the major works, we get the flavour of the man himself and see him in his leisure moments in some French town, such as Rouen, or idling in Paris on the Left Bank, probably having spent the morning peering at manuscripts in the Bibliothèque Nationale. . . .

Richard Hayes's complex character was well summed up by General Richard Mulcahy in *The Irish Sword*, the organ of the Military History Society which Hayes helped to found, and of which he was a vice-president. 'Physician, Soldier, Historian, Artist, Philosopher, "Fire-Sider". Many people of different mould knew Dick Hayes in one or several of these roles. All experienced his gentleness, his reticence; some found that there were things which drew his flash of anger.'

Hayes confided to Frank O'Connor that as a young man he had fallen in love with a girl who had tuberculosis. He knew that she would not live long but he was afraid that if they married and had children the disease would be passed on; unromantically he gave her up. For years he remained a bachelor, but in 1939 he married Mrs Hilda Shaw.

A director of the Abbey Theatre from 1934, Richard Hayes was a member of the Royal Irish Academy and of the Irish Academy of Letters; the National University of Ireland conferred on him the honorary degree Doctor of Letters in 1940 and the French Government made him a member of the Legion of Honour. He died at Woodlands, Rochestown Avenue, Dun Laoghaire, on 16 June 1958.

From *Brief Lives of Irish Doctors*, Blackwater Press, 1978

Feathery Bourke
Jim Kemmy

The marriage of Michael (Feathery) Bourke came as a big surprise to his neighbours in High Street and Cornmarket Row. His brother-in-law Leonard O'Grady played a leading part in the affair. When he first came to Limerick, O'Grady had stayed in the same house as a woman named Maude Guerin, before he married Feathery's sister, Annie. He introduced Maude Guerin to Feathery and, after a fifteen year friendship, they got married in 1945. Both were then nearly 50 years of age and the marriage was more a business arrangement than anything else. They got married secretly at St Michael's Church after 8 a.m. Mass. Two hours later Feathery was back in his shop buying and selling scrap.

Feathery was not over-generous to his wife and kept a tight control over her few financial transactions. Money and food were strictly rationed and both lived in frugal circumstances. Many stories are told about Feathery's relationship with his wife. One tale describes a novel method devised by him to husband their household stock of tea. Every morning, following breakfast with his wife, and before his departure for the scrap store, Feathery would go through a carefully thought out, elaborate ritual. He would catch a fly on the kitchen walls and would then place the fly inside the tea-canister, firmly replacing the lid. On his return to his home at lunch-time Feathery would immediately check to see if the fly was still buzzing around inside the tea-canister. If the fly had escaped, he would know that his wife had made some tea for herself in his absence and would admonish her for doing so.

After about six years of marriage, Feathery's wife died. Her funeral, like her wedding, was a quiet affair, with only the same small number of people in attendance. After his wife's death, Feathery withdrew further into himself and continued to live a spartan existence. His relations with his three brothers and two sisters had never been easy. . . . Rather than allow himself to be under a compliment to one of his sisters who lived next door to him in Cornmarket Row for many years, he ordered his daily lunch from the Stella Restaurant and had it delivered to his store by a messenger-boy on a bicycle.

Another example of Feathery's attitude to money, clothes and people was given on a wet May morning in the early 1940s when one of the seven sons of his brother Frank made his First Holy Communion and was doing the 'rounds' of his relatives. The well-scrubbed and well-dressed young nephew called to see his Uncle Feathery at his High Street store. As the eager and excited boy approached in the rain, Feathery briefly glanced at him and brusquely directed: 'Run along home sonny and take off that new suit before you ruin it.' Uncle Michael never believed in giving money away — not even on a First Communion day.

From the *Limerick Socialist*, Vol. 3, No. 4, April 1974

Gerard Ryan
From: With a Tip of the Cap to Horace
Peter Donnelly

In the heel of a night from an empty cask
Some atavistic voice may ask
About me: then tell the unheeding bar
I'm one who followed a falling star,
Rubbed smooth by sixty winters' rime,
With hair gone white before its time;
A countryman, though city-bred,
Who knows a ditch where white violets spread
Their innocence on the unheeding air:
Whose life goes down another's stair —
O! breath that passes. O! diet of tears.
O! shuttled thread in a warp of years —

> By Plassey waters remembering Sion,
> The last romantic, Gerard Ryan.

From *Castle Poets*, 1966

Robert Herbert
Benedict Kiely

That old bilingual wall-map of Ireland that used, in the days of my boyhood, to be on view in schoolrooms, even in the six counties, I saw again recently: each of the thirty-two counties a distinct colour and no indication at all of the line (it is still called the Border) that cuts off the six from the twenty-six. . . .

The last time I looked on a copy of that old map I was in Limerick city in the company of a dear friend, the city librarian, the never-to-be-forgotten Robert Herbert who was among other things, the greatest authority ever on the works of Michael Hogan, the Bard of Thomond. Robert Herbert, tall and bony, with the beard and visage of Don Quixote, and a sense of humour like crazy, and a tongue that at times could be as exact as I have heard, that of James MacNeill Whistler.

Overwhelmed by books in his office in the great library, he found time to write for the *Limerick Leader* the series of articles, *Worthies of Thomond*, which were afterwards collected in book form. And he talked of everything and everybody, from Johnny Connell,

> who stood tall and straight,
> in every limb he was complate,
> and could pitch a bar of any weight
> from Garryowen to Thomond Gate,

to the splendid description of Garryowen at the beginning of Gerald Griffin's novel *The Collegians*. . . .

For Bob Herbert and myself, and many of our generation, Gerald Griffin and *The Collegians* and Garryowen came to us, for the first time and even the second time, in a second-hand or third-hand way. In my case it was with a group of local amateur players doing Boucicault's *The Colleen Bawn*, in the Forester's Hall in Omagh town. And, next time round, with a week of opera — opera in the townhall from O'Mara's travelling company who brought with them the *Lily of Killarney*. Who else? And where else should she come from?

Were O'Maras the last people ever to wander the roads of Ireland with a caravan loaded with operas? That week they spent in the townhall was better for me and many others, than two years at school. . . . And the Lily of Killarney was present with the smile of forgiveness softly stealing o'er her beautiful face . . .

Eily, mavourneen; I see thee before me,
fairer than ever with Death's pallid hue . . .

And looking at the old map I remembered the laughter of Herbert and myself at
our memory of such things. And I remembered, also, a story that I never did or could
tell him while he was alive. For once in those days I was showing an American visitor
around the scenic beauties of the Glen of Aherlow. This was how I set about it.

He was a man by the name of Kevin Sullivan, a distinguished professor in
Columbia, and he had written notably about James Joyce among the Jesuits. He
was also, God help him and rest him, one of the closest friends I ever had. He had
heard a lot about Robert Herbert, the great librarian, and wanted to meet him. So
we set off for Limerick. It was the second journey on which I acted as guide for the
distinguished Dr Sullivan. The first journey I had recalled, or used, in a story called
'The Dogs in the Great Glen'. . . .

But here is how I managed the later journey to introduce Sullivan to Herbert
and, on the way, to surprise and even startle him with the Glen of Aherlow, where
my father's father's people came from: my own great grandfather from a place called
Lisvernane. It's still there.

He was a tough man to startle was Sullivan. But I managed to do so. This was how.

From the heart of Tipperary town there was then, and still is, a quiet unassuming
road that led you, tall trees on either hand, and convinced you that you were going
nowhere: just through quietude and trees. The Road to Nowhere. . . . Nowadays
that road is not completely anonymous. There's a signpost in Tipperary town. But
it was not there when I directed Sullivan and he, as a lot of Americans could not
help doing, driving on the wrong side of the road. And I assured him the road was
a shortcut to Limerick city. It may be or may have been. I never measured it. It was
a narrow road. We met little or no traffic.

Up and up. Trees on either side of us: and quietly bending above us. Then a
sudden twist, a brief steep ascent and the Wonderland hit you in the face: the great
Glen and the Galtee Mountains beyond. The view from Mount Tabor.

Sullivan was shaken. He said that, by God or Somebody, I had sprung this on
him and, and . . .

But I bought him a Black Bushmills in the Glen Hotel, which is still there and
splendid, and we renewed our friendship. The sun blessed us. On we went and
slowly downward towards the Shannon land. But we made a few more stops. There
were hospitable houses by the wayside and pleasant, talkative men within. They
delayed us. We were easily persuaded. The skies darkened. When we left Galbally
and headed for Limerick city to pay our respects to Robert Herbert the heavens
opened and the rain came down in sheets, shaking the car on the road. Visibility
was poor. We overtook a man on an autocycle, rod and net and gaff or something
strapped on his back: and, as we did so, we struck a puddle or a minor lake that the
storm had made, and we deluged the man from head to toe with dirty water.

'What do we do?' says the polite American.

'Drive on,' I said. 'Don't stop to apologise. He'll do us with the gaff.'

So on we drove and stopped for one drink in a Limerick hotel. Then round to the fine stone house beside the library in Pery Square to pay our respects. Much ringing and knocking, and the door opening slowly and the head of a very angry Don Quixote emerging. I am recognised. We are admitted. He is in vest and long drawers, a towel in his hand, his hair and beard in chaos.

'Some gentleman,' he says, 'in a motor thoroughly drenched me on my road back from fishing in the Mulcaire river.'

His words were not quite as polite as that. He spoke well on the matter for another few minutes. With the muddy water in his eyes he identified nothing or nobody. We did not tell him then, nor did I afterwards ever tell him. For there were times, as I've said, when he had a tongue as exact as that of James MacNeill Whistler. But it is odd the things that come back into your head when you're simply looking at an old map.

From *Asylum*, Winter 1996

Maggie
Maureen McAteer

Seeking sustenance, she came to our Garryowen home each evening
on a vague pretext of helping my mother;
An innocent abroad in the alien territory
of mischief, deviously deployed by boisterous brothers,
when her notoriously wayward dishcloth undid
yet another meticulously constructed pyramid of cards;
Bittersweet revenge was extracted
while she dozed beside the fire;
They fastened the fringes of her all-enveloping shawl
to the chair-legs, causing chaos when she rose to go.

Now I would ask of her a thousand questions:
Was she loved and lusted after,
and what colours fired her in her ripened youth,
before the decades slipped away
weathering her all-anaemic grey?

Distance, marriage, babies separated our lives.
Later I learned that no arrangement of arum lilies
nor carpet of cardinal red festooned the altar

when Maggie's funeral Mass was said.
Being a woman of great gentleness and no property,
three mourners marched behind the hearse
when her bones were finally laid to rest.
Sometimes on the radio I hear a crackled rendition
of 'She is Far from the Land' and I see her rotund,
flaccid face and curious, vulnerable eyes;
Then the haunting sound of her wistful voice
trickles, warmth, into the remote cold corners of my heart,
down all the long years.

From *Force 10*, Autumn 1994

The Poet Ryan
Desmond O'Grady

We met one quiet afternoon in that hostelry in Limerick where I first learned why
my grandmother was called Feathereye Bourke, or Feathery, as it is locally pronounced.
I sat alone, my back to the leaded window panes, after a long journey. I had been away
for several years. A gentleman in late middle age came in. He ordered his pint and
sat, slightly bowed, in the far corner. We were the only customers in the pub.

It was early summer and the clean light glanced off the gentleman's tousled grey
hair, delineated his sculpted head, his lined features. His dress was respectable, even
if it had seen better days. He made a strong presence.

After some silence he made a neighbourly comment on the fine weather and the
summer's prospects. His voice was refined, resonant, rhythmical. Conversation
caught until, stretching forward, he asked me if I might not be Desmond O'Grady.
Surprised, I said I was, and straight away he joined me, saying that although we had
not met till now he knew about me from mutual friends and introduced himself.
While we sat there for an hour or so he told me more history of my own family
than I had ever heard at home.

For the rest of the day, until late that night, we wandered together through the
streets of old Limerick talking of poetry and poets, local history, local characters,
the dreams that are born and die in small provincial places. He made music with
every phrase, humour with every turn in a story. From that day, we were inseparable
companions and shared the innocent adventures of the provincial's imagination
that rarely get recorded.

Devoted to the art of good conversation, story-telling and high song, he spoke
only of people and poetry, the human affair and those mad enough to try to record

it through art. Every time thereafter I returned from my wanderings we would meander about Limerick swapping tales of the adventures that befell us in our separation.

In those days he lived with two bedridden old pensioners in one room of a small cottage in Chapel Lane. We called it the 'poop of that scuttled Spanish galleon'. At night the four of us would huddle there, telling stories that transformed the place. Later, after the two older men died, Gerard moved to what he grandly called the 'Winter Palace' but which was known to the burghers of the town as the 'poor-house'. From there, he would sally forth daily and we would meet at the White House bar to start the day's wanderings. He would frequently begin a conversation with: 'Desmond, let me tell you something for nothing' and launch into a Limerick story like 'Shawn-a-Scoob' or the historical background to 'Drunken Thady and the Bishop's Lady', quoting liberally from Hogan, the Bard of Thomond, as he proceeded. He loved talk and, like the Gaelic poets of the past, he knew all the wild flowers and birdcalls, their good and evil associations and all manner of riddle. These monologues were his true poems but were never written down.

Poor in pocket, he was rich of heart and pure of tongue. I never heard him speak ill or angrily of anyone but I knew he loathed, and in silence could terribly curse, any manifestation of philistinism. His encouragement of the young who showed interest in good reading, art and nature never tired. He loved an occasion, like Limerick Races, for the life, the colour, the people. . . . He received postcards from foreign poets like Ezra Pound, Pablo Neruda, Yevtushenko and many others. He had the vision to see that Limerick was to him what Alexandria was for Cavafy, Buenos Aires for Borges, Leningrad for Achmatova. To be in Limerick and not see him was to be in Venice and not see Pound, in Dublin and not see Kavanagh.

Like the troubadours of the south of France, Gerard made his poems in praise of nature and the wildlife of Clare and to honour those ladies who moved him as the physical presence of the Muse moves. He never thought of publication. He recited to those friends who knew him as the Poet Ryan.

Now that he has passed into the light that radiated from him in his last years, those who loved him have gathered together what poems he committed to paper for his memorial. He lived a full life. He left some record.

He was my friend and for me he was the last in spirit of the poets in the true Gaelic tradition. Kinsale marked the beginning of the end. Aughrim and Limerick finished it. Yet something of the spirit lingered on, no matter how thinly dispersed, even into our childhoods. For me Gerard was a living covenant of that tradition. Through his life, work, talk, he passed it on to those fortunate to have known him. Our covenant with him is to do likewise.

From *A Memoir: Introduction to an April Morning Walk*, The Limerick Poetry Circle, 1974

Remembering Mr Toppin
John Liddy

Out of the mouths of crows he swooped,
A red faced wing commander,
Low flying over the big house,
His landlord's eye upon us.

In him we felt the crack
Of his Anglo-Irish whip whenever
He rode to hounds or snapped
In his once great laundry rooms.

He was a world of ponies and traps,
Of dance bands on moonlit lawns,
Keeper of the sweetest apples,
A hide-away among the gardens.

Now only elm and sycamore stand
Like sentries with nothing to guard
As factories edge
To where the front door was.

From *The Old Limerick Journal*, No. 22, 1987

Pat Kinnane
Flann O'Connor

He was delicate we were told
When we were children
In the summers at Crean,
Only years later to discover
How he had been beaten
By the Tans at Caherguillamore
And never fully recovered.

He taught us how to thatch
From sapling branches

Miniature huts, traps for birds,
And how to prop them up in the grass
Beside a crust of bread,
And how to recognise
In the orchard the sweetest apples.

He was married to a cousin
They had no children,
The flagstones in the kitchen
Were cool under our feet,
We ate brown bread and drank strong tea
And were shy
Of his calm country courtesy.

From *Poems*, The Cecil Press Ltd, 1993

Liston from Knockaderry
Michael O'Toole

In the true traditions of Burgh Quay, I had barely sat down that first morning when I was given a job. Sean Ward called me up to the newsdesk, handed me a small bundle of newspaper cuttings from the library, and said: 'Give me six or seven paragraphs of an obituary on this fellow, and remember the first edition deadline is 10.30.' . . .

I had scarcely finished my obituary notice that morning when behind me a great and strange voice boomed out: 'They tell me we have a decent man from Limerick here at last.' Turning, I found myself looking at a giant of a man with a face like an enormous turnip out of which shone two mischievous blue eyes. The huge frame was covered with a Denis Guiney gaberdine coat and on its head was a grey felt hat which had been sat on in many a snug. 'I'm Liston from Knockaderry', the strange voice said as I got a playful thump between the shoulder blades.

I had, of course, heard of Maurice Liston, doyen of the agricultural correspondents and founding member of the NUJ (National Union of Journalists in Ireland), who was at that time one of the outstanding figures of Irish journalism. He didn't normally frequent the newsroom, he told me, but he had come this morning as a fellow Limerick man to mark my cards. It was true, he said, that Burgh Quay was a cruel and a dangerous place but one shouldn't believe everything one heard about it. 'Expect a good kick in the balls every two hours or so and you won't be too far out,' Maurice advised. 'And always be nice to the copy-boy, because, as sure as

Jesus, he'll be the news editor next year.' The grin turned into a belly-laugh and the great frame heaved with mirth. . . .

At this time Maurice was well established as one of the legends of Irish journalism. When he joined the *Irish Press* in 1932 he was a highly trained reporter who, like myself, had cut his teeth on the *Limerick Leader*. He had also served the cause in the West Limerick Brigade of the IRA and after escaping from the Curragh was never recaptured. He took no pension and rarely talked about his exploits. The only time I ever heard him discuss them was when he came into the Scotch House one evening after having a chest X-ray and he told me that the specialist on looking at the film said: 'I see that you had pneumonia, Mr Liston.' Maurice insisted that he had never been treated for pneumonia but as he was leaving the hospital he suddenly remembered a hideous week of coughing and fever as he slept in ditches while he was on the run. For his services to the NUJ he had received the union's highest and rarest accolade, being made a 'member of honour'.

One of the many remarkable things about Maurice Liston was his voice. No one I ever met before or since spoke even remotely like him. It was as if the words were being sucked up from his throat and filtered through coarse gravel as they came out. His was truly a language that the stranger did not know. Once, at an annual delegate meeting of the NUJ in Brighton, the English delegates called for a speech from the father figure of the union in Ireland. Maurice had been in search of what he liked to describe as 'formidable drink' and he rose somewhat unsteadily to respond. As the applause faded he began to speak. 'For five years of my life,' he began, 'I fought the fucking British.' Then he sat down. The delegates, understanding not a word he had said and believing that he was overcome with emotion, gave him a standing ovation.

It wasn't only the voice that contributed to his unique delivery. Though by no means taciturn he was economical with words and often arranged them oddly. One anecdote about him which I have heard recounted by newspaper people in many parts of the world concerns a fire in a Dublin convent during the 1940s. William J. Redmond, the managing editor, was then at the height of his powers as a disciplinarian and as they were both departing to their separate pubs for a nightcap he ordered Maurice to get a taxi and follow the brigade. Half an hour later WJR left the Scotch House for Mulligan's where he found Maurice propped up at the corner with 'a formidable drink'. 'Mr Liston,' he demanded (WJR was always formal in confrontation), 'what about the fire in the Dominican Convent?' Maurice was unruffled. 'I was speaking to the reverend mother,' he said, 'and she told me personally that there was fuck-all in it.'

Yet despite this and other displays of bravado, Maurice, like most of the reporters of his generation, was essentially a timid man. They had reason to be. From the foundation of the state until well into the 1960s Irish journalism suffered from the general paralysis that afflicted Irish society. There was an almost complete failure on the part of newspapers to apply decent critical analysis to practically any aspect of Irish life. In *Ireland: A Social and Cultural History 1922–1985*, Terence Brown says:

Regrettably, almost all Irish journalism in the period had contented itself with the reportage of events and the propagandist reiteration of the familiar terms of Irish political and cultural debate until these categories became mere counters and slogans often remote from actualities.

The reporting, more often than not, was on the terms and under the control of the authority figures — which is the real reason why ageing politicians, prelates and sundry potentates pine for the days of the old-style journalism. The journalists in the main were poorly educated, poorly motivated and poorly paid. They went about their work in the sure knowledge that in the event of any complaint from the great and powerful they would almost certainly get no backing. . . .

Maurice and many of his contemporaries were journalists of a kind which, though still common in the sixties, is now virtually extinct. Bohemian by temperament, they had drifted into a little world which, though frequently called a profession, imposed no qualifications for entry and enforced no real standards for remaining. In Maurice's case he had run away from a farm and endured the splendid irony of being made into an agricultural correspondent. Many of his peers had tried other vocations and either found them wanting or had themselves been found wanting. A number had been in the religious life. Some could be classified among the incorrigibly eccentric — if not the mentally unbalanced. Many were improvident and impecunious and lived in dread of their bank managers.

Many failed to understand that being called to the banquet is not the same as being part of the feast and foolishly forgot that a journalist is always an outsider looking in. They knew that by observing a few ground rules they could just about survive and preserve their sense of their own courage as well. Above all, they observed the rules of that special Geneva convention of Irish public life which declares: thou shall not queer the pitch. Like Mark Twain, they would have liked nothing better than to blow the gaff on the whole world — except that they were acutely aware of the perils of so doing. They were not so much paper tigers as tissue-paper tigers.

I am not trying to deprecate them. Like all of us, they were children of their own times and it was not their fault that they lived in an age of brutal stagnancy. Nor do I wish to convey that the slicker, better-educated, better-accoutred journalists who followed them are invariably superior. Very often the opposite is true. The call to the rich man's table is as attractive and as fatal as ever and the line between fact and propaganda is often blurred now as it was then. Despite all the advantages by way of education, decent salaries, training and trade union protection there is still too much mediocre journalism in Ireland. A large number of Irish journalists still fail to make the fundamental distinction between the 'news' that is handed to them along with a gin and tonic by some PR person and that which has to be painfully and skilfully prised from a hostile and unwilling source. Northcliffe's dictum that 'news is what someone somewhere wishes to suppress' and that 'everything else is advertising' seems to have little effect on a large number of Irish journalists. . . .

Maurice Liston and his contemporaries travelled far and wide — first class, on free passes provided by the railway companies — far more than reporters do today. The assignments were usually mundane — agricultural shows, amateur drama festivals, the consecration of some bishop — the stuff of which Irish national newspapers of the day were chiefly fashioned.

These excursions were admirably suited to the bohemian temperament. They entitled the traveller to viaticum in the form of advance expenses, often grudgingly handed over, which wouldn't have to be paid back for weeks and which were sometimes severely dented in Mulligan's bar prior to departure. They ensured a temporary respite from the tyranny of the newsdesk and provided the opportunity of looking up old friends and acquaintances. For, like all commercial travellers, these men had an extensive network of cronies and like-minded souls to be found in all sorts of nooks and corners throughout the country. . . .

On Wednesday, 22 January 1958, the Roman Catholic Archbishop of Dublin, the imperious Dr John Charles McQuaid, set out from his episcopal palace in Drumcondra to bless a vocational school recently erected in the south city suburb of Dundrum. Two of the three Dublin dailies sent reporters to cover the event. The *Irish Press* was represented by Maurice Liston, one of its senior and most colourful reporters. The *Irish Independent* sent John Healy, its aviation and diplomatic correspondent, then a junior recently arrived from the *Sligo Champion*. *The Irish Times*, still clearly identified as the Protestant paper, was not represented.

The Archbishop was known to be impatient of newspapers and their representatives. His Lenten pastorals were submitted with the proviso that they be printed in full or not at all. His Grace disliked being photographed and some press photographers believed that his enthusiastic sprinkling of holy water in their direction as he blessed churches and other buildings was as much intended to blur their lenses as to bring them special graces. Only in the most exceptional circumstances would a reporter dare approach the Archbishop on public occasions. If the Archbishop wanted publicity for his public utterances a script would be prepared in advance and handed to the waiting reporters by his chauffeur.

On this occasion the chauffeur had no script to offer so the two reporters — both expert shorthand writers — took a note of the Archbishop's public speech and typed it up while the reception was going on. Healy was anxious to get back to the office but Liston insisted that the report be shown to the Archbishop for vetting. Healy's protests were in vain. Liston, aware of the special relationship between the Archbishop and Major Vivion de Valera, was taking no chances.

As Dr McQuaid was about to leave, Maurice's bulky figure broke from the ranks of the attenders like the soothsayer in Caesar's triumphal procession. Having made his obeisance, he started to address the prelate in the booming, guttural tones which were a source of wonderment to all who heard them. He explained that as no script had been made available he and his colleague had taken a verbatim shorthand note and would His Grace be so kind as to look over what they had written so as to make sure he was happy with it.

His Grace took the foolscap page and, scanning it, appeared to be amused rather than annoyed. 'Is this what I really said?' he asked with a grin. Much encouraged, Maurice assured him that it was indeed what he had said as his words had been taken down by two men with top-class shorthand. The Archbishop then slowly folded the foolscap paper twice and tore it into neat quarters. Handing them back to the astonished Maurice he said: 'If that was what I said, then I hadn't intended saying it.' And after giving a final benediction to the little group, he disappeared in a flash of purple into his waiting car.

With a few honourable exceptions, the established reporters of that era were a docile lot, over-zealous in their desire to please the proprietor, the advertiser, the prelate and the politician. The era was characterised by an unhealthy willingness to accept the prepared statement, the prepared speech and the public relations handout without demanding the opportunity of asking searching questions as well. Irish newspapers were largely a conduit through which government, Church and commercial interests fed their messages and their ideas to the masses. The sixties changed much of that.

From *More Kicks Than Pence: A Life in Irish Journalism*, Poolbeg Press, 1992

Outsider
From: Blow-In
Johnat Dillon

Little change here;
Hard work by
The light of day.
Our snug village pub
Passes time on dark,
Nothing-to-do nights.

Wealthy farmers talk
About their sick cattle,
High prices of dry land.
Daily weather forecasts
Come and go with
The monthly moons.

I'm out here for years,
But in close, chatty babble

They always label me
Strange outsider, Limerick greenhorn,
With my boggy acre
And 'Derryfada Cottage'.

But I come from
That old city
Of the broken treaty
Where love still breeds
Good, healthy stock —
I'm here to stay!

This Limerick man
Is deep rooted
In the human spirit —
Nothing will change him!
This Johnny-come-lately
Has made a new start.

From *Paper Poems 1978–1983*, Thomond House Publications, 1983

Memories of Michael McNamara
Mae Clancy-Leonard

I found it in a second-hand bookshop in Ottawa: *The Vision of Thady Quinlan*. I liked the title but it was the author's name that really excited my attention — Michael McNamara.

I knew three Michael McNamaras and I wondered if it could be one of them. . . . I read the biographical notes on the dust-jacket — never! But it was — our own Michael Mack from Limerick. It was years since I'd seen him. He was one of our group way back when we were teenagers and the least likely one, I would have thought, to become an author. He was shy, whilst we were boisterous, but he was always there: a solid shoulder to cry on — a good friend. We went places together: there were picnics in summer, the 'hop' at St Patrick's on Saturday nights, and the very daring uptown Ceili and Old Time at St Michael's Hall.

In that bookshop in Ottawa I remembered that he had joined the American Army. In fact, he called in on one of his trips home. He looked a dream in the khaki uniform; his blonde curls shorn to a half-inch crew-cut. We went to a dance at the Stella — me in my oh-so-sophisticated blue skirt, white shirt-blouse and long string of coloured wooden beads.

It was the Royal Showband and we rock 'n rolled until midnight. . . . 'See ya', he said, giving me that lopsided smile of his when we parted. We never discussed our life's ambition and I had no idea that he had 'the gift'.

In that musty-smelling bookshop in Ottawa I found him again as I read that Michael McNamara had left the army and that his GI ticket had bought him American citizenship and a B.A. in English at the University of Colorado. There was a fellowship to Oxford and marriage to an American called Mary.

I bought *The Vision of Thady Quinlan* and read it high above the Atlantic on the way home to Ireland. It filled me full of confusion. The careful disguising of people I knew, familiar Limerick street names in wrong locations and — this was a shock — I recognised myself.

I wrote to him and he replied. He was the same old Michael Mack. I treasure his letter. *Thady Quinlan* didn't make him rich, he said, but it had received excellent reviews.

Fame and fortune, he felt, would come from his new book called *The Dancing Floor* and he had been offered a 'fat' contract by his publisher. And there was talk about a film script. In the meantime Mary and he were expecting their second child within weeks. He wrote of meeting some of our friends on his last trip home and was surprised at the changes in the old home town. In closing he asked me to keep in touch.

I bought a copy of *The Dancing Floor* and in my opinion it is a far better written story than *Thady Quinlan*. It seemed to me that Michael Mack was cutting the ties and moving out into the big time. I saw a couple of reviews: the *New York Times* called it 'a fine book'; another said, 'a compulsive drama, superbly crafted'; and 'A gifted writer — McNamara's fast-paced narrative holds the reader's attention while he tightens the plot to the breaking point.'

Hot on its heels came *The Sovereign Solution*, and I read in the notes that he then had two children. I still hadn't replied to Michael Mack's one and only letter to me. I meant to write to him again. I really did. But it is too late now. The man, the talent, and his fame and fortune were all wiped out one night by a drunken driver.

From *My Home is There*, Isle Publications, 1996

Kevin Hannan
Jim Kemmy

Last month Kevin Hannan died. For almost five decades he had been one of the leading local historians in Limerick. During that time, he has maintained a ceaseless flow of articles and letters to newspapers and magazines, as well as contributing to radio and television programmes, and had done much to sustain public interest

in the history of the city and county. By any standard Kevin Hannan was a remarkably gifted and versatile man — historian, tailor, writer, nature-lover, traveller, poet,
fisherman, story-teller, artist — he filled all these and many more roles with distinction. . . . His affection for the scenes of his childhood has been vividly reflected in
his writings on the Shannon, Abbey, Groody and Mulcaire rivers, on the Irish town
and the market-place, on Garryowen, Park, Corbally and Plassey, and in his
memorable vignettes of the characters who vividly impressed themselves on his
youthful, fertile mind. He was a most delightful companion on a 'day out' when his
vast fund of knowledge flowed naturally, as he discoursed on churches, castles,
graveyards, flowers, rivers, local events and people.

From the start Kevin Hannan was an avid reader with a phenomenal, ency-
clopaedic memory. The historians, Maurice Lenihan and Canon John Begley, were
his mentors and he also read all the great poets of the age. To his last day, he could
quote effortlessly the whole of Michael Hogan's *Drunken Thady* and the poetry of
Browning, Burns, Wordsworth, Tennyson, Gerald Griffin, as well, of course, as
chunks of Lenihan and Begley. . . .

Kevin Hannan set his face firmly against modern poetry and art, and had been
a severe and vocal critic of the sculpture that has appeared on our streets in recent
years. He saw little merit in most post-1900 poetry and prose, and dismissed almost
all of modern art as dross. In recent times, he became a controversial figure in
Limerick life because of his public stances. When embroiled in battle he enthusiastically tackled all-comers and brought the full range of his formidable Victorian
vocabulary into play in these encounters. Despite his shy, self-effacing private
persona, he had come to enjoy his new-found notoriety and to savour his television,
radio and press outings. Many of his friends found themselves poles apart from him
on a variety of issues. Fortunately, these differences never blinded them from
recognising his unique and tireless contribution to his native city and in admiring
his zest for life, his boundless energy, his writing verve and his mental serenity.

Up to the very end, having attained the biblical life-span of 'three score and
ten,' plus nine more years, and despite the debilitating death of his wife, the loss of
his right eye and a dreadful illness which necessitated major surgery, Kevin Hannan
remained as vigorous as ever and his writing lost none of its force or vitality. His
death is an incalculable loss to local historical studies.

From *The Old Limerick Journal*, No. 33, Winter 1996

FIVE

THE COUNTY

Natural History
Maurice Lenihan

Neither in the fauna, flora, nor sylva of this county is there anything that requires particular notice. Wood is scarce, though in this and the County Clare the county is famous for orchards, producing the cider called Cacagee. Two of these near Loughmore, have of late years been cut down. The eagles that once frequented Lough Gur are hardly ever seen now, and even the singing birds and other small birds have been nearly annihilated by the severity of past winters. The wild swans have forsaken the marshes of Cahercorney, Carrickee, and other parts of the county, and the flights of wild geese are no longer so numerous as of old. The county must have been formerly well wooded, if we are to judge from the oak, fir, beech, and other trees, which we find in the bogs, and which, from their bearing the marks of fire, seem to have been cut and burned by the natives. A 'moving bog', like that which created such a sensation about 1822 near Clara, in the King's County, occasioned similar excitement at Kilmallock on 7 July 1697. Bones and horns of the Irish elk have been found near Lough Gur, at Castlefarm, Rathcannon, and at Knockee, one of which, a perfect specimen, Archdeacon Maunsell sent to the Royal Dublin Society. Flint instruments, including celts, spear heads, etc. have been found at Lough Gur. . . .

Several fine specimens of fossil deer are preserved in Adare Manor. Numerous specimens of these huge animals have been found by William Hinchy of Thomond Gate, in Kilcullane Bog, within two miles of Lough Gur, in which a great number of the bones of the Fossil Cow have also been found. Hinchy had lately one of these deer measuring twelve feet eight in a straight line from the tail to the mouth, and ten feet across the antlers. He had two others of somewhat lesser size. He sold two of them to the Dublin Society for the sum of £60. They were male and female. Lord Powerscourt gave him fifty guineas for another.

From *Limerick; Its History and Antiquities, Ecclesiastical, Civil, and Military, from the Earliest Ages*, Hodges, Smith and Co., 1866

Farewell to the Maigue
Aindrias Mac Craith
(Translation by Edward Walsh)

A long farewell I send to thee,
Fair Maigue of corn and fruit and tree,
Of state and gift and gathering grand,
Of song, romance and chieftain bland.

Och ochone! dark fortune's rigour —
Wealth, title, bribe of glorious figure,
Feast, gift, all gone, and gone my vigour,
Since thus I wander lonely.

Farewell to her to whom 'tis due,
The fair skin, gentle, mild-lipped, true,
For whom exiled o'er the hills I go,
My heart's own dear love whate'er my woe.

Cold, homeless, worn, forsaken, lone,
Sick, languid, faint, all comfort flown,
On the wild hill's height I'm hopeless cast,
To wail to the heath and the northern blast!

Forced by the priest my love to flee,
Fair Maigue through life I ne'er shall see,
And must my beauteous bird forgo,
And all the sex that wrought me woe!

And och ochone — my grief, my ruin!
'Twas drinking deep and beauty wooing
That caused through life my whole undoing
And left me wandering lonely.

From the *Labour Party Conference Magazine*, April 1997

Fairy Lawn
William Griffin

During the latter part of our residence in Limerick, my father had taken a place in the country, and was occupied in building a house upon it according to a design of his own, the principal character of which was internal comfort. To this we removed about the year 1810. . . .

Our new residence, to which the name of Fairy Lawn was given, was situated on the Shannon, about eight-and-twenty miles from Limerick, and having left the city finally, we entered on our life there with all the freshness of a new beginning, and cheered by the novelty and the natural charms of a country home. The river, which grows wider by degrees in its onward course, expands a little above this spot into a vast sheet of water, separating the shores of Limerick and Clare by a distance of three miles, and giving the last named county, when viewed from the Limerick side, the appearance of a thin line of land stretching away to the westward, where the shores seem to meet, and the river becomes again land-locked. Nothing can be more glorious than the magnificent floor of silver it presents to the eye on a fine evening in summer, when the sun is setting, and the winds are at rest. The prospect from any elevated ground in such circumstances is quite enchanting. Indeed, there is no river in these countries that at all approaches it in magnitude. Viewed from the heights of Knock-Patrick on a clear day, when the tide is full, and from whence one can see the broad Fergus, one of its tributaries, dotted with islands, and the Shannon itself as far as the distant island of Scattery, with its round tower and ruined churches — that bright spot, where the stern saint sang his inhospitable melody:

> Oh! haste and leave this sacred isle,
> Unholy barque, etc.;

and where its waters mingle with the Atlantic, it is precisely what the poet Spencer has described it:

> The spacious Shenan, spreading like a sea.

To the minds of those who have spent years on its margin, and enjoyed its ever-changing beauties, this oft-quoted eulogy is ever present. . . .

It was on a lovely evening, just such as I have alluded to, that Gerald and I first arrived there. . . . Nothing could exceed our transport on beholding the grounds, the house, the garden, the river, the boats, with their sails of glossy black, passing up and down; and the enchanting views of the western sky. In the fever of our ecstasy . . . we skipped off and raced about, until we became heated with exercise in our eagerness to see and examine everything. . . . It may be easily judged with what fondness and warmth of feeling Gerald (Griffin) was accustomed to look back to these scenes of his boyhood, from the opening stanzas in 'Shanid Castle', one of his late poems.

From *The Life of Gerald Griffin by His Brother*, James Duffy, 1857

Fare thee Well, my Native Dell
Gerald Griffin

Fare thee well, my native dell,
Though far away I wander,
With thee my thoughts shall ever dwell,
In absence only fonder.
Farewell, ye banks, where once I roved
To view that lonely river —
And you, ye groves so long beloved,
And fields, farewell for ever!

Here once my youthful moments flew,
In joy like sunshine splendid,
The brightest hours that e'er I knew
With those sweet scenes were blended —
When o'er those hills, at break of morn,
The deer went bounding early,
And huntsmen woke with hounds and horn
The mountain echoes cheerly.

Fare ye well, ye happy hours,
So bright, but long departed!
Fare ye well, ye fragrant bowers,
So sweet, but now deserted!
Farewell each rock and lonely isle,
That make the poet's numbers;
And thou, oh, ancient holy pile,
Where mighty Bryan slumbers!

Farewell, thou old, romantic bridge,
Where morn has seen me roaming,

To mark across each shallow ridge,
The mighty Shannon foaming.
No more I'll press the bending oar,
To speed the painted wherry;
And glide along the woody shore,
To view the hills of Derry.

There's many an isle in Scariff Bay,
With many a garden blooming;
Where oft I've passed the summer day,
Till twilight hours were glooming.
No more shall evening's yellow glow
Among those ruins find me;
Far from these dear scenes I go,
But leave my heart behind me.

Fast, fast we ride by bridge and tree,
Fast fade my loved bowers;
Still through the bursting tears I see
Thy hills and hoary towers.
'Tis past! my last faint glimpse is o'er,
My last farewell is spoken;
I see those loved scenes no more —
My heart — my heart is broken.
Fare thee well, my native dell,
Though far away I wander,
With thee my thoughts shall ever dwell —
In absence only fonder.

From *The Poetical and Dramatic Works of Gerald Griffin*, James Duffy, 1891

Blossom Gate, Kilmallock
J.F. O'Donnell

The ancient town of Kilmallock had, once upon a time, as the storytellers say, four gates. Of these two still remain, namely, the tall, square, castellated one which defended the road leading towards Limerick; and the smaller and more compact structure, beneath whose rounded arch the way towards Charleville still passes. Why this latter building was called the Blossom Gate we were never able to discover with any positive certainty. On examining it, however, a few summers ago, we were struck with the profusion of wall-flowers and other similar plants that decorated its roof and every chink and cranny from battlement to base, which were seen in their full glory in each revolving season by the inhabitants of the town for many successive generations, and may, perhaps, have given origin to the name to which we have alluded.

Be the above supposition as it may, the Blossom Gate, from time almost immemorial, served successively as a place of habitation, free of rent, for certain individuals of the town and its vicinity, who, having lost their home and substance either by misfortune or extravagance, were sent thither, to make their dwelling by the influence of one or more of the neighbouring gentry.

From *Duffy's Hibernian Sixpenny Magazine*, No. 1, January–June 1862, James Duffy

A Legend of Lough Gur
From: Garadh Earla and the Two Coopers
Michael Hogan

The sun went down, with burning blushes;
The song-birds sought the sheltering bushes;
The corncreak commenced his croon,
And up the blue east stole the moon.
Large pitch-black clouds, with inky fringe,
Gave the lone lake an ebon tinge;
The billows rolled with moanings drear,
Like suffering spirits in despair;
The gale blew with a sullen howl,
Shrill screamed the restless waterfowl;
Black grew the rayless brow of night,
As if the moon had lost her light.

Midway upon the lake's dark breast,
The boat a moment seemed to rest,
As if some hidden thing of force
Had stopped her in her drifting course;
The fishers leaned upon her side,
And looked into the deep, dark tide,
And saw an armed chieftain stand,
Beneath the waters, stern and grand;

His breast was clad with silver mail,
His limbs were sheathed in burnished steel,
And a gold helmet, on his head,
Such burning rays of glory shed,
That all the brightest polished gems
Of Europe's kingly diadems
Seemed in a blazing halo rolled
Around the ornamented gold.
Awhile the craftsmen speechless gazed,
With wonder, in the sun-bright tide,
That like a mine of jewels blazed,
In rings of light, on every side,
As if the brightest orbs that hung
In the dim, blue crystalline sphere,
Were melted in one mass, and flung
In fiery waves of splendour there.

From *Lays and Legends of Thomond*, M.H. Gill and Son, 1880

Glenosheen
Patrick Weston Joyce

In my early time Glenosheen had a mixture of Catholics and Protestants (chiefly Palatine), about half and half, and we got on very well together: in recalling the kindly memories of my boyhood companions, Palatines come up as well as Catholics. . . .

The Ballahoura Mountains extend for several miles on the borders of the Counties of Cork and Limerick. Commencing near Charleville, they stretch away towards the east, consisting of a succession of single peaks with lone and desolate valleys lying between, covered with heath or coarse grass, where for ages the silence has been broken only by the cry of the heath-cock or the yelp of the fox echoing among the rocks that are strewn in wild confusion over the sides of the mountains. They increase gradually in height towards the eastern extremity of the range where they are abruptly terminated by the majestic Seefin, which, projecting forwards — its back to the west and its face to the rising sun — seems placed there to guard the desolate solitude behind it.

Towards the east it overlooks a beautiful and fertile valley, through which a little river winds its peaceful course to join the Funsheon; on the west 'Blackrock of the Eagle' rears its front — a sheer precipice — over Lyre-na-Freaghawn, a black heath-covered glen that divides the mountains. On the south it is separated by Lyre-na-Grena (the valley of the sun), from 'the Long Mountain' which stretches far away towards Glenanaar; and immediately in front, on the opposite side of the valley, rises Barna Geeha, up whose sides cultivation has crept almost to its summit. Just under the eastern face of Seefin, at its very base and extending even a little way up the mountain steep, reposes the peaceful little village of Glenosheen. . . .

Gentle reader, go if you can on some sunny morning in summer or autumn — let it be Sunday morning if possible — to the bottom of the valley near the bank of the little stream and when you cast your eyes up to the village and the great green hill over it, you will admit that not many places even in our own green island can produce a prettier or more cheerful prospect. There is the little hamlet with its whitewashed cottages gleaming in the morning beams, and from each a column of curling smoke rises slowly straight up towards the blue expanse. The base of the mountain is covered with wood and several clumps of great trees are scattered here and there through the village, so that it appears imbedded in a mass of vegetation, its pretty cottages peeping out from among the foliage.

The land on each side rises gently towards the mountain, its verdure interspersed by fields of blossomed potatoes, or of bright yellow corn, or, more beautiful still, little patches of flax clothed in their Sunday dress of light blue. Seefin rises directly over the village, a perfect cone; white patches of sheep are scattered here and there over its bright sunny face; and see, far up towards the summit, that long line of cattle, just after leaving Lyre-na-Grena, where they were driven to be milked, and grazing quietly along towards Lyre-na-Freaghawn. The only sounds that catch your ear are, the occasional crow of a cock, or the exulting cackle of geese; or the softened low of a cow may reach you, floating down the hillside; or the cry of the herdsman, as with earnest gestures he endeavours to direct the movement of the flock.

But hear that merry laugh. See, it comes from the brow of the hill where the women of the village are just coming into view, returning from Lyre-na-Grena after milking their cows. Each carries a pail in one hand and a spancel in the other, and as they approach the village, descending the steep pathway — the 'Dray Road', as it is called — that leads from 'the Lyre', a gabble of voices mingled with laughter floats over the village, as merry and as happy as ever rang on human ear. Observe now they arrive at the village, the group becomes thinner as they proceed down the street, and at length all again is quietness.

Happy village! Pleasant scenes of my childhood! How vividly at this moment do I behold that green hillside, as I travel back in imagination to the days of my boyhood when I and my little brother Robert and our companions — all now scattered over this wide world — ranged joyful among the glens in search of birds' nests, or climbed the rocks at its summit, eager to plant ourselves on its dizzy elevation.

From *The Wonders of Ireland, and Other Papers on Irish Subjects*, Gill, 1911

Shanid Abu
T. Costello

Here other guests than screaming owl,
And other music thrilled the soul,
Of Chieftains high on Fame's bright roll,
In former days . . .
Here Chiefs, and Bards, and Kerns sat round,
Broad boards with golden goblets crowned,
And proudly trod yon airy mound,
Where now yon cattle graze.

From an estate map of 1837, with a watercolour of Shanid Castle

Pastoral Memories
Charlotte Grace O'Brien

It remains throughout one's whole life a beautiful thing to have been born and reared in a rich pastoral country. Images of beauty lie hidden in the mind; sweet scents and homely sounds return even to the dulled senses of after life. Deafness itself, even, does not wholly separate one from a consciousness of those simple sounds to which one has been, as it were, born. The imagination has so strong a hold it gives hearing to the brain even when the ear is useless. I am deaf, I know, but the great sweep of the scythe through falling grass repeats its rhythm of sound to me still. This is individual, but to all, I think, a richer and fuller enjoyment of the mere earth surface must accompany the familiarity of childhood with every sight and sound of the sweet brown clay and its produce. For one thing, we country-bred folk understand it all so much better than those to whom the multitudinous growth and leafage is all one in meaning, like the surface of a carpet.

I recall from the early days of my own life (I can remember just after the Great Famine) the farm life in the cottages round my home. I was then a very independent little fair-haired mortal, and was very much given to trotting off through the fields quite alone to my farm friends. Well, they did welcome me! The bowls of cream and solid sour milk, which I liked so well, that I got through were surprising. There was the dark but clean dairy, the large, dark, thatched kitchen, with the old palsied mother in the corner, and two or three fine, handsome, buxom girls. There was a big spinning wheel, and many a time I tangled and broke the woollen thread. But they had patience. Everything I might do they had patience to suffer. Time was no great value, and the skein was easily joined by the skilled hand of the spinner. . . .

But the shadow of the flowering limes was all over, and hanging in the branches thereof I seem to see a dainty snow-white cloth full of cream slowly dripping away its superfluous moisture, slowly hardening into the delicious solidified happiness called a cream cheese. Why do we not have such cream cheeses now? Ivory white, exquisite in texture, delicately suggestive of all green fresh things — beautiful to look at and perfect to the taste. It seems to me we lived on cream cheese in old times; now they are unheard of.

What is worthy to be spoken of now after them? One little tender remembrance of a long, thin young man called Dan, holding whose hand I used to toddle round after the cows and learn to milk. I loved him sincerely, and respected him deeply, for why? Because a rumour was afloat — true or false, I know not — that Dan was 'in with the White Boys'! What more was wanted to make him a hero, when he was so kind and affable as to teach me to milk? Farewell, Dan; farewell, the heaps and mountains of blazing hot potatoes, butter and eggs, and sour milk!

> *Have you seen, have you seen in the grey and misty morning*
>   *When the golden sun is up and peeping o'er the lea,*
> *When the thrushes and the larks without a note of warning*
>   *Break into a rush of singing, fresh and wild and free —*
> *Have you seen the farmer treading through the nodding grasses,*
>   *Or seen him with his cattle when the girls have come to milk —*
>
> *Patting their moist heaving sides, and joking with the lasses,*
>   *While pressing to his heart of hearts his daughter's head of silk?*
> *And oh! but there is joy in the brightness of the earth,*
> *Oh, but God has blessed its goodness and its mirth!*

June 1898

From *Charlotte Grace O'Brien: Selections from her Writings and Correspondence*, with a Memoir by Stephen Gwynn, Maunsel and Co. Ltd, 1909

Ounanaar, the Glenanaar River
Robert Dwyer Joyce

> I gained a valley lone and deep,
> Where Ounanaar's bright waters leap
> And fill the thick green woods with song,
> Wild tumbling through the dells along.
> I sat me by the voiceful stream —

I sat me in a pleasant dream;
For who could pass that valley fair
And stop not for a moment there?
The green ash o'er the torrent grew,
The oak his strong arms upwards threw
To the blue heavens, as if to clasp
Some wandering cloudlet in his grasp.
The leafy branches thick and green
On all sides made a shadowy screen,
Save where a little vista showed
Beneath me where the torrent sheen,
A mimic lake, all smoothly flowed,
With many a sparkling ripple stealing
Over its breast of radiancy,
Wild beauties on its banks revealing;
And, O, what it revealed to me!

From *Ballads of Irish Chivalry*, The Talbot Press Ltd, 1872

My Own Home
Charlotte Grace O'Brien

Many are the lovely places in Ireland of which the tourist knows nothing, and of them the wide-spreading, far-reaching, blue-glancing distances of our grand Lower Shannon are most worthy of loving praise; or, at least, I thought so, for the fates of my life made me a true lover of the Shannon before I well had sense to know my right hand from my left. First, in mere babyhood, from the heads of the high towers of Dromoland Castle, Co. Clare, I remember the beautiful blue distances, but am not sure if the river itself showed; anyhow, the river country left on my mind a vision of distances of blue and purple. Then later, when we lived in County Limerick, ten miles inland, the first joy of our lives was a long day spent on the shores here; therefore no sooner did I, at 21, begin to handle my own money than a vision of a cottage at Foynes, my own building and my own forming, began to hover before me. If it had not been that a man-of-war was permanently in Foynes at the time I was able to take the work in hand, I fear my too wise friends would have gone further than remind me that 'fools build houses' etc. However, my folly gained the day, and proved good wisdom in the long run. . . .

So I was thinking as I lay in the sun under my pinus looking far out over the island, beyond to the Beeves Lighthouse, and away and away, and my heart sank at the thought of even attempting to speak of our river, of our ever varying, ever wonderful Shannon, which lay before my eyes, it and its country spread wide in its sweeping magnificence of tender, frost bright colour. . . . You see indeed the garden and the island, and the Port of Foynes all right, but you do not see even in a suggestion the great plains of Limerick and Tipperary extending thirty, forty, fifty, perhaps even sixty miles, where the Golden Vale intervenes between the Galtees and Lough Gur hills to the south-east, and the Keeper range, Limerick, Cratloe and Clare hills to the north-east, at the foot of which the Shannon loses itself to our view after spreading up to the Fergus estuary to a width of five miles or more. The Port of Foynes is enclosed by the island, which occupies a sort of corner. North of the island the main water flows three miles wide before it divides as you go up the river. It is salt water, so the tides give a constant variety, sometimes brimful to the green edges, again leaving apparently only the real river in its oozy channel.

From *Charlotte Grace O'Brien: Selections from her Writings and Correspondence, with a Memoir by Stephen Gwynn*, Maunsel and Co. Ltd, 1909

Mary from Murroe
Anonymous

If I was at home in Lackamore,
My pencil I'd take and write,
My thoughts commenting, dear, of you,
That my Mary had taken flight;
When first I came to this country,
My thoughts were all of you,
And set my memories back again
To my Mary from Murroe.

One evening near the farrier's,
At the cross above the forge,
'Twas there I spied my Mary,
An' she comin' down the road.
Alas our courting was cut short,
For her mother came in view,
'Twas then I kissed the ruby lips
Of my Mary from Murroe.

So we jogged along together
Till we came to the Boiling Well,

We both sat down and began to talk
Till night upon us fell;
And as we sat there side by side,
The darkness hid our view,
But not enough to hide the smile
Of my Mary from Murroe.

If I had all the money
That lies in Lackamore;
Or all the earthly treasures
That King Billy had in store,
'Tis wishing I'd be giving them
As presents back to you,
I'd give my life, she were my wife
In the thatched house near Murroe.

We jogged along together, till
We came to the painted gate,
'Go home at once, dear Mary,
For I fear it's getting late.
I'll try and earn a fortune,
And your footsteps I'll pursue,
And when I gain fame, I'll call again
And court you in Murroe.'

From the *Limerick Leader*, 24 April 1948

The River Shannon
Charlotte Grace O'Brien

When I walk here along by the river in the midst of this glory of May, I say to myself — 'What infinite beauty must this world show to those who have entered the "beatific vision" and can embrace its varied loveliness in one human consciousness.' It is a splendid conception. . . . The daily aspect of things is, in a sense, also a concealment. Men come and go by this great river (too few of them indeed), and the revelation of its beauty is not made to them fully, often not at all; but let one live by it and it is 'the most beautiful place in the world'. A friend quoted to me the other day — 'Ad ogni uccello suo nido è bello.' Even so, to each of us comes the realisation of the hidden beauty that lies all round.

But tonight it was no hidden beauty. I went down by the river in the evening. It was full, the tide just past the turn, and sweeping down the great mass of water at an extraordinary pace, and yet, though the whole river was swinging along at many miles an hour, the surface was a marvellous mirror. The glowing masses of furze on the island, a quarter-mile away, were so near and distinct in the wave one could almost stretch out a hand to gather them. Every cloud and every shade of light and colour in the sky were again in the river, but far more intense. At my feet, and twenty yards down and across the channel, was a dense black cloud reflected; this formed an unbroken mass of shadow in front. Its crenellated edge cut sharp against the reflection of silver, blue, grey and intense white light stretching far away westward. I stood, as the old books used to say, 'entranced'. And still the river swept down, and still the furze and the wonderful green and the dark cloud bar were, as it were, under my hand, and the glorious 'gates of the Shannon', as the Elizabethans called this Foynes, were opened to heaven's light beyond my touch.

> We, thy children, love thee, noble river;
> For us thy tides flow ever;
> For us o'er all thy solitudes
> Eternal beauty broods.
> For us thy faint, pale distances extend —
> With the far heavens to blend.
>
> Oh, river! river! Home of the wild cloudland,
> Home of the restful woodland;
> We ask not beauty from thee — being ever
> Our own eternal river.
>
> We know the secret of thy tides, we know
> The swell, the fall, the pantings of thy bosom;
> Thy passions and thy restings and thy strife —
> Even as the weed tossed idly on the flow;
> Even as the flowers that on thy marges blossom,
> We are fed from thee and nourished from thy life.

May 1898

From *Charlotte Grace O'Brien: Selections from her Writings and Correspondence, with a Memoir by Stephen Gwynn*, Maunsel and Co. Ltd, 1909

The Falls of Doonass
Anonymous

As I roved out one evening as Sol cast his rays,
Behind yon Western mountains and the wide Western seas:
I carelessly roved out, my leisure hours to pass,
For to view the Shannon water that flows through Doonass.
My mind was enraptured at this enchanting scene,
Such a place in all Ireland there is not I ween;
Proud, beautiful and crystal bright, shining like glass,
Is that pure Shannon water that flows through Doonass.

In Doonass I was born and 'tis there I'd like to die,
And down in its old churchyard my old bones lie:
For if fortune proves in favour the seas I ne'er will cross,
Nor bid adieu to Clonlara, Castleconnell or Doonass.

Have you been to Killarney, the Causeway or Quay,
The proud bay of Dublin, Loophead or Kinsale?
The city cove of Cork seems but shadows or gas,
When compared to the proud rolling falls of Doonass.
And if you're not tired of walking proceed on further still,
To the right of Massey's mansion 'tis there you'll get your fill;
And when you reach the summit, come fill up your glass,
Drink a health, wealth and honour to the falls of Doonass.

Go into the rock-gardens to take a refreshing breeze,
Where the holy hand of time has spread beneath its trees;
'Tis there you'll see the anglers, both bonny, bright and gay,
With their artificial flies in the sweet month of May.
Go eastward and westward and into the churchyard,
Quiet, sober and silent, 'twould win your regard,
With its crumbling walls of ivy and graves of green grass,
And the dead lying beneath them near the falls of Doonass.

And if you are not tired of walking, proceed on still,
Until you come up with St Senan's holy well,
Where the lame, blind and weary a cure ever has,
In that healing gift from heaven near the falls of Doonass.
Oh, when shall that day come, that dear and happy hour,
When I'll walk undisturbed 'neath the turret's green bower,

With my mind free from care, and by my side a lass,
And she lives in a cottage near the falls of Doonass.

From the *Limerick Leader*, 23 December 1967

Glin Castle — Not For Burning
J. Anthony Gaughan

Desmond Fitz-John Lloyd watched with impotent horror the radical changes in Ireland during the revolutionary period from 1913 to 1923. He and those of his class realised that these changes would in the long term make their survival extremely unlikely. He remained resident at Glin Castle during the Anglo-Irish War. Early in January 1920 he received a visit from some members of the Ballygoghlan company of the IRA. They demanded the guns that were in the castle. Anticipating such an incident, his son had hidden these and the visitors went away empty-handed. However, when they returned a week later he ordered that they be given the guns. Subsequently, he and his property was not interfered with. In fact, at this time the only harm he suffered was at the hands of the Crown forces. On the night of 1 April 1921, in a search for arms at Kilfergus cemetery by the Crown forces, a tomb, in which John Fraunceis Eyre and his wife, Clara Anne, were buried, was demolished. (The tomb was restored by the next Knight, Desmond Windham Otho, in 1931, and in 1976 a carved plaque with the FitzGerald arms was placed on it.)

During the Civil War, Glin Castle was saved from destruction only by his courage. He let it be generally known, especially after those who opposed the treaty had destroyed a number of the great houses of Ireland, that Glin Castle would have to be burned literally over his dead body. In February 1923, three local men arrived at the castle to set it on fire. They ordered everyone to leave the castle but Desmond Fitz-John Lloyd refused to move and resisted attempts to put him outside. (At that time, due to his paralysis, he was confined to bed or a chair and had become a recluse, meeting only his valet John (Jack) Parry and his housekeeper Sarah MacNamara who attended him.) He remained sitting in his wheelchair in his smoking room and the would-be incendiarists, faced with the prospect of having the Knight burned to death in his castle, permanently postponed its destruction. However, at this time, some trees were felled and a wall and a sundial were damaged in the demesne. Subsequently, the Knight received some £5,000 compensation for this.

From *The Knights of Glin: A Geraldine Family*, Kingdom Books, 1978

From Shannon to Sea
E.G.A. Holmes

The Shannon bore me to thy bosom wide:
I wandered with it on its winding way
By fields of yellow corn and new mown hay,
And far blue hills that rose on either side,
And low dark woods that fringed the ebbing tide:
And ever as its waters neared the west,
Out of the summer of its broadening breast
Faint momentary ripples rose and died: —
And rose again before the breeze and grew
To wavelets dancing in the noonday light,
And these were changed to waves of ocean blue,
And creek and headland faded from the sight,
And oh! at last — at last I floated free
On the long rollers of the open sea.

From *The Book of Irish Poetry*, edited with an Introduction by Alfred Perceval Graves, The Talbot Press Ltd, 1914

Unrequited Love
James Kennedy

A story is told about a middle-aged bachelor farm-labourer who fell off a roof he was thatching in Plaukerauka in our parish sometime in the 1930s. When the nurse in Barrington's Hospital asked him how the accident happened he had to go back to the year 1900 to begin his story. He walked from north Kerry then, he said, as a spalpeen for the digging of the spuds in Limerick and, on a cold night, ended up in a house in Kildimo where he was taken on for a few days.

When he was going to bed in the loft the only daughter of the house climbed up the ladder and put her head in the small door. In a husky voice she asked, 'Are you all right, Brendan? Can I do anything for you?'

'Oh, I'm great,' he replied, 'my belly is full and there's a pleasant tiredness on me from all the walking. Thanks very much!'

Next night when the old folks were gone to bed she did the same again only this time she added, 'Are you sure you're all right? Can I do anything for you?'

He protested that he couldn't have been better treated, said goodnight and blew out the candle.

The third night she came into the room, sat on the edge of the bed, held his hand and with great concern whispered, 'Are you all right, Brendan? Do you really want me to do anything for you?'

'Of course, I'm all right,' he insisted. 'That rhubarb cake you made today was as good as my mother ever made. I'll miss ye when I go tomorrow.'

At this stage the nurse in Barrington's intervened. 'What the hell has this story of thirty years ago to do with your breaking your leg?' she asked.

'When I was above on the roof yesterday,' he explained, 'it dawned on me what the Kildimo woman was up to and with the shock of it I slithered down and fell off.'

My love life from the age of 4 to 18 was something like Brendan's. Things never dawned on me until the opportunities had passed.

I lived in some sort of never-never land. Whatever romance was in me, fuelled by books like *The Blue Lagoon, Coral Island*, those of Maurice Walsh and Zane Grey, stayed in the realm of fantasy. Anytime it came out it was as horseplay or else I backed away from it with the alacrity of a cut cat.

There was a period during secondary school — around the age of 16 — when women became the rage for many of us. The cinema in the village of Doon became the rendezvous place. It was only a short distance from the Christian Brothers where I went to school and the Mercy convent down the road. Since I lived five miles away and was only allowed to go to the pictures the odd time I had to listen to my contemporaries in the village of Doon talk about sessions with convent girls, some of whom were boarders who would slip over the wall at night. It was mouth-watering, he-man stuff.

Eventually my great moment arrived. After the pictures, one night, the hard men from the village were pairing off with girls and disappearing into the moonlight. I was left with this girl from the mountains who was very pretty.

'Will you go with me?' says I.

'I will,' says she.

'Get up on the carrier so,' says I.

It was a time for quick breathing. I raced down the Togher road with her on the carrier in case I'd lose any of the occasion's momentum.

I turned in the narrow bohreen towards Kilmoylan bog, threw the bicycle up against the ditch and then . . . I didn't know what to do.

It was a regular feature of country life for courting couples to find a 'nest' free of briars in a ditch and lie up against it in one another's arms. I had seen them many times. One night I even greeted a couple in Croughmorca who were locked into one another with a 'God bless the work.' . . .

The whole business of love and courtship was never talked about at home which was a great pity. I never understood, and still don't, what there is in it to be secretive about. Perhaps it was because of its association with the sexual side of it — the part to do with the sixth and ninth commandments. My mother never mentioned what she thought about love, sex and marriage to me. . . . There seemed to have been a conspiracy to keep the strongest impulses of adolescence in fantasyland.

I have no idea whether that was widespread but I do know that, later on in life, other forces were at work to impede the natual instinct of healthy, well-adjusted men and women to mate. It wasn't the Church which one could always side-step by admitting a liaison in confession. It was the class structure.

I knew of women in the parish — fine women whom any man could be proud of — who never married because the only marital options open to them were to men who might have a farm thirty acres less than their own. The number of eligible single men with land and livelihood, even now, is incredible.

From *The People Who Drank Water from the River*, Poolbeg Press, 1991

Maiden Street, Newcastle West
Michael Hartnett

Everyone has a Maiden Street. It is the street of strange characters, wits, odd old women and eccentrics: also a street of hot summers, of hop-scotch and marbles: in short, the street of youth. But Maiden Street was no Tír na n-Óg. It was one of the remnants of those depressed areas to be found in every city and garrison town, such as the many 'Liberties' and 'Irishtowns'. Human warmth and poverty often go hand-in-hand: well-to-do suburbanites do not intermingle at home as much as the poor do: in country places, this intimacy (manifested in the 'rambling house') still exists, but is dying out. Maiden Street, of course, is a memory distorted by time in the minds of all who lived there. In the period 1948–51 the scheme of new houses, 'The Park', was seen as a kind of enemy, though it was not really so. Like the battle of Aughrim, it dealt the death-blow to a society which was dying, an inbred, poor and weak society. But it also introduced the people of the street to electric light and flush toilets. . . . For a good many years people have asked me to write about Maiden Street, to produce a kind of 'Cannery Row': this is the closest I could get to it. I used the metre of 'The Limerick Rake', the best Hiberno-English ballad ever written in this county. . . .

The object of this ballad is to invoke and preserve 'times past' and to do so without being too sentimental. Too many songs gloss over the hardships of the 'good old days' and omit the facts of hunger, bad sanitation and child neglect.

From the Preface to *Maiden Street Ballad*, Observer Press, 1980; *Collected Poems*, The Gallery Press, forthcoming

The Moat in Kilfinane
Gabriel Rosenstock
(Translated by Jason Sommer)

I think I understood
Even back then that it would outlive us
That it was more ancient, more permanent
Than the sweet clash of hurleys.
There were things around us when we were growing up
That blessed us with sweetness and terror:
A holy well . . . do they still visit it?
A Protestant church; (chains were heard in the graveyard
In the dead of night!)
And the moat —
Mute, mysterious echo
Of the forgotten historical pageant.
You had a view from the top
Of the fertile plains of Limerick
A flighty cloud over a wooded hill
A miserable old greyhound sunning himself in front of the grotto
And at night the stars
Looking down on the moat
As though on their orphan.

It was our own Tara, if the truth be told,
The deep heart of the universe.

From *Portrait of the Artist as an Abominable Snowman*, Forest Books, 1989

SIX

SPORT

The Scarteen
Alastair Jackson

The 'Black and Tans' have been hunted by the Ryan family for over 300 years and, as far as most people are concerned, these unique hounds have always been there. . . . The breed is known as the 'Kerry Beagle', but the term is misleading, since these hounds have no beagle blood in them. They are in fact miniature foxhounds, the doghounds standing 22–23 inches at the shoulder and the bitches nearly 2 inches shorter. They are all black, with head and legs of rich deep tan and most of them have amber-coloured eyes. They do not have the classic 'neck and shoulders' of the modern foxhound, but their shoulders are built for speed and were described by Ikey Bell as being like a cheetah's. They carry great muscle over their rather long back and loins and their well-let-down hocks are built for speed. They have longish natural feet and indeed they have never been known to let a toe down. Their most extraordinary asset is their cry — their antecedents are described by no less an authority than Sir John Buchanan-Jardine as having 'absolutely the finest music of any hounds in the world', and Ikey Bell describes them as being remarkable in the field: 'They go top speed; their noses are out of the ordinary, as also is the volume of their cry. I have heard people declare them to be out and out the best working hounds with which they had ever hunted.'

Thady Ryan, Master and huntsman since 1946, has recently handed over to his son and emigrated to his wife Anne's home country of New Zealand. They have turned the family home of Scarteen into a hospitable guesthouse for foxhunting visitors, many of them from America and Europe. A brilliant horseman who has judged on both sides of the Atlantic, Thady has also worked hard on various committees for the advancement and improvement of the Irish horse. The country is all grass and many of the enclosures are separated by formidable 'doubles' — wide banks with ditches on both sides.

There are similar Kerry beagles kept by farmers all over the south-west of Ireland and many of them are collected after Mass on a Sunday to form 'trencher-fed' packs. It is to these hounds that the Ryans have had to go for outside blood, as other outcrosses, such as the Dumfriesshire, were not a success. It is remarkable how these hounds have kept their constitution in spite of being so inbred. It is certain that they are of Gascon-Ariègeois stock from south-west France and it had been popularly thought that some of them were brought back to Ireland by the 'Wild Geese' — those persecuted Catholics, who were persuaded by King Louis to fight the English on continental soil. However, Thady Ryan maintains that they came to Ireland long before this via the great Spanish-Irish trading island of Valentia, off Kerry. It has been said that the same type of hound had been bred in neighbouring Aragon, Catalonia and Navarre, and it would not be surprising if the Spanish had brought hounds to Valentia, as well as the sheep, black cattle and beautiful women that are still to be found in this part of Ireland.

In 1781 John Ryan handed over the Black and Tans to Tha' Ryan; the family's eldest sons have alternated down the generations between a John and a Thaddeus ever since. Tha' moved house from Ballyvistea to Scarteen in 1798, thus giving the Hunt its principal name. At a later date, when there was a financial crisis due to the collapse of Sadler's Bank in Tipperary, the family pack was taken on trust for seven years by John Franks of Ballyscadane. Clement Ryan, whose elder brother was constantly away soldiering, hunted hounds until his nephew John took over in 1904.

This John Ryan owned the Black and Tans for over fifty years, and was already a most popular Master when he joined the 16th Lancers at the outbreak of war in 1914. When he and his gallant company were blown up and buried in a trench, he was listed as 'missing, presumed dead'. A local fund was started to erect a memorial to him in Emly village square. In fact, when he was dug out, he was found to be alive, and a high-ranking German officer, who had been hunting with the Black and Tans before the war, recognised him and saw that he was treated well. When this good news reached Ireland there was great rejoicing in Emly, and the committee who were arranging the memorial decided that the easiest way to dispose of the money would be to celebrate the wonderful news in whiskey! . . .

Towards the end of his Mastership, various Joint Masters acted as huntsman, but he hunted hounds himself for one more season before the war, Captain C.C. Thompson joining him for the duration. In 1946 Thady Ryan, then aged 23, took over the horn, joining his father in the Mastership until the latter's death in 1955. From 1971 to 1982 he was Joint Master with Mrs Dermot McCalmont, widow of Kilkenny's celebrated Master, and then with Mr Wolf and Mr Hobby from the United States. In 1985 his son Christopher became a Joint Master and is hunting the hounds with great flair today, helped by kennel-huntsman, Tommy O'Dwyer, who has held the post since 1954, when he succeeded his father, Jack, who served the Ryans for thirty years himself.

With yet another young member of the Ryan family — Masters of the Scarteen since time immemorial — in control of this pack — one of the oldest in history — the future of the Black and Tans must be well assured.

From *The Great Hunts: Foxhunting Countries of the World*, David & Charles, 1989

A Disciple of Old Isaak
W.R. Le Fanu

In the year 1826, my father having been appointed Dean of Emly and Rector of Abington, we left Dublin to live at Abington, in the County of Limerick. Here our education, except in French and English, which our father taught us, was entrusted to a private tutor, an elderly clergyman, Stinson by name, who let us learn just as much, or rather as little, as we pleased. For several hours every day this old gentleman sat with us in the schoolroom, when he was supposed to be engaged in teaching us classic lore, and invigorating our young minds by science; but being an enthusiastic disciple of old Isaak, he in reality spent the whole, or nearly the whole, time in tying flies for trout or salmon and in arranging his fishing gear, which he kept in a drawer before him. Soon after he had come to us, he had wisely taken the precaution of making us learn by heart several passages from Greek and Latin authors; and whenever our father's step was heard to approach the schoolroom, the flies were nimbly thrown into the drawer, and the old gentleman, in his tremulous and nasal voice, would say, 'Now, Joseph, repeat that ode of Horace', or 'William, go on with that dialogue of Lucian.' These passages we never forgot, and though more than sixty years have passed, I can repeat as glibly as then the dialogue beginning, ῏Ω πάτερ οἷα πέπονθα, and others. As soon as our father's step was heard to recede, 'That will do', said our preceptor; the drawer was reopened, and he at once returned, with renewed vigour, to his piscatory preparations, and we to our games. Fortunately my father's library was a large and good one; there my brother spent much of his time in poring over many a quaint and curious volume. As for me, under the guidance and instructions of our worthy tutor, I took too ardently to fishing to care much for anything else. I still profit by those early lessons. I can today tie a trout or salmon fly as well as most men.

The appearance of our venerable preceptor was peculiar. His face was red, his hair snow-white; he wore, twice-folded round his neck (as the fashion then was) a very high white cravat; his body was enclosed in a bottle-green frock coat, the skirts of which were unusually long; a pair of black knee-breeches and grey stockings completed his costume. In addition to his other accomplishments he was a great performer on the Irish bagpipes, and often after lessons would cheer us with an Irish air, and sometimes with an Irish song. But, alas! how fleeting are all earthly joys; our happy idle days with our reverend friend were soon to cease. My father found that we were learning absolutely nothing, and discovered, moreover, some serious delinquencies on the part of the old gentleman, who was summarily dismissed in disgrace. For some years we did not know what had become of him, and then heard that he had become a violent Repealer, and sometimes marched, playing party tunes on the pipes, at the head of O'Connell's processions. The Repealers were of course delighted to have a Protestant clergyman, no matter how disreputable, in their ranks.

In his old age our quondam tutor led, I fear, a far from reputable life in Dublin. I never saw him but once again. It was many years after he had left us; and oh, what a falling off was there! I beheld my friend, whom I had known as the prince of anglers for trout and salmon, sitting, meanly clad, on the bank of the River Liffey, close to Dublin, engaged in the ignoble sport of bobbing for eels.

From *Seventy Years of Irish Life: Being Anecdotes and Reminiscences*, Edward Arnold, 1893

Frank 'Scurry' Hewitt
Keith Dunstan

7 March 1870

Mr George Coppin, the celebrated theatrical entrepreneur, has brought to Australia, the champion sprinter of the world, Frank 'Scurry' Hewitt, who hails from Limerick, Ireland.

His idea, of course, is to match him against John Gregory Harris, the champion colonial athlete. Hewitt is 25 years old and five feet eight inches. Harris is 24 and five feet ten inches. Harris is the perfect physical specimen, and, we like to think, the pure local product. He was born in 1846 in Collins Street, no less, Melbourne's oldest street.

The Australasian has been philosophical about this. It says many Australians believe that the colonial climate is more favourable for the perfect development of the human frame. But there is also the suggestion that the colonial youth, while bigger and more precocious in his development, might not have the stamina of the product from 'home'.

The organisers arranged five races from 100 yards to 440 yards and there were all sorts of rumours about their capabilities. Harris's team said he could run 150 yards in fourteen seconds, while Hewitt's backers counter-attacked with a rumour that he had done it in thirteen.

The races were at the Melbourne Cricket Ground and on Saturday. We had 20,000 people, the biggest crowd since the days of Mr Stephenson's cricketing XI. There were attempts to climb over the outside fence and fifteen men climbed on the roof of the stable inside the reserve, causing it to collapse. The *Argus* reported that a horse inside the stable escaped injury, but the paper did not concern itself about the fate of the spectators.

Harris, the local boy, won the 150 yards by three yards in $15^1/_4$ seconds, he won the 220 by three yards in $20^1/_2$ and the 300 was a dead heat in $33^1/_4$. The races continued today. His excellency, Viscount Canterbury, was present and *The Australasian* commented: 'Even the most sanguine of admirers of muscular Christianity could hardly have expected such a crowd. However, the day belonged to Hewitt. He won the 100 yards in $9^3/_4$ seconds, and the 440 in $51^1/_4$. Harris was angry. He said the 100 yards was a dead heat and he had accusations about the umpires. One of them was a 'well-known heavy bettor'.

Nor was the Melbourne Cricket Club over-pleased. There was a very disdainful letter to the morning press:

'Amateur pedestrianism and athletic sports are all very well, but the professional element is not wanted. We don't want our ground rushed by roughs, our pavilion invaded by members of the ring, trainers etc. The ground was granted for cricket, all cricketers, and although we tolerate amateur pedestrianism, it is toleration only.

Why should the dressing room of private members be rendered unbearable by a steaming mob of runners.' (The writer did not give his name, but signed the letter as 'A member of the MCC'.)

So what happens now? It looks as if the next race will be in the Friendly Society Gardens by the Yarra, opposite the Botanic Gardens.

From 'A Day in the Life of Australia', *The Age*, 7 March 1988

Carol Carroll: Mountain-Climber
Eric Bardon

It was on a winter sports holiday in Wengen in January 1939 that we met Carol Carroll. She was from Limerick and was the first woman to climb Mount Kenya, a fearsome climb of 17,058 feet. Just over the Tanzanian border is Kilimanjaro which, although 19,348 feet, is a much easier climb, the only trouble to climbers is the altitude. . . .

Carol was an ebullient character with fun and high spirits just bubbling out of her. She was of medium height, with a round face and a mop of lovely black hair. She tried her hand at any job; if it involved travelling, so much the better. She told us she was engaged once, but the man broke it off when she dangled him on the end of a rope down the side of Table Mountain! . . .

Carol was in England when the war came, and joined one of the services. She married a serviceman and in 1943 was joined by her mother for a visit to London. One day she and her mother-in-law were walking over Westminster Bridge. It was a cloudy day and suddenly a lone raider burst through the clouds with his guns blazing. The two women threw themselves into the gutter, but the German had spotted them and, with fatal accuracy, killed them both.

When we heard that news my wife and I felt as if we had lost one of our own family.

I feel that Carol's climbing achievements should be known here in Ireland. She got credit for her ascent of Mount Kenya in serious books on climbing. Her lovely character has been only a memory for a very long time.

We named one of our daughters after her.

From an article on Carol Carroll by Eric Bardon, in the possession of the Editor

A Shannon Fisherman
Ernest Phelps
T.C. Kingsmill Moore

They talk of Master Ernest still beside the Shannon shores,
Leaning upon their idle spades, and over closed half-doors;
And tales go round of distant lies that he alone could reach,
Of Lame Man's Rock, and Counsellor's Throw, and Fifty-Pounder Beach.

From Back of Leap to Fork of Weir, from Landscape to Doonass,
By Cock, and Cloon, and Commodore, they watched for him to pass,
True, constant, tireless as his own stout Castleconnell rod,
He bore each ill that fate assigned, served man, and worshipped God.

The waters where he plied his craft are gone, as he is gone,
Shrunken, dispirited and maimed, the Shannon stumbles on:
But through the gates of memory the great, grey waters roll
And — 'Master Ernest's in a fish, down by the Dancing Hole!'

From A Man May Fish, Colin Smythe, 1979

Plassey Regatta
P.J. Ryan

An annual regatta was held at Plassey Mills . . . being two miles from the city, it had the attraction of country air and scenery. . . . It was attended by family parties who started out around ten in the morning with ample stocks of food and cooking implements. They made a picnic day of the event. The roaring torrents of water rushing through the broken sluices and tailrace of the ruined Plassey Mill gave the place a memorable air of romance and danger. In the afternoon, while the children sported or slept in the sun, some parents thirsty for adventure could cross the narrow black bridge to the Clare side of the river. They needed no mariner's compass to swing to the right by the river's bank. Two hundred yards from the bridge and fifty feet from the river, set in green fields, was a small low thatched house of refuge — Shanny's Pub. Some drank their pints in the pub or outside on benches; others filled some three-quart tin cans with the flowing gold and drank at leisure among the greenery.

From 'The Fourth Siege of Limerick', Limerick Socialist, Vol. 5, No. 2, February 1976

An Old Angler's Dream
Anonymous

I oft times think as my days draw nigh
Of a pub near Plassey Mill,
Of a field and hedge, all blossom starred,
Where the anglers drank at will;
And when the dark would shroud the scene,
Hushing the merry din,
Ann Shanny would look around and ask:
'Well, boys, are ye coming in?'

'Tis many and many a year since then,
And the pub near Plassey Mill
No longer echoes the anglers' feet
In the place so still, so still.
I see it all as the shadows creep,
Though many a year has been
Since last I heard Ann Shanny ask:
'Well, boys, are ye coming in?'

Those memories cling as the waters ring
O'er the falls midst rocks and sand;
Those islands small, past the Garrison Wall,
And the angler with rod in hand.
As the salmon leaps and the wild life peeps
From shuttering rock and rill,
I can hear Ann say, in her old dear way,
'Well, boys, are ye coming in?'

I wonder when the great shadow falls
On that last short earthly day,
When we say goodbye to the riverside,
All tired with fishing and play,
When we step out in that other land,
Where Peter so long has been,
Will we hear him say as Ann Shanny of old:
'Well, boys, are ye coming in?

From the *Limerick Socialist*, Vol. 5, No. 2, February 1976

The 1940 All-Ireland Hurling Final
Breandán Ó hEithir

In the autumn of 1940 life was still reasonably normal. My father took me to Dublin for a long weekend and I saw my first All-Ireland hurling final. While shopping in Elvery's he was offered two Cusack Stand tickets for the match between Limerick and Kilkenny. It seemed too good to be true and I spent the night sleeping fitfully, worried that my father would lose the tickets and that the two of us would be left standing outside Croke Park, listening to the roars of the crowd and pleading in vain with stony-faced officials.

But everything went smoothly and unlike my previous visit, when I found the surroundings more interesting than the performance, I was clearly aware that I was in the presence of some of the greatest hurlers of all time. I was by now reading the sports pages almost as eagerly as I read the murder trials. On to the field came the Mackeys, Mick and John, Dick Stokes, Paddy Scanlon (the great goalkeeper who worked in McDonough's of Galway), Paddy Clohessy, Jim Langton, Paddy Grace, Jimmy O'Connell, Jackie Power, Jack Mulcahy and the others who had previously been only names on Michael O'Hehir's lips or smudgy photographs in the newspaper.

I got into the swing of Croke Park in no time at all and even took issue with a large priest from Kilkenny who was sitting behind me. He took grave exception to a stroke which felled Jack Gargan and began to roar, 'The line! The line!' at the referee and Paddy Clohessy simultaneously. In a manner far too advanced for my years, and for his level of tolerance, I told him it was an accident and voiced concern for his eyesight. I got a dig of an umbrella from the priest and was advised by my father to keep my eyes on the field and my mouth shut.

But I had the last laugh. My favourites, Limerick, won by two clear goals. Little did anyone present imagine that internal dissension and strife would soon relegate Limerick hurlers to the lower depths inhabited by both Clare and Galway for so many years. Limerick won a National League final in 1946 but did not win another Munster senior championship until 1955 and had to wait until 1973 to win another All-Ireland.

From *Over the Bar: A Personal Relationship with the GAA*, Ward River Press, 1984

Bud Aherne
Stephen McGarrigle

Thomas Aherne, known to everyone as Bud, played senior hurling for his native Limerick and played for Carrigaline in the South East Cork Junior Championship while stationed with the army at Fort Camden, Crosshaven. He began his senior soccer career in the League of Ireland with his hometown club Limerick before moving north to join Belfast Celtic in 1945.

A quick player with excellent positional sense which 'planted him in the right place at the right time', Bud was described as 'hard as nails'. He figured prominently in the closing chapters of the great Belfast side, winning an Irish League Championship medal in 1947–48 to add to the Irish Cup winners medal he'd won the previous season.

During his career Aherne played in some magnificent sides, including the Irish side which inflicted England's first home defeat by an overseas side, at Goodison Park in 1949. He was also a member of the Belfast Celtic team which the same year achieved an even more unexpected victory over Scotland, who had been dubbed the 'wonder team of 1949'. The Scots were Home International champions and believed they had little to fear from the Irish club side when they met in America's Triboro Stadium. The result was an astounding 2-0 victory to the Belfastmen.

In March 1949 Aherne was signed by Luton Town after they watched his performances at left-back for Belfast Celtic and for Northern Ireland against Wales. Bud's signing — for a fee believed to be over £6,000 — proved a shrewd piece of business for the Hatters. He claimed a first team place immediately and over the next decade at Kenilworth Road he became a cult figure. The Luton faithful admired his tough tackling and his intelligent use of the ball from defence.

Luton was Aherne's only Football League club. He made a total of 267 League appearances for them and made a telling contribution to their 1954–55 promotion-winning season, after which they became a First Division club for the first time in their history. He left Luton in 1961 to become coach to the London Spartan League club Vauxhall Motors.

During his time in Belfast, Bud was a regular in the Irish League representative side. He was also one of only a handful of players to represent both 'Irelands'. He made four appearances for the North, all at left-back, between September 1946 and March 1950, at a time when the North could choose players from the South for Home International fixtures.

Bud made his debut in the first post-war international, against Portugal, in an Irish team which contained ten debutants and Manchester United's Johnny Carey. Bud became his country's regular left-back in September 1949, playing in thirteen consecutive games. He won his sixteenth and final cap in a World Cup qualifier against France in Dublin in October 1953.

From *The Complete Who's Who of Irish International Football, 1945–1996*, Mainstream Publishing, 1996

Impressions of the 1951 Limerick Regatta
Professor King-Griffin

The vagaries of the climate are sometimes disconcerting, but the brilliant sunshine, gentle zepher and moderate temperatures of yesterday afternoon made ideal summer weather which was truly delightful. Under such meteorological conditions the Limerick Citizens' Regatta was successfully held, and the presence of large crowds along the quays and the embankments was indicative of a revival of interest in rowing.

The regatta meeting, a very popular fixture, provided an agreeable mixture of enjoyment, sport, and pleasurable social intercourse. Many enthusiastic patrons ardently descanted with vertiginous volubility on the merits of their favourite crews, regardless of grammatical exactitude. A surge of spontaneous friendliness pervaded the festive atmosphere, and often during the progress of the races the rigid formalities of etiquette were relaxed as the antics of over-zealous supporters of crews compelled spectators to cling together in strenuous effort to preserve an attitude of equilibrium.

In general, nothing exceptional was recorded to render the day memorable, and as the fame of most of the winning crews had preceded them no great sensation was experienced. Some oarsmen instinctively felt the strength of their muscles inadequate to the courage of their hearts, while others, bewildered by the rapidity of unforeseen circumstances, just failed to reach the high standard set by their aspiring souls. Many crews gave creditable performances that were loudly applauded, and a few crews produced remarkable spectacular splashing that passed unappreciated. With keen rivalry among the competing crews, all the races were eagerly contested, and the impartial observer had no difficulty in discovering the qualities and the foibles of the various contenders.

The welcome appearance of the numerous visiting crews created a very favourable impression. Occasionally they ably displayed their prowess in watermanship, and with confidence rowed gamely in admirable combination. The home crews rarely taxed their physical capacity, and not one of their performances was considered a criterion of stamina. They manipulated their boats according to mood and temperament, and seldom unnecessarily burdened themselves with trophies.

During the intervals between the races a diverting feature which caused much merriment was the hilarity with which persons on the river banks familiarly greeted, with modern sobriquets, pleasure parties that lolled in cushioned ease, and promptly returned compliments in appropriate idiom as they leisurely cruised about the river.

From the *Limerick Leader*, 21 July 1951

John Gavin
Stephen McGarrigle

John Gavin joined Division Three (South) Norwich City from his hometown League of Ireland club, Limerick City, in August 1948 for £1,500. At Carrow Road he gained a reputation as a high-scoring winger. His tally of 122 goals in 312 League games in two spells for Norwich still stands as a club record. In October 1954 he left Carrow Road for First Division Tottenham Hotspur.

Gavin had already won four Irish caps before arriving at Spurs, scoring on his debut in the 3-0 defeat of Finland in September 1949. He gained two more caps during his 13 month sojourn in north London, becoming the first Spurs player to represent the Republic of Ireland. Johnny's 15 goals in 32 League games for Spurs were the only interruption to a ten year stint with Norwich, for he returned to Carrow Road in November 1955. He won his seventh and final cap during his second spell at Norwich before departing for the Canaries' divisional rivals Watford in July 1958. He had scored 12 goals in 43 League appearances for Watford when he transferred to Fourth Division Crystal Palace in May 1959.

He ended his League career with 15 goals in 66 League appearances for Palace; and then he spent some time in non-League football with Cambridge City and Newmarket Town. Johnny became a publican and later went into the painting and decorating business. He now lives in Cambridge.

From *The Complete Who's Who of Irish International Football, 1945–1996*, Mainstream Publishing, 1996

Tom Reid
Barry Coughlan

Who was it coined the phrase that the All Blacks were 'lucky to get nil' when beaten 12-0 by Munster at Thomond Park on 31 October 1978? Well, whoever used it on that occasion, was actually stealing from Tom Reid, the Garryowen and Irish forward. Tony O'Reilly, who toured with Reid on the 1955 Lions tour to South Africa, tells the story:

Having seen Tom in action on tour when he was the 'cement' of the side, the 'mortar' that pulled us all together, I had not realised he was not noted for the avidity with which he trained. I'd last seen him in Pretoria as we boarded the plane to fly home and the following February we met again in London for the match against England.

I noted in the dressing room that Tom was extremely vigorous in the pre-match warm-up and I said, 'For God's sake you'll exhaust yourself.' His reply was, 'Jesus, Reilly, this is the first run I've had since Pretoria.' He went out and, like all of us, proceeded to prove it was the first run since Pretoria, for we were hammered 20-0. Coming off the pitch pursued by every hospital orderly, fly-over constructor and trench-digger in the greater London area, I said to him, 'Wasn't that awful?' Back came the reply: 'Yes, Reilly, and weren't we lucky to get nil?'

O'Reilly has a very definite affection for Reid, respecting him far more than most of his colleagues on that tour and his subsequent tour to New Zealand in 1959. He comments:

I should think the 1955 tour was the first time in his life that Reid was really fully fit and he played a major role in the success of the tour. We had won one and lost another of the first two tests and then we went 2-1 up in the series with a 9-6 win in the third game. In my opinion, Tom Reid effectively won that game for us because of his dominance at the back of the lineout. He proved more than once that he was something other than a quick tongue and a golden voice and was one of the major successes of the tour, doing superbly in the two tests in which he played.

Reid was one of five Irish players on that side which drew the series 2-2 with South Africa.

From *The Irish Lions 1896–1983*, Ward River Press, 1983

Our Sporting Heroes
Críostóir Ó Floinn

Political Border and sporting Ban
Were equally abhorrent to the valiant clan
In my native Parish by Shannon shore,
Where names were honoured in folklore
That made us proud of Limerick town
When on the field they won renown

For club or county or national team
In any sport. Our boyhood dream
Saw glory beckon for the cause
No matter the code or who made the laws.
Our fathers' hearts with pride filled up
When Young Munster won the Bateman Cup.
We thrilled to the hurling deeds of Mackey,
And young and old were equally happy
When Ireland twice won the Triple Crown,
Tom Clifford and Paddy Reid gained renown
As part of a true All-Ireland team.
In soccer we all could glorious deem
Our hero from Thomondgate, Bud Aherne,
Who, like many another, was forced to earn
A living in sport across the water
In exile never dreamed or sought for.
With Luton Town he soon won fame
And at Dalymount Park was oft acclaimed
When bold as a lion he was seen
A sportsman true in Ireland's green.

From *Centenary: A Poem*, Foilseacháin Náisiúnta Teo., 1985

Days in the Sun
Karl Johnston

Growing up in Limerick, we lived beside the Catholic Institute Club where cricket, alas, now no longer is played, and where today that peculiar manifestation of suburbia, pitch and putt, has taken over. There, as kids, we used to sit on the boundary, and there, one day shortly after the war, I saw my first black, who happened to be Leary Constantine, the great West Indian Test player who was afterwards knighted for his services to cricket. From his position in the outfield, he talked to us as we gaped at his coloured skin and gold teeth. When asked, we replied that no, we hadn't ever played cricket, and the Great Man advised us that we should at least give it a try.

Soon afterwards, my elder brother fashioned a home-made bat, with which, a heavy rubber ball and a wicket chalked on a barn door, we took to cricket. . . .

My ambitions to conquer the cricket world received added stimulus from a series called 'It's Runs That Count' in a comic called 'The Rover'. . . .

But by then cricket was in my blood, and I read every book about it which I could lay my hands on in the local library, reliving in the printed word the momentous events of other days. . . .

By now I was playing real cricket; being unable to afford to join Catholic Institute, a group of us formed a team which we called 'Limerick Unknowns', a name which turned out to be a true description of the way we were destined to remain. We played games against Institute, Glenstal Abbey, Limerick Protestant Young Men's (known locally as 'LP'), and made at least one foray to distant Cork.

With Unknowns, I had the odd distinction of playing on the same team as Harold Pinter, and note from the score book which I still possess that he took four wickets and made 26 runs. He was touring the country with a fit-up company at the time, and overhearing us talking in a coffee shop, asked if he could have a game. Since we were invariably short of players, we were only too glad, and he turned out to be — by our standards, at any rate — a very useful fastish bowler and solid batsman. But theatrically, Harold then was an Unknown, in more than one sense.

Apart from ourselves, Institute and LP, there was another team playing occasional matches in Limerick at that time, known as 'Hilarys', because, like the conqueror of Everest, they had to climb over a series of walls to get into the meadow they used as a playing-field. (It's odd to think that today, some twenty-five years on, there is just one team in Limerick, and lack of facilities and coaching over the years must surely have lost many a boy to the game.)

Soon, I joined Institute, and spent many of the happiest summers of my life playing cricket for that club. One of the highlights of our season was the annual visit paid by Railway Union, a fixture which always seemed to be played in cloudless hot weather. Our club had no bar licence then and on Sundays — the day the game was played — the pubs closed at 7.30 p.m., so a stock of booze would be laid on in a shed where the groundman's gear and roller were kept, since drink was not allowed on the club premises. The beer I drank from the bottle on those long-ago summer nights I still can savour; and later, I would relive the memories of the match as I walked home to our house across the moonlit fields.

From *Hibernia*, 4 May 1978

Bill Mulcahy
Barry Coughlan

Ronnie Dawson formed an all-Irish front for partnership with the redoubtable Sid Millar and Gordon Wood, two players of contrasting styles. . . . Wood was not spectacular, but solid to the core, very fit and very strong — pretty immovable, in fact — and both made quite an impression when they played together.

In the second row was Bill Mulcahy, who despite his lack of height was one of Ireland's most successful forwards, winning himself 35 caps. He was arguably too small to be a second row, but yet had a high rate of success as a player. Cecil Pedlow, when asked by Tony O'Reilly what the lineout calls were before one international, replied: 'Ah, just throw to the hole in the middle. They are crouching in a private trench.' And Mulcahy himself, when asked how he would like the ball, is said to have reacted by saying, 'low and crooked'.

Mulcahy suffered his share of injuries in New Zealand, in 1959, but he was, according to O'Reilly, 'never less than good and sometimes was superb. He was one of the most courageous footballers I have ever played with.' The County Limerick man played in one test against Australia and one against New Zealand. . . .

Bill Mulcahy had been to Australia, New Zealand and Canada in 1959 and, four years later, he was, with Sid Millar, the only Irishman to appear in all four tests. Mulcahy won himself a large fan club in 1962. He led a big pack into battle with the Springboks and much of the credit for their success up front has been attributed to him. Long before the end of the tour, the pack were being referred to as Mulcahy's 'Boyos'. Mulcahy had, after his student days in UCD, moved on to Bohemians in Limerick, and he was the second player from that club to be honoured with selection for the Lions — the first being Mick English, who had joined him three years before.

From *The Irish Lions 1896–1983*, Ward River Press, 1983

Frank O'Mara Takes Gold
Noel Carroll

'On this particular night I knew I was getting it all right. I was running fast. It came early and I was winning. I was putting self-doubt out of my mind. I knew no matter what Boutayeb did he couldn't get rid of me. With two laps to go I was going to kick for home. But I remembered my coach [John McDonald] telling me to wait until the last lap. I had to hold myself back. I felt that good. I could go when I wanted. It was my race.'

I was talking to Frank O'Mara in Seville the day after he won the World Indoor 3,000 metres title. We talked about the race, his training, his injuries and his plans. He was happy, elated even, about the race he had just run, and more so by the floating feeling of the race than the euphoric feeling of the victory, he told me.

He had 'seized the day', as his friend and warm-up partner on the night, Marcus O'Sullivan, had urged him. . . .

Frank was ready. His training was razor sharp. He ran 10 x 400 metres in 57.3 seconds, with a 75 second recovery ten days before Seville. In the heats he felt great. He was so much in control (in spite of running at 7.50 pace) that he calculated and inflicted a psychological victory over local hero Gonzales as well as a physical one. And on the night of the final he was deliberate and pointed. He was last out on the track but put his ASICS training gear in the first basket. While the others lined up for pre-race introductions and camera shots, he walked out in front, strolled behind the camera and took his place in the line-up, precisely when it suited him. He then proceeded to demolish a class field and win the World Championship!

Such a performance was not achieved without considerable hardship, struggle and setback. His undoubted class as a runner was often offset by his anxiety to train too hard, get injured and try to get back too quickly. . . .

In spite of all his injuries, he still has had one big win every year since he started racing seriously. 'This is what has kept me going.' And, mind you, some of his wins have been in the big league: the NCAA Mile title in 1983, the 5th Avenue Mile in 1985, the World 4 x 1 mile record in 1986 and the World Indoor 3,000 m title in 1987. He has also run an Irish record 5,000 m of 13.13.02 and has a range of world-class times from 800 m (1.46.04) to 10,000 m (27.58.74).

In truth, Frank O'Mara is one of the world's great runners. His range of world-class times from 800 metres to 10,000 metres is surpassed only by Said Aouita and he has a devastating turn of speed which is the indispensable need of today's world beater. Frank has all the equipment.

Here are his best times:

800 metres (hand timing)	1.46.04
800 metres (automatic)	1.47.17
1,500 metres	3.34.02
1 mile	3.51.06
1 mile (indoors)	3.52.30
1 mile (road)	3.49.60
2,000 metres	4.59.00
3,000 metres	7.40.41
3,000 metres (indoors)	7.41.14
3,000 metres steeplechase	8.42.00
5,000 metres	13.13.02
10,000 metres	27.58.74

Is it possible to talk of a man who has won two world titles as an under-achiever? In Frank O'Mara's case it may well be. Yet most runners would envy his achievements. And rightly so.

From *The Irish Runner*, Vol. II, No. 3, May 1991

J.P. McManus: The Limerick Leviathan
Hugh McIlvanney

If a discernible warmth crept into Peter O'Sullevan's voice as The Fellow galloped powerfully up the Cheltenham hill last week ahead of Jodami, we should not suspect that it had anything to do with the financial loyalty he had shown to his old ally (ante-post at 100-6). He was delighting in an overdue victory for a 9-year-old. . . . In fact, O'Sullevan was in superb form throughout the three days, as this reluctant absentee from the Festival can testify. . . . Having the Voice bring the thrills of Cheltenham into the living-room through the television set was one thing. Having him elaborate on the day's excitements by phone was a marvellous bonus, especially when he was reporting on his regular visits to the box of J.P. McManus, the agreeable Irishman who has long been a matchless leviathan in the betting ring.

Last week, J.P.'s exploits stirred the customary swirl of myths and rumours, notably the tale that he had backed his 7-year-old Gimme Five to win £1 million in the last race on Tuesday afternoon. 'It's not even half-true,' the man himself insisted on Friday morning. He was speaking from his 400 acre farm between the towns of Limerick and Tipperary, having just driven the youngest of his three children to school, a homely chore for someone more often associated with coming down on bookies like a wolf on the fold. As usual, the realities of his betting were extraordinary enough without embellishment. He did have a major lunge at Gimme Five. It started when Stephen Little, in a single bet, laid him £250,000 to £30,000 — and there were other spectacular onslaughts. Gimme Five's sluggishness was expensive even by J.P.'s standards. But resilience is the essence of his nature and when Danoli, Ireland's banker of bankers in Wednesday's Sun Alliance Hurdle, lived up to the advance billing, the McManus bombardment included bets of £155,000 to £80,000 and £60,000 to £30,000. 'That put the wheel back on the bike,' he told me.

He was then poised to wreak havoc, as he sent his brother to seek 10-1 or better about his own contender, Time for a Run, in the Coral Handicap Hurdle. But sevens or eights was the best he was offered. Then, when the horse duly won, the starting price was announced as 11-1. 'If you don't get on an 11-1 winner of your own at Cheltenham, you reckon it's time to down tools and that's what I did,' he said. Charlie Swan kicked home another winner in his colours, Mucklemeg, in the 5.50 on Wednesday but McManus did not back her. He maintained the truce with the enemy throughout Thursday, making Danoli his last wager of the meeting. 'I finished a little ahead,' he confirmed.

From *McIlvanney on Horseracing*, Mainstream Publishing, 1995; *The Observer*, 20 March 1994

SEVEN

HISTORY

The County Boundaries
P.J. Meghen

The Fifth Interim Report of the Limerick Rural Survey which appeared this year represents an effort on my part to collect as much information on the origin and development of the county as could be found in the printed sources available. It does not presume therefore to be new historical research; it is rather a collection of facts about the county which came my way in twenty years of administration in Limerick. I would like to devote this article to a discussion of some of the ideas which came to me from a consideration of this material and to explain perhaps more fully what influenced me in the selection of material.

First, one may ask why was it necessary to go back to discuss the first inhabitants of the area, the people who found their way here almost 4,000 years ago. My reason for doing this was my belief that the descendants of these original inhabitants were in occupation of the land in County Limerick for many hundreds of years. The researches of the late Professor Sean O'Riordan indicate how important the settlement based on Lough Gur was for many hundreds of years. It seems to have been a sacred place of the ancient religion, and one can be sure it was the scene of religious ceremonies and festivals to which the people of other settlements would gather. Ultimately these people were conquered by the invading Gaelic tribes, but the authorities seem satisfied that while the Gaelic invaders provided an upper-class minority strong enough to rule the older race, the original inhabitants lived on as workers on the land. This was to happen many times in the history of County Limerick. Yet always the invaders — Danes, Normans, Elizabethan planters or Cromwellian planters — were never large in number and the older race always remained to till the soil. This is a fact which is sometimes forgotten but the detailed figures given for the various plantations in Canon Begley's *History of the Diocese of Limerick* indicate that these intrusions brought little change in the blood of the Limerick people. Finally, in the nineteenth century, these people were tough enough to win back their lands.

In County Limerick I was fortunate to find these researches of Professor O'Riordan and the volumes of Canon Begley's *History*. But these works are not easily accessible and I felt that it would be a help to many students of social affairs to give some idea of the tenacious survival of the people of the county over the long years of plantation and persecution.

Another point that I was anxious to underline was that the boundaries of the county date back very many hundreds of years. On the north, the River Shannon has provided the main boundary always but the other boundaries — roughly the three remaining sides of a rectangle — do not generally coincide with any natural physical feature. We know that the first known maps — dating back to about A.D. 1600 — show the county boundaries much as they are today; but there is reason to believe that they are much older than that. We know for instance that the boundaries of the diocese of Limerick, which coincide with the county boundary in the west, were fixed in A.D. 1110 at the Synod of Rathbreasail and that they coincided with those of the ancient territory of Hy Fidhgente, as set out in the ancient tracts. One could say therefore that the boundaries on the west and south date back for a thousand years. In the east and south-east, the final settlement was not until 1609.

The county boundaries are therefore of considerable antiquity. The county administrations may be said to have started in 1254, when the county was given a separate sheriff. From then onwards, the records in Dublin Castle endeavoured to keep track of the sheriffs and courts in County Limerick. Thus for the past seven hundred years men and women could have called themselves 'County Limerick people'. Again while we are inclined to think that the democratically elected County Councils established in 1898 were the first County Councils, we can find in the history of the Confederation of Kilkenny after 1642, that there were County Councils set up by then and such a council was functioning in County Limerick in 1643. These councils were composed of two representatives of each barony and I was glad to be able to include a map of these baronies, as they were at that time, in the Interim Report. The history of these barony boundaries would require a book to itself. They were well settled at any rate in 1642. The baronies were used in the work of the Grand Jury for road administration and for county cess calculation. They remained as administrative divisions up to the Local Government Act 1898 and for census purposes before the census of 1901.

From *Rural Ireland*, 1964

Sarsfield Captures the Guns (1690)
Thomas Babington Macaulay

When it was known that the French troops had quitted Limerick, and that the Irish only remained, the general expectation in the English camp was that the city would be an easy conquest. Nor was the expectation unreasonable: for even Sarsfield desponded. One chance, in his opinion, there still was. William had brought with him none but small guns. Several large pieces of ordnance, a great quantity of provisions and ammunition and a bridge of tin boats, which in the watery plain of the Shannon was frequently needed, were slowly following from Cashel. If the guns and gunpowder could be intercepted and destroyed, there might be some hope. If not, all was lost; and the best thing that a brave and high-spirited Irish gentleman could do was to forget the country which he had in vain tried to defend, and to seek in some foreign land a home or a grave.

A few hours, therefore, after the English tents had been pitched before Limerick, Sarsfield set forth, under cover of the night, with a strong body of horse and dragoons. He took the road to Killaloe, and crossed the Shannon there. During the day he lurked with his band in a wild mountain tract named from the silver mines which it contains. In this desolate region Sarsfield found no lack of scouts or guides: for all the peasantry of Munster were zealous on his side. He learned in the evening that the detachment which guarded the English artillery had halted for the night about seven miles from William's camp, on a pleasant carpet of green turf under the ruined walls of an old castle; that officers and men seemed to think themselves perfectly secure; that the beasts had been turned loose to graze, and that even the sentinels were dozing. When it was dark the Irish horsemen quitted their hiding-place and were conducted by the people of the country to the place where the escort lay sleeping round the guns. The surprise was complete. Some of the English sprang to their arms and made an attempt to resist, but in vain. About sixty fell. Only one was taken alive. The rest fled. The victorious Irish made a huge pile of waggons and pieces of cannon. Every gun was stuffed with powder, and fixed with its mouth in the ground; and the whole mass was blown up. The solitary prisoner, a lieutenant, was treated with great civility by Sarsfield. 'If I had failed in this attempt,' said the gallant Irishman, 'I should have been off to France.'

Intelligence had been carried to William's headquarters that Sarsfield had stolen out of Limerick and was ranging the country. The King guessed the design of his brave enemy, and sent 500 horse to protect the guns. Unhappily there was some delay, which the English, always disposed to believe the worst of the Dutch courtiers, attributed to the negligence or perverseness of Portland. At one in the morning the detachment set out, but had scarcely left the camp when a blaze like lightning and a crash like thunder announced to the wide plain of the Shannon that all was over.

Sarsfield had long been the favourite of his countrymen; and this most seasonable exploit, judiciously planned and vigorously executed, raised him still higher in their estimation.

From *Ireland in Prose and Poetry*, Junior Book, M.H. Gill and Son Ltd, n.d.

A Death March to Cork
Padraig Ó Maidin

On 31 October 1691, the remnants of the Irish army began marching out of Limerick through the English town, out the West Watergate and took the road to Cork. They were on their way to exile in France. On 28 September the terms of the Treaty of Limerick had been agreed and on the same evening an order had been signed directing a portion of the transport ships in Cork to sail for Limerick to take some of the Irish forces on board. The articles of the treaty were signed on 3 October and on Saturday, 5 October, the Irish Army was assembled on the King's Island to be addressed by Patrick Sarsfield. On Sunday morning they were addressed by members of the clergy who urged them to volunteer for service in France, where they would have opportunity of fresh fields for their bravery, that they might return again in a short time to vindicate the rights of the old land. English officers went amongst them telling them of the advantages of joining the English Army. When the time came, however, few of the Irish went over to the English side.

One of the contemporary accounts states: 'Hundreds of the soldiers were in rags and unshod, but all bore themselves well and had a dauntless aspect. It had been agreed that the men who were to take service in France were to defile beyond an appointed spot; those who were willing to remain were to turn away. The choice of the immense majority was soon seen; some 11,000 passed beyond the selected point; some 2,000 went quietly to their homes; scarcely 1,000 threw in their lot with Ginkel. Sarsfield looked with pride at the spectacle exhibiting the noble spirit of our race. "These men," he said, "are leaving all that is most dear in life for a strange land in which they will have much to endure, to serve in an army that hardly knows our people; but they are true to Ireland and have still hopes for her cause; we will make another Ireland in the armies of the great King of France." The transports from Limerick were soon under way; loud wailing was heard from the adjoining shores as the departing sails glided down the Shannon; a few of the soldiery on board escaped by swimming, but nearly all remained faithful to their heroic choice.'

The contemporary account continues: 'Some regiments, however, had to march a long distance to Cork; I was in the company of Sarsfield with these. The temptation was too strong for some failing hearts; hundreds deserted and were never seen again. A woeful sight was seen on the Lee when the transport set sail; Sarsfield had promised the exiles who had embarked that their families were to go with them to France. There was no room in the ships to enable the pledge to be fulfilled. Loud cries and lamentations broke from the wives and children who had been left behind; some dashed into the stream and perished in its depths; some clung to the boats that were making off from the shore; many of the men, husbands or fathers, plunged into the waters. Not a few lost their lives in their efforts to reach dry ground. Nevertheless the mass of our army reached France in safety.'

From the *Cork Examiner*, 15 October 1981

The Poetry of the Wild Geese
Jeremiah Newman

I cannot conclude this essay on the literature of the Wild Geese without some treatment — however inadequate — of the poetry which they inspired. This is almost entirely Irish in origin, a great deal of it in fact in the Irish language. The greater part of the Gaelic poetry was produced in the eighteenth century and most of it was produced in Munster, much of it from around Limerick and its neighbouring counties. . . .

Some of these poems are known as songs (amhrain), although meant to be read rather than sung. Some are difficult to date. Some are lineal precursors of the songs about the Wild Geese. One such is 'Sean O Duibhir a' Ghleanna', composed to commemorate the departure to France of Colonel John O'Dwyer and 500 followers after the disastrous Cromwellian war. . . .

Another such song is 'Eamonn an Chnoic', about a relative of the O'Dwyers, who opted to stay at home as a rapparee rather than to go into exile. As in the case of many others, it is by a nameless poet. It was versified later in English by Mangan. So too was a version of one of the first real Wild Geese lyrics, 'A Lament for Patrick Sarsfield', again by an unknown Gaelic poet. Frank O'Connor made a fine English translation of it:

> So goodbye Limerick and your homes so fair,
> And all the good friends that quartered with us there,
> And the cards we played by the watchfires' glare,
> And the priests that called us at night to prayer . . .

The greatest Gaelic poet of the Williamite war is Daithi Ó Bruadair (1630–98), who settled near Dromcollogher and from whom a large number of pieces have come down to us. He was desolate after Limerick. . . .

The Munster poets who lauded the Jacobite cause came, most of them, from around Limerick or not altogether that far from its hinterland. . . . Sean Ó Tuama of Croom (1708–75) produced an aisling too, as did his friend Andrias Mac Craith in 1746, a poem hopeful of an eventual Stuart victory and the restoration of the churches, even though he himself died around 1791, in his own words 'neither a Protestant nor a Papist'. . . .

The events surrounding Limerick are the focus of much of this literature, from poets of whom many were themselves from Limerick. I refer especially to Michael Hogan, the Bard of Thomond (1832–99), who wrote copiously on what he called 'The Battle of Limerick', especially on the heroines of the breach, on Sarsfield and his men's farewell, and on the need at the time that he wrote for a memorial in Sarsfield's honour:

> There let him stand with sword in hand,
> and flashing arms of steel, In bright array,
> as on the day he made the foeman reel.

Today, one might say:

> Long may he stand there;
> Just trim round the site, and let him be seen.

Robert Dwyer Joyce from near Ardpatrick (1830–83), in his *Ballads, Romances and Songs* (1861) and *Ballads of Irish Chivalry* (1872), has left us many poems on the Siege of Limerick, the march out from there of the Wild Geese, and some of their exploits abroad. . . .

Aubrey de Vere (1814–1902) added his own pieces to these poems. . . .

To end: despite overstatement of the prowess of the Wild Geese, and in the revisionism that is sometimes in order in that regard, I am sure that I may suitably finish with four lines from Davis on the death of Sarsfield:

> Sarsfield has sailed from Limerick Town,
> He held it long for country and crown; . . .
> Sarsfield is dead, yet no tear shed we —
> For he died in the arms of Victory.

From *From Out of Limerick: Glimpses of the Wild Geese*, Diocesan Offices, Limerick, 1991

Old Times! Old Times!
Gerald Griffin

> Old times! old times! the gay old times!
> When I was young and free,
> And heard the merry Easter chimes
> Under the sally tree.
> My Sunday palm beside me placed —
> My cross upon my hand —
> A heart at rest within my breast,
> And sunshine on the land!
> Old times! Old times!

It is not that my fortunes flee,
Nor that my cheek is pale —
I mourn whene'er I think of thee,
My darling, native vale! —
A wiser head I have, I know,
Than when I loitered there;
But in my wisdom there is woe,
And in my knowledge care.
Old times! Old times!

I've lived to know my share of joy,
To feel my share of pain —
To learn that friendship's self can cloy,
To love, and love in vain —
To feel a pang and wear a smile,
To tire of other climes —
To like my own unhappy isle,
And sing the gay old times!
Old times! Old times!

And sure the land is nothing changed,
The birds are singing still;
The flowers are springing where we ranged,
There's sunshine on the hill;
The sally, waving o'er my head,
Still sweetly shades my frame —
But, ah, those happy days are fled,
And I am not the same!
Old times! Old times!

Oh, come again, ye merry times!
Sweet, sunny, fresh, and calm —
And let me hear those Easter chimes,
And wear my Sunday palm.
If I could cry away mine eyes,
My tears would flow in vain —
If I could waste my heart in signs,
They'll never come again!
Old times! Old times!

From *The Poetical and Dramatic Works of Gerald Griffin*, James Duffy, 1891

The Palatines
Mainchín Seoighe

Glenosheen — Gleann Oisín — is an interesting little place, that lies in a lovely setting. It had a colony of Palatines, descendants of some of the 3,000 Germans who had come as refugees from the Rhenish Palatinate to Ireland in 1709. The largest Palatine settlement was that on the Southwell estate, near Rathkeale, in County Limerick; and it was from there that a number of Palatine families came to Glenosheen, as well as to nearby Ballyorgan and Garrynlease, on the invitation of the local landlord, the Right Honourable Silver Oliver. P.W. Joyce remembered hearing the following lines being recited by neighbours:

> In the year seventeen hundred and nine,
> In came the brass-coloured Palatine,
> From the ancient banks of the Swabian Rhine.

In Glenosheen, the land given to the Palatines was unoccupied, so that there were no evictions or clearances to make room for them, and, consequently, no ill feelings among their Irish neighbours. In his book, *The Wonders of Ireland* (p. 205), Joyce says:

> In my early time Glenosheen had a mixture of Catholics and Protestants (chiefly Palatine), about half and half, and we got on very well together: in recalling the kindly memories of my boyhood companions, Palatines come up as well as Catholics.

When they first came to Glenosheen, he tells us, the Palatines had to clear large areas of wood and scrub to prepare their little farms for cultivation. At that time, and for many years afterwards, their dress, and even their shoes — with the exception of the soles — were made of canvas; they ate sauerkraut, and slept between two feather beds, that is, between a feather tick and what we now call a continental quilt. Mostly, they were Methodists — the original Palatines who came to Ireland were Lutherans — but they generally attended the Protestant church. They were steady, sober and industrious, were good farmers, understood gardening, kept bees, and were fond of making pastry.

The principal Palatine surnames in the Glenosheen district were Altines, or Alton, Barkman, Bovenizer, Delmege, Fizzel, Glaizier, Heck, Ligier (Ligonier), Ruttle, Shoultiss, Strough, Struffle (Stroffel), Young. The spelling of many of these names varied considerably from that of the original forms: Barkman, for instance, was originally Berghmann; Young was Jung; Delmege was Dolmetsch.

Of considerable interest is a description of his native district that Joyce wrote when still a young man. Apart from the pleasing picture it unfolds, the description shows how every feature of the landscape, as well as the placenames and the doings of the people had impressed themselves indelibly upon him.

'The Ballahoura Mountains,' he wrote, 'extend for several miles on the borders of the Counties of Cork and Limerick. Commencing near Charleville, they stretch away towards the east, consisting of a succession of single peaks with lone and desolate valleys lying between, covered with heath or coarse grass, where for ages the silence has been broken only by the cry of the heath-cock or the yelp of the fox echoing among the rocks that are strewn in wild confusion over the sides of the mountains. They increase gradually in height towards the eastern extremity of the range where they are abruptly terminated by the majestic Seefin, which, projecting forwards — its back to the west and its face to the rising sun — seems placed there to guard the desolate solitude behind it.

Towards the east it overlooks a beautiful and fertile valley, through which a little river winds its peaceful course to join the Funsheon; on the west "Blackrock of the Eagle" rears its front — a sheer precipice — over Lyre-na-Freaghawn, a black heath-covered glen that divides the mountains. On the south it is separated by Lyre-na-Grena, the "valley of the sun", from "the Long Mountain" which stretches far away towards Glenanaar; and immediately in front, on the opposite side of the valley, rises Barna Geeha, up whose sides cultivation has crept almost to its summit. Just under the eastern face of Seefin, at its very base and extending even a little way up the mountain, reposes the peaceful little village of Glenosheen.'

From *The Joyce Brothers of Glenosheen*, Coiste Scoil na Seoigheach, Cill Fhionáin, Co. Luimnigh, 1987

How Plassey Got Its Name
Jim Kemmy

The name Plassey has a romantic origin, being derived from the palas tree or 'flame of the forest' which, in turn, gave its name to a village in India, about 80 miles north of Calcutta. But, for all the sylvan attractions of the surrounding countryside, Limerick's Plassey owes its title to a combination of other factors, military and political.

On 23 June 1757, Robert Clive, the son of a Shropshire squire, led an army of the East of India Company to a decisive victory at the Battle of Plassey. This event was to be crucial in the establishment of the British Indian Empire.

In 1760, at the age of 34, Clive returned to England to a less than enthusiastic reception. Ill health and his failure to wield sufficient political influence prevented him from obtaining an English peerage. For all his past glories, he had to be content with a second best honour. Through the intercession of the Duke of Newcastle, he procured a scattered Irish estate in Limerick and County Clare which involved the purchase of lands and a manor house from Thomas McMahon at Ballykilty, on the banks of the River Shannon, just outside Limerick city.

Thus Clive became Baron of Plassey, and the district was renamed after its new owner. It is doubtful, however, if Clive lived in the house for a long period. In 1774 he ended his life in a lavatory by cutting his throat with a penknife.

Through the centuries Plassey has been a paradise for fishermen, boatmen, artists, nature-lovers, picnickers and riverside strollers. And a variety of writers, some of whom lived in neighbouring townlands, have fondly described the spot in prose and poetry.

The University of Limerick and its campus are located at Clive's old house and estate — an ideal setting for this place of learning.

From *Plassey Arts Days*, April 1985

The Examination of Barry St Ledger

5 March 1797

The Examination of Barry St Ledger, now a Lieutenant in the 2nd Battalion of the 2nd Legion of France, says that he was born near Limerick in the Kingdom of Ireland, that his Father lived upon his Property, which was in Land, and a Distillery. Examinant is near 20 years old, says he left Ireland when he was about 12 years old, in order to go to America, to his Uncle, who, having no Children, wished for Examinant to live with him. His Uncle's Name was Bryan Smith, and he resided about 46 miles from Charlestown in South Carolina, that he lived with his said Uncle till November 1795, when he quitted him, in order to come to London to sell Rice, and remit the money to Ireland to his Mother, his Father being dead. That on his passage, the Ship called the *Hope of Charlestown*, Captain Le Monte, losing her Rudder, was wrecked on the West Coast of Ireland, near Limerick, on which Examinant went to his Mother, and staid with her a month or six weeks. In consequence of the wrecking (of) the Ship, Examinant lost all his Papers and all his Property which was on board. That he afterwards took his passage from Limerick to Baltimore, by the way of Lisbon, the *Sally of Boston*, Captain Webber, and after being at Sea three days, was captured by a French Privateer, called Le Vengear, and carried into Brest. That there he met Col Tate, whom he had seen in America, who, proving to the French Government, that Examinant was an American Citizen, he was set at liberty. That soon after, the Irish Brigade in the Republican Service, marching into Brest for the Irish Expedition, under the command of Col O'Meara, Examinant finding him to be his Relation, was persuaded by him to enter into that Regt as a Sub Lieutenant. That he went on board the *Eole* a 74 Gun Ship to the Coast of Ireland, that said Ship was the first that anchored in Bantry Bay, where she staid six days, that she never parted her Cable, having a new one at leaving Brest, that there were 1,500 men in the Irish brigade, chiefly French excepting the Officers, and Genl Harty, General of the Brigade. That on weighing anchor, they sailed for Brest, and came back quite unhurt. That the Brigade then marched to Morlaix, 33 miles from Brest, and Examinant stayed in Brest. That soon after the Hussars, who were aboard the *Surveillante*, which was scuttled in Bantry Bay returning in the *Cocade*, an Officer named O'Naughtin, an Irishman from Galway, persuaded Examinant to go into the Army of the Sambre and Meuse, where he was himself going, which Examinant had partly determined to do, when finding Col Tate had the command of an Expedition, which Examinant heard was going to Dunkirk to join an Expedition, which was to sail from thence. Examinant chose to go with him, received his Commission as Lieutenant from General Moyer. That he went aboard the *Vengeance*, and sailed from Brest last Friday fortnight, and next morning came in sight of Lizard Point. That they then sailed for the Bristol Channel, and anchored abreast of Lundy Island, and scuttled a small vessel. That the Wind being adverse they could not get up the Channel, says that as he was on the Poop, he heard a dispute between Tate and Categne [sic] the Commodore, but cannot tell what about. That they then sailed for the Welch Coast, and the next day anchored in Fishguard Bay. That Colonel Tate then came to him and said 'You must go ashore in the first Boat with the Grenadiers', which Examinant did. That he then went to a farm house with 25 Grenadiers. The farm house belonged to one Mortimer. That he formed the Grenadiers in the Yard. That he told the Grenadiers they must not enter it to plunder it, but they said they would. That he declared he would shoot the first Man that did so, but they said they could shoot as well as the Examinant. That they then went into the House, and plundered it, and broke everything, and drank all the Liquor, on which Examinant quitted them. That he afterwards returned, and found them quite drunk and about to set fire to the Ricks &c. Which with great difficulty he prevented. That next day he spoke to Morrison to tell Col Tate that he and Morrison and Tyrrell would leave him immediately; when Tate replied do not yet, for I mean to capitulate. Says that he has heard his Uncle say, that Tate was a Virginian, and that he was much talked of in America, where he raised a Body of Men to go against the Spanish Colonies. Says that when Col Tate saw the Ships sail, he made signals by firing Guns, and hoisting a white Flag. Says that he was at the advanced Post, and when he heard the English Drums, and thought they were going to be attacked, he drew up his Men and ordered them to fire by Platoons, and to retreat slowly to the Main Body.

(Signed) Barry St Ledger

Taken at Whitehall before
me this 5th day of March

Richd Ford

From the Public Record Office, London, PC.1/37, A.114, 5 March 1797

Kilmallock
Sir Aubrey de Vere

What ruined shapes of feudal pomp are there,
In the cold moonlight fading silently?
The castle, with its stern, baronial air,
Still frowning, as accustomed to defy;
The Gothic street, where Desmond's chivalry
Dwelt in their pride; the cloistered house of prayer;
The gate-towers, mouldering where the stream moans by,
Now, but the owl's lone haunt, and fox's lair.
Here once the pride of princely Desmond flushed.
His courtiers knelt, his mailed squadrons rushed;
And saintly brethren poured the choral strain:
Here Beauty bowed her head, and smiled and blushed:
Ah, of these glories what doth now remain?
The charnel of yon desecrated fane!

From *Irish Poets of the Nineteenth Century*, selected with introductions by Geoffrey Taylor, Routledge and
Kegan Paul, 1951

Father Mathew in Limerick
Elizabeth Malcolm

It is not clear exactly when Father Mathew began to issue temperance medals,
possibly late in 1838 or early in 1839. . . . The *London Morning Post* claimed on 20
October 1839 that Father Mathew was 'driving a profitable trade; he gets one
shilling from each penitent . . . and gives him or her his blessing, and a pewter
medal value half a farthing'.

That the visit to Father Mathew was a form of pilgrimage, the medal being a
relic thereof, seems to have been a popular view. A Limerick priest told the *Dublin*

Evening Post that, while not seeking to 'imitate' Father Mathew, the clergy did not restrain those wishing to visit Cork, 'as it is supposed that the fatigue of the journey, the change of place and circumstances have the effect of making a stronger impression on their minds'. Batches of ten, twenty or even thirty pilgrims could be found waiting in Father Mathew's parlour in Cove Street at nearly all hours to take the pledge. According to J.F. Maguire (the biographer of Father Mathew), some came 'sober and penitent', but others were obviously under the influence of drink and needed the goading of wives or mothers. 'We doubt', wrote Maguire, 'if there was a tap-room in Cork in which a more decided odour of whiskey and porter . . . was apparent.' Father Mathew's willingness to administer the pledge to those in a state of drunkenness caused considerable unease within the temperance movement and led critics to ridicule the sincerity of many pledges. . . .

By late 1839 Father Mathew was being pressed by numerous temperance societies to visit their towns. Many, as in the case of Belfast, he refused, pleading that it was impossible for him to leave Cork for any length of time given the large numbers arriving there to take the pledge from him personally. Some requests, however, he found it impossible to reject; these came from close at hand and from the hierarchy of his own church. A branch of the Cork society had been established in Limerick in July 1839, though many still travelled from the city to take the pledge from Father Mathew himself. In September the mayor, Alderman Garrett Fitzgerald, wrote inviting Father Mathew to visit, and this request was seconded by Bishop Ryan, an old friend. With some hesitation, Father Mathew agreed to preach a charity sermon in Limerick on behalf of the schools conducted by the Presentation nuns. The choice was significant: Nano Nagle, who had founded the Order in the 1770s, was a connection of the Mathew family; moreover, Father Mathew himself had long been interested in the education of poor Catholic children. A visit to Limerick also afforded an opportunity to see one of his sisters, married to a merchant called Dunbar. Given his commitments in Cork, however, he could only spend from Saturday, 30 November, to Tuesday, 3 December, in Limerick. He wanted no 'invitations, addresses and such like', for, as he wrote to the organisers, 'I am resolved not to make a spectacle of myself, except in the pulpit'; and for the whole of Monday he was determined to put himself at the disposal of Bishop Ryan, to do as the Bishop desired. His anxiety to involve the local clergy in his visit and thus not give offence is obvious. McKenna, his secretary, was to accompany him, bringing some 2,000 medals and cards for distribution. If 4,000 were joining each week in Cork, then an estimate of 2,000 for the three days in Limerick doubtless seemed reasonable.

What happened during his three days in Limerick astounded even his most ardent supporters. By Friday, according to the *Limerick Reporter*, the city was packed with people and 5,000 were without a bed. Fortunately, though it was winter, the weather was relatively mild and many slept out of doors. On Saturday the road to Cork was lined with people for two or three miles outside the city, as Father

Mathew's arrival was anxiously awaited. When he finally appeared late in the afternoon the crowds were such that he had great difficulty in getting from the coach to his brother-in-law's house in Upper Mallow Street. The next afternoon he preached the planned sermon at St Michael's and then proceeded to the county courthouse, near the present Mathew Bridge, where he began to administer the pledge from the steps. The *Limerick Reporter* estimated that in the quarter of a mile from Denmark Street to the courthouse, 30,000 people were gathered. To put such a figure in perspective we should perhaps note that, according to the 1841 census, the population of Limerick city was only 48,000.

He returned to his brother-in-law's house for a meal at about 5 o'clock, after which he continued to administer the pledge there until 9 p.m. On the Monday morning he resumed his labours at 5 a.m. But the crush around the house was so great that one woman was trampled to death, many others were injured, and substantial damage was done to the house itself. Father Mathew returned to the courthouse at 9 a.m. and continued uninterrupted there until 3 p.m. Again crowding became a serious problem, and a number of people were pushed into the river. Finally his friends, fearing for his safety, were forced to call for aid. A troop of Scots Greys cleared the way so he could return to Upper Mallow Street. There, according to the *Reporter*, 10,000 people knelt in the street to receive the pledge, while Father Mathew went among them with a military escort. On Tuesday he again spent most of the day in Mallow Street until 5 p.m. when, with difficulty, he boarded the coach for Cork. Later Father Mathew was to refer to this, his first mission outside Cork, as 'glorious' but 'awful'. According to the local paper, during these three days some 150,000 people took the pledge.

From 'Ireland Sober, Ireland Free': Drink and Temperance in Nineteenth-Century Ireland, Gill and Macmillan, 1986

Castleconnell
Sir Aubrey de Vere

Broad, but not deep, along his rock-chafed bed,
In many a sparkling eddy winds the flood.
Clasped by a margin of green underwood:
A castled crag, with ivy garlanded,
Sheer, o'er the torrent frowns: above the mead
De Burgho's towers, crumbling o'er many a rood,
Stand gauntly out in airy solitude
Backed by yon furrowed mountain's tinted head.

Sounds of far people, mingling with the fall
Of waters, and the busy hum of bees,
And larks in air, and throstles in the trees,
Thrill the moist air with murmurs musical.
While cottage smoke goes drifting on the breeze;
And sunny clouds are floating over all.

From *Irish Poets of the Nineteenth Century*, selected with introductions by Geoffrey Taylor, Routledge and
Kegan Paul, 1951

Hunting the Wren in Park
Kevin Hannan

The Parkmen could not allow themselves the luxury of a rest even during Christmas-
tide. But the most important and strenuous event in their festive activities had
nothing to do with their daily work. Though the Wren's Day is still regarded as a
special occasion throughout the country, in Park it had a significance all its own.
The market-gardeners had little time to waste on the birds all round them during
the rest of the year but for two days the wren dominated their thinking. And this
was no celebration of the little bird's triumph over the hostile elements. No; for the
Parkmen, at this time, the only good wren was a dead one.

So, every Christmas Day morning, men of all ages came together to hunt the
wren. About twenty Lower Parkmen would meet at the Bun Ard, come rain, frost
or snow. A similar number from Rhebogue and Singland would assemble at Singland
Cross. All the men made sure to be well fortified against the wintry conditions.
Each man armed himself with two stout wattles, especially cut for the occasion.

The quarry was one of the frailest and most inoffensive of all birds, a miracle of
symmetry and song, with its gossamer feathers arrayed in a beautiful pattern on its
tiny body. This was the wren, 'the king of all birds', which was to forfeit its life on
this Christian day of all days. . . .

The itinerary of the journey over the traditional hunting-grounds never varied.
The Bun Ard contingent always started off towards the 'Bottoms' remorselessly
beating every hedge on the way. Moving downstream from the water meadows of
the Shannon Fields, past the tail of the Bealavunna, and the river draughts of
Swan, Feehib and Poulahurra, the men crossed the Pike Bridge to the high ground
of Athlunkard, before entering the broad plain of Clouncaree, with its long hedges,
sloping up from Altabugga and the 'Heights and Hollows' to the 'Range' and the
Bog Road. The hunt went on through Annabeg and usually came to an end at
Gillogue, whence, after some seasonable refreshment, the weary, sated Lower
Parkmen returned home by the easier route of Plassey Bank.

The Singland Cross group simultaneously traversed the valley of the Groody river, taking in the sloping hedges of Kilbane, only pausing to say a prayer at the holy well of St Mary Magdalen, the patroness of the parish. The fields around the Bloodmill were usually finecombed, and the force then swept on through Towlerton and 'Maags', where thirsts were often slaked and strategies reviewed. After this rest, the homeward journey was made by way of the Singland Road.

During the hunt, ten or twelve men would line up in formation on each side of the ditch and methodically beat the bushes. At times, when wrens were scarce, the pursuit took on the appearance of a military operation, with the men deployed on the two flanks, a scouting party and a rearguard. Once the victim was 'raised', there was no let-up. . . .

The wren's range of flight, being in proportion to its size, was never far, fast or high enough to put a distance between itself and its enemies. If it escaped the first barrage of flying wattles, it could only flit in short, fitful spurts along the hedge, or to an adjoining thicket. And its movements were always followed by the deadly, well-trained eyes of the Parkmen. Flushed out, again and again, amid the thunder of half-crazed yells, to run the gauntlet of the murderous wattles, the tiny creature's flights became shorter and shorter. The men relentlessly closed in on the terrified bird until it could no longer fly through sheer exhaustion. One more furious fusillade and the wren was finally released from its terrible terror. The ritual went on until about four o'clock in the afternoon, when usually two or three wrens would have been killed by each group.

The number of birds killed varied from year to year, the decisive factor being the nature of the weather in the months before Christmas. A hard, cold winter, with a lot of frost, meant that even the hardy wren would be weak and hungry from the sheer struggle for survival. After a brief flurry of low flights, the worn-out bird became completely exhausted and, having been driven to a standstill, was a sitting target for the hunters. On such a day, five or six wrens would be done to death with the crashing wattles. A mild winter saw the wren in sprightly condition and difficult to corner. But the Parkmen were not easy to shake off and would be loath to give up the chase until at least one bird had been killed.

From *The Old Limerick Journal*, No. 20, Winter 1986

Tait's Clock
Michael Hogan

That splendid pile of noble stone,
With its grand clock and graceful cone,

Was founded to commemorate
The matchless worth of generous Tait,
A public testimonial made
To honour Limerick's Prince of Trade
The fine perfection of its plan
Is like the grandeur of the man;
And while it charms the public view,
It does a public service too;
The rich-toned bells that grace its tower
Hymn the advance of every hour,
And in their sweet alternate chime
We hear the warning voice of time.

From *The Story of Shaum-a-Scoob*, by the Bard of Thomond, No. 5, 1871

The Advent of the Creameries
P.J. Meghen

There are several economic problems associated with agriculture which have produced great social changes in County Limerick and to which only a brief reference could be made in the Fifth Interim Report of the Limerick Rural Survey. I have indicated that from the earliest available records the tendency in County Limerick farming was towards dairying. This may have dated from the great Cistercian monastic period but the soil and climate suited this development. When the farmers gained their own lands on reasonable terms, many of them concentrated on it. This form of farming associated with home butter-making gave considerable employment. . . .

This was soon to be changed by the advent of the creamery system. In the report, some details are given but I would like here to stress two features in particular which marked this change in County Limerick.

In the first place, there was in a few years an almost complete change-over to the creamery system. From the opening of the first creameries in the county about 1884, there was a constant spread of the idea so that it is recorded that there were 110 creameries in the county by 1896. This marked the end of butter-making on the farms. The second feature was that with this number of creameries available, the farmer was able to bring his own milk to the creamery every day. This tradition has never changed in the county. The recent report of the survey team established by the Minister for Agriculture on the Dairy Products Industry (1963) showed that 99.9 per cent of the milk supplies are still delivered by the farmers in County

Limerick to the creameries. The report also showed that this was possible because 96.5 per cent of these farmers in the county reside within a distance of 4 miles from one or other of the 83 creamery premises still working in the area.

The departmental report however sounds a grave warning about this practice. In par. 81, it says:

> While the system of individual-farmer delivery of milk to creameries located within short distances from the farms was appropriate in the early years of the creamery industry, it is largely outmoded in present-day conditions and the balance of economic advantage lies with the rationally-organised milk haulage.

While it recognises the difficulties likely to be encountered in changing a system so long established, its final recommendation is that the effort must be made. Here is what it recommends:

> Arrangements should be made as expeditiously as possible to introduce multi-can haulage schemes in all creamery areas; these schemes should replace completely all farmer deliveries of milk.

From what I have noted here, one can see how big a problem faces the County Limerick farmer. It is not for the social historian to indicate how the change is to be made but it would seem that a long period of education and pilot schemes of one kind or another will be needed. I have selected this one aspect of social life in County Limerick to indicate how some of the problems of the present day have their roots deep in the past.

From *Rural Ireland*, 1964

Selective History
David Hanly

When I was a schoolboy, I worked during the summer holidays as an office boy in Matterson's bacon factory in order to make enough money to . . . well, once it was to buy a new three-speed Raleigh for £22, which represented 11 weeks' wages.

The job was not exactly intellectually demanding and it had its less enjoyable moments: having to run the gauntlet of the cannery girls — 'Would you like a roll?' — and feeling my face grow crimson with tongue-tied embarrassment.

But there were also chores to look forward to, and one of them was to be sent, for whatever reason, to the back gate of the factory, where the pigs were taken in for slaughter.

The white-haired man in the green coat who supervised this daily operation was Johnnie Cox, a pipe-smoking Canadian with a passion for salmon-fishing. Johnnie talked to me on equal terms, and I appreciated this, but what I treasured more were those occasions when he talked about his experiences as a young soldier in the Canadian Corps in the Great War.

He didn't do this often, and the references were brief. But they had all the more impact for that.

I didn't know enough about the Great War to ask informed questions: *Stair Sheanchas na hÉireann* was not brimming with information, and especially not about the Irishmen who took part in it.

Our next-door neighbours were a childless couple named Parkinson. He was a gentle, quiet-spoken man who polished his boots until they sparkled outside his back door on summer mornings.

He was a veteran. Of Paschendaele? The Somme? I don't know. He never spoke about it. Neither did his frequent visitor, a Mr Robinson, who had lost an arm in battle and who was also a gentle quiet-spoken man of great dignity. Were they in battle together? Was that what they talked about when Mr Robinson visited? I wasn't privy.

Mr Robinson lived in Bengal Terrace, built by the British to house the veterans. In another house lived the family of the late Seán Burke, who was later provided with a different kind of accommodation by the British and thanked them by springing George Blake. The ironies abound.

I'm sure there were ironies in my own family, as there were in thousands of families, but I was never made aware of them. One side — my father's — is a complete blank: he never talked about his family one way or the other, and, except for the occasional rueful remark ('and they told us it was for the freedom of small nations') he was an utterly pacific and apolitical man. On my mother's side, and at a distance, there were three Curragh internees, all of whom went into exile in New York upon release. One of them refused to set foot in his homeland until de Valera was dead. . . .

Was anyone in my family ever a member of the British Army? Do we have a Munster or any other kind of Fusilier in our escutcheon? Perhaps. But if so, they have been air-brushed from the family memory. Just as they have been air-brushed from the national collective memory. . . .

I don't know whether the occlusion was deliberate. . . . But I do know that when the bravery and sacrifice of 1916 are invoked, nobody is thinking of the Somme.

It is understandable, but that does not make it right. The Robinsons and the Parkinsons were just as brave, their sacrifices just as great, as their cousins' back home. They were just as Irish, and they deserve not to be forgotten.

From *The Sunday Tribune*, 21 July 1996

A Civil War Ultimatum
Cmdt Gen. Michael Brennan

Oglaigh na h-Éireann

DEPT
Ref. No.

4th Southern Division,
Headquarters, Limerick

20 July 1922

To the O/C
Executive Forces
Strand Barracks

1. As you may have noticed I now have guns in position to shell the Strand Barracks.

2. Having no desire to shed further blood I am giving you the opportunity of surrendering before opening fire.

3. If a white flag is not hanging out through one of the Barrack windows within five minutes of the receipt of this my gunners have instructions to open fire. In the event of your deciding to surrender immediately after hanging out the flag all your men will line up in front of the barrack gate unarmed. Unless these conditions are immediately carried out the responsibility for your men's lives will rest on you.

4. Your men fired last night out of the house where you have the Red Cross Flag flying. This house and the two next it will be treated as part of the Strand Barracks if you have to open fire.

5. My conditions are unconditional surrender. You and your men will get prisoners of war treatment if you surrender.

(Signed) M. Brennan
Comdt Gen.

From a copy of a document in the possession of the Editor

Second Death
Mainchín Seoighe

Close by the fireside they would sit
In those remote pre-wireless days,
Recalling neighbours they had known
And discoursing on their ways.
Paddy Hogan he would be there,

My father surely, and Jack Wall —
Oh they could talk the whole night long
As the dead men they'd recall.

We'd hear of ould Bill Hennessy,
And Matt Loughlin and Thomas Wall,
Of ould Dwane and ould Carey,
Dick Walsh and the Tuohys all.
And though I had never known them,
And each slept in his bed of clay,
They still lived full in memory
An after-life in our day.

But Paddy Hogan is no more,
Nor my father nor Jack Wall,
And no one now speaks the names
Of the men they used recall.
The life they lived in memory
Was dependent on others' breath,
And when those others passed away
They died a second death.

From *Castle Poets*, 1977

The Drumcollogher Cinema Fire
Barney Keating

The advertised programme for the Assembly Rooms Picturedrome, Cork, for Friday and Saturday, 3 and 4 September 1926, was a cowboy film entitled *The White Outlaw*. It was described as 'A very remarkable drama of the open, starring Jack Hoxie and Scout the Wonder Horse'. The supporting film was a two-reel comedy, *Baby be Good*. There was no programme advertised for the Sunday because the Assembly Rooms remained closed on the Lord's Day. This strict observance of Sunday was to contribute indirectly to the fire tragedy in Drumcollogher. Patrick C. Downing was employed at the Assembly Rooms as the assistant projectionist. One of his responsibilities was to pack the films after the evening show and get them ready for dispatch to Dublin by train early on the following Monday morning.

Patrick Brennan was the owner of a two-storey shed at Church Street, Drumcollogher. A quantity of timber and glass was stored on the ground floor. At one side a wooden ladder with a hand-rail led up to a narrow door, through which one gained access to an upstairs room, which measured about 60 ft in length and some 20 ft in width. At the far gable-end two small windows, barred on the outside, flanked a small, narrow room which was partitioned off from the rest of the floor and was used, on occasions, as a dressing-room for amateur dramatics. Portion of the room was covered with felt.

William (Baby) Forde, a hackney-car owner in Drumcollogher, decided to rent this upstairs room from Brennan for a film show. Five 'Cinematograph Entertainments' had already been staged, mainly by Hurleys of Charleville, in the same venue. This seems to have been Baby Forde's first venture into the travelling cinema business. He arranged with Downing to travel from Cork by train on Sunday afternoon. Forde collected Downing at Charleville, the films being carried in a Gladstone bag. To lighten the load, the films' metal cases were left in Cork. The show was scheduled for that evening, Sunday, 5 September 1926.

Sergeant Long, from the local Civic Garda barracks, hearing of the proposed film show, contacted Brennan, Forde and Downing, separately and on different occasions during the week or so preceding the film show. He informed them of the various safety regulations to be observed under the Cinematograph Act, 1909. Long, who had been trained as a fireman while in the British Army at Aldershot, placed special emphasis on the provision of blankets, buckets of sand and water, and exits. It was to be shown subsequently that these regulations were not observed.

At least 150 men, women and children climbed up the ladder that fateful night and passed through the narrow door in single file. Forde was just inside the door collecting the money and was standing at the end of a long table which lay lengthwise across the centre of the room. He had two lit candles on the table beside him when the first film started. This enabled Forde to examine the money coming in and to give change. Once inside, the patrons sat on forms and some wooden chairs.

Downing stood further up at the centre of the table operating the projector. Around him lay rolls of film completely exposed; the engine of a lorry parked outside on the footpath was kept running during the performance — this provided the only electric power for the projector.

From evidence later, it would appear that the film show started at about 9.10/9.15 p.m. Some twenty-five minutes later the supporting film — the two-reel comedy — concluded and the main picture commenced. The two reels of the first film were left lying loose on the side of the table nearest Forde when portion of one film was ignited by a candle. Being celluloid, it flared immediately and burned furiously.

Sergeant Long was on duty that night in the hall and was standing beside the table. He stated later that, as he was about to make a grab at the burning film, somebody pushed past him and struck it with a cap, spreading the flames and setting fire to the rest of the films. Before he was pushed out of the door in the stampede, Long managed to kick one of the blazing reels out through the door where it fell and lay burning on the bottom step of the ladder.

In the hall, the flames spread rapidly over the top of the table and across the floor. Panic reigned in an instant. Most of those sitting behind the projector and immediately in front of it managed to escape, while those up in front, near the screen at the rear of the building, were trapped. The fire blocked them off from the only door and, as it took hold, forced them back to the rear wall where the barred windows were.

One survivor, John Gleeson, the local parish clerk, who had been sitting with his wife up in front of the projector, described what happened:

> Everything happened so quickly that it seemed as if it were but three minutes before the whole hall was in a blaze. The flames in front of the door cut us off at the back of the hall, from the only exit. I thought of the windows and rushed to the one near the screen. I knew that there were iron bars on the window but that they would not be hard to remove. I worked frantically at them while my wife stood by my side. I could feel the heat growing intense. My ears were deafened with noise and the crackle of the flames and burning wood, while my eyes and mouth were full of smoke. I got my wife through the window at last and then turned to assist a grey-haired woman whom I could hear moaning at my feet. I helped her to the window and pushed her through. I made to help another woman through but, quite suddenly, flesh came off my hands in chunks. I looked and saw the flesh all wrinkled and shrivelled — yet I had not been touched by the flames. The heat and suffocation were so terrible that I then made for the window myself and got through on to a rick of hay outside.

Dan O'Callaghan, retired principal of Drumcollogher National School, told me that this small partitioned room at the end of the hall had been used as a venue for local IRA meetings during the Troubles. To guard against a surprise raid by the British forces during such meetings, the bars in the windows had been sawn through in the middle. This would have helped any of the 'boys' present to escape immediately if there was a sudden raid by the Black and Tans. Luckily, for the six people who escaped through these windows on the night of the fire, Gleeson, being in the local IRA, had been the person responsible for originally cutting through the bars many years before.

Garda Davis had also been on duty in the hall that night. His fiancée had been there as well and had lost her life in the fire. Davis had been badly injured while making rescue attempts. He later told how he had been separated from his fiancée in the mad rush for the door. 'I saw a terrible sight, where the people were behaving like savage beasts, mauling, tearing and struggling with one another. They were holding one another in a frenzied deadly grip. They were shouting, screaming and fighting. I did not know where the girl was, the crowd had knocked her out of my hands and separated us. By then the hall was a blazing inferno. The smoke was terrible and it was a miracle that I was not suffocated. The crowd at the back were behaving like a hive of beasts — the men knocking down the women and children in their frenzy.'

From various reports afterwards it would seem that a stout woman got jammed in each of the two small windows — thus blocking off the last remaining routes of escape. Those still trapped inside were quickly overcome and suffocated. First, the ladder to the upper room, then, the floor and, finally, the roof collapsed. Within ten minutes from the start of the fire the whole building was a raging inferno. Within half an hour it was gutted. Forty-six people lost their lives in the fire, while two of those seriously injured died later in hospital.

From *The Newcastle West Observer*, July 1980

Welcome to John F. Kennedy
Frances Condell

In welcoming you here this afternoon on this race course, Mr President, I would like you to know, however, that we of Limerick have a lovely city, away in there, beyond the trees and the hills, a city of which we are very proud, steeped as it is in history and antiquity with its charter and its first Mayor, reaching away back to the year 1197. It was from our docks, Mr President, that many emigrant ships set sail for your shores, and from which point of departure our people became yours. That time of great exodus is over, thank God, and I am sure you will agree with me that you have enough of us over there to keep you happy, and to assure you of our faithful support at all times. The day has come when the point of departure and arrival has transferred itself from us, some 15 miles distant, and in keeping with modern times, to an airport. . . .

Mr President, we the women of Limerick city and County, feel that we have a special claim on you; we claim the Fitzgeralds. May I repeat, we claim the Fitzgerald in you, Sir, and we are extremely proud of that heritage. Over there you see a large number of your relatives and connections who have come to greet you on the distaff side. . . .

And now, Mr President, on behalf of my fellow councillors and citizens, I ask you to accept the honorary freedom of our city of Limerick. In our full recognition of the great honour you have done us in coming to visit us and in support of your distinguished leadership in aims vital, necessary, united and determined, may God bless you and your family. . . . I ask you, Mr President, to accept this scroll and casket which makes you a freeman, and gives you the freedom of the city of Limerick.

From press reports of the Limerick visit of John F. Kennedy, President of the United States, 30 June 1963

'Beautiful Women and Fast Horses'
John F. Kennedy

Mr Mayor, Clergy, Members of the City Council, fellow citizens of Limerick, I want to express my thanks and also my admiration for the best speech that I have heard since I came to Europe. I asked your distinguished Ambassador to the United States, Dr Kiernan, what is this county noted for, and he said it is noted for its beautiful women and its fast horses, and I said 'You say that about every county', and he said, 'No, this is true about this county.' I want to express my pleasure in seeing the Fitzgeralds — I wonder if they could stand up. . . .

This is a great country, with a great people, and I know that when I am back in Washington that I can, while I may not see you, I will see you in my mind, and feel all of your good wishes as we all will, in our hearts. Last night somebody sang a song which says, the words of which I am sure you know. 'Come back to Erin Mavourneen, Mavourneen, Come back Arue to the land of thy birth, Come with the shamrock in the springtime, Mavourneen.' This is not the land of my birth, but it is the land for which I hold the greatest affection. . . .

Last night, I sat next to one of the most extraordinary women, the wife of your President, who knows more about Ireland and Irish history, so I told her I was coming to Shannon and she immediately quoted this poem, and I wrote down the words, because I thought they were beautiful. ''Tis the Shannon's brightly glancing stream brightly gleaming, Silent in the morning beam, oh! the sight entrancing. Thus return from travels long, years of exile, years of pain to see old Shannon's face again, O'er the waters glancing.' Well, I am going to come back and see old Shannon's face again.

From press reports of the Limerick and Shannon Airport visits of John F. Kennedy, President of the United States, 30 June 1963

The Limerick Tumbler
Paul Hogan

In the early 1950s Michael McDonnell travelled to England with his good friends, Paddy and Imelda Lowe, to attend a bird show. While there, they met a man who bred the English Short-Faced Tumbling Pigeon (a bird so-called because of its peculiar, tumbling flight-pattern) and bought two pairs from him. At the time it was illegal to bring pigeons into Ireland from abroad, so the story goes that Imelda succeeded in smuggling the birds home by putting them down the leg of her drawers!

After almost thirty years of selective breeding, Michael McDonnell had changed the original species into a more 'showy' type of bird. Unfortunately, in 1986 his pigeon-loft was vandalised, and only two of the birds survived. Disheartened, Michael gave them away to someone, who in turn passed them on to me. I was very impressed by them and decided to enter them in the National Pigeon Show in Dublin. This was the first time that the birds were shown and the reaction was overwhelming, with breeders wondering what they were and where they could be obtained. Up to this point the breed was still nameless and so, because of their origin, I came up with the Limerick Short-Faced Tumbler, or the Limerick Tumbler for short. In 1989, it was officially recognised as a true breed and was given a class of its own at the national show. It is now highly sought after among breeders, with birds being exported to places as far afield as Scotland, Belgium and South Africa.

To the best of my knowledge, this is the first time that a breed of pigeon has been honoured by having music and dance commissioned in its name. On behalf of pigeon-fanciers everywhere, but especially breeders of the Limerick Tumbler — many thanks.

From the Programme of *The Limerick Tumblers*, a Celebration of New Irish Expressions in Music and Dance, University of Limerick Concert Hall, 26 September 1996

EIGHT

THE STAGE

Limerick Theatre in the 1770s
William Smith Clark

In 1768 Henry Mossop, the new manager of the combined Dublin theatres, transferred his touring company from Cork to Limerick on the last weekend of September and played at Peter's Cell until 29 October. This, his first, experience at the antiquated playhouse prompted him to think of improving Limerick's stage facilities in accord with the spirit of progress now pervading the city. Recent demolition of the old walls had made way for the extension of main thoroughfares and for the construction of new quays along the Abbey River: George's Quay (1763); the South Mall, later known as Charlotte's Quay (1766); and Sir Harry's Mall (1767). The introduction of handsome buildings commenced with the erection of the City Court House in 1764 and the Custom House in 1769. A year later the elegant Assembly House, containing shops on the ground floor and vaults underneath, was completed at a cost of £4,000. It stood towards the eastern end of Charlotte's Quay near the old West Water Gate of the Irish town. All these large edifices rose on the edge of Newtown Pery, a splendid tract of land owned by the Right Honourable Edmond Sexton Pery, son of a wealthy Limerick merchant and Speaker in the Irish House of Commons, in 1768. Pery, showing the vision of a modern city planner, laid out his ground in a design of broad straight streets, cutting across one another to form spacious blocks. Newspaper advertising of 1769 described the Newtown Pery sites in the picturesque style of eighteenth-century landscape painting that Irish stage settings of the time often copied:

> An extensive view up and down the river, commanding a full prospect of many agreeable objects, particularly the romantic grandeur of the County Clare mountains. — A large Cascade and spacious Basin alternately as the tide ebbs and flows. — All the shipping, etc. passing and repassing, and at the several Quays and the Pool. — The Ruins of Carrig O'Gunnell, etc. . . . In short, the most elegant Town Residence in the Kingdom, or perhaps in the World, cannot boast such rural Beauty or so fine a Landscape, and the Variety is daily increasing.

The rapid development of Newtown Pery into a district of handsome brick residences and shops for well-to-do mercantile families as well as for the gentry from the surrounding country beautified the face of Limerick to an extent which no Irish town other than Dublin enjoyed in the eighteenth century. . . .

No matter what local subscriptions may have been forthcoming in the autumn and winter of 1768, the grave difficulties which Mossop soon encountered in the management of his Dublin theatres made it impossible for him to carry on with the Limerick project. Within the next year and a half the Dublin manager sold his theatrical rights in Limerick to a native of that city, Tottenham Heaphy, who had been connected with the Irish stage for over twenty years. In the spring of 1770 Heaphy proceeded to erect a theatre, since he had secured £600 towards the venture from twenty-four subscribers, each of whom paid £25 for a silver transferable admission ticket valid indefinitely. The new building, located at the south-west corner of Cornwallis Street (now Gerald Griffin Street) and Playhouse Lane (now Little Gerald Griffin Street), presented in its inelegant appearance and arrangements a great contrast to the Assembly House finished a little earlier in the same year. Heaphy's structure lacked a conventional theatre facade with centre doors, because the forward section, abutting on Cornwallis Street, was designed for dwelling and business purposes. Edward Gubbins, noted carriage and coach builder, for years occupied these front premises. Access to the playhouse boxes could be gained only by a long and inconvenient passage that ran from Cornwallis Street through Gubbins's kitchen to the theatre in the rear. Often so many persons crowded together in this narrow corridor that it was very difficult, especially for ladies, to get out without being hurt. The entry leading to the pit door opened off Playhouse Lane; perhaps it survives in the small old passage on the west side of Little Gerald Griffin Street a short distance north of the corner. The theatre itself measured 80 feet by 40 feet wide, less than two-thirds the size of the Theatre Royal in Aungier Street, Dublin, built forty years before. It had a small stage in comparison with the area of the house and no green-room for the actors; but it did possess, adjoining one gallery, a second tier of side-boxes termed 'lattices' as in Dublin. The prices for seats Heaphy established at the prevailing Dublin scale: 4s. in the boxes and lattices, 2s. 6d. in the pit, and 1s. in the gallery.

As late as April of 1770 the old playhouse in Peter's Cell was still being used. *The Limerick Chronicle* carried advertisements of a performance to be given there on 14 April by an unnamed group of players, presumably local amateurs. Heaphy opened the new theatre in Cornwallis Street during the summer of 1770 either before or after his company's visit to Cork, 24 August to 6 September. The personnel, drawn mostly from Dublin, included besides Manager Heaphy and his wife, Mr and Mrs William Dawson, the youthful light comedian William Thomas Lewis, and Mrs Spranger Barry as the principal figures. Of their bills, none is on record; of their playing, a Limerick resident said 'tolerably decent'.

The following year Heaphy and many of 'His Majesty's Servants' from the Crow Street Theatre, Dublin, played Limerick before Cork. . . .

The new theatre did not wholly cure the Limerick audience of the unruly conduct in which it had so freely indulged at Peter's Cell. On Thursday, 10 October, *The Limerick Chronicle* took prominent space to express the public's appreciation 'to the gentlemen who corrected a most clamorous, indecent, troublesome young man in the Gallery of the playhouse last Tuesday night'. By now the local playgoers had invented a more subtle form of misbehaviour; they forged the special printed tickets which were issued in advance for the benefit nights of both individual actors and local charities. In connection with the end-of-season performance on behalf of Limerick's Poor a stern warning had to be published a day ahead that 'Mr Mayor has marked all the Tickets, and any Person who attempts to pass a Counterfeit one, will be severely punished.' Not only the customers but also the physical plan caused difficulties for Heaphy. The long, dark playhouse required constant attention. . . .

In 1772, Heaphy with most of the chief performers from Crow Street, Dublin, occupied 'the New Theatre Royal, Limerick', at the beginning of July. Soon afterwards an anonymous Limerick troublemaker berated the manager: 'Do you imagine a city so considerable will tacitly suffer such actors to mock so rational an amusement with impunity? . . . What greater indignity could you offer than bringing here that animal O'Keeffe, who dared to inscribe some indecent lines under a picture in a publican's at Monasterevan to the Ladies of Limerick?' This attack only succeeded in arousing a greater public interest in the local season. Business proved so good that the company did not leave for Cork until mid-August and then returned again for Assize Week, 14–19 September. In fact, the habit of playgoing had grown to such a point among the common people that prices for gallery seats were raised during the season another sixpence to 1s. 6d.

Even if irate letter writers did not prove disturbing, other matters did cause Heaphy concern. Numerous male patrons, as in Dublin and other towns, insistently desired to penetrate backstage. . . . At last the manager promised that 'for the future the Curtain will rise exactly at seven o'clock'. In return, the Limerick ladies and gentlemen were requested to send servants to keep places at five o'clock instead of the former hour of six.

From *The Irish Stage in the County Towns 1720 to 1800*, Oxford at the Clarendon Press, 1965

The Praises of Limerick
Dr MacDonnell

O! what a dainty, sweet, charming town Limerick is,
Where neither sly nor slippery slim trick is;
For true generosity, honour, fidelity,
Limerick's the town, ne'er doubt it — I tell it you.

Of smart pretty fellows in Limerick are numbers; some,
Who so modish are grown, that they think good sense cumbersome;
And, lest they should seem to be queer or ridiculous,
They affect not to value either God or old Nicholas.

You neighbours of Ennis, of Kerry, and Galway,
Whose characters justly are taken by all away,
Come hither among us, we'll make honest men of you,
For, in every respect, one of us is worth ten of you.

Though fame has given out our shopkeepers have a cant,
And in selling their goods they charge us extravagant;
Yet I, the other day, heard an honest man swear it,
That he never charged more than his conscience could bear it.

Our wives behind counters, not saucy nor slatterns are;
For meekness, politeness, and goodness, they patterns are;
It would do your heart good, on the mall where they walk at eve,
To see them so dressy, so flirtish, so talkative.

From *Anthologia Hibernica*, 3 February 1793, reprinted in *Popular Songs of Ireland*, collected by Thomas Crofton Croker, George Routledge and Sons, 1886

A Thespian Society
William Griffin

Beside the beauty of its scenery, Adare had other advantages. Being within 10 miles of Limerick, he (Gerald Griffin) was enabled frequently to consult such works as his taste inclined him to, and had opportunities of meeting there occasionally, persons whose pursuits were similar to his own. It was in Limerick he first met his friend Mr Banim, who afterwards, by many important services in London, proved the warmth and deep sincerity of his attachment. Mr Banim was then in the commencement of his literary labours, and was, I believe, scarcely yet known to the world. There was a Thespian Society established at the time in Limerick, which consisted of several respectable young men of the city, assisted by two or three professional persons. They used to perform two or three times a week, and the receipts were applied to charitable purposes. During his occasional visits to the city, Mr Banim was accustomed to write critiques on their performances, under the signature of 'A Traveller', which displayed considerable knowledge of the stage, and from the superiority of their style attracted very general attention. It was during the progress of these that he became acquainted with Gerald, who had the highest admiration of his talent, and who, young as he was, was excited by his literary tastes to similar attempts. . . .

Up to this time, the passion for literature which had been gradually growing upon him, had only shown itself by the intense interest he took in the poets, especially in dramatic poetry, and in the production of occasional short pieces, such as I have noticed, together with others which were principally of a pastoral character, but now it developed itself so strongly, that all idea of the medical profession was entirely given up; he became very fond of theatricals, and soon began to occupy himself in writing tragedies. I am uncertain whether he completed any regular piece at this period, at least if he did, none of them came under the observation of the elders of the family. He used, however, with the assistance of some of his cousins, to enact scenes from those he wrote; and on one occasion, when it was necessary to poison one of the characters, he made a niece of his, who played the heroine, drink off a glass of infusion of quassia, in order, probably, to deprive her of all pretext for hypocrisy in the contortions of visage that were to usher in death.

From *The Life of Gerald Griffin, By His Brother*, James Duffy, 1857

The Colleen Bawn
Julius Benedict

It is a charming girl I love, she comes from Garryowen;
She's gentler than the turtle dove, her hair is brown and flowing!
Her eye is of the softest blue, her breath as sweet as morning dew,
Her step is lighter than the fawn, and 'Och', she's called the Colleen Bawn,
Botheration, botheration, her likeness I never shall see;
There is but one Colleen Bawn, and she does not love me!

You asked me what I'm looking for, then listen to the sequel: —
The Colleen Bawn I'll love no more when I can find her equal;
Mayhap now such a girl is here with step as light, with eye as clear,
Ah, she'll be welcome as the dawn although she's not the Colleen Bawn,
Botheration, botheration, her likeness I never shall see!
There is but one Colleen Bawn, and she does not love me!

From *The Lily of Killarney*, first produced in 1862; from the Stephen O'Shea music collection

The Royal Albert Saloon
Julius Rodenberg

I proceeded to the Royal Hotel, where I intended to rest. As I sat down to my dinner I felt as if I had been walking through centuries, I seemed to myself so old, so grey, so superannuated, like a man returning from the other shore. . . . Cruise's coffee-room was arranged on the English model. The waiters were stiff and grand, although the green island peeped out at times at their elbows, or through some treacherous holes. Gas-lights were burning and striving to display their brilliancy through dusty globes as well as they could. Wearied travellers were seated at tables, like myself, and shouting for newspapers, very few of which were to be had. My dinner was in the meanwhile brought in under covers, as in England; but the peculiar tricks the cook plays in this way, both with the hunger and imagination of the diner, were not so pleasantly terminated as is the case there. The fish was half raw, and red; the joint — mutton, of course — was uneatable from the opposite fault. The mutton patriotism becomes, from this point westward, always more and more opposed to the demand a well-regulated stomach must make for a reasonable variety. At last, you rise with mutton, and go to bed with mutton, and the whole world seems to exhale a smell of mutton. Wherever I looked and felt, the same discomfort; the porter bottles were badly corked, the cheese was utterly decayed, and the butter was ornamented with bread-crumbs; the plates and dishes were strongly plated, on the other hand, and the waiters' cravats of the most aristocratic stiffness. Fortunately, my appetite was not alarming, and I was soon out again, with a cigar between my lips.

It was Saturday evening, and George-street was extremely animated. This street is the promenade of Limerick, and by the light of the gas-lamps — which burnt here at very considerable intervals — the promenading crowd walked up and down. A few ladies in crinolines, a few gentlemen in hats — but the majority of the women walked about with naked feet, and the men wore tail-coats and torn trousers, the national costume of Ireland. In the cellars things went on jollily enough. In one of them — a store and a barber's at once — one sat at the door being shaved by gas-light, while another was drinking whiskey. In other cellars roasting and baking for the Sunday were going on, and producing a far from agreeable smell. Limerick looked far more cheerful and lively by night than by day. It seems as if the Irish, after the fashion of nervous men, only awake to a consciousness and use of their strength with the first evening lights. Women sat at the street corners selling fruit and potatoes, and little girls with black hair and southern faces lay on the pavement asleep, fantastically illumined by the flickering flame of the torches. Here and again, a member of the Irish constabulary was posted, in his shako and black tail-coat, and gradually the watchmen also made their appearance with their long sticks.

But between the first evening light and the long sticks of the watchmen lay a peculiar pleasure which I was to enjoy. I had naively looked about and inquired for something that would fill up the idle portion of the evening. There was certainly a theatre in Limerick, but there were no actors. Places of amusement, in our sense, must not be looked for in Ireland; but at last I heard of the 'Royal Albert Saloons', in which concerts took place every night. I had, I grant, lost confidence in all 'Royal' things in Ireland, still I decided on not leaving this sole place of public amusement in Limerick — for such it proved — unvisited. I certainly had trouble enough in finding it: some declared that they knew nothing about it, while others knew its name and position in the most general way. At length I was directed to Arthur's Quay.

Here, by the water-side, matters were tolerably lively. Several vessels lay close to the wharf, and only a few lights from the shore lit up their tackling. There was a sea smell when turning towards it, and a herring smell on looking landwards. All, therefore, kept to its element. The sailors seemed to be roaming about; they lounged in their tarry jackets against the posts, or lay on the steps of the subterraneous whiskey shops. They smoked and laughed and talked, while barefooted boys were playing among the piled-up casks and ships' ropes. A gas-lamp, with broken panes — the only one visible — flickered restlessly in the breeze, and before one of the houses on the quay a tar fire burned in a dish. I was directed to this house when I asked for the 'Royal Albert'. In front of the house was the ordinary public, with its doors opening on the street. The saloons were in the yard. In royal matters it is allowable to talk in the plural; in everyday life the 'Saloons', however, were nothing more than a wretched dirty hole, filled with smoke and stench; in the background a species of stage, below it a place for the common folk, above, a far from secure gallery for the gentry. Of such there were three or four present besides myself. They appeared travellers, like myself, but more probably for commercial reasons. Of travellers for amusement there was at this time only one in Limerick, possibly in all Ireland, and that was I. In the room sat about ten men at nailed-down tables. They represented the people, smoked long clay-pipes, and filled the intervals with curses, because they broke so often in their mouths. Matters were managed in a free-and-easy style here, I must confess. A lady came to meet me, when I entered the gentlemen's gallery, and what a lady! She was the prima donna of the 'Royal Albert', and wore a large flowered cotton dress, and a tin diadem on her brow. She was past those years in which prima donnas are wont to be dangerous, and seemed to have experienced the joys and sorrows of life in every shape. She offered me her hand, and led me to a wooden chair; she then mixed hot whiskey and water with brown sugar, and had no objection, when I asked her to drink the mixture.

In the meanwhile, the singing had begun, most of the songs in a primitive condition, without accompaniment, some with the orchestra. This consisted of a violin soloist, at whose performance the gentlemen's hair of the gallery audience stood on end; and, on specially solemn occasions, a boy came forward, who treated us to the piano. Most of the notes of this unhappy instrument no longer struck, and the boy, whom I had seen not long before chasing others at the water-side, had no idea of the sweet science. The former did no harm, and the latter was not needed; for the violinist pointed out to the boy, before the beginning of each piece, two keys, which, at an agreed-on nod, he had to strike incessantly till the end. According to his master's hints, he struck them slower, quicker, softer, or louder, sometimes with both thumbs, and then, when these had grown tired, for a variation, with the two middle fingers.

The time arrived when the prima donna was compelled to leave us. She went downstairs into the lower room, and her garments rustled between the tables. The rustling certainly sounded like calico, but the more aristocratic was her carriage, the more proudly did the tin diadem flash. She did not deign a glance to the mob of ten; and her eye, her smile, her heart, were directed to the five 'gentlemen'. The violinist had pointed out the two keys to the boy, and the latter sat, afraid of losing them, with outstretched fingers and half-turned face, that he, too, might notice her first appearance on the boards. At length she stepped forth, and stepped so heavily that the thin framework of boards grumbled, and the boy in his fright lost the two keys he had hitherto pressed. The maestro first gave the boy a box on the ears, and showed him the lost keys once more; then he passed the bow over the strings, while she employed her handkerchief. Then she began singing: it was the song of 'Bonnie Dundee', the dauntless Highland chief, and his tartan bonnets. It is a Scottish song, and the mountain daring of the Highland clan is recorded in the peculiar, abrupt melody. But what did the Limerick prima donna make of this song! Oh, Lord! With her shrill soprano voice she marched into the field against harmony and bravery, and they, with Bonnie Dundee, and fiddle, and piano, fled from it in dismay. It is true that the boy tried to make a fight of it for a while with his thumbs, but the two notes grew gradually weaker and more undecided, and at length died out in a help-less whine. The violinist, too, attempted in vain what a powerful bow could do against a prima donna. It was of no use, she kept her position, and arm, bow, and violin sank, wearied to death. It was a life and death struggle for the hegemony in the kingdom of false notes, and flight was the only chance of salvation. But her tartan bonnets and the thunder of applause from the ten of the people and the four gentry, under which the Valkyre of song seemed to quit the battle-field, pursued me through two streets.

The Sunday bells awoke me next morning. It was a rainy day, cold and uncom-fortable. I shivered all over in the dark, gloomy bedroom allotted to me. I had put on my over-coat, and yet shivered. I felt as if a world and an eternity lay between me and the golden season of the lakes. All had changed, all had another colour, another tone. Poor, bare, naked, all seemed to have been submerged in dirt and irregularity. My window offered a prospect of Arthur's Quay and the Shannon. In spite of the piercing cold of the autumn morning the river was crowded with men and horses bathing together: and that took place in front of the most fashionable and lively streets in Limerick; and on the quay stones the men performed their toilet, while the horses coolly shook off the water drops. No one who has not witnessed it can form an idea of such a state of nature. It is almost as if the wild inhabitants of Ireland, who, according to Giraldus, had goats' beards and bulls' feet, and, accord-ing to Bernard of Cirencester, smeared their bodies with blood, had risen from their peat graves to bathe in the Shannon in the foggy October morning, in ridicule of the Sunday propriety and George-street. At the same time, all these men looked ugly rather than otherwise: their faces were flattened, their features coarse, their build disagreeable. A fable about the prettiness of the 'Limerick lasses' certainly runs through all guide-books, and a French tourist, in no way distinguished for his politeness to Ireland, not even for his compliment to the Limerick ladies, says 'that they are more remarkable for great beauty than their husbands are for good sense'. But my *Picturesque Tourist* was the only place where I saw anything of this belauded beauty.

The streets were wretched enough; the Sunday and the Sunday clothes even produced no material change in them. In all its classes the people was shabby and poverty-stricken, as usual. There was not a trace of the comfort, pious monotony, and religious retirement of an English Sunday. Trade went on in the streets as on any week-day, and though the large shops of the English in George-street were closed, the women stood at the corners with apples and plums, and cabbage and fish, and the retail trade, which always produces the greatest and most disagreeable noise, filled the low districts and the cellars.

From A *Pilgrimage through Ireland or the Island of the Saints*, Charles Griffin and Co., 1860

Limerick is Beautiful
Anonymous

Oh, Limerick is beautiful, as everybody knows;
The River Shannon full of fish beside the city flows.
'Tis not the river, nor the fish, that preys upon my mind,
Nor with the town of Limerick have I any fault to find.

Oh, the girl I love is beautiful, and fairer than the dawn,
She lives in Garryowen, and she's called the Colleen Bawn,
But proudly as the river flows beside the fair city,
As proudly, and without a word, that colleen goes by me.

Oh, if I was the Emperor of Russia to command,
If I was Julius Caesar, or Lord Lieutenant of the land,
I'd give my fleet, my golden store, I'd give up my army,
The horse, the rifle, and the foot, and the Royal Artillery.

I'd give my fleet of sailing ships that range the briny seas,
I'd give the crown from off my head, my people on their knees,
A beggar I would go to bed and proudly rise at dawn,
If by my side, all for a bride, I found the Colleen Bawn.

From the *Labour Party National Conference Magazine*, April 1997

A Country Concert

One of those admirably arranged concerts, which in country localities are so difficult of arrangement, came off on the evening of Thursday last at Ballingarry. It was,
we believe, originally at the suggestion both of the Protestant rector and the
Roman Catholic parish priest that the matter first had its origin, and it is gratifying
to perceive that combining upon the broad basis of Christian charity the efforts of
these gentlemen to raise a fund for the poor of the locality have been crowned with
no ordinary success.

The weird old building known as Grove House, in which for a considerable
number of years, anterior to the erection of the present beautiful Roman Catholic
church, the usual religious services were held, was beautifully decorated for the
occasion by Captain and Mrs Wilkinson, Mr and Mrs Moroney and Mrs and Miss
Atkinson. This large room is capable of holding from 700 to 800 persons.

Miss Massy of Stoneville presided at the piano with her usual skill and effect.

The concert opened with an exquisite chorus, the 'Spring Song' (Pinsuti), which
gave evidence of what was to follow. 'Come into the garden Maud' was exceedingly
happily rendered by Mr McCallum, Bruff, whose sweet tenor voice was in admirable
condition.

Mr C.B. Barrington, who was enthusiastically received by the audience, then
gave 'Cleansing Fires' with happy effect, after which was rendered in most exquisite
style, two Orpheas Glees — 'The Chapel' and 'Evening', sung by Mr C. McCallum,
Mr W. Hall, B.E., Mr D. Tidmarsh and Mr D. Purcell.

'The Reason Why', a charming song rendered by Mrs Furnell, elicited deserved
applause, as did 'She Wore a Wreath of Roses', delivered by Mr Herbert Sullivan.

Of a duet, 'Of Fairy Wand' (Maritana), sung by Mrs Hall and Mr Tidmarsh, we
cannot speak in terms sufficiently eulogistic. 'Hail Smiling Morn' (Spoffort), chorus
from 'HMS Pinafore' (Sullivan), 'The Village Choristers' (Mochelles), and 'You
Stole My Love' (McFarren) was in strict truth the happiest effort of the evening.

A duet by Miss Dennehy and Mr Kearney 'Ie'l Ramenti', was also everything
that could be desired, nor must we omit mentioning the rendering of 'The Village
Blacksmith' by Mr D. Tidmarsh, or the comic effects of 'Mediane Jack' by R. Hill.
'The Pinafore' chorus closed the first part of the programme.

The second part opened with an admirable chorus, 'Village Choristers', which
was followed by a song given in no amateur style by Miss Wilkinson. This lady we
seldom have heard in more perfect voice than upon this occasion.

Substituting 'The Diver' for 'The Bedouin Love Song', Mr D. Purcell made one of
his happiest and best appreciated 'hits' of it. Subsequently Mrs Furnell and Mr
Sullivan, in a beautiful duet, 'When the Wind Bloweth', produced a charming effect.

That most spirited of pieces, 'Let Me Like a Soldier Fall', was done more than
amateur justice to by Mr R.R. Kennedy, RM, following which we were again
gratified to receive from Miss Dennehy 'His Home Across the Sea'. Mr Barrington
gave with splendid compass and power 'Saved from the Storm'.

'O Erin My Country', charmingly rendered by Miss Browne, is deserving very high eulogium, and was evidently much appreciated. A comic song by Mr D. Browning brought the agreeable evening to a close.

We must not forget to add that ample refreshments were provided for the amateurs at the expense of several local gentlemen, so that the entire proceeds of this most successful of concerts, which amount to a considerable sum, will be allocated to the poor of the district.

From *The Limerick Chronicle*, 20 January 1880

Where the River Shannon Flows
John L. Russell

There is a pretty spot in Ireland,
I always claim for my land
Where the fairies and the blarney,
Will never ever die,
It's the land of the shillelagh,
My heart goes back there daily,
To the girl I left behind me,
When we kissed and said good-bye.

Where the dear old Shannon's flowing,
Where the three-leaved shamrock grows,
Where my heart is I am going,
To my little Irish Rose,
And the moment that I meet her,
With a hug and kiss I'll greet her,
For there's not a colleen sweeter,
Where the River Shannon flows.

There's a letter I'll be mailing,
For soon I will be sailing,
And I'll bless the ship that takes me,
To my dear old Erin's shore,
There I'll settle down for ever,
I'll leave the old sod never,
And I'll whisper to my sweetheart,
'Come and take my name asthore.'

From the Joe Neiland music collection

'The Catch of the Season'
Kate O'Brien

I remember that when I was a child some amateurs ambitiously played *The Catch of The Season* in the Theatre Royal in Limerick. It was a stupendous success and we ageing creatures can talk with pleasure of it still. My eldest brother played 'the Catch' and was so much more attractive and goodlooking than poor Seymour Hicks could ever have tried to be that it was unfair; and my eldest sister was one of the glamorous chorus of twelve 'Gibson Girls'. Only a few of us now, sitting in the shade, can remember the style and type of those Dana Gibson heads and figures that were everywhere, on magazine covers, on postcards and pinned up in our brothers' rooms — but they were a very chic and romantically sweet ideal of the time — and the twelve who were picked from among the débutantes of Limerick to personify them were, one thought, stunning, perfection. 'We realise the pictures, tall and divinely fair . . .' I can hear the twelve singing away — and divinely fair they were.

But here's my point. We can all allow for local enthusiasm when it is a matter of amateur theatricals — and Limerick was, I think, that winter beglamoured by its *Catch of The Season* — but there is an old photograph somewhere of those Gibson Girls in their great hats and long robes, and one can see little in it now but faded youth and absurdity — unless you can name each one by her own Limerick name, and so remember her as in fact she was in daily life. And each of those girls truly was, by any standard anywhere, of exceptional beauty. To the names the faces — many vanished now — come back in their flower — and one is surprised to realise that our chorus of twelve was in face far more beautiful than we were able to understand. And if twelve could be picked to that quality of beauty out of one little social set, they remind us of many more among their friends and sisters who were beautiful too. And that old photograph has always seemed to me a good argument for the standard of female handsomeness in Limerick. So I do not contradict the old saying now . . . merely I observe that the girls there seem nowadays very pretty indeed and the men look fine, to match.

From *My Ireland*, B.T. Batsford Ltd, 1962

Ballinamona
Anonymous

In the sweet County Limerick one cold winter's night,
Oh the turf fires were burning when I first saw the light,

And a crazy old midwife went tipsy with joy,
As she danced round the floor with her slip of a boy
Singing *Bainne an bo is na gamhna*,
And the juice of the barley for me.

When I was a young lad of eight years or so,
With my turf and my primer to school I did go,
To a dirty old schoolhouse without any door,
And the schoolmaster lying dead drunk on the floor.

At booklearnin' I wasn't a genius I'm thinkin',
But soon I could beat the schoolmaster at drinkin',
At wakes and at weddings for nine miles around,
In a corner blind drunk I was sure to be found.

Till one morning the priest read me out from the altar,
And said I would end all my days in a halter,
I'd dance a merry jig between Heaven and Hell,
And his words they did scare me the truth I now tell.

So the very next morning my way I did make,
Along to the vestry the pledge for to take,
I peeped in the window saw three priests in a bunch,
'Round a great roarin' fire drinkin' tumblers of punch.

So from that day to this I have lived all alone,
Jack of all trades and master of none,
The sky is me roof, the earth is me floor,
And I'll spend all me days drinkin' poteen galore.

From the *Labour Party National Conference Magazine*, April 1997

A Season in Limerick
Carolyn Swift

Not long after the Shaw Season finished in the Gaiety, a young couple approached
Alan Simpson. They explained that they had been left the sum of £200 in the will
of some relative and wished to use it to found a professional theatre company in
their native city of Limerick.

Even in those days, £200 was a ludicrously inadequate sum — just how ludicrous
can be seen by the fact that it was less than twenty-nine weeks' salary for the Gate

stage-director. Clearly, Alan should have pointed this out to them but, in fairness to him, he probably never stopped to think about it because, for him, it was an answer to prayer. . . . Alan told Ward Lloyd and Catherine Wainwright that he would get together a first-class company with himself as producer and myself as stage-manager. Ward and Catherine had both had amateur acting experience and were as interested in playing roles on stage as they were in playing at being a theatrical management for, having no idea of the worries and responsibilities involved in this most risky of businesses, that was really what they were doing.

Thus, with them and myself to cover the smaller roles, Alan set about collecting leading players. Here his experience with the Gate came in useful, for he was friendly with many talented young people who had worked for Edwards-Mac Liammóir, but were often out of work for long periods. . . . From these sources, he assembled such people as Daphne Carroll, Denis Brennan and Barry Cassin. From Radio Éireann he lured the late Una Collins. . . . Alan then set about picking his repertoire. This was to consist of a G.B. Shaw (*Arms and the Man*), an Oscar Wilde (*An Ideal Husband*), a Séan O'Casey (*The Plough and the Stars*) and an English thriller, recently successful on the West End stage (*Uncle Harry* by Thomas Job). It was decided that these would all have a few initial rehearsals in Dublin and then be given a week's rehearsal each in Limerick, so that while one play was running the second would be rehearsed. In other words, it was to be the old system of weekly rep., with the advantage that, prior to the week's rehearsal given to play no. 1, plays 2, 3 and 4 would at least have the moves mapped out so that the cast could start to work on their lines knowing the moves that would accompany them. If the first four weeks were successful, other plays would be added in due course. . . .

As designer, Alan engaged Gene Martin, now well known as a radio producer with RTE and, as acting stage-carpenter, Gerald FitzGerald, whose son Jim was afterwards to become well known as a producer. As a final touch, Alan persuaded Cyril Cusack to appear as guest artist for one week as Bluntschli in *Arms and the Man*, a part for which he was already famous. I am sure Cyril appeared for a very nominal fee, but how anyone ever imagined that a company of this size and calibre could be launched and maintained until it was established on a sum of £200 is a total mystery.

The first task was to inspect the venue and Alan, Gene Martin and I set off for Limerick. The theatre was the Playhouse, home at that time of the College Players, the highly successful local amateur group. It belonged to, and was at the back of the O'Connell Street offices of, the Irish Transport and General Workers' Union, but has since been destroyed by fire.

We measured the dimensions of the stage and noted all the facilities and lack of them. We also made contact with the Players, arranging that some of their members would, as was then the custom for Dublin companies visiting the provinces, play small roles in any play which had a cast too large to be filled by members of our own company. Before the day was out, we had already established our unofficial headquarters in Gleeson's pub, on the corner almost opposite the ITGWU office.

Needing to stay overnight, we put up at Cruise's Hotel. In 1947 this hotel was very different from what it is today, although the exterior has changed little, apart from being repainted. In those days it was cheap, old-fashioned and used mainly by commercial travellers; and the only accommodation they could offer us was a double room with a single leading from it. Given the quite Victorian approach to such matters in Ireland at the time, particularly in Limerick, we were somewhat taken aback, but in the end Alan and Gene took the double room, through which I had to pass to reach my own. No doubt our acceptance of this offer caused a few raised eyebrows and I was ill at ease until we left next morning. But by the time the company arrived in Limerick, we had thrown caution to the winds and, on the advice of Ward and Pat, Alan and I booked into a double room in a seedy little hotel in Catherine Street called Commercial. . . .

The Mercury Theatre Company, as we decided to call ourselves, opened at the Playhouse on 26 May 1947, with *Uncle Harry*. I can no longer remember why we should have chosen to start with the least prestigious of our plays, but I daresay there was a reason, perhaps connected with Cyril Cusack's availability for *Arms and the Man* the following week.

The *Limerick Leader* drama critic commented on 'the sparse attendance', but added: 'The show is worthy of an overflow attendance and before the week ends bookings should show a big improvement.' He was an optimist. They did nothing of the kind. After the snows of January and February, a sudden heatwave arrived in May and what seemed like the whole population of Limerick headed off each evening to the mill race to disport itself in the river or on its banks.

Moreover, there was distinct customer-resistance to the fact that we had increased the price of seats from that charged for local amateur productions, from 2s. 6d. to 3s. 6d. (or $12^1/_2$p to $17^1/_2$p). When I pointed out that it cost more to stage a professional production, since the cast had to be paid, and that it was surely not too much to ask for an extra shilling to see actors like Cyril Cusack, I was told: 'The Limerick players are very good too, you know!'

This, however, was not the attitude of the local drama critics, who could hardly have done more to encourage audiences to support us, the *Limerick Leader* repeating yet again at the close of the long double column notice of *Uncle Harry*: 'It is altogether a great show, worthy of the patronage of all local devotees of the art.' More important to me was the fact that the *Limerick Leader* also wrote that 'the Mercury Theatre Company did an excellent bit of business when they secured a brilliant cast and a gifted producer in Alan Simpson, former stage manager for Hilton Edwards-Micheál Mac Liammóir Company', while *The Limerick Chronicle* said: 'Alan P. Simpson must be congratulated on his production and lighting. These were treated with strong individuality and careful attention.' . . .

Arms and the Man brought even more enthusiastic notices, but the audiences remained thin. The *Limerick Leader*, under its heading 'Cusack brilliant in *Arms and the Man*' said:

The spell of fine weather that has come to our shores must be considered as the deterrent which has deprived the Playhouse of full houses since last night week. What other thing could it be? The Mercury Theatre Company has brought to Limerick an array of outstanding personalities and is providing a treat in stage entertainment. . . . One feels beggared to describe the magnificence with which a great cast treats Shaw's easy-flowing wit. . . . Alan P. Simpson again showed his genius by his adept direction of both production and lighting. . . .

Our third week at the Playhouse was climactic. *The Limerick Chronicle* reported:

At one period last night during the performance of *The Plough and the Stars* by the Mercury Theatre Company, the action of the play was completely held up, so great was the enthusiasm of the audience. . . . We have come to expect good effects from this company and . . . neither the staging nor the lighting last night could be surpassed. It was an achievement in itself to present four totally dissimilar settings and the lighting of the fourth act was a treat to watch. . . . We again offer congratulations to Alan Simpson for a scintillating production, with full knowledge of the difficulties which had to be overcome to make this the memorable performance it was.

Everyone was praised: Barry Cassin in 'a star performance' as the Covey; Una Collins 'excellent' as Mrs Gogan; Patricia Kennedy 'brilliant as the inimitable Bessie Burgess'; Daphne Carroll 'deeply moving' as Nora Clitheroe; Denis Brennan 'solid and convincing' as Fluther Good; Ian Sainsbury 'surmounted many of the pitfalls' as Jack Clitheroe; James Gould (of the College Players) 'very effective' as Uncle Peter; Catherine Wainwright 'impressed' as Rosie Redmond; Lister Skelton 'a brilliant shaft of light' as Corporal Stoddart; and Gerald FitzGerald 'made Sergeant Tinley a very credible character'. And 'minor roles were capably filled by Ward Lloyd, Kevin Larkin, Andy Butler and Cyril Gallivan' (the last three being members of the College Players, who had also provided Kevin Dinneen as a Glee Club member in *Uncle Harry*).

From *Stage by Stage*, Poolbeg Press, 1985

Sive Storms the Playhouse
Gus Smith and Des Hickey

Limerick was ill prepared for the arrival of *Sive*. The tiny Playhouse Theatre, which housed the Féile Luimní productions, was taxed to its limit of 200 seats on St

Patrick's night. Keane and his friends had to push their way through the crowds in the narrow laneway to get to the theatre. When the doors were firmly shut at 7.30, half an hour before curtain up, more than one hundred people were outside, clamouring for admittance.

P.J. (Paddy) Fitzgibbon, a local journalist and playwright, was demanding angrily of a priest to let him through. 'I'm an Abbey playwright,' he protested. 'You must let me in!' Fitzgibbon and his colleagues were eventually admitted to the auditorium through the O'Connell Street entrance but, to their chagrin, were told they must stand in the wings because there were no seats in the auditorium.

Gardaí were called to avert a confrontation in the laneway as hotheads tried to fight their way into the theatre. The growing reputation of *Sive* was creating problems not normally associated with festival occasions. 'We were all caught up in the excitement,' said Keane. 'The Playhouse was simply too small to cater for everybody.' Yet the cramped size of the theatre only added to the atmosphere, ensuring that the audience missed nothing. The terrifying beat of the bodhrán filled every corner and each word was clearly heard. At the final curtain, there was prolonged applause and stamping of feet. Keane stood applauding the cast as the adjudicator, the broadcaster H.L. (Harry) Morrow, appealed for calm.

Morrow told the audience, 'I am still staggering from this prodigious play and its equally prodigious production by Brendan Carroll. There is no question of it being the play and the production of the Féile. I shall be very much surprised if it doesn't prove itself to be the play and the production of the year in drama festivals all over the country, and it will be more than interesting to see how it fares at Athlone, for which I have no hesitation in nominating it.' . . .

Having paid tribute to the producer and the cast, Morrow remarked, 'I do not salute the management of the Abbey who, I am told, had the stupidity and impertinence to reject the manuscript of this play without a word of explanation or apology. I despair!'

To seasoned Limerick playgoers it seemed absurd that *Sive* was being hawked around the amateur circuit before it could gain national recognition; in their opinion it should have been accepted by the Abbey and so given the young playwright the spur he badly needed. It was these same playgoers who roundly applauded H.L. Morrow's stricture of the Abbey management. Some people wondered if, in the long run, a festival success would be the best thing for Keane, for it would not help him learn craftsmanship or technique.

Amid the euphoria in the auditorium Keane could hardly hear Morrow's words. It was to be another night of celebration after the event. The adjudicator gave the premier award to Listowel.

From *John B: The Real Keane*, Mercier Press, 1992

Where the River Shannon Meets the Sea
Anonymous

Tho' my feet are planted in a far off land,
There is somewhere they would rather be,
Faith, 'tis firmly planted in the dark brown sand
Where the Shannon River meets the sea.

My heart is e'er returning to my darling,
Whose blue eyes mean all the world to me;
Sure 'tis heaven and someone placed an angel there
Where the Shannon River meets the sea.

Tho' my father told me other lands were fair,
I'm afraid with him I can't agree;
For I always long to breathe the scented air,
Where the Shannon River meets the sea.

There are no lips so sweet and so beguiling
As the lips that sure belong to me:
Tho' I go on roaming, faith, my heart remains
Where the Shannon River meets the sea.

From the Stephen O'Shea music collection

Terry Wogan
Gus Smith

Terry Wogan has gone out of his way to facilitate the press. Millions of words have been written about him, most of them complimentary, some bizarre, others banal. 'You can't be loved by everybody,' sighs Terry philosophically. Yet many have found the private Terry a replica of the public image. . . . There was the priest-columnist from Ireland who visited his dressing-room at the BBC Television Theatre in Shepherd's Bush and tackled Terry in the nicest way imaginable about the state of his religious beliefs in 1986. Few, if any of the Fleet Street people, had thought up that one. . . . The irony in this particular case was that the priest would be published in an Irish Sunday tabloid that more resembled the *Sun* than the *Universe*. Wogan, the priest noted, was 'embarrassed by his question. He gave a nervous little laugh. It was obviously a question he hoped I wouldn't ask.'

But Terry, who is never lost for a word, confessed that he was brought up in a good Irish Catholic family. 'I have difficulty in believing in the existence of God and I'm not a terrific supporter of religion. That doesn't mean I'm against religion or that I have no religion.'

As they talked, it struck the priest that Terry had rejected an image of God rather than rejecting God. 'There is too much goodness, too much decency in the man to call him irreligious.'

Terry's confession wasn't finished, 'When I was growing up, we were always told that faith meant you had an unquestioning belief. I have never accepted that kind of faith since I was about 16 years old. I still find it hard to think of myself as a non-believer and yet I know I am not a believer in any accepted sense. I'm at best an agnostic.' . . .

He was cheerful and responsible whenever he was confronted by the press and continued to give three or four interviews every week. Some of the writers went away disappointed; they had sought to find chinks in the Wogan armour; instead they discovered few flaws. He wasn't, as far as they could discern a hypochondriac, insomniac, puritan, hellraiser, bisexual, drug addict, cynic, conceited, temperamental, manic depressive, woman fancier, or a bombast. Nor did he possess those self-destructive characteristics that made Brendan Behan notorious. The guy was simply normal. He was happily married and regarded his glamorous career as just another job to be done. He liked a drink but wouldn't run a mile for a bottle of stout; he liked good food and good wine but swore to all and sundry he wasn't a glutton.

There was a story told in Fleet Street that a hardened news editor of a tabloid was furious with a young woman reporter who came back from an interview with Terry and said she could not find warts on Terry. 'Ridiculous!' boomed the news editor. 'There must be warts on the fellow. Everybody's got warts somewhere. Don't tell me Wogan is an exception.'

'There are none,' reiterated the reporter.

'Ask his wife, ask his doctor,' bellowed the news editor. 'I tell you there must be warts.' . . .

Limerick humour is at once warm, hurtful and mischievous and practical jokers abound; where sport and commerce transcend art; where the rugby deeds of Tom Clifford, Gordon Wood and Ginger McLoughlin are more likely to be remembered than the novels of Limerick authors, Kate O'Brien and Gerald Griffin, or the operatic achievements of tenor Joseph O'Mara and diva Catherine Hayes. A pretty place of water and spires, fitting Bernard Levin's essentials for the picturesque city, small or big — water, spires and heart. . . . Maligned, misunderstood, often uninviting to the outsider, yet treasured by its citizens. . . . An engaging place in summer as boat crews practise on the River Shannon for regattas; a place where poverty and wealth live . . . side by side, where Catholics and Jews and Protestants enjoy games of golf together. A city that has grown more tolerant with each passing decade. . . . It was here in a quiet, unobtrusive terraced house, 18 Elm Park, that Michael Terence Wogan was born on an August day — the 3rd — in the year 1938. No church bells pealed out over the city to mark the occasion. Nor did his name appear in the births columns of the national or local newspapers. Like other babies born in Limerick on that day, he arrived unheralded and unsung. He was the first child born to Michael and Rose Wogan and his arrival brought great joy to his parents, his father in particular being thrilled that the baby was a boy.

Elm Park is a respectable middle-class area situated a mile or so from the city centre and skirting the main road to Shannon Airport. Wogan senior worked as manager of a city grocery store, Leverett and Fry, but couldn't afford a car, so he cycled to his work. . . .

Life in Limerick was relatively quiet. On the previous day, 2 August, there had been car races around the streets, otherwise the citizens were more concerned about holidays. Traditionally, it is a month when thousands of Limerick people go to the County Clare seaside resort of Kilkee for two weeks' vacation, turning the resort into a miniature Limerick. The more well-off Limerick people have their summer houses there. Because of the birth of their first child, the Wogans decided to take no holidays that month.

They had already decided to call their son Michael Terence Wogan. He was a healthy baby and caused his mother little trouble. When young Wogan was 6 years old a second child was born and he was named Brian. By now Michael Terence was attending the Salesian nuns. . . . At the age of 8 he was sent to Crescent College which was then located in the city centre. The college catered for the sons of middle-class and professional people and was labelled 'snobbish' by some Limerick citizens who had their sons at the Christian Brothers. The Crescent had a good academic reputation and a fine sports tradition. The Jesuits ran a strict school where discipline was the letter of the law. They gave the boys 'lots to do and you were expected to do your homework efficiently and have it in time'. . . . Young Wogan was studious and invariably had his homework ready for inspection each day. . . . He continued to show his innate flair for the English language with the result that his essays were always amongst the best.

Today, Terry Wogan recalls with a certain pleasure those early days of his life in Limerick: 'It was a very happy fourteen years. I was glad I experienced it, very glad I was born in Limerick, because the city has a kind of individuality. I suppose anyone who comes from a small place thinks it has. I liked Limerick. I made a lot of friends there; they were important years for me, the formative years of my life. I liked Crescent College.'

Discussing the Jesuits and their influence, if any, on his early life, he reflected: 'I don't think, though they made a lasting impression on me, I never found them to be particularly impressive or indeed to live up to the reputation they had with some people. Perhaps it was an advantage for me being at a day school where we hadn't them all the time. However, I found the Jesuits good teachers and I did like my particular teachers. My early life was, I suppose, made up of sport and education. . . . I became orientated towards city life and that was important for the future.'

From *Wogan: Chat Show Host Extraordinary*, Madison Publishers, 1986

Re-Railroading The Cranberries
Colm O'Callaghan

It's been one curious trip around the houses, minding the dressers, for The Cranberries, the only Irish popular music act to have positively travelled and translated to any extent in almost ten years. Little over six years since their first beguiling cassette memo to a wonderful world outside of their window, the still gorgeous 'Nothing Left At All', and they're untouchable enough to be this country's first great pop whipping-toy since The Saw Doctors.

It only seems like yesterday, or at least the day before, since a distinct handful of us, lippy would-bes with far too much attitude and bile, hailed them from wherever we found ourselves, be that on radio or television or in print or, as was more often than not, on mammoth telephone calls to each other. The Cranberries were diamonds in a crucial regional pop cluster and were very steadily on their way. And they were ours, all ours, which is where this particular problem may very easily begin and end.

The Cranberries, in retrospect, very positively suited our own petty agendas — they were far from outside of Dublin and they couldn't have cared less, so gawky and awkward, so lacking in presence or poise that they simply had to trade on the might of their songs because the options were never going to run. Or, in a nutshell, they had their priorities intact, consciously or not.

And they came over like the last great gang in town, an out-and-out guitar pop troop spun up in classic colours, led by a black and white, right and left, two-way writing team, shaped out by what Noel Hogan had read in papers like *Melody Maker* and had heard on late-night radio, and spurred on by The Smiths and The Sundays and The Cocteau Twins. Back then it was about influences and records and guitars, and the vision was Noel Hogan's. The voice and the face, however, belonged elsewhere.

Last year, on their third album, *To The Faithful Departed*, The Cranberries sank to a brand new low, both in terms of output and style and taste as if, almost, their hands had been tied and they'd been forced against their own wills and their better judgments. From the sleeve artwork down to the guitar sounds and back-up through the words and the laziest/easiest arrangements, *To The Faithful Departed* sounded for all the world like a tired band playing through the motions of falling apart at the seams which, for a band still to even touch on their promise, is a problem.

Browsing the disc sleeve tells us everything and more, one imagines, because right now the vision and the voice and the face are all Dolores O'Riordan's, and that's that. Elsewhere Feargal Lawler's mammoth thrust and heave and Noel Hogan's grace are lost to O'Riordan's voice, by now no more than pastiche and an easy-escape wail that masks the writing damp. These days she dominates her own songs — and these are very positively *her* songs — like she dominates the sleeve credits, like she dominates the live show and the photographs and the band's press.

And right now, well, it's just that little bit overplayed.

Which is why, looking outwards and upwards, the next twelve months may easily be so important to The Cranberries. Because while we can excuse *To The Faithful Departed* on the grounds of rigour and lethargy — even REM's record/tour/record/tour schedule isn't always that watertight — its lack of breadth and dimension and scope is, even now, far smellier to pardon. But far more arrogant still is the band's own reluctance to concede on this, ironic given the on-our-sleeves, no-holds-hidden influences that The Cranberries wore defiantly up to three years ago.

In the meantime, of course, they've become even more remote to those of us who've been around the block with them, preferring the counsels of a fawning and over-loyal critical coterie to one that actually *worries* for them. Like they've almost wrapped themselves in their own hyperbole and entertain the real world only when it's warm outside. In tandem, of course, they've also become tired and dull like they've become mammoth and mainstream, so that the truth is always far harsher when it bites.

The fact is, however, that the essence of pop-writing, like a primal athletic ability, is innate and, by and large, more about genetics than key-tunings. Something that, when push comes to shove, is far harder to acquire than to lose. And whatever the current state of play, The Cranberries have already impacted with a snowball-speed like no one this country's ever seen before, U2 included, regardless of how and why. On the back of two false-starts, they've already handed a handful of pop-crackers — 'Dreams' and 'Linger', 'Put Me Down' and 'Sunday', 'Zombie' and 'Twenty-One' and, whatever the source, even 'Forever Yellow Skies'. They've already done three mammoth, box-office albums like they've spun America and Europe around their fingers and could, if they weren't still in their middle twenties, throw it all away without a single regret in the whole world. But then that's never been their form and they've been through enough already to respect what they hold and where they stand. And they've never been late starters.

Which is why fate might easily have fallen on their side this time around, forcing them into a corner where they can finally see themselves in context and at least buy themselves the space to regroup. Because the thing is that The Cranberries, with all of the potential and will in the world, have yet to fully realise themselves and have yet to make the record which delivers their promise to its optimum loudest. So that maybe one full year spent doing nothing really in particular will help them to re-railroad back to primals and basics, to all intents the only real option when you're staying true to yourself and to where you've always come from.

Provided, of course, that this is what and where The Cranberries really want to be.

From *The Sunday Tribune*, 12 January 1997

NINE

THE CITY

The Blacksmith of Limerick
Robert Dwyer Joyce

He grasped his ponderous hammer — he could not stand it more,
To hear the bombshells bursting and thundering battle's roar;
Said he, 'The breach they're mounting, the Dutchman's murdering crew:
I'll try my hammer on their heads and see what that can do.'

'Now swarthy Ned and Moran, make up that iron well,
'Tis Sarsfield's horse that wants the shoes, so mind not shot or shell.'
'Ah, sure,' cried both, 'the horse can wait, for Sarsfield's on the wall,
And where you go we'll follow, with you to stand or fall.'

The blacksmith raised his hammer and rushed into the street,
His 'prentice boys behind him, the ruthless foe to meet:
High on the breach of Limerick with dauntless hearts they stood,
Where bombshells burst, and shot fell thick, and redly ran the blood.

'Now look you, brown-haired Moran, and mark you, swarthy Ned,
This day we'll try the thickness of many a Dutchman's head —
Hurrah! upon their bloody path they're mounting gallantly;
And now the first that tops the breach, leave him to this and me.'

The first that gained the rampart he was a captain brave, —
A captain of the grenadiers with blood-stained dirk and glaive;
He pointed and he parried, but it was all in vain,
For right through skull and helmet the hammer found his brain.

The next that topped the rampart he was a colonel bold,
Bright through the dust of battle his helmet flashed with gold.
'Gold is no match for iron,' the doughty blacksmith said,
As with that ponderous hammer he stretched the foeman dead.

'Now here's for God and Limerick!' black Ned and Moran cried,
As on the Dutchmen's leaden heads their hammers well they plied.
A bombshell burst between them:— one fell without a groan;
One leaped into the lurid air and down the breach was thrown.

'Brave smith! brave smith!' cried Sarsfield, 'beware the treacherous mine:
Fall back, fall back on th' instant, or death is surely thine!'
The smith sprang up the rampart and leaped the blood-stained wall,
As high into the shuddering air went foemen, fort, and all!

Up, like a red volcano they thundered wild and high —
Brave Brandenburghers, spears and guns and standards, to the sky;
And dark and bloody was the shower that round the blacksmith fell;
He thought upon his 'prentice boys — they were avengèd well.

At that mighty roar a deadly silence instant settled down:
'Twas broken by a triumph shout that shook the ancient town:
Again its heroes forward dashed, and charged, and fought, and slew,
And taught King William and his men what Irish hearts could do.

Hurrah, for the brave defenders! They've hurled the foeman back!
The blacksmith rushed on the flying ranks; his hammer ne'er was slack.
He's tak'n a Holland captain beside the red pontoon,
And 'wait you here,' he sternly cries, 'I'll send you back full soon.'

'Dost see this gory hammer? It cracked some skulls to-day;
And yours 'twill crack if you don't stand and list to what I say:—
Here, take it to King William straight, and you may tell him too,
'Twould be acquainted with *his* skull, if he were here, not you.'

The blacksmith sought his smithy and blew his bellows strong;
He shod the steed of Sarsfield but o'er it sang no song.
'Ochone, my boys are dead,' cried he; 'their loss I'll long deplore;
But comfort's in my heart — their graves are red with foreign gore!'

From *Ballads of Irish Chivalry*, Gill, 1908

The Bishop's Lady
Críostóir Ó Floinn

When I was growing up in Limerick city in the 1930s, we lived in one of a terrace
of three old cut-stone houses situated on the island in the Shannon which is
formed by a narrow loop of the river. That island, which was the historic nucleus
of the now much expanded city, is still known as 'the King's Island' from the fact
that King John of England reserved it for himself when he ordered a castle and a
stone bridge to be built. Later, the fortified island came to be known as the 'English
Town' to distinguish it from the shanty 'Irish Town' outside the walls where the
Irish were allowed to live (those terms were still in common use in my boyhood).
When the 'Irish Town' also became part of the walled city, Limerick assumed the
form of a miscast hour-glass, its two parts linked by the narrow Baal's Bridge across

the 'Abbey River', as the loop of the Shannon is called. Just a stone's throw from our house, the towers of King John's great Norman castle stood guard over Thomond Bridge, the link not only between County Limerick and County Clare but between the provinces of Munster and Connacht. Our terrace of three two-storey houses adjoined a large old mansion built in the same solid stone-block style. This was let out in family apartments, *cottered*, to use my mother's word. Later, like many of the nearby cottage-type houses which had housed large families in my boyhood, the old mansion became entirely derelict; but in recent years, along with King John's Castle, it has been restored to something like its pristine glory as a precious item in the architectural heritage of Limerick, although King John might be puzzled to find a modern 'glasshouse' monstrosity cluttering up the courtyard of his Norman castle.

Although then providing accommodation for so many families, the old mansion was always referred to as 'the Bishop's Palace'. This anomaly was explained to us as part of our fireside folklore — the building had formerly been the episcopal residence of the Protestant bishops of Limerick, the three houses attached to it were for minor clergy, the large building behind the houses had been the Bishop's coachhouse, stables, and servants' quarters. Adjoining our terrace on the other side was the churchyard of the old Protestant church named after Limerick's patron saint, Mainchín ('the little monk' — his Irish name, or nickname?, like many other native personal and placenames, has been mangled into an appalling English phonetic version, 'Munchin'). Beyond the church and churchyard, at the other end of the street, a Protestant widows' home and the Villiers School completed what must have been an episcopal enclave on that part of the King's Island in the post-Reformation period of Limerick's history.

The old mansion next door was of even more interest when we heard that among its former residents there had been a certain 'Bishop's Lady' who was so wicked that after her death her spirit was sentenced to haunt Thomond Bridge. And before ever we were subjected to the formal learning of poetry in school, we were privileged to hear poetry in its natural use and setting when our maternal grandmother, Mary Connolly, who lived in nearby Crosby Row, used to quote lines by a man she called 'the Poet Hogan', whom she had known personally, to reinforce her warning that anyone who dared to try to cross Thomond Bridge too late at night, or in a less than sober condition, was in danger of being thrown into the river by the Bishop's Lady — 'just like what happened to Drunken Thady'. And when we crossed that bridge even in broad daylight, we were still subjected to the thrill of terror when our older siblings fitted our nervous fingers into the actual grooves on the parapet of the bridge where the ghostly lady's hand had left its mark, so they told us.

As we grew older, we came to accept that in our fireside entertainment on a winter's night, or as part of some social event such as a wedding or a christening, a person who could neither sing nor play an instrument would contribute a recitation, and the piece frequently offered was the Poet Hogan's *Drunken Thady and the Bishop's Lady*, all 438 lines of it. And if the performer's memory lapsed here and there, the necessary prompt was always forthcoming from one or other of the listeners. Hearing such dramatic renderings of the Bard's poem, especially on a winter's night with the wind howling down from the Clare Hills around Thomond Bridge and King John's Castle, reinforced our fears of the Bishop's Lady to such an extent that we dreaded even the unlighted hallway and stairs of the old 'palace' next door where so many of our neighbours lived. . . .

> Each night she roamed with airy feet
> From Thomond Bridge to Castle Street,
> And those that stayed out past eleven
> Would want a special guard from heaven
> To shield them with a holy wand
> From the mad terrors of her hand.

From *The Bard of Thomond: Selected Poems*, Obelisk Books, 1994

Billy Carr's Garden in 1809
Francis Wheeler

> You may travel the nation all over,
> From Dublin to Sweet Mullingar,
> And a garden you will not discover
> Like the garden of Sweet Billy Carr;
> 'Tis there that the tall trees were planted
> In the days of the old Tommy Parr;
> And the soft winding Shannon is flowing
> Round the garden of Sweet Billy Carr.
>
> 'Tis there the big praties are growing,
> Enough to supply all Dunbar,
> Where the soft winding Shannon is flowing,
> 'Round the gardens of Sweet Billy Carr;
> His sisters like sweet pretty posies,
> More beauteous than roses by far,
> They bloom like carnations and roses
> In the gardens of sweet Billy Carr.
>
> O! may they be happily married,
> To a mayor, and a lawyer, and tar,
> How blest will they be when they're wed,
> With the sisters of Sweet Billy Carr!

Now if you have a mind to live frisky,
And trouble and grief would you mar —
I'd advise you to go and drink whiskey,
Along with the Sweet Billy Carr!
In a room, Sir, he keeps a big bottle,
Without either crack, flaw, or star,
Which is often applied to the throttle,
Of that thirsty gay soul Billy Carr.

From *Limerick; Its History and Antiquities, Ecclesiastical, Civil, and Military, from the Earliest Ages*, by Maurice Lenihan, Hodges, Smith and Co., 1866

Daniel O'Connell in Limerick
Maurice Lenihan

There was no city in Ireland for which O'Connell had entertained more affection than for Limerick. Some of his best speeches were delivered at Catholic meetings held in Limerick, and at the Court House in the defence of prisoners. He lodged, during his periodical visits, at the house No. 6 Patrick Street, then occupied by Mr Sheehan, a saddler, where he was constantly besieged by attorneys and clients; and his appearance, as he walked with a thorough air of complete independence, 'kicking the world before him', to and from Court, or through the city, always attracted a large and enthusiastic crowd of admirers. Going to or returning from his beloved mountain home in Kerry, he usually rested for a night in Limerick; and it was his usual habit on these occasions to address the throngs by whom his carriage was ever surrounded, when he never began a speech without, in the first place, attacking the local Tory journal, and asking, 'How is Andy Watson?' its proprietor. He retained a strong hold on the affections of the citizens up to the very last visit which he paid to Limerick, which was towards the close of the summer of 1846, when, breaking down in health, and sorely disappointed in hope, he was no longer the eloquent and enthusiastic orator that he had been. During the Clare election, in 1828, Limerick was as it were the centre of operations of O'Connell and his friends. The citizens were absolutely wild with excitement. As O'Connell proceeded to Clare, to open that great county, and strike the final blow for Catholic freedom, the entire population of Limerick became well nigh frantic in their demonstrations in favour of the cause in which the nation and its avowed leader had embarked.

From *Limerick; Its History and Antiquities, Ecclesiastical, Civil, and Military, from the Earliest Ages*, Hodges, Smith and Co., 1866

Curragower Falls
Michael Hogan

Hark! hark! like tigers roaring to devour
A quivering carcass howls wild Curragower
As if its thunders, groaning in the gloom,
Would wake the tenants of each lonely tomb!
Sweet Curragower, I love to hear thee roar
Like billows beating 'gainst the shuddering shore,
I love to hear thy wild cyclonic shocks
Burst with fierce fury o'er the rattling rocks.
Careering madly 'neath the moon's pale glow,
Like wrathful rebels plunging on the foe.
How soft and sweet the mellow moonbeams rest
On noble Shannon's palpitating breast,
That regal river, that far-flashing flood
Which once grew ruddy with the foeman's blood,
When Celt and Saxon swayed in deadly lock
And freedom's pillars shuddered at the shock.

From *Continuation of Poetical Satire on the Limerick Corporation and Other Sordid Citizens* by Oliver Twist, Bard of the Brand (Michael Hogan), *circa* 1875

Leamy's School
John Fleming and Seán O'Grady

On 24 March 1814, on the island of Madeira which is situated off the coast of North Africa, William Leamy, a native of Limerick who had spent a lifetime at sea and who had amassed a large fortune allegedly through piracy, made his will in which he left the residue of his estate 'to be applied to the education of the poor in Ireland, principally those in and about Limerick city: or as they, my executors, in their better judgment should deem meet to give this bequest the most extensive efficacy'. For a considerable time after his death, his executors failed to carry out his wishes and it was only in 1839 that the residue of the will could be applied for educational purposes. In 1842 the scheme for a school was drawn up. In his will, Leamy made no distinction between poor children on the grounds of religion. However, the 1842 scheme clearly acknowledged the possibility that tension would arise because Protestant and Catholic children attended the same school. Two years later Leamy's School opened in Hartstonge Street.

From the outset, it went through a very difficult period and in 1865 it closed for some years. While Protestants tended to support it, the number of Catholic children attending the school was never greater than twenty-five. In 1874 a modified scheme was introduced but the number of Catholic children attending the school never reached the expected level. The Protestant presence dominated the school, despite the preponderance of Catholic children among the poor of Limerick. Because of this, in 1885, shortly before his death, Bishop Butler forbade Catholic children to attend the school and, by 1887, when the Educational Endowments (Ireland) Commission sat in Limerick, Leamy's School provided intermediate education mainly for the children of affluent Limerick Protestants. Catholic anger began to arise on the issue and it found its protagonist in Bishop Edward Thomas O'Dwyer, who was personally convinced that William Leamy died a Catholic and, therefore, could be presumed to have been particularly concerned that poor Catholic children should have benefited from his estate.

By 1887, shortly after his appointment, the lines of conflict emerged. On the Protestant side the Dean of Limerick, the Rev. Bunbury, who was also the Chairman of the Board of Governors of Leamy's School, became the chief protagonist and on the Catholic side the Bishop took the matter into his own hands. Within a very short time it became apparent that this dispute was not simply about the running of a school but encompassed the entire religious, social, educational and political atmosphere in Limerick. Central to the core of Protestant anger was the belief that Catholics, whom many equated with Jesuits, had taken over the University College at Mungret. The Rev. Baxendale summed this up before a meeting of the Educational Endowments Commission on 25 October 1889 when he said: 'The Roman Catholics have a larger thing in Mungret than we have; and they should let our ewe lamb alone, and we would not have attacked their sheep.' In suggesting that Leamy's go to the Protestants and Mungret to the Catholics, he was at pains to point out, however, that Catholics could not be equated with the Jesuits and that, by implication, Mungret should not be the sole concern of the Order. Another source of Protestant anger was their assertion that Leamy himself was a Protestant and would have principally wanted his co-religionists to benefit from his will. With the exception of Rev. Walter Baxendale, they also advocated denominational education and held that both the Model School and Leamy's should be theirs.

Edward Thomas, on the other hand, believed that Leamy died a Catholic. He recognised that Catholics in Limerick outnumbered Protestants by eight to one and among the poor by about twenty to one. He also held that the vast majority of poor children in Limerick at that time were being educated by the Christian Brothers, the Presentation Sisters and the Sisters of Mercy, none of whom were in receipt of government monies. A key assertion made by O'Dwyer was that an endowment which did not specify the denomination of those who were to benefit from it could be equated with non-denominational education. He was convinced that denominational education was essential and declared: 'I will never allow the Catholics of Limerick, while I am Bishop, to attend a mixed school.' Another key factor in this debate was his own background. Educated mainly by the Christian Brothers, O'Dwyer's sympathies lay with them rather than with the Jesuits, whom he associated with the wealthier classes, and who were also a target of Protestant anger.

The dispute lasted for almost seven years. A simple solution to the issue would have been to have given the Model School to the Protestants and Leamy's to the Catholics but legal issues prevented this. Finally, on 13 April 1894, a new scheme for Leamy's School was drawn up, whereby the Protestants got a quarter of the assets of the school and the Catholics got the property and the remainder. O'Dwyer then became Chairman of the Board of Governors, a post which he occupied until his death in 1917.

This dispute established O'Dwyer as a leading figure in education as well as in political life. It demonstrated his ability to enter the cut and thrust of political battle, as well as his commitment to Catholic principles in education, which he held dear. His preferences also began to emerge, as well as his prejudices. In particular his concern for the education of the poor showed a leaning towards the Brothers and Sisters and away from the Jesuits.

From *St Munchin's College, Limerick 1796–1996*, published by St Munchin's College, Limerick, 1996

The Devil's Address to the Merchants of Limerick
Sean O'Faolain

Well here ye are
and ye didn't come far
or need a car
for the smell of hell
is from Pennywell
and out to the ridge
of Thomond Bridge
anyway I'm proud as hell
to see ye so well
but what makes ye so bold
come out of the cold
and not be shaking and chattering
like a priest at a pattern
come in a bit nigher
and enjoy me fire
not like boys in a quire
wisha is that Sexton Pery

with lashings of sherry
and I suppose I can't avoid
taking wine from Lord Lloyd
or persuading Maggoty Quin
to go slow with his gin
and will ye look at Halpin and Spaight
behind each side of the gate
manufacturing mate
and Bateman and Hogges
with turf, coal and logs
to drive off the fogs
they're all here by dogs
Boyle, Roche, and Fox
the Halpins and Houghs
with every fish
your heart could wish.
We're the grandest variety
of Limerick society
and we'll make it a feast
to welcome ye east
call up on the trumpets
the best of my strumpets
the Countess of Clare
and Dame Castlereagh
King James and King Bill
can drink with a will
Cromwell and Pitt
and all that will fit.
Then rubadubdub
on the drum and the tub
drink lads and be merry
the finest of sherry
but what the divil is that
tastes like me ould hat
I'd rather a kick in the shin
do you call that stuff gin?
Come on Mister Pery
out with yer sherry
here's a can for it
and I'm the man for it.
Oh! may Cromwell then curse on ye
this stuff is worse on me.

And look at my fire
is it the way ye desire
for to make it expire
it's as good as a byre
what have I done
to ask ye to come
to my house was so spicy
ye Limerick lice ye
I'll teach ye be civil
and not be cheating the divil
let this be yeer fates
ye Halpins and Spaights
for selling bad meat
both early and late
to sit on yeer rumps
under red-hot pumps
with boiling stout
into yeer mouth
and ye Boyles and ye Roches
ye Houghs in yeer coaches
and Maggoty Quin
with your gutrot gin
and fine Sexton-Pery
I'll make them merry
in Broad Street and Dock Street
and Bridge Street and John Street
and Clare Street and where street
to bate ye and rate ye
down west Watergate with ye
with yeer rumps in lumps
and harrows for barrows
boiling, smelling
bubbling, yelling
roasting, ghosting, toasting Limerick
merchants to the Judgment Day.

And so, in after years at night should men inquire
What may it be that causes Limerick's smell,
Point down the Shannon to the ghostly fire
Of the fifteen Limerick merchants burning out of hell.

From *A Nest of Simple Folk*, New York Viking, 1934; reprinted in *The Old Limerick Journal*, No. 27, 1990

A Limerick Encounter
V.S. Pritchett

I travelled across Tipperary to Limerick, arriving there in one of those long soft brown and yellow sunsets of the West, with the white mists rising from the Shannon. The Celtic twilight was working on me. I sat up drinking with a satanic engineer; and, thinking it was about time, I tried that night to write one of my articles. I found that after two or three whiskies my pen swept across the paper. When I read the thing in the morning, I saw it was chaotic and I tore it up. That is the last time I ever wrote on alcohol.

Limerick was in an edgy state. It had just been relieved of a siege and there was still a crack or two of sniping at night. There was a strike on at the bacon factories; and there was an attempt to start a soviet. I went to see the committee and politely took my hat off and made a small French bow when I went into their room. The leader told me to put my hat on: they had finished, he said, with bourgeois manners. We had a wrangle about this because, although I am shy, I am touchy and argued back. We had a rapid duel of sarcasms. He was one of those 'black' Irishmen one occasionally comes across; there was another, a waiter at the hotel in Limerick who threw a plate of bacon and eggs at a customer. He was a big fellow who looked murderous every time he came into the dining room with a plate.

There occurred in Limerick one of those encounters which — looking back on it — I see as a portent. I found there a very serious young Englishman, in fact a Quaker, who took me to a house outside the town. As we climbed up on an outside car, he whispered to me not to talk on the long ride out because, he said, his situation was delicate. He had caught the Irish love of conspiracy, even the whisper. When we got to his house he told me he had been in the fighting against the Sinn Féiners, but had lately married an Irish girl. I think he had been in the Auxiliary Police. Except for having his tennis court shot up now and then, he said, when he and his wife were playing in the afternoons, there was not much trouble now. The English have stubborn natures but, I saw, could get light-headed in Ireland. Into the sitting room, which was furnished in faded Victorian style, with pictures of lakes and vegetation on the walls and the general Irish smell of rising damp, came an elderly woman wearing a wig of black curls and with a sharp, painted face; and with her a pale little girl of 12 — I thought — one of those fey, unreal Irish children with empty blue eyes and untidy russet hair. She looked as if she had been blown down from the sky, as, in her tiny skirt, she sat bare-legged on the floor in front of the fire. She was *not* a child of 12; she was the Quaker's wife, and very excitable. The shooting, she said, livened up the tennis and they were afraid for the strings of their rackets, because in these times you might have to send them to Dublin to be re-strung. A brother-in-law came in, a man who sat in silence breathing sociably, as Guinness after Guinness went down. I gazed from the old lady to the girl, from brother-in-law to the ascetic looking young Quaker soldier, and could not see how they could be together in the same house. In how many Irish families was it to seem to me that the people had all appeared accidentally from the wheel of fortune, rather than in the course of nature. The old lady chattered about balls and parties, about Lord this and Lady that, about the stage — was she an actress? In her wig, paint and her rings, bracelets and necklace, and her old-fashioned dress of twenty years before, she was nimble and witch-like. Indeed, she got out a pack of cards and told my fortune. I dropped the Queen of Spades. She sprang on it with glee:

'You will be surrounded by women who intend to harm you.'

I walked back to Limerick late, feeling, as I was so often to do in Ireland, that I had stepped into a chapter of a Russian novel. The smell of turf smoke curled among the river fogs and I was not sure of the way in the dark. I waited for a shot or two, for the Irregulars liked to loose off at night to keep the feeling of war alive, from behind a friendly hedge. There were no shots that night. It was an eerie and pleasant walk, like a ghost story told in the dark.

From *Midnight Oil*, Chatto & Windus, 1971

The Leaving of Limerick
Anonymous

As I strolled out one evening
Down by the Assembly Mall,
I heard two lovers speaking,
As me and my love passed on.
And the words that passed between them
They were but very few.
'Tisn't the leaving of Limerick that's grieving me,
But my darling leaving you.

In the morning, when I am going,
I will wave my lily white hand.
I will wave it over my shoulder
In adieu to the Limerick Strand.
And farewell to the girls of Thomondgate
'Tis to them I bid adieu,
'Tisn't the leaving of Limerick that's grieving me,
But my darling leaving you.

And now that we must be parted,
I know you'll understand
Why I must go broken-hearted
Away from the Limerick Strand.
Though my fond love I must leave you,
You know my heart is true.
'Tisn't the leaving of Limerick that's grieving me,
But my darling leaving you.

From the *Labour Party National Conference Magazine*, April 1997

Shanny's Pub
Kevin Hannan

Those who remember Shanny's pub will not easily forget 'the parlour splendours of that festive place'. It had a peculiar attraction for all those who came to Plassey. Perhaps it was its unique location, its fairy-tale approach along the towpath by the river, across the plank over the drain and through the big field. It was a very special place to shelter in during squally October days, when the bridge was obscured by the incessant sheets of rain driving up from the south-west. The warmth within the walls, the lively conversation, the smell of stout and sawdust, and the friendliness of the Shanny sisters made the pub a haven for every Waltonian that ever plied line and lure in the river there. Known colloquially as 'The Thatch', the house was a refuge of hospitality for every pilgrim out of Limerick and out of farmhouses and cottages from the surrounding countryside.

Perched boldly close to the river's edge, just above the Plassey Bridge on the Clare shore, the pub was a spiritual and temporal oasis for wayfarer and fisherman. A stranger might pass it by, pausing only perhaps to admire the lilac trees, or the roses that reached right up to the thatch, if his attention was not arrested by the legend painted on a wine-covered board and fastened on the wall between the parlour window and the front door. 'Catherine Shanny, licensed to sell beer, wine and spirits to be consumed on the premises.'

From *The Old Limerick Journal*, No. 7, Summer 1981

Dear Old Thomondgate
Tom Glynn

Oh Thomondgate, my native place, so beautiful and grand,
To see the Shannon's purple tide come rolling down the Strand,
And when you walk out the New Road, you can view the hills of Clare,
They are nicer than Killarney or the plains of old Kildare.

We are noted in this old place for large funerals and great wakes,
Some people call us Munchin boys, more call us Soda Cakes;
Let them call us what they like, no parish in this state
Can compete with the noble spot, called dear old Thomondgate.

Now the merry boys and merry girls, wherever they may roam,
You will always know that they have come from where the Shannon flows;
In singing they are famous, great songs they can relate —
'Tis little wonder we are proud, of dear old Thomondgate.

There was a man named Billy Lee, he came from Irishtown;
He used to go out every night and knock the people down;
The police couldn't take him, his strength it was so great,
'Til one night he came and met his match in dear old Thomondgate.

Oh, Thomondgate is nigh well gone from what it used to be;
Long ago we made fine whiskey in the distillery;
The crumbling walls are standing yet, the shaft is tall and straight,
It commemorates the good old days in dear old Thomondgate.

From the *Labour Party Conference Magazine*, April 1997

Windmill Ways
Gerry Gallivan

The Henry Street that I knew during the 1920s and early 1930s was a comfortable, down-to-earth place to grow up in. Of course, one cannot just take the street itself in isolation; the whole locality, with Henry Street as the focal point, is what I have in mind. Running into it at various points, like tributaries to a river, were Frederick Street, Clontarf Place, the Windmill, Newenham Street, Hartstonge Street and several others but Henry Street was the common denominator, being the bread-basket of the area, with its wide selection of shops. . . . Even in my own section, bounded at one end by Clontarf Place and by Hartstonge Street at the other, we had more than enough to go on with. . . .

Two of the joys of those days were 'the pens' at the bottom of O'Curry Street Hill, and the billboard beside Whelan's corner shop. The pens were a kind of partitioned stockade where herds of cattle were driven on designated days and, naturally, we kids would be there in our dozens hanging over the railed fences. . . . The billboarding was reserved for advertising future and current cinematic attractions. A man with dungarees, a step ladder, a large brush and a bucket of paste would come at regular intervals and, with rapid, expert slashes of the brush, would unfold before our popping eyes, in gloriously coloured posters, the secrets of the coming week . . . Bebe Daniels in *She's a Sheikh*, John Boles in *Rio Rita* or Maurice Chevalier in *Innocents of Paris*.

When I think back, names keep tumbling . . . Lynches, Simpsons, O'Conners and O'Briens. Around the corner in Clontarf Place lived the Madigans, the Carmodys, the Bensons, the Cooneys, the O'Dohertys and the Halls. . . . Gladys and Lovie added glamour to the locality, while their brothers, Jack and Sammy, gave loyal service to the Limerick Boat Club. My brothers, Cyril, Jim and Eddie, and I also rowed for the club . . . as did Joe White and Charlie O'Connor.

Joe O'Sullivan who, like my brother Cyril, was one of the leading amateur actors in the city, lived in Frederick Street, as did the brothers Eugene, Timmie and Jackie O'Sullivan, all seagoing officers with the Limerick Steamship Company. Seafaring and the dock connection was part and parcel of the Windmill tradition though there were, of course, other occupations too. Among the people I recall are the Kirby, Houlihan and Douglas families.

One feature of life indelibly associated in my memory with the Windmill is the singing at the corner of the street. Around eight or nine o'clock at night, young men would gather on the steps near Bridie Brown's to swap yarns and to sing the old songs in natural untutored harmony. I have only to close my eyes in moments of nostalgia and I'm back once more in the drowsy calm of still summer evenings hearing them again, and the words of the old favourite, 'Heart of my Heart', could have been written specially of them:

> 'Heart of my Heart', how I love that melody,
> 'Heart of my heart', brings back a memory,
> When we were kids at the corner of the street,
> We were rough and ready guys, but oh how we could harmonise.

All right, so if it's easy to be sentimental looking back from a distance of fifty years and more I readily admit it. There had to have been problems, disappointments, disruptions . . . of course there were, but none of it changes the fact that Henry Street was a good place for a youngster to be when feeling his way towards life.

From *The Old Limerick Journal*, No. 21, Autumn 1987

The Death and Wake of Eugene
Frank McCourt

I know Oliver is dead and Malachy knows Oliver is dead but Eugene is too small to know anything. When he wakes in the morning he says, Ollie, Ollie, and toddles around the room looking under the beds or he climbs up on the bed by the window and points to children on the street, especially children with fair hair like him and Oliver. Ollie, Ollie, he says, and Mam picks him up, sobs, hugs him. He struggles to get down because he doesn't want to be picked up and hugged. He wants to find Oliver.

Dad and Mam tell him Oliver is in heaven playing with angels and we'll see him again someday but he doesn't understand because he's only two and doesn't have the words and that's the worst thing in the whole world.

Malachy and I play with him. We try to make him laugh. We make funny faces. We put pots on our heads and pretend to let them fall off. We run across the room and pretend to fall down. We take him to the People's Park to see the lovely flowers, play with dogs, roll in the grass.

He sees small children with fair hair like Oliver. He doesn't say Ollie anymore. He only points.

Dad says Eugene is lucky to have brothers like Malachy and me because we help him forget and soon, with God's help, he'll have no memory of Oliver at all.

He died anyway.

Six months after Oliver went, we woke on a mean November morning and there was Eugene, cold in the bed beside us. Dr Troy came and said that child died of pneumonia and why wasn't he in the hospital long ago? Dad said he didn't know and Mam said she didn't know and Dr Troy said that's why children die. People don't know. He said if Malachy or I showed the slightest sign of a cough or the faintest rattle in the throat we were to be brought to him no matter what time of day or night. We were to be kept dry at all times because there seemed to be a bit of a weakness in the chest in this family. He told Mam he was very sorry for her troubles and he'd give her a prescription for something to ease the pain of the days to come. He said God was asking too much, too damn much.

Grandma came over to our room with Aunt Aggie. She washed Eugene, and Aunt Aggie went to a shop for a little white gown and a set of rosary beads. They dressed him in a white gown and laid him on the bed by the window where he used to look out for Oliver. They placed his hands on his chest, one hand on top of the other, bound in the little white rosary beads. Grandma brushed the hair back from his eyes and forehead and she said, Doesn't he have lovely soft silky hair? Mam went to the bed and pulled a blanket over his legs to keep him warm. Grandma and Aunt Aggie looked at each other and said nothing. Dad stood at the end of the bed beating his fists against his thighs, talking to Eugene, telling him, Och, it was the

River Shannon that harmed you, the dampness from that river that came and took you and Oliver. Grandma said, Will you stop that? You're making the whole house nervous. She took Dr Troy's prescription and told me run over to O'Connor the chemist for the pills, that there would be no charge due to the kindness of Dr Troy. Dad said he'd come with me, that we'd go to the Jesuit church and say a prayer for Margaret and Oliver and Eugene, all happy in heaven. The chemist gave us the pills, we stopped to say the prayers, and when we returned to the room, Grandma gave Dad money to bring a few bottles of stout from the pub. Mam said, No, no, but Grandma said, He doesn't have the pills to ease him, God help us, and a bottle of stout will be some small comfort. Then she told him he'd have to go to the undertaker tomorrow to bring the coffin back in a carriage. She told me to go with my father and make sure he didn't stay in the pub all night and drink all the money. Dad said, Och, Frankie shouldn't be in pubs, and she said, Then don't stay there. He put on his cap and we went to South's pub and he told me at the door I could go home now, that he'd be home after one pint. I said, No, and he said, Don't be disobedient. Go home to your poor mother. I said, No, and he said I was a bad boy and God would be displeased. I said I wasn't going home without him and he said, Och, what is the world coming to? He had one quick pint of porter in the pub and we went home with the bottles of stout. Pa Keating was in our room with a small bottle of whiskey and bottles of stout and Uncle Pat Sheehan brought two bottles of stout for himself. Uncle Pat sat on the floor with his arms around his bottles and he kept saying, They're mine, they're mine, for fear they'd be taken from him. People who were dropped on their heads always worry someone will steal their stout. Grandma said, All right, Pat, drink your stout yourself. No one will bother you. She and Aunt Aggie sat on the bed by Eugene. Pa Keating sat at the kitchen table drinking his stout and offering everyone a sip of his whiskey. Mam took her pills and sat by the fire with Malachy on her lap. She kept saying Malachy had hair like Eugene and Aunt Aggie said no he did not till Grandma drove her elbow into Aunt Aggie's chest and told her shut up. Dad stood against the wall drinking his stout between the fireplace and the bed with Eugene. Pa Keating told stories and the big people laughed even though they didn't want to laugh or they weren't supposed to laugh in the presence of a dead child. He said when he was in the English Army in France the Germans sent gas over which made him so sick they had to take him to the hospital. They kept him in the hospital a while and then sent him back to the trenches. . . . when he came back to Limerick the only job he could get was in the gas works shovelling coal into the furnaces. He said there was so much gas in his system now he could supply light to a small town for a year. Aunt Aggie sniffed and said that was not a proper story to be telling in the presence of a dead child and Grandma said it was better to have a story like that than to be sitting around with the long face. Uncle Pat Sheehan, sitting on the floor with his stout, said he was going to sing a song. More power to you, said Pa Keating, and Uncle Pat sang 'The Road to Rasheen'. He kept saying, Rasheen, Rasheen, mavourneen mean, and the song made no sense because his father dropped him on his head long ago and every time he sang that song he had different words. Grandma said that was a fine song and Pa Keating said Caruso better look over his shoulder. Dad went over to the bed in the corner where he slept with Mam. He sat on the edge, put his bottle on the floor, covered his face with his hands and cried. He said, Frank, Frank, come here, and I had to go to him so that he could hug me the way Mam was hugging Malachy. Grandma said, We better go now and sleep a bit before the funeral tomorrow. They each knelt by the bed and said a prayer and kissed Eugene's forehead. Dad put me down, stood up and nodded to them as they left. When they were gone he lifted each of the stout bottles to his mouth and drained it. He ran his finger inside the whiskey bottle and licked it. He turned down the flame in the paraffin oil lamp on the table and said it was time for Malachy and me to be in bed. We'd have to sleep with him and Mam that night as little Eugene would be needing the bed for himself. It was dark in the room now except for the sliver of streetlight that fell on Eugene's lovely soft silky hair.

From *Angela's Ashes: A Memoir of a Childhood*, HarperCollins Publishers, 1996

In the People's Park
Gerard Ryan

From the topmost branch of a copper beech
Facing the setting sun in early April
A mistle thrush sings loud and clear
As my brother and myself walk
On a moss grey path between twin ilexes
In the People's Park
Talking of the day's happenings,
Testing each other's memory of things past,
Of people loved and otherwise;
My brother silent for a while
Caught in the enchanted web
Of some ecstatic dream of childhood;
Of such was his best thoughts and talk
Of that blest time — for him so blest,
Fresh as the dawn of a May white morning
When we first heard that bird's progenitor
On that same tree in that sweet April's prime,
The same wild rapture.

'Tis evening now — our life's evening
And singing time is over,
Lost in the vanished years,
Echoed in memory only.
'Tis twilight now —
Blue dusk falls pensively
Among the silhouetted trees.
The ranger rings his handbell
And soon the gates must close.

From *An April Morning Walk*, Limerick Poetry Circle, 1974

Upstairs, Downstairs
Frank McCourt

Malachy and I are back in the bed where Eugene died. I hope he's not cold in that white coffin in the graveyard though I know he's not there anymore because angels come to the graveyard and open the coffin and he's far from the Shannon dampness that kills, up in the sky in heaven with Oliver and Margaret where they have plenty of fish and chips and toffee and no aunts to bother you, where all the fathers bring home the money from the Labour Exchange and you don't have to be running around to pubs to find them.

Mam says she can't spend another minute in that room on Hartstonge Street. She sees Eugene morning, noon and night. She sees him climbing the bed to look out at the street for Oliver and sometimes she sees Oliver outside and Eugene inside, the two of them chatting away. She's happy they're chatting like that but she doesn't want to be seeing and hearing them the rest of her life. It's a shame to move when we're so near Leamy's National School but if she doesn't move soon she'll go out of her mind and wind up in the lunatic asylum.

We move to Roden Lane on top of a place called Barrack Hill. There are six houses on one side of the lane, one on the opposite side. The houses are called two up, two down, two rooms on top, two on the bottom. Our house is at the end of the lane, the last of the six. Next to our door is a small shed, a lavatory, and next to that a stable.

Mam goes to the St Vincent de Paul Society to see if there's any chance of getting furniture. The man says he'll give us a docket for a table, two chairs, and two beds. He says we'll have to go to a second-hand furniture shop down in the Irishtown and haul the furniture home ourselves. Mam says we can use the pram she had for the twins and when she says that she cries. She wipes her eyes on her sleeves and asks the man if the beds we're getting are second-hand. He says of course they are, and she says she's very worried about sleeping in beds someone might have died in, especially if they had the consumption. The man says, I'm very sorry, but beggars can't be choosers.

It takes us all day to haul the furniture on the pram from one end of Limerick to the other. There are four wheels on the pram but one is bockety, it wants to go in a different direction. We have two beds, one sideboard with a mirror, a table and two chairs. We're happy with the house. We can walk from room to room and up and down the stairs. You feel very rich when you can go up and down the stairs all day as much as you please. Dad lights the fire and Mam makes the tea. He sits at the table on one chair, she sits on the other and Malachy and I sit on the trunk we brought from America. . . . Dad says nothing. He finishes his tea and looks for a nail to hang our one picture. The man in the picture has a thin face. He wears a yellow skullcap and a black robe with a cross on his chest. Dad says he was a Pope, Leo the Thirteenth, a great friend of the workingman. He brought this picture all the way from America where he found it thrown out by someone who had no time for the workingman. . . .

Two weeks before Christmas Malachy and I come home from school in a heavy rain and when we push in the door we find the kitchen empty. The table and chairs and trunk are gone and the fire is dead in the grate. The Pope is still there and that means we haven't moved again. Dad would never move without the Pope. The kitchen floor is wet, little pools of water all around, and the walls are twinkling with the damp. There's a noise upstairs and when we go up we find Dad and Mam and the missing furniture. It's nice and warm there with a fire blazing in the grate, Mam sitting in the bed, and Dad reading the *Irish Press* and smoking a cigarette by the fire. Mam tells us there was a terrible flood, that the rain came down the lane and poured in under our door. They tried to stop it with rags but they only turned sopping wet and let the rain in. People emptying their buckets made it worse and there was a sickening stink in the kitchen. She thinks we should stay upstairs as long as there is rain. We'll be warm through the winter months and then we can go downstairs in the springtime if there is any sign of a dryness in the walls or the floor. Dad says it's like going away on our holidays to a warm foreign place like Italy. That's what we'll call the upstairs from now on, Italy. Malachy says the Pope is still on the wall downstairs and he's going to be all cold and couldn't we bring him up? but Mam says, No, he's going to stay where he is because I don't want him on the wall glaring at me in the bed. Isn't it enough that we dragged him all the way from Brooklyn to Belfast to Dublin to Limerick? All I want now is a little peace, ease and comfort.

From *Angela's Ashes: A Memoir of a Childhood*, HarperCollins Publishers, 1996

Plassey — A Vignette
Gerard Ryan

We cross the bridge at Plassey Mill
When swans float down the day's last beams
Below the singing waters;
Then through a chancel of green boughs
Into a small lock garden,
The lock-gates spurting showers,
With courting linnets playing
In dance of light and shadows
Around a white-crowned guelder rose;
The scent of night flowers clinging
To the twilight's loosened tresses;
And through the wide spaced willows
A haze of gold and amethyst
Mantles the brow of Keeper.

From *An April Morning Walk*, Limerick Poetry Circle, 1974

Sentenced to Daingean
Seán Bourke

It was a cold October morning in 1947. Mr Justice Gleeson gazed down from his lofty perch on the judicial bench at the three cold, hungry and ragged boys standing huddled together in the well of the court. He spoke to the other two first and there seemed to be some confusion about which of us had done what. I hadn't been with the other lads all the time and they sometimes did things on their own but now we were all charged with everything. Finally the judge turned his attention to me. 'Have you anything to say for yourself?' he asked severely. 'No, sir,' I answered.

He turned to the superintendent. 'It seems to me, Superintendent, they've been doing so much mischief in the streets of Limerick for the past few months that they don't know what they've done and what they haven't done.'

'I took the bunch of bananas out of the car, sir,' I said weakly.

'I agree with you, Your Honour,' the Superintendent answered, ignoring me. 'They seem to have lost track of what they did.' He smiled as he spoke.

The worst part of it was the turmoil within, the conflict of inexplicable feelings. Was it possible for a 12-year-old boy to stand here and not care what happened to him? Was it natural? The streets outside were so hateful to me I knew deep down I did not want to go back to them. But how could I *want* to be sent away? Oh God, help me to understand! These are not the thoughts and feelings of a young boy. I cannot *want* to go away and yet I do. Please, Justice, please don't send me away! If I could only *understand*. Why do I *want* to go? Oh God, tell me why I feel this way. . . .

The young boy was standing in the middle of the playground at Sexton Street. It was the mid-morning break and he was surrounded by a hundred other boys laughing and pushing. The tears were streaming down his face hot and large and hurried as if they were impatient to escape till it seemed they must leave, river beds behind them. The schoolmaster was Lefty Kelly and he had the boy's left arm gripped tightly with his right hand and his knuckles stood out big and white. He had a long thick round stick in his left hand and was tapping it against the side of his lame leg in time to the rhythm of his words.

'How-many-times-does-nine-go-into-eighty-one?' he shouted. He wasn't angry at all and smiled all the time.

'Eight t . . t . . times, sir,' the boy sobbed.

Lefty Kelly threw his head back and laughed. 'Did ye hear that, lads?' he demanded, looking around at the sea of young faces. 'We did, sir,' some of them answered. He turned back to the sobbing boy. 'I'll teach you to do your homework, boy!' He shifted his weight away from his lame leg. 'Hold out your hand!' The boy slowly stretched his hand out and closed his eyes tightly and for the tenth time Lefty Kelly, still smiling, brought the heavy stick down on the bruised palm.

Brother Andrews, the Head Brother, was standing over near the wall with three other brothers and two of the schoolmasters, Spud Murphy and Jack Danangher, were with them. And they were all laughing at Lefty Kelly and the boy. The boy's hand was turned blue and was all swollen up, but Lefty Kelly kept hitting it with the stick till the boy's knees started bending with the weight and the pain and the shame. . . .

Justice Gleeson's voice sounded far away, as if in a dream. 'I don't see what else I can do, Superintendent. I'll have to send them to Daingean.'

Daingean! The word was like a sword-thrust. *Daingean!* The times we had talked about it and laughed about it and joked about it. And heard about it from boys who had been there. *Daingean!* Would he really send us there?

Fully awake now, hanging on his every word. He shuffled the papers decisively into a neat bundle in front of him. Not Daingean! Oh God, please God, not Daingean!

'I am committing all three of you to Daingean for a period of three years each!'

I looked at the other two. They didn't seem to be distressed. Perhaps it wasn't just me. But surely they couldn't want to be sent away too? It wasn't right. It wasn't natural. Nobody could have thoughts like mine, feel the way I did. It was a curious elation that came over me and completely enveloped me as I walked from the court with the two policemen.

The other two boys would not be leaving for Daingean for another week so I would be making the journey on my own. Four hours in a cell in William Street Barracks to wait for the three o'clock train to Tullamore in Offaly. My mother called at dinner time with a can of tea and I drank it out of the lid as I ate the bread and jam sandwiches. She stood in the middle of the cold, damp cell watching me, and then she cried. 'You'll have no mother by the time you get back! Oh God, you'll have no mother!' I didn't cry and I wondered if she was puzzled by my silence. I was glad to be leaving Limerick.

A young policeman in civilian clothes with a white belted raincoat collected me from the cell at half past two and told me that he would be escorting me to Daingean.

As we sat in the third-class carriage at Limerick station I could see my mother making her way along the platform and looking in all the windows of the train to see where I was. When she found me she reached in and handed me two bars of chocolate. The train started to move and she cried again and said something but I couldn't hear her words above the noise of the hissing steam and the chugging engine.

'Would you like a piece of chocolate?' I said to the policeman as we approached Limerick Junction. He smiled. 'Thanks very much,' he said. 'I didn't have time to get anything myself.'

That curious feeling of elation came over me again. I was glad to be leaving the claustrophobic poverty of Limerick and the mindless cruelty of Sexton Street. I would hate those Christian Brothers till my dying day.

We got off the train at Tullamore and walked to the police barracks, where my escort made enquiries about how to get to the village of Daingean where St Conleth's Reformatory School was situated. The station sergeant got us a taxi and we went out on the last lap of our journey. Dusk was falling as we drove through the flat, dull boglands of Offaly. We passed through the village of Ballynagar and finally arrived at Daingean (known as Philipstown in the days of the British) at seven o'clock that night.

The car pulled up near the stone bridge over the Grand Canal and the driver spoke to a passing villager. 'Could you tell us where the . . . er . . . Industrial School is?' he asked, choosing his words out of politeness to me. The villager frowned. 'You mean the reformatory?' he said. He pointed to a high stone wall on the other side of the bridge close by the canal. 'That's it,' he said. We crossed the bridge and drove through the iron gates.

The part of St Conleth's school visible to the public gaze on the other side of the gates was a two-storey, symmetrical building consisting of three wings that embraced well-tended lawns. The main wing faced the gates and the other two wings were connected to it at right angles and faced each other across the expanse of lawns, so that the entire building resembled a giant letter 'E' with the centre bar missing.

The driveway up to the main door was interrupted by a large marble plinth surmounted by a statue of St Conleth. The car weaved round to the left of the statue in a semicircular motion and then straightened out and went on for another twenty yards before coming to a halt.

I got out with the policeman and we stood for a moment on the gravelled driveway. I glanced back towards the gate but it was already hidden by the winter darkness and the bogland mist. Then the policeman nodded at the big solid door. 'This is it,' he said. 'Let's go in.'

From the *Limerick Socialist*, Vol. 6, No. 2, February 1977

Introduction to a Pub in Limerick
Knute Skinner

Once a sexton's hose, constructed on
a burial ground,
this pub houses the quick and the dead.
And those who mark time

in the snug bar tipple by the bones
of Seán a Scuab.
A twelfth-century brush peddler, he
had the luck to cross

the Shannon bridge into Limerick
at the right moment.
He found himself, John of the Brushes,
Limerick's first mayor.

The pub itself forms part of the walls
of St John's Churchyard
and against one of the gables stands
a vault, house high, built

long ago by a Limerick miller.
He spent his old age
in the vault, sitting and drinking tea,
getting used to it.

Come now, let us go into the pub,
order a porter,

and raise our glasses in a toast to
mayor and miller.

From A *Close Sky Over Killaspuglonane*, Dolmen Press, 1968

A Letter to an Only Aunt
Seán Bourke

26 Perryn Road
East Acton
London, W.3.

19 September 1966

Dear Mrs O'Grady,

Your curiosity may have been aroused a few weeks ago by a neighbour telling you
that a stranger by the name of Bourke had called to see you in your absence. That
stranger was me, Seán Bourke, of the Bengal Terrace clan. The neighbour in
question is the owner of a little huckster shop just a short distance from your home,
and she told me that you had gone to the seaside for the weekend with your
daughter Betty.

Why did I call to see you? There was no particular reason. It just suddenly
occurred to me when I was visiting Limerick for one of my rare home holidays that
you were my one and only aunt and that I had not seen you since the day I made
my first Holy Communion and my father, your brother, took me and my twin to see
you in our new grey flannel suits to collect the traditional piece of silver. I
remember that you gave us sixpence each, the largest single donation that we were
to receive on that glorious, memorable day. That was twenty-five years ago next
month, and I thought it was time to renew the acquaintance. . . .

My God, it has been so long that I remember when we called at your house in
High Street next to Mick Bourke's shop I was fascinated and overawed by the
elephant's foot which stood in your hall as a walking-stick stand; it was the most
exotic thing I had ever laid eyes on. I remember telling my mother afterwards about
the thick, crazy-paving skin like the bark of a tree and the big yellow toenails still
intact. And there was a carpet in your front room — a carpet! The likes of which
nobody in Bengal Terrace had ever seen. And the sweet, luxurious scent of freshly
cooked custard pervaded the air and danced magically around in my nostrils — and
custard surely goes with jelly and custard and jelly is for mansions and priests and
bishops in their palaces. What a day that was! A magical oasis in a vast desert of

poverty and deprivation. And it was twenty-five years ago and so much has changed.

As your brother Frank had seven sons, you may have some difficulty in placing me in particular but I think I can easily help you. I am — to use that charitable euphemism so often employed by my exasperated neighbours in Limerick — the 'wild' one. The police, the judges and the probation officers have used other descriptions for me over the years; for, alas, my 'wildness' did not end in Limerick. Indeed, only a very short while ago I finished a seven-year sentence in one of London's greatest jails for allegedly attempting to blow up a policeman with a bomb. The policeman in question was not even scratched, but he was given a tremendous fright, and of course the attempt *had* been made. However, that is all water-under-the-bridge, as the unpoetic English would say. Still, that experience in Wormwood Scrubs Prison was so interesting and so rich in terms of sheer human *living* that I am almost glad I went there. . . .

I enjoyed my holiday in Limerick immensely. The beauty of Irish speech is something which we take for granted when we are living in Ireland and after a few years in an English community (nobody corrupts the English language more than the English themselves) it is a great pleasure to go back home and just listen to the sheer poetry which every Irish man and woman seems to make of otherwise ordinary language.

I was sitting in Kirby's public house in William Street with Ger Nash, a chap with whom I went to school and who was in Limerick on holidays at the same time as me. A big fat man with a railway uniform and a vigorous growth of white hair protruding out at all angles from under his ill-fitting peaked cap came into the bar. He plodded across the boards with a heavy deliberate tread made all the noisier by his hob-nailed boots.

'Hello there, ladies,' he hailed the two young barmaids, 'what's the name of this pub?'

'Kirby's,' answered one of the girls.

'Never heard of it,' said the old man as he lodged his great weight on a creaking stool. 'A pint of porter,' he added when he had settled down comfortably.

The girl gave him his pint of Guinness. As he reached out a huge hand to envelop the glass, he accidentally knocked an empty bottle to the floor. It was a big bottle and when it hit the bare boards it made a very loud noise that could be heard in every part of the building.

'Jasus, me false toot is after fallin' out!' he exclaimed. . . .

I was pleased and relieved to be told by the teacher Jack Danagher in a pub one night that the Christian Brothers have got less vicious and sadistic with the passing of years. This will mean, of course, that there will now be less young men leaving Ireland with hatred in their hearts for these unholy teachers of the poor. When I think of the poverty of those days and the callous indifference of the Christian Brothers to the plight of their suffering pupils, I cannot help wondering what their founder, Brother Rice, would have thought of those frustrated little tyrants.

However, to finish on a more cheerful note. During my holiday in Limerick I made a point of revisiting some of the old haunts of my schooldays, including the Courthouse where I had on more than one occasion been hauled before the late Mr Justice Gleeson for various outrageous transgressions against the community. This day, for the first time in my life, I was a spectator at the judicial proceedings rather than an unwilling participant. As I sat there for the first ten minutes unheedful of what was going on around me, my mind went back to that day long ago when I was 12 years of age and I stood in this very same room accused of stealing a pot of jam from a railway wagon. . . .

Anyway, when I called this day the presiding Justice was Mr de Burca. The erring citizens on the hard wooden benches at the back of the tiny courtroom nervously awaiting their fate had not changed much in appearance with the passing years except perhaps that they looked less hungry and better dressed. . . . Anyway, the humour is still there, even if Mr de Burca is not prepared to share in it. After I had been sitting in the courtroom about an hour a fellow with the very grand Christian name of Sebastian was brought in and charged with disorderly conduct.

'What are the details, Superintendent?' asked Mr Justice de Burca, as he rested his elbows on the arms of his huge mahogany chair and placed his fingertips together in front of him to form his hands into the shape of a church steeple.

'Well, your honour,' said the Superintendent, standing up and reading from a typed sheet, 'at one o'clock in the morning on the 28th instant, acting on information received, a number of garda surrounded the Protestant cemetery in St John's Square. A search was made of the cemetery itself and the accused was found lying on top of the flat roof of a tomb in the grounds. He smelt of drink. When asked by the garda what he was doing there, he replied: "I felt like a climb"!'

Well, Mrs O'Grady, I had better bring this letter to a close. I fear I have rambled on rather too much as it is and perhaps taken up more of your time than I should. I intend to be in Limerick again at Christmas; would you mind if I called in to see you? In the meantime, every good wish to you and Mr O'Grady and all the family.

Yours sincerely,
Seán Bourke

From a copy of a letter in the possession of the Editor.

Spring Rice
Finbar Crowe

Once again youth comes to frolic,
Sportive seedlings sapped with joy.

Mothers, purling, knit their future —
Dreams that melt in a clear spring sky.

New life bursting through the old wood,
Oozing sprays of luscious green,
Sickly saplings sprout new vigour,
Nature stirs through my demesne.

Over yonder emerald ivy
Slowly scales the Georgian wall;
Cut, yet gripping, clipped, advancing,
Running crimson in the fall.

And in November Poppies marching,
Hiding old wounds, bodies frail,
Braving scorn to honour comrades,
Dead, interred at Passchendaele.

I see, but keep my stony silence,
Who would heed me if I spoke? —
'Spring Rice, stylite* Lord Monteagle,
What can *he* know of Irish folk?'

I meddle not, but ripening watch,
The rose that made a thorn crown,
The rich red berry filled with bitter,
The thistle's tears of soft white down.

* A statue of Thomas Spring Rice, Lord Monteagle, MP for Limerick 1820–32, stands in the People's
Park.

From *The Old Limerick Journal*, No. 12, Autumn 1982

The Wounded King
Christopher Somerville

The September sun shone hot on the streets of Limerick, bringing the publicans in
shirtsleeves to their doors for a breath of air and putting a rosy glow on the noses
of the shopgirls eating their lunchtime sandwiches in the park. The girls munched
and chatted as they sat on the grass, their backs to a wildly painted statue of some

Celtic god or other straddling a wheeled chariot, twice life-size, stark naked, a line of silvery flames blazing on his out-thrust arm. Handsomely, even improbably endowed, he made a potent backdrop to the carefree girls and their chummy exchanges. None of them so much as glanced up at his protuberances dangling overhead. Evidently the month or so that had passed since his erection had drawn the sting of controversy. Early in his reign some impudent vandal had made off with his wedding tackle — 'Statue Loses Crown Jewels' trumpeted the headline in the local paper — but now his dignity had been restored. A couple of late-season tourists, strolling past, pointed, snorted and collapsed into laughter, and the shop-girls looked up from their sandwiches in bafflement. Limerick people can handle these things.

Lines of bunting were strung across the streets, and 'Limerick 300' banners fixed to the lamp posts. The city was in the middle of celebrating the three hundredth anniversary of the signing of the Treaty of Limerick, and doing its best to attract the attention of newcomers fresh off the planes at Shannon Airport.

From *The Road to Roaringwater: A Walk Down the West of Ireland*, HarperCollins Publishers, 1993

Little Old Ladies
Ciaran O'Driscoll

Adept at the furtive knee in the groin
and the elbow in the solar plexus,
little old ladies jump the bus queue
waving their out-of-date passes.

On the sixteen-forty to Raheen,
foraging gangs of three or four
little old ladies surround the conductor
and tell him to stick his peak-hour fare.

Little old ladies conspire to bring
the economy crashing down
by blocking supermarket checkouts
and driving weekend shoppers insane

with an endless supply of pennies counted
out of their moth-eaten purses.
Little old ladies spend their pensions
on knuckledusters and karate courses.

Little old ladies read poems, my foot!
The little old ladies I have seen
on the sixteen-forty to Raheen
were leafing through manuals of guerrilla warfare

and would spit on the *Penguin Book of Contemporary Verse.*
I have seen grown men break down and cry
on the sixteen-forty to Raheen
when fixed by a little old lady's eye.

From *The Poet and His Shadow*, Dedalus, 1990

Séamus Ó Cinnéide: Wounded Warrior
Cormac O'Connor

Séamus and I sat on the same bench in school. His fascination with poetry was infectious. It was tragic, and indeed ironic, that because of a teacher who did not understand poetry, Séamus left the school before he obtained any certificate. He never returned. But our friendship survived the years. I would meet him on the street and his conversation would be about Yeats or Ferguson, or Bobby Burns, or of some new play in the theatre. Or perhaps he would show me some lines he wrote himself.

Séamus worked in the local library. His knowledge of the books was extensive. He would steer me towards some new writer or some 'old reliable' when I came to borrow. I would go away with an armful of reading, but not before we had some vigorous conversations on things literary. Inevitably a group would gather around him as we discoursed on the arts. He delighted in such gatherings. . . .

I would meet him in the street, without a tie, even in the coldest of weather, and wearing an old sports jacket that had seen better days. We would go and have coffee together and his conversation still would be of Eliot or Chaucer or the Abbey Theatre. . . . As the years passed he wrote for a local newspaper, 'to make a contribution', as he put it. The few pounds he earned were meagre but sustained him. . . .

Séamus had deep wounds to bear, wounds he never spoke of but which had left their mark, wounds that came from we knew not where. Knowing him over many years I knew the wounds were deep but I could never open so sensitive a subject. . . .

A few more years passed by and, by a twist of fate, we had to move to another county. . . . We would enquire about him from time to time and learned that he had 'gone into himself', that he rarely was 'out and about' now. He who in the early

days was a familiar figure walking the river bank now was seen no more. . . .
Eventually I got news that Séamus had died.

He who saw the nature of things, and never asked anything of the world, was
gone, without the world's farewell, as if released from a cold and unlistening prison
to go and pluck daffodils in higher fields. He was, indeed, as he described himself
in one of his cherished letters, 'a warrior without banners'.

From *The Messenger*, July 1997

TEN

POLITICS

King John's Charter

Steps are being taken in Limerick for the celebration of what is described as the Seventh Centenary of the Charter of Incorporation of the City. Irish history, broadly speaking, is a much neglected study, otherwise such a celebration would not be proposed, and the fact of its having been proposed indicates the process of anglicisation we are undergoing, and which in time might substitute West Britonism for Irish nationality. The charter we are asked to celebrate is not a charter of incorporation in the sense of constituting a body for municipal administration: street cleansing and road making, and gas and water were not in King John's line. His was a genius of a higher order, and his charter an instrument of a more fateful purpose. It is a symbol of that dominant influence of English authority over Irish affairs against which for seven hundred years the strength of Irish nationality has been fighting. It provided for the appointment of a mayor and two bailiffs to govern Limerick in the absence of John, then Lord of Ireland, and thus typifies the military subjugation of the country which John and his Anglo-Norman followers were so zealous to accomplish. It is most singular at the present moment to find that Irishmen have been asked to celebrate the granting of this Charter, and that, too, by a nationalist mayor and Corporation who have thus appealed to the national instincts of our people to render homage to the works of a dishonourable English king, in whose favour no historian of England has a good word to offer, and whose memory no Englishman would even dream of revering.

The installation of John as Lord of Ireland coincides with the extinction of the Kings of Munster, the last of whom, Donald O'Brien, died bravely in the struggle against the Normans. Donald was the representative of a kingly line. He had vowed that 'Limerick should no more be a nest for foreigners.' He had devoted himself to his religion and his country, and to this day, through all the change and havoc of centuries, his memory is preserved in the Cathedral of St Mary, which he himself founded on the site of his royal palace. His death in 1194 removed at that time the ablest opponent of the English colonisation of the country, and Limerick did not come under the English Government till his decease. The establishment of that authority began with John, then Earl Moreton and Lord of Ireland, and the charter now so much spoken of was issued by him from Killaloe and dated 18 December 1197. Ordinarily that charter might be taken as an honour conferred upon Limerick; in reality it implied the subjection of the people. It was not a concession to the mere Irish, but a privilege to the 'superior' English who in the train of John flocked into Limerick and helped themselves to whatever spoliation the conquest enabled them to gather. It is well to quote the description of these events given by a historian of the period, and a writer, too, who was ever ready to preserve the English sentiment.

'Immediately after the death of Donald', says this writer, 'the English appear to have recovered their authority in the city of Limerick. We find that in 1195, the seventh of Richard I, an English magistracy was established in Limerick, John Strafford being appointed to the office of Provost. In 1198 the title of Provost was changed to that of Mayor, when Adam Sarvant was appointed to that office. The citizens were also permitted to choose two bailiffs for the better government of the city. But the English in the same year were forced to abandon Limerick for a third time by M'Carthy of Desmond. King John on his accession to the crown was so sensible of the necessity of regaining possession of this important place that he renewed his grant of the lands of Thomond to Broasa, while he committed the recovery and custody of the city to William de Burgo. From this period, for more than four centuries, the English, though surrounded by enemies on every side, remained undisputed possessors of a prize which had been so forcibly contested. John gave orders for the adoption of every measure for its security. Thomond Bridge was built and strongly fortified to secure a passage at all times into the territories of Thomond, and a castle of great strength was erected which commanded the bridge in its full extent. English settlers now flocked to Limerick in great numbers, and arrangements were made, consistent with the policy of the times, to preserve tranquillity among the three distinct races — Irish, Danes and English — by which the district was now inhabited. Treaties of amity were concluded with the neighbouring chieftains; the suburb now called the Irishtown was allotted to the residence of the native inhabitants, and some portions of the adjacent territory were granted to the Ostmen, while, to secure the allegiance of the new English colonists, many immunities were conferred on the citizens by charter in the second year of John's reign. Amongst these privileges, the most important were that the citizens were not to be impleaded outside the walls, that they should be free of toll and passage through the King's dominions, and they might yearly elect a Mayor, a discreet and proper person, and faithful to the Crown, etc.'

Here we have the acknowledgment that John's charter was conferred on the English colonists in order to secure their allegiance. With characteristic English haughtiness, they are styled the citizens who were not to be impleaded (arraigned) outside the walls, while the native inhabitants, the Irish, were condescendingly permitted to remain in the suburb called the Irishtown, which was not walled till a later date. During the reign of John that portion of the city inhabited by the colonists was surrounded with walls and it is recorded that this king made several grants to his followers, within and without the walls. During the reigns of subsequent sovereigns the terms of John's charter were preserved and enlarged, only however in the English interest. In 1582 by charter of Elizabeth the subjugated area was raised to the dignity of a city. This charter sets out that 'considering the fidelity and obedience which the citizens of that city to us in all things freely showed, and were ready to show at their own very great expenses, labours and charges, especially in the most wicked rebellion by Gerald, Earl of Desmond and his Confederates, against us and our Royal power, very lately attempted and perpetrated. We have willed that our city of Limerick shall be, and remain for ever hereafter, a city in itself, and the citizens of the said city be, and for ever hereafter, shall remain one body corporate and politic in deed, fact, and name, by the name of Mayor, Bailiffs and Citizens of Limerick.' Who the citizens were may be gathered from the provision that 'no person who is by blood an Irishman or who shall live as an Irishman etc., etc., shall be preferred to any dignity, etc.' This provision was excluded from the Charter of James, 1609. The names of some of the mayors are not very Irish: Adam Sarvant, Thomas Cropper, Roger Maij, John Cambilor, Samuel Minuter, Sewardus de Ferendona, John Avenbrugger, etc. The succession of mayors and bailiffs continued uninterrupted from King John's reign. 'Limerick was formed into a state consistent with the ideas of its English rulers, whose policy was to have each city and town in Ireland thoroughly English, for nearly all outside the walls continued absolutely hostile to the Crown and interest of England.'

The light of the history here quoted dispels the idea so erroneously set up, that John's charter was a privilege conferred upon the Irish. It was, as indicated, an English instrument of power, and why Irishmen should be now called upon to celebrate it sur-passes comprehension. The subsequent history of the mayoralty and the Corporation, for a lengthened period, is distinguished by the rule of the ascendancy party in Ireland down to the period of the reform of the municipalities, when, thanks to the spread of better ideas and the struggle for religious equality, some of the disabilities that denied office to Irishmen were removed, and this good work crowned by O'Connell being elected Lord Mayor of Dublin.

By these reforms power passed into the hands of the people, and to that alone, and not to the charters of John or any later sovereign, must be attributed the honour and prestige which in a popular sense now attaches to the mayoralty of Limerick in common with that of other Irish cities. In sympathy with the enlightened progress which these reforms indicate, no Irishman can participate in the homage which it is sought ingloriously to bestow on this charter in Limerick. If we honour the charter we cannot but consistently honour the King, who is described, not by a mere partisan Irishman, but by the English historian, Hume, as 'equally odious and contemptible in public and private life; he had affronted the barons by his insolence, dishonoured their families by his gallantries, and enraged them by his tyranny', while of his tyranny we have an exquisite sample in the words of Professor Gardiner, the most notable of modern English historians, who writes that while in Ireland, John amused himself by pulling the hairs out of the beards of the Irish Chiefs.

From *Reading For The People, No. 1, King John's 'Charter' to Limerick: What Irishmen are Asked to Celebrate,* O'Connor and Co., 1898

The Corrupt Corporation
Maurice Lenihan

The battle of independence was nobly fought in Limerick, nor could it ever have been fought so well, were it not for the wanton plunder of the Corporation, which, stimulated by the apprehension that its days were numbered, left no stone unturned to make the most of the time of respite, from a doom which all honest men heartily desired to see it receive. Daniel O'Connell had already denounced the misdeeds of the Corporation, the annals of which, at this time, were nothing more than malversation of the public funds, outrageous infringements on public liberty, corruption of the worst character, manufacture of freemen, etc. For some time Thomas Spring Rice, Esq., who had attained a prominent place in the public eye, by energy and attention to public business, had identified himself with the popular struggles. This gentleman, connected with the city by family ties of ancient duration, and born in Mungret Street, threw himself heart and soul into the ranks of the Independents; and well did he advance his own interests by the part he took, in promoting those of the citizens against the conspiracies of an unscrupulous faction. A Protestant, Mr Spring Rice carried with him his influential connections and friends of that persuasion. Early in 1815, he wrote a pamphlet, in which he vehemently denounced the Grand Jury Laws. The Corporation had become rank in the nostrils of all classes, and every man wished to see an end to its ignominious reign of audacity and spoliation. Mr Tuthill had fought the good fight, but was defeated by a combination of the most discordant elements. . . .

The battle of independence continued to wage in the city. Mr Rice, already the champion of the popular cause, was looked upon as the future representative in parliament of Limerick. At every meeting of the Independents he took a prominent part. — He aided all who stood forth against the irresponsible iniquity of the Corporation. As each sum was doled out by that body for corrupt purposes, he and the Independents took note, and exerted themselves to check the wrongdoings of their honours, but it was all in vain for a time; the manufacture of freemen by the Corporation was such, that nothing could resist its bad effects in interfering with the exertions of the citizens, who, nothing daunted — persevered, knowing that truth and justice were on their side. '*Magna est veritas et prevalebit.*'

Mr Tuthill was chaired after a contest between him and Major Vereker, in which, however, the gallant Major was victorious. The local Tory organ did not publish a report of the popular ovation, because it had been always ranged on the opposite side; but in a Dublin paper of the day, the chairing was described as an unparalleled popular triumph, during which Mr Tuthill was surrounded by at least 30,000 people.

On the chair were four labels in letters of gold; the first was, God save the King; the second, the Man of the People; the third, the Champion of our Rights; and the fourth, Tuthill and Independence. He was presented with favours from the several trades: with a beautiful sash from the clothiers. What heightened the scene, and excited the greatest enthusiasm, was the presenting him with a branch of laurel, the leaves of which were edged with gold, by Mrs Russell, of Glentworth Street. This was done amidst loud huzzas, waving of handkerchiefs and hats. The procession, in the following order, then moved on: first, the different tradesmen with cockades and favours, amounting to some thousands, their respective banners in front, and walking arm in arm, indiscriminately united. Next came a square car, with high railing, interwoven with shrubs and flowers; in the middle was planted the tree of knowledge, representing the garden of Eden; two children were standing at the step of the garden, dressed in buff to represent Adam and Eve in their innocent state; a large eel was twined round the tree, in imitation of the serpent who alights on it, and was anxiously expecting Adam would take the apple from Eve that she was presenting him with. Then came the chair, preceded by gentlemen bearing banners, on which were inscribed, 'Our Music is the Voice of the People': and now our longing eyes beheld Mr Tuthill surrounded with nearly all the wealth, talent, and respectability of Limerick. On the platform were Mr William Roche, the banker, Mr Mathew Barrington, and other respectable gentlemen; and the chair was followed by about 800 respectable citizens with wands, to which branches of laurel were bound. The procession was closed by an innumerable concourse of people, and proceeded through every quarter of the city, even to the liberties; but in going through George's Street, Major Vereker stepped out on the balcony at the Club-house, respectfully bowed to Mr Tuthill, and remained uncovered until the procession passed by. (Mr Tuthill, who had been the man of the people, fell, in some short time afterwards, from his high estate, and went over to the enemy, which he had expended such enormous sums, and so much energy and determination in opposing.) . . .

Such was a chairing in the times at which our history has arrived, and such was the enthusiasm of the citizens, though success did not smile on their exertions. The Corporation, in the face of these demonstrations, proceeded in its iniquitous and spoliating courses. Hundreds of freemen continued to be manufactured. (The petition referred to the manufacture of non-resident freemen, and to the fact that multitudes of men were not granted their freedom who had the right.) . . . No wonder that the 'rising star' of Thomas Spring Rice should be regarded under auspices so favourable to the interests he undertook to promote. . . .

It is no wonder that legalised vengeance should have befallen the Corporation. In the history of the world there has been seldom heard of such malversation, spoliation, and unblushing plunder.

From *Limerick; Its History, Ecclesiastical, Civil and Military, from the Earliest Ages*, Hodges, Smith and Co., 1866

The Politics of Aubrey de Vere
John P. Gunning

In politics the poet belonged to the Edmund Burke school of thought: and was always an ardent admirer of that political philosopher. Though Mr de Vere has written some interesting political treatises, he was, however, never publicly identified himself with party interests. It is well, perhaps, that the bard did not openly attach himself to party. No good man can do it with impunity. The best men will suffer most because the conviction of their cause is deeper. And how much more must be the sufferings when one with the sensibility of a poet throws himself into the excitements of fierce political struggle. The endowment of feeling and imagination which qualifies him to be the ideal interpreter of life, wholly unfits him for participation in that real life where imagination and feeling are misplaced. He must inevitably go under in a flame of fire.

Mr de Vere, like Burke, had strong conservative tendencies. He had the greatest reverence for old institutions, habits and traditions; and down to the last moment of his life he dreaded and hated anything approaching organic change in the constitution. He feared, perhaps, too strongly and without sufficient justification, the elements of evil and discord which might arise from the establishment of pure democracy. On the achievement of a separate political nationality the poet foresaw, as it were, the downfall of the Catholic faith in Ireland; hence that remarkable expression of his when speaking of O'Connell's Repeal of the Union: 'There exists a much nobler one — the Catholic ideal — and they are inconsistent.'

Politics or politicians had never much interest for the poet, and he often spoke of both in a jesting sort of way.

Speaking of a marble group of Bailey's, representing 'Maternal Affection', he remarks: 'It is the most perfectly lovely thing I ever saw, of a beauty so absolute that it would tranquillise in a moment wild beasts fighting for food, or even politicians in the House of Commons.'

Many recent critics — lady critics, probably, as Mr de Vere was a bachelor — in the newspaper press have characterised the poet as 'eccentric' in his manner. Nothing is further from the truth than this. In his later years the bard loved solitude and retirement, and found much consolation among his books. In these years books and solitude were his solitary pride. He was seldom abroad until evening, except on Sunday, when he went in the morning to Adare to divine service. Let the weather be what it might, he never resisted the temptation of going out. The fact of his being so retiring and apparently exclusive, led many, from want of thought, to believe that the man was odd, if not eccentric. In these years, too, his hearing and memory . . . were slightly impaired, and this, with a great fastidiousness of moral taste, gave an appearance of shyness and reserve to his manners, towards the curious and other acquaintances, and caused a quick rejection of their approaches, which, in the eyes of the ordinary observer, had all the semblance of eccentricity. No doubt in appearance, dress and conversation he was different from the ordinary type of humanity, and in the company of farmers and tradesmen, whose only thoughts are of bullocks, the price of stocks, interest on money, dividends, Mr de Vere would have been taken for a simpleton. . . .

If we might attempt to sum up in a sententious phrase the characteristics of the poet, the last upholder of the Wordsworth tradition, to name the informing spirit of his life and work, I should do it in the words — the spirit of charity. In an age characterised as it is by hurry, doubt of the future, literary jealousies, poetic namby-pambyism, there is something refreshing in watching this spirit animating, as it were, every thought of the poet. . . .

The want of appreciation troubled him — and what poet would it not — but still he would not truckle to the animalism of the public house, the delectation of the 'man in the street', or the catch-penny sensationalism of our day. Nor was he indifferent to the fame which he might well think was his just due. . . . Anxious as our poet may have been of securing fame, yet it was not altogether fame or any lower motive that induced him to hold an unwearied pen. . . . No man holding such high rank in the literary world made so little out of his works. In fact he had to reprint the latest editions of his poems at his own expense. 'If I left down my pen', said the genial poet, 'I would double my income.'

Mr de Vere did not write solely for money. He loved his art and he revelled in it. He did not belong to the new race of poetical jargonists, whose barbarous and unmeaning effusions have struck at the essential existence of genuine productions in poetry and literature. Absorbed in the contemplation of material objects, and rejecting whatever does not enter into their restricted notions of utility, these cold, mercenary, poetic seers, with nothing but millions in their imaginations, and whose choicest works of art are the ballads of the music hall, have no conception of the sublimity of genius except the question of 'demand and supply', which rules their intellectual tasks. The spirit of levity and immoral suggestion which at the present time is shaking the columns of society by detracting from or burlesquing its elevating moral principles, our poet abhorred and condemned. Mr de Vere's inspiration was drawn not from the barrack room, the public house, or the baser side of human nature, but from a purer and deeper source: from the mysteries of his faith, from the patriotic and historical legends of his country. Without these movements of the soul and of the heart how poor and artificial a thing is that sparkling composition, which flashes with the cold vibrations of mere art and artifice.

The *Saturday Review* of 14 September 1861 called our author severely to task on this score: 'Mr Aubrey de Vere', it writes, 'has cultivated with creditable and profitable care a genuine poetical faculty. His verses are skilfully constructed, his language is polished and accurate; and he has always a definite meaning. But we

regret that so much taste and ability should be wasted on uncongenial controversy.'
Needless to say our poet did not truckle to his English critics.

From *Aubrey de Vere: A Memoir*, Guy & Co. Ltd, 1902

Dr O'Dwyer and the Plan of Campaign
Laurence M. Geary

A minority among the Catholic hierarchy strongly disapproved of the Plan of
Campaign, notably Dr O'Dwyer, Bishop of Limerick, described by Wilfrid Blunt as
a 'shaky kind of patriot' who had gone over bag and baggage to the enemy. . . . In an
emotional and self-righteous response to a charge in the *Freeman's Journal*, O'Dwyer
denied that he was a unionist or a 'landlord' bishop and proceeded to condemn
boycotting and the Plan of Campaign, one, because it was sinful, and the other, on
account of its manifest unjustness. He felt conscience-bound, he wrote, to stand
aloof from a movement which he castigated as politically stupid and morally wrong.

The vast majority of the bishops, however, supported the Plan of Campaign,
albeit with varying degrees of enthusiasm. Some feared the pull of the secret
societies if the episcopacy refused to align themselves with the popular agitation.
Others considered the Plan to be a desperate remedy for a desperate situation. . . .
Most of the bishops followed the example of the two most influential churchmen
of the day, the formidable Archbishop of Dublin, Dr Walsh, and his ebullient
colleague in Cashel, Dr Croke, who, after initial doubts, gave their unequivocal
support to the agitation. In early December 1886, Walsh publicly defended the
Plan of Campaign on moral grounds. The result of his archiepiscopal blessing was
to convert the waverers in the nationalist ranks. As the Bishop of Clonfert wrote
to his nephew in Australia a fortnight later, '*practically* the priests, bishops and
people are united'.

A lone, dissenting, though not entirely unexpected, voice was now raised. Dr
O'Dwyer had stated in a letter to the Mayor of Limerick that the papal rescript,
condemning the Plan of Campaign and boycotting, was binding on the conscience
of each Catholic and, while it was a grievous sin to disobey, it was an even greater
one to deny the Pope's authority to issue the circular.

Dr O'Dwyer was publicly and roundly condemned. Speaking in Limerick, the
Bishop's own diocesan centre, William O'Brien called him 'an arrogant ecclesiastical official'. At Kildare, John Dillon denied the right of Dr O'Dwyer to speak
on behalf of the Catholic Church in Ireland, insisting that the majority of Irish
bishops supported the Plan of Campaign and that Dr O'Dwyer spoke for himself
alone. Dillon cast him as

the champion of the landlord interest in Ireland. . . . He is the supporter and the champion of rack-renting and landgrabbing in Ireland. . . . He represents a small minority of the Roman Catholic Church in Ireland who are on the side of the oppressor against the oppressed, of the rich man against the poor man, of the landlord against the tenant.

Throughout the country, successive speakers drove home the point that Rome had no right to interfere in Irish politics. . . .

The most emphatic refutation of the papal rescript was delivered by William O'Brien at Glensharrold, in the diocese of Limerick, on 29 May. 'We will stick to the Plan of Campaign', he pledged. 'We will stick to boycotting and will treat every landgrabber and every exterminator as a public pest and a public enemy more dangerous to society than a leper is.'

On the following day, the Irish hierarchy met at Clonliffe College. . . . The only member of the hierarchy to publicly break ranks was the unrelenting Dr O'Dwyer. At a diocesan synod on 11 June, he repeated the points he made in his letter to the Mayor of Limerick a fortnight earlier. O'Dwyer insisted that the rescript was binding on both the clergy and laity of his diocese and said that those who agitated against it were committing 'heinous offences'.

With the exception of the Limerick diocese, the papal rescript had little or no effect on the agrarian agitation. In general, at local level, the clergy who had pledged themselves to the Plan of Campaign continued to support it. . . .

A resumption of evictions on several Plan of Campaign estates in the early months of 1890 not only added to the Plan's financial difficulties but led directly to a bitter public clash between John Dillon and Dr O'Dwyer, Bishop of Limerick. In January 1890, eviction decrees were obtained against a number of tenants on the estate of John Christopher Delmege, Glensharrold, Co. Limerick. In mid-May, the receiver of the property offered a clear receipt to August 1889 to all tenants who, before 27 May 1890, paid a year's rent, less thirty per cent. The question of arrears, which averaged three and one-half years' rent, would thus be disposed of. In a circular letter, which was read out to the tenants on 24 May, Dr O'Dwyer appealed to them to accept the receiver's generous offer and thereby save themselves from eviction. Should they act otherwise, he added, they would be 'guilty of reckless folly' and would be unable to convince anyone in the future that they were 'the victims of rapacious landlordism'. During a debate on the Irish estimates in the House of Commons on 11 July, Dillon described the Bishop's action as scandalous and denounced his epistle as 'one of the most infamous, cowardly, dastardly letters ever penned by ecclesiastical hand'. Three days later, the letters columns of the *Freeman's Journal* carried O'Dwyer's reply. He deprecated 'Dillon's outburst of outrageous language', claiming that it was 'the conduct of a coward and a dastard to use such language to any man, but most of all to a bishop, behind his back'. He charged Dillon with personal and political cowardice, implicitly accused him and the members of the parliamentary party of financial dishonesty and concluded by roundly condemning boycotting and the Plan of Campaign.

Nationalist opinion was enraged. Under the heading, 'An Episcopal Swashbuckler', the *Roscommon Herald* editorialised: The prelate of Limerick flooded a column and a half of the *Freeman* with a quantity of language which proclaimed its author as a past master in the art of abuse. The *Sligo Champion* denounced O'Dwyer's letter as 'utterly false and shameless', while the *Westmeath Examiner* proclaimed it to be 'outrageous'. The leader writer of the influential *Freeman's Journal* opined:

> We cannot recall anything of later days, in a public argument between two gentlemen of standing, so lofty, more unwarranted and unfair than Dr O'Dwyer's charges of a personal nature against the trusted, the honourable and the fearless John Dillon. To twit with cowardice or dishonesty a man of the character of Mr Dillon . . . was so absurd that were the thoughts not penned by a bishop they would be passed unnoticed as the frothings of impotent malignity.

Dillon believed that O'Dwyer had, for the first time, fully revealed himself to the public in his true character and that the Bishop's intemperate outburst would benefit the nationalist cause. A monster protest meeting was held in O'Dwyer's own cathedral city of Limerick on 24 August. William O'Brien, Tim Harrington and Dillon, among others, addressed the huge assembly and the latter's speech was, in effect, an unrepentant defence of boycotting. The Bishop's reply was immediate and characteristically forthright. Once again, he condemned the 'utterly sinful character' of boycotting and the Plan of Campaign, and stressed, in the wake of the papal rescript, that it was his duty to speak out against them.

Several of O'Dwyer's more conservative episcopal brethren supported his stand. Bishop Coffey of Kerry described the language of the lay Catholic leaders, both inside and outside of parliament, as deplorable and complained to Tobias Kirby in Rome that they seemed determined 'to subvert ecclesiastical authority'. Similar views were expressed by Dr Michael Logue, Archbishop of Armagh, and by Bishop Laurence Gillooly of Elphin. Bishop T.A. O'Callaghan of Cork and Bishop Lynch of Kildare reminded their flocks of the papal condemnation of boycotting and the Plan of Campaign. The more nationalistic members of the hierarchy, however, strongly deprecated O'Dwyer's actions. The two most influential Irish churchmen, the Archbishops of Dublin and Cashel, believed that the Dillon-O'Dwyer contretemps reflected little credit on either man but they were equally convinced, in Croke's phrase, that 'the Bishop erred ever so much more grievously than the layman'. In a letter to the Bishop of Elphin, Dr Walsh bitterly criticised O'Dwyer for pursuing 'a crotchety line of his own'.

From *The Plan of Campaign 1886–1891*, Cork University Press, 1986

The 1901 Mayoral Election
Padraig Ó Maidin

It was recognised even at the time that the election of a mayor for Limerick city in 1901 was a throw-back to the early 1870s when open voting had first been introduced and caused many a lively and occasionally rowdy scene in the Council Chamber in Patrick Street. One of the contemporary accounts stated: 'There was an attempt made to debauch the constituency and a fairly successful manoeuvre to defeat the nationalist candidate, James F. Barry, T.C., who was thrown out as a result of the second poll.'

John Daly, who had held the office of mayor for the previous two years, was again a candidate. He had returned to Limerick in 1896 after having served twelve years in English prisons on charges arising out of the dynamite campaign at the time. After a gruelling lecture tour in America he had founded a successful bakery firm in the city and was elected to the City Council. In 1899 he was elected Mayor and was re-elected the following year. Few thought that he would go forward again in 1901.

The most favoured candidate at the time was Sir Thomas Cleeve, a loyalist and a Unionist, proprietor of the well-known Cleeve's factory which had given considerable employment to the citizens. The rate of wages paid in the factory was to be an element in the election of 1901, one of the councillors stating that a girl employed there had received only 1s. 1½d. after six days' work.

The reports published on 24 January 1901 agree that a mob in favour of the Unionist candidate, Sir Thomas Cleeve, besieged the City Hall long before the hour fixed for the election. 'A mob violently favourable to the Unionist candidate were outside the Council Chamber, shouting themselves hoarse, cheering for Cleeve, or groaning those to whom they took exception. Eight or nine men, with a banner, which was stated to be at one time the flag of the defunct Dock Labourers' Society, was borne up and down Patrick Street, and the shouting and uproar went on until the crowds thought it was time to get into the Council Chamber.'

The night patrol of the Corporation were powerless to prevent the mob from getting into the Town Hall and from swarming up the stairs. The patrol then attempted to keep them out of the Council Chamber. 'To no purpose, for the mob smashed the door from the hinges and gained admission.' The efforts of the patrol were then confined to getting the members of the Corporation into the chamber in comparative safety.

There were originally five candidates for the mayoralty: John Daly, the outgoing Mayor; James F. Barry; Sir Thomas Cleeve, City High Sheriff; James Kett; and Alderman Joyce, MP. Joyce retired in favour of Barry. Kett then gave notice of his intention to retire and requested permission to explain his conduct when a vote was being taken. Mayor Daly said that he did not see any reason why they should have a silent vote and granted the permission.

Councillor Donnellan then proposed Cleeve, amid cheers and hisses. He said that he could see no hope for the resurrection of the labour and trades interests of the city, nationalism was at a low ebb, and therefore he was supporting Cleeve who represented the commerce of the city. Many things had been said against the firm of Cleeve's but he had been shown proof that they paid as much wages as any concern in the city. He was interrupted by a question as to the number of hours a day worked by the employees of the firm, to which he did not reply.

Councillor Begley seconded the proposal, but his remarks could not be heard because of the cheers and the counter-cheers for Daly and Cleeve. When Councillor O'Brien of the Irishtown intimated that he was supporting Cleeve there were rowdy interruptions of: 'Oh, you traitor' and 'You are only a crawler.' There was confusion and uproar at this point as the crowd in the public gallery attempted to get through the barrier into the chamber proper but they were prevented by the night patrol and the Mayor's sergeants, one fellow at least getting a broken nose.

One of the councillors demanded to know: 'Are we in Ireland or in England? If we are in Ireland let us behave like Irishmen.' Councillor Whelan then proposed Alderman John Daly, the outgoing Mayor for re-election, denouncing Cleeve who 'belonged to that section in Ireland who had exterminated the people and brought famine and ruin on the distracted'. He was seconded by James Moloney, amid further uproar.

Councillor Vaughan then proposed Barry. 'It was with pain he saw an English rabble there purchased with porter. They would weep and wail yet for this.' Councillor John Slattery supported the candidature of Barry, 'an honest labour candidate'. He wanted to know why Daly would not stand down and allow Barry to be elected. At this point Jack-in-the-Box O'Brien from the Irishtown was effectively silenced by Councillor Donnellan who put his hand over his mouth.

On the first poll there were 11 for Barry, 12 for Daly and 15 for Cleeve. Two members did not vote. Barry was then eliminated and the second poll resulted in 21 for Daly and 15 for Cleeve, 4 not voting. Amid increasing uproar the town clerk declared Alderman John Daly elected for his third term. He was to add to the mayoral chain a gold medallion as large as a crown piece, recording his conviction and sentence to life imprisonment in 1884.

From the *Cork Examiner*, 24 January 1973

An Easter Message
Kathleen Clarke

On Holy Thursday (1916), I was sent to Limerick with despatches. I took my three children with me to leave them with my mother, so that I could be free to take on the duty assigned to me in the Rising. On arriving in Limerick I presented the despatches to the men there, and also a verbal message: 'Tell them that John MacNeill has agreed to sign the Proclamation and is quite enthusiastic.' After delivering both to Colivet and another man, who I think was Ledden, I was told that they were holding a meeting, at the end of which they would give me a message to bring back to Dublin. I told them that I had orders to take the mail-train back to Dublin that night, and that they must have the message ready by then. Someone would be at Kingsbridge station to meet me, as the train would be arriving in the early hours of the morning.

Before train time arrived, Colivet, Ledden and another man, who I think was George Clancy, came in from the Fianna Hall at the rear of my mother's house, where the meeting was being held. They asked me to wait over until next day, as they had not yet reached a decision on the message I was to take back. I said that I thought I should obey orders to return that night. I agreed to stay, very reluc-tantly; I had a full day's work waiting for me on Good Friday.

The three men stayed for a while chatting before returning to the meeting, and told me some of their difficulties. Listening to them, it occurred to me that they were of a nature which should have been considered and settled long before. I was exasperated when, after waiting overnight, I still got no message to bring. I was told that they were sending a lorry to Dublin for some things, and that the message would go with the lorry. The trains on Good Friday ran on a Sunday schedule, and it was too late for the morning train when I got this message from Colivet. I had to wait for the evening train, and it was very late when I arrived home.

Cumann na mBan were in my mother's house in Limerick that day, making first aid outfits, so I decided to give them a helping hand while I was waiting for the train. Though none of them except my sisters knew that the manoeuvres which were to take place on Easter Sunday were really a rising, they seemed to sense a crisis, which made them very anxious and troubled. To cheer them up I started to sing a popular pantomime ditty, 'One grasshopper jumped right over another grasshopper's back, and another grasshopper jumped right over another grasshopper's back.' It was sung in fugue form, and by the time the last girl joined in we were all laughing like idiots. A stranger coming in might have been excused if he thought he had inadvertently entered a mental home. It was all very silly, but it broke up the tension. My sisters knew the position, but were not depressed. On the contrary, they were in a wild, but suppressed, state of excitement and enthusiasm, and quite sure of success. It amazed them when they found I did not feel the same way.

When I arrived in Dublin, I went home to Richmond Avenue. Seán MacDermott was there with Tom (Clarke). I gave them an account of what had happened in Limerick, and why I had disobeyed orders in not returning to Dublin the previous night. Seán asked me to get him some tea. Before leaving the room to do so, I said that I had not been impressed with the men I had met in Limerick. Seán turned on me in a rage, saying, 'For Christ's sake shut up, you are always croaking!' I said, 'I am very sorry, Seán, but I considered it my duty to let you know the impression they left on me. I had not met them before, and they struck me as slow and hesitating, especially for the work before them.' It was the first time in our acquaintance Seán had spoken to me in that way, but I understood the strain he was under and forgave him.

From *Revolutionary Woman: My Fight for Irish Freedom, Kathleen Clarke 1878–1972*, edited by Helen Litton, The O'Brien Press, 1991

The Betrayal
A Poem for My Father
Michael D. Higgins

This man is seriously ill,
The doctor had said a week before,
Calling for a wheelchair.
It was
After they rang me
To come down
And persuade you
To go in
Condemned to remember your eyes
As they met mine in that moment
Before they wheeled you away.
It was one of my final tasks
To persuade you to go in,
A Judas chosen not by Apostles
But by others more broken;
And I was, in part,
Relieved when they wheeled you from me,
Down that corridor, confused,
Without a backward glance
And when I had done it,
I cried, out on the road,
Hitching a lift to Galway and away
From the trouble of your
Cantankerous old age
And rage too,
At all that had in recent years
Befallen you.

All week I waited to visit you
But when I called, you had been moved
To where those dying too slowly
Were sent,
A poorhouse, no longer known by that name,
But in the liberated era of Lemass,
Given a saint's name, 'St Joseph's'.
Was he Christ's father,
Patron saint of the Worker,
The mad choice of some pietistic politician?
You never cared.

Nor did you speak too much.
You had broken an attendant's glasses,
The holy nurse told me,
When you were admitted.
Your father is a very difficult man,
As you must know. And Social Welfare is slow
And if you would pay for the glasses,
I would appreciate it.
It was 1964, just after optical benefit
Was rejected by de Valera for poorer classes
In his Republic, who could not afford,
As he did
to travel to Zurich
For their regular tests and their
Rimless glasses.

It was decades earlier
You had brought me to see him
Pass through Newmarket-on-Fergus
As the brass and reed band struck up,
Cheeks red and distended to the point
Where a child's wonder was as to whether
They would burst as they blew
Their trombones.
The Sacred Heart Procession and de Valera,
You told me, were the only occasions
When their instruments were taken
From the rusting, galvanised shed
Where they stored them in anticipation
Of the requirements of Church and State.

Long before that, you had slept,
In ditches and dug-outs,
Prayed in terror at ambushes
With others who later debated
Whether de Valera was lucky or brilliant
In getting the British to remember
That he was an American.
And that debate had not lasted long
In concentration camps in Newbridge
And the Curragh, where mattresses were burned,
As the gombeens decided that the new State
Was a good thing,
Even for business.

In the dining-room of St Joseph's
The potatoes were left in the middle of the table
In a dish, towards which
You and many other Republicans
Stretched feeble hands that shook.
Your eyes were bent as you peeled
With the long thumb-nail I had often watched
Scrape a pattern on the leather you had toughened for our shoes,
Your eyes when you looked at me
Were a thousand miles away,
Now totally broken,
Unlike those times even
Of rejection, when you went at sixty
For jobs you never got,
Too frail to load vans, or manage
The demands of selling.
And I remember
When you came back to me,
Your regular companion of such occasions,
And said, They think that I'm too old
For the job. I said I was fifty-eight
But they knew that I was past sixty.

A body ready for transportation,
Fit only for a coffin, that made you
Too awkward
For death at home.
The shame of a coffin exit

Through a window sent you here,
Where my mother told me you asked
Only for her to place her cool hand
Under your neck.
And I was there when they asked
Would they give you a Republican funeral,
In that month when you died,
Between the end of the First Programme for Economic Expansion
And the Second.

I look at your photo now,
Taken in the beginning of bad days,
With your surviving mates
In Limerick.
Your face haunts me as do these memories;
And all these things have been scraped
In my heart,
And I can never hope to forget
What was, after all,
A betrayal.

From *The Betrayal: Poems by Michael D. Higgins*, Salmon Publishing, 1990

Sinn Féin Intrigue
Kathleen Clarke

When I came out of prison, I heard the reason why I had not been selected or elected. I had been nominated by the North City, Dublin Comhairle Ceanntar (constituency council) for that area. When my name had been sent to Sinn Féin HQ for ratification, Harry Boland and Dick Mulcahy called on John R. Reynolds, Chairman of the Comhairle. They asked him to have my name withdrawn in favour of Dick Mulcahy, as I had been ratified as a candidate for Limerick City and I was sure of election there. John R. Reynolds told them that he had no power to do so, but that if the matter stood as they said he would summon a meeting of the Comhairle, and place the matter before them. The meeting was called and the matter put before it, and the members said they did not wish to change. According to Reynolds, Harry Boland told the meeting that literature was already out for my election in Limerick, and that I was sure of being elected there. The meeting very reluctantly agreed to the change.

Harry Boland was one of the Honorary Secretaries of the Sinn Féin Executive and must have known the exact position at the time, which was that Micheál Colivet had been ratified by headquarters as the candidate for Limerick City, and his election literature was already out. I was very angry when I heard all this but was glad to know it was not the fault of the people. My sisters knew all about it, and were also very angry. Dick Mulcahy was not then the well-known figure he became afterwards.

From *Revolutionary Woman: My Fight for Irish Freedom, Kathleen Clarke 1878–1972*, edited by Helen Litton, The O'Brien Press Ltd, 1991

Donogh O'Malley
Proinsias Mac Aonghusa

The dull Second Coalition was in office when Donogh O'Malley was familiarising himself with parliament. Unimaginative and rather frightened men were trying to cope with economic problems which they mostly did not understand. The Government totally lacked the glamour, magic and novelty of the initial and glorious Inter-Party Government of 1948. Fianna Fáil was quite effective in opposition, and among those who helped make life difficult for the overwhelmed Coalition ministers was the holy terror from Limerick. He took rather a while to adjust himself to parliamentary procedure and his early activities in the Dáil were very much like those of the traditional bull in the china shop.

He was not very long in parliament when the first of many noted incidents occurred. One day the Division Bells began to ring while he was having some refreshments. He took his time to finish his drink so that by the time he reached the Chamber door it was locked. He was upset, he fumed, he became articulately and imaginatively angry. He tried to push the door open and when he failed he proceeded to kick it, to the amazement and horror of the Deputies inside. It is said that Éamon de Valera, then Leader of the Opposition, sat quietly in his seat enjoying the situation with an amused grin on his face, apparently under the impression that the offender was a certain Labour deputy. But when he discovered who, in fact, was responsible, his attitude rapidly changed. The 33-year-old O'Malley was paraded before him and lectured severely about behaviour and decorum; it was to be the first of many such schoolmaster/schoolboy meetings.

Another man's political career might have been ruined by an ugly public incident of this kind. But already the large, good-looking, open, cheerful, friendly and, somehow, rather lost, Donogh O'Malley had made a lot of friends in the Dáil; even the most staid were willing to stand by him and explain to critics that the holy terror had a great and generous heart, that he was his own worst enemy and not to be hard on him.

Even the Chief, who had a history of dealing harshly with Fianna Fáil parliamentarians thought to be guilty of unfortunate conduct, had a soft spot for him and was willing to forgive much. One of O'Malley's stories was that once when carpeted by de Valera, the Chief said 'Do you know what they are saying about you?'

'No,' Donogh claimed he said, 'but I never believed any of these stories they used to spread about you. I remember one story that . . .' That ended the carpeting. . . .

He swept through the corridors of the 1954–57 Dáil every inch of him the wild, untameable playboy of the western world painted by the stories from Limerick. He was an engineer by profession, though hardly by inclination, but in these years not many hours were left to devote to his business: the serious work of carousing had to be looked after, and so had his constituents, in particular the older people and the have-nots of Limerick. His concern for these people was no one-night-growth, invented for publicity reasons. It was real and basic and genuine and his acts of personal charity to poor people in that town were legion.

A small number of people in Dublin began to notice a tremendous difference between O'Malley boozed and O'Malley sober, and it was not merely the normal difference between a drunk man and a sober person. The sober O'Malley talked and acted like a man of some intellect, of ideas, of idealism mixed with real and legitimate political ambition. The contrast between him and the holy terror was astounding and, occasionally, in the dining room at Leinster House someone would suggest that Donogh might one day be a member of a Government if he were to sober up. But few believed him capable of sobering up and most people regarded the idea that he could, perhaps, one day be in Government as an impossible and quite ridiculous joke. 'I was drunk for ten years', he once said. To many who knew him it seemed longer. . . .

He half expected a job in the new Government and was bitterly disappointed when de Valera passed him over. His escapades continued and stories about him abounded in every corner of Ireland, some of them untrue but most all too near the bone. Friend and foe expected some disaster to overcome him but his luck held; he showed an amazing talent for survival. Doubtless his athletic years, when he played inter-provincial rugby for three provinces, Munster, Leinster and Connacht, and also represented both Munster and Leinster, at different times, in inter-provincial swimming tournaments, helped him and allowed his body to stand up to the tough time it was receiving. . . . O'Malley achieved the near-impossible and in so doing showed what tremendous will-power he possessed and what amazing strength of character he had. He gave up drink. It is practically impossible to overestimate the change this wrought upon his life. Much of his time for many years had been spent with a bottle; now the bottle was finally set aside and a new life started to be built.

Years before that Donogh O'Malley invented an alter ego whom he called Dum-Dum. Whenever he erred and was relating what happened he always referred to Dum-Dum as the culprit. Dum-Dum was blamed for a great deal, Donogh was always the innocent victim of fate. The danger was that Dum-Dum would take over completely and that Donogh would disappear. That the opposite happened, that Dum-Dum was sent into oblivion and that Donogh survived and totally rehabilitated himself is one of the greatest and most crucial factors in O'Malley's life and the necessary clue to any understanding of him. . . . By the time he reached Marlborough Street and the Department of Education there was little trace left of the weak, difficult but somewhat lovable Dum-Dum. Donogh O'Malley, the man with ambition, the man with a mission, was emerging. Time for cod-acting was over; the new man was a politician going places, having proved by disciplining himself that he was a man to be reckoned with. The new man was one about whom insiders spoke as a possible future Taoiseach or Leader of the Opposition. No one jeered anymore when this was suggested. But it took the public quite a while to accept that the book was now open at a totally different page and that, though there was much of the funny man left, the foolish lad had finally vanished.

O'Malley was always a man of considerable activity and long hours, but now these long hours were to be spent far from the loud and gay and irresponsible companions of a quarter of a century and used instead in national and political work. . . . His lovely wife and two children saw less than ever of him as he became more and more involved in the public welfare. Politicians' wives and children are by definition neglected, and see less of their husbands and fathers than most other women and children. The sad fact is that the more dedicated to the public good the politician is, the harder life is bound to be for his wife and children. O'Malley became a copybook example of the hard-working and absolutely restless politician and his family paid the penalty.

From *Scene*, 1968

A Vision of de Valera from a Bus in Bruree
John Liddy

It was as though he cloaked
The land again and all past events
Seemed to melt with a sudden burst of sun.
From where I sat high above the Maigue
History was less than truth
And fact a thing of plastic consumed
By the smallest flame.

What matter then that he tried
To shape a country with his own hands,

Or once transformed villages
Into Greek arenas when playing
Homer at political rallies.

In the darkness of his last years
Perhaps this is what he wanted:

An old man and a boy
Walking by the river of his childhood,
The sun tossing fish into the sky,
Green fields spread out like Paxton's
Chatsworth, a warm eternal peace
In Bruree where people could
Sit and drink Guinness,
Not always at ten to three.

From *The Angling Cot*, Beaver Row Press, 1991

Steve Coughlan
John Horgan

It is difficult to identify an archetypal right-wing Labour Party rebel, as they form a relatively homogenous group. What is certain is that the tensions between them and the newcomers created such friction within the Parliamentary Labour Party that during the 1969–73 Dáil meetings of that grouping were more volatile than at any time before or since.

Their commonality resided in part in a hawkish stance on republican issues, trenchant conservatism on social issues, and a strong pro-coalition stance, conditioned no doubt in part by the sixteen barren years of parliamentary opposition which their left-wing adversaries within the party had not shared. . . . They tended to come from west of a line drawn roughly between Galway and Waterford, and Stevie Coughlan, if not archetypal, was certainly one of the most colourful of them. . . .

These more conservative party members in the provinces were never without power or influence, no matter what official line had been decided by the party. This power and influence could, on occasion, be exerted in the crudest possible way — and for all one knows, still is. A classic, if minor example of this occurred in late 1975, when the PLP witnessed a confrontation between Stevie Coughlan and the leadership which involved basic questions of party loyalty. On that occasion, Coughlan argued that because a decision had been made to hold the party's annual conference in Dun Laoghaire rather than in Limerick (where his son was Mayor), his constituency delegation would not be coming to conference, and would probably be withholding national collection funds as well. If any of this meant that the Left swamped the platform, he said, it wouldn't be his fault, but the fault of a 'clique' which had 'rigged' the Administrative Council. To his credit, Corish took him on immediately, indicating that Coughlan's duty to conference was to make sure that his delegation was present, challenging him to be more specific in his allegation about 'cliques', and warning him that if he planned to carry out his threat about finances, the AC would obviously have to take some remedial action. . . .

One of the major problems facing Labour is that, given the party strength, it has almost never achieved more than one TD per constituency. This has meant, especially outside Dublin, that the constituency organisation and the TD have become synonymous. Axe the TD on ideological grounds, and you have also lost an entire constituency organisation — and the votes which they can bring to conference to support a beleaguered leadership. Anybody who doubts this power should be in attendance in the seventies and early eighties. Frequently at conference — before registration formalities were tightened up to prevent the undignified scrum that used to ensue — it would be possible to see despots like Coughlan or Michael Pat Murphy paying delegate fees, and all the arrears of affiliation fees due by branches whose existence in non-election years was always a matter for conjecture, from immense wads of notes produced with a flourish from back pockets — and woe betide any hapless party official who queried any of the delegates' credentials. . . . A person with a Dáil seat, however acquired, speaks with some kind of authority, no matter how deficient his ideology may be.

Coughlan first achieved political prominence in his native city of Limerick as a member of Clann na Poblachta. . . . This party was formally dissolved in 1965, but Coughlan was by that stage already a member of Labour, having joined in 1961. . . . No sooner had the election taken place in 1969, however, than Coughlan was in the wars with the new boys, his first public brush coming after Barry Desmond . . . had tweaked the Limerick deputy's nose by parading in protest outside a rugby match involving a South African team in Limerick — a match which Coughlan made a point of attending. . . . Conor Cruise O'Brien was not the only cross that Stevie Coughlan had to bear. The influx of activists into the party were frequently appalled by some of his statements and actions, and a hint of things to come was provided in the same year when a group of Irish Maoists (a forgotten breed of mostly student agitators whose direct action techniques made them something of a political nine days' wonder at the time) opened a bookshop in Limerick the better to propagate their gospel. After an unknown Limerick defender of the faith had discharged a gun at these premises, ordinary Labour Party members were horrified, for all that they did not share the views of the small group of Maoists. Their anger, however, was rapidly turned on Coughlan when, instead of condemning the outrage, he took a potent, sideways swipe at the victims. 'Any fellow with one eye open and the other closed', he averred stoutly, 'could see this coming. I am vehemently opposed to these people.'

The matter was not allowed to rest there by left-wing (and indeed by many Centre) members of the party, but Coughlan refused to recant, and indeed this was not the only offence he had given. In another speech around the same time, dealing with historical aspects of the Jewish commercial presence in Limerick (a city from which they had been expelled forcibly in the early years of this century after a number of inflammatory sermons by a local priest) Coughlan used the words 'bloodsuckers' and 'extortionists'. The impact on rank and file members of the party can be imagined. This time, an apology was inescapable, and it was tendered less than a week before a critical PLP meeting at which a bitter debate would undoubtedly have taken place, followed by the removal of the whip. . . . By now the AC wanted to expel him, not just from the PLP but from the party itself. The manoeuvrings within that body were hectic. . . .

But, like the US Fifth Cavalry, Coughlan again came charging to his own rescue, issuing in Limerick an extraordinary speech — extraordinary, that is, in the light of his record — in which he called for a new Ireland under a secular, liberal constitution. 'Never before', muttered the political correspondent of *The Irish Times* in evident disbelief, 'have such sentiments been uttered by Mr Coughlan.' Nor were they to be again. Coughlan's star was already on the wane in Limerick. Mick Lipper, who had proposed Coughlan for the mayoralty successfully in June 1969, was chosen as a by-election candidate in February 1973 and, after an astonishing showing, secured the backing of many anti-Coughlan elements in the party organisation in the city. He ran and was elected as an independent in 1977, effectively taking Coughlan's seat, with the blessing of the same bishop who had — through Coughlan — sent a message of greeting to the party when it had staged its annual conference in Limerick!

Such was the relief in the PLP that Lipper was welcomed back into the fold with what Coughlan would have plainly regarded as indecent haste. In April 1979, two years after they had last appeared at a Labour Party Conference, both he and his son, whom many people supposed he had been grooming in the dynastic tradition, announced formally that they were severing their connections with the Labour Party. As a Parthian shot, Stevie announced that he was writing his memoirs.

From *Labour: The Price of Power*, Gill and Macmillan, 1986

A Solo Run
Eamon Cregan

It was in the early eighties, 1981 to be precise. This was the time when governments rose and fell like sports personalities; one minute you were riding high, the next you were flat on your back. Oh the fickleness of sports writers!

Anyway, to get on with my sceal, the FFers had a general election coming up in May/June. Limerick East was the venue and all the big guns were there: Des O'Malley, Peadar Clohessy, Michael Noonan, Jim Kemmy, Willie O'Dea, etc. Fianna Fáil would win two seats, but it was the third they wanted. But Michael Noonan and Jim Kemmy had things to say about that.

Kemmy had a strong city base and Noonan was the rising star for Fine Gael.

Then I realised how stupid a person can be, or was it ego?

I got a telephone call from a guy called Wall (no, nothing to do with the Walls of Limerick) at 12.40 p.m. on Tuesday. Would you stand for Fianna Fáil? Need to know by 1 p.m.. Imagine Fianna Fáil headquarters ringing me about this. I know I had been asked some time before and refused, but I suppose ego is a terrible thing if it runs rampant. No one to discuss this with except Ann. I did not know where Des O'Malley was. In a panic, I got a mad rush of blood to the head and said yes by telephone. Ann naturally thought I was mad and sure I was. . . .

HQ was in my office in O'Connell Street, maps of the city and the east plastered on the wall. Blindly, I started. My auctioneering business was handled by Ann Broderick from Athea (she has since died tragically in Australia) and we started canvassing. I was going to sweep all before me for Fianna Fáil. They would get their third seat, but it wouldn't be me — either O'Dea or Clohessy.

After ten days it was announced that the 'Big Chief' was coming. Haughey was coming on a 'grand tour'. This was going to upset our schedule. We had people to see and hands to shake; this was disruption.

The Eagle landed in Sarsfield Barracks and came out to meet the plebs. I was knocked down in the rush to shake the great man's hand; O'Malley shuffled over, a limp handshake; O'Dea, a big O'Dealing smile on his face; Peadar, half-shy.

I was about to meet the leader of Fianna Fáil; I had taken three weeks off work, did no training with Limerick even though we were meeting Tipp in Thurles; spent whatever bit of money I had just to help get the third seat; and here he was, 'Our Leader'.

Being the last to shake his hand (I suppose he was tired) I took his hand and shook it. Very limp. I did not realise I was that tall. He looked at me for about two seconds and turned away to start his cavalcade through Limerick.

It suddenly dawned on me on that sunny day in Sarsfield Barracks, that this man had not a clue who I was. The embarrassment was all over my face, but he did not see it because he was gone.

I decided there and then that never ever would I put myself in that position again.

From *Egg on my Face*, edited by Seán Power, Gill & Macmillan, 1996

ELEVEN

TRAVELLERS

Taking the Waters
Caroline, Countess of Portarlington

Limerick, Wednesday, 31 August 1785
To Lady Louisa Stuart

We came to Mr Heads, which is a charming place in the middle of rocks and mountains, and just upon the banks of the Shannon, which is one of the noblest rivers I ever saw.*

Here we were entertained very hospitably by the family above mentioned. They have eleven fine children, Mrs Head a very pleasing woman, and two good-looking daughters; grown up, both very good musicians, particularly the eldest, who has a very fine voice; these with an old maiden aunt (Miss Cassandra) make up their family. They have just built a large good house, and have charming walks along the riverside. They have also the ruins of an old castle upon a rock, which is an island, except when the river is low, which was the case then, so we walked over to it, and had a delightful view from it. We remained there till after breakfast this morning, and then proceeded to a place called Castle Connel, where there is a very good spa. It is a very romantic little spot upon the banks of the same river, and another much larger ruin in the midst of the river. The houses are chiefly built for lodgings, so are very neat and dispersed about in the manner of Tunbridge, all commanding a view of the water surrounded by very rich ground well planted and backed by mountains, and here and there a bleach yard close to the river, which forms a very picturesque appearance. They have just built rooms, where they have balls twice a week. We tasted the spa, and it appears to me just like the Tunbridge. They say it has done wonderful cures. We walked about their walks, and were proceeding to look at a waterfall when we were accosted by a gentleman, who said he fancied we were strangers, and begged he might attend us, which we accepted, and he took us through his own grounds, where he had a charming little cottage. They were just making hay, and it was delightful. He took us to the place where there has always been a great cascade till this dry summer; there we found another romantic-looking rock, great part covered with ivy, and a house upon it built in the form of a tower, which is inhabited by a gentleman who is building a large house upon a hill looking down upon the river. All these rocks and things in the river make me suppose that the river formerly was not near so large, but has forced its way over rocks and places that were inhabited. This gentleman we found afterwards to be a councillor Reeves. He was excessively civil, and would fain have persuaded us to stay and dine with him in his pretty little cottage, but we begged to be excused. He told us every house there was taken all the summer, and that people gave from three to six guineas a week for lodgings. After thanking him for his civility we proceeded to this town, which is a second Dublin. After we had dined we sallied forth to see what was to be seen, but the wet and dirt was terrible; however there is a part they call

Newtown Pery, which is as well built as Harley Street, and people's names over the doors quite like a city. There is a very fine Custom House, and in the course of our walk we arrived at the Parade, where the band belonging to a regiment were playing upon the top of a wall, like the ruin of a castle, to the people below, who were walking backwards and forwards, and I suppose when it is fine it's quite the fashion. We saw people driving about full dressed in their carriages. I suppose there is a number of balls and assemblies every night. . . . We are going by Mr L___'s, and I dread *their civility*, as they have got relations settled in our neighbourhood, and I fear we shall become intimate at any rate. . . .

— Ever your   C. PORTARLINGTON

---

* Michael Head of Derry. The Heads were relatives of the Cootes, Lady Carlow's neighbours. In 1778 the eldest daughter, Maria, married the eldest son of the Right Rev. W. Gore, Bishop of Limerick, whose first wife was Mary, eldest daughter of Chidley Coote of Coote Hall, and relict of Guy Moore, Esq.

From *Gleanings from an Old Portfolio containing some correspondence between Lady Louisa Stuart and her sister Caroline Countess of Portarlington and other friends and relations*, edited by Mrs Godfrey Clarke, privately printed for David Douglas, 1896

The House of Industry
John Carr

The inns have not kept equal pace with the prosperity of the town: they are dirty and ill attended, but as usual furnish excellent wine at four shillings per bottle. We also partook of some excellent cow-beef, I wish I could object to nothing more than the inconvenience of ill-conducted inns; but alas! a subject of much deeper interest, and truly afflicting to every feeling mind, is to be found; if the traveller will take the trouble of walking over Thomond's bridge and enter the house of *Industry*, as it is called. He will quit a noble city, gay with novel opulence and luxury, for a scene which will strike his mind with horror. Under the roof of this house, I saw madmen *stark naked* girded only by their irons, standing in the rain, in an open court, attended by *women*, their cells upon the ground-floor, scantily supplied with straw, damp, and ill-secured. In the wards of labour, abandoned prostitutes, in rags and vermin, each loaded with a long chain and heavy log, working only when the eye of the superintending officer was upon them, are associated throughout the day with respectable old female housekeepers, who, having no children to support them, to prevent them famishing, seek this wretched asylum. At night, they sleep together in the same room; the sick (unless in very extreme cases) and the healthy, the good and the bad, all crowded together. In the venereal ward, the wretched female sufferers were imploring for a little more covering, whilst several idiots squatted in corners, half naked, half famished, pale and hollow-eyed, with a ghastly grin, bent a vacant stare upon the loathsome scene, and consummated its horror. Fronting this ward, across a yard, in a large room, nearly thirty feet long, a raving maniac, instead of being strapped to his bed, was handcuffed to a stone of 300 lb weight, which, with the most horrible yells, by a convulsive effort of strength, he dragged from one end of the room to the other, constantly exposed to the exasperating view and conversation of those who were in the yard. I have been well informed that large sums of money have been raised in every county for the erection of mad-houses: how has this money been applied?

The building of this lazar-gaol is so insecure, that the prostitutes confined in it, although ironed and logged, frequently make their escape. No clothing is allowed to these poor wretches but what they bring into the prison, or can earn, or beg. Upon enquiry I found, what I need scarcely relate to my reader, that the funds are very inadequate, that it is supported by presentments and charity, and very seldom visited by those whom official duty, if not common humanity, ought to have conducted there. The number of miserable wretches in this house amounted to one hundred and thirty-eight. The Governor appeared to be a humane man, and seemed deeply to regret what he could not conceal.

One of the naked subjects which I mentioned, lost his senses by an excess of mathematical research, the other by a disappointment of the heart, and the third, who was in the same yard, by drunkenness: a more affecting and expressive group for the pencil, could never be presented. In one cell, covered to his chin in straw, lay a hoary-headed man, who would never speak, nor take any thing unless conjured to do so by the name of 'the Most High'.

From *The Stranger in Ireland; or, A Tour in the Southern and Western Parts of that Country in the Year 1805,* Richard Phillips, 1806

A Coach Journey
Richard Fitzgerald

Early in the summer of 1819, I doffed my cap and gown in my rooms at dear old Trinity, and, with elastic step and buoyant spirits, issued from the ancient gateway of *Alma Mater,* anticipating with feelings of no ordinary delight, the sweet society of the loved relatives of home, which I hoped to enjoy during the long vacation, now commenced. Having bidden a kind farewell to the college porters, I bounded off, accompanied by my skip (the students' servants were called 'skips' in my college days) with my trunk on his back, and reached the office of the two-day coach for Limerick, just as my old friend Jim Dempsey had taken his seat on the box. No sooner had I taken the place which Jim had so adroitly provided for me, than 'crack went the whip, round went the wheels', and away we bowled at the rate of six Irish miles an hour, a slapping pace fifty years ago, when railroads were not so much as thought of. After a comfortable journey of about nine hours, not marked by any particular incident, but very much enlivened by the racy and amusing jests of my jolly and good-humoured companion Jim, we arrived at Mountrath in time to partake of a most substantial and well-served dinner; and, after it, to enjoy for the evening the society of the passengers of the up, as well as those of the down coach, which for many years had daily met at that provincial town.

We started precisely at six next morning and arrived at Dunkerran at nine, well prepared for a hearty breakfast, for which we paid two tenpennies, with a trifle to the waiter, and, depend upon it, left little profit to the *Maitre d'hotel*. Having arrived safely at Limerick at three p.m., I walked about the town until six o'clock, when I enjoyed a hearty dinner at Moriarty's, now Cruise's Hotel, and looked forward with earnest longings for the morrow at the close of which, after a sail down the Shannon, I hoped to clasp to my bosom the beloved friends for whom my youthful heart for the last nine months was deeply and intensely longing.

From *True History of the Colleen Bawn*, Moffat, 1869; The Kerryman Ltd, 1927

Kilmallock
T. Crofton Croker

When first I saw Kilmallock's walls,
'Twas in the stillness of moonlight;
And lofty towers and stately balls
Frowned darkly then enwrapped in night;
Just touched with tinsel, streaks and gleams,
Mysterious as a town of dreams!

But morning with its rosy sky
Dispelled this visionary pride;
All greatness did in ruin lie,
Mean hovels stood on every side;
The peasant held the lordly pile,
And cattle filled the roofless aisle.

Kilmallock in the pensive mind
Wakens many a solemn thought;
There will the heart this lesson find —

That human strength and power are nought;
Today, a boast; tomorrow, gone,
A moral deep to muse upon.

From *The Story of Kilmallock*, Kilmallock Historical Society, 1987

'The Ancient City of Kilmallock'
T. Crofton Croker

Many Irish villages boast a post-chaise, the horses for which are not unfrequently taken from the plough, and the chaise itself submitted to a temporary repair before starting, to render it, if the parody of a nautical phrase may be allowed, road-worthy; but the defects are never thought of one moment before the chaise is required; and the miseries of posting in Ireland have, with justice, afforded subject for the caricaturist. Tired horses or a breakdown are treated by a driver, whose appearance is the very reverse of the smart jockey-like costume of an English postilion, with the utmost resignation, as matters of unavoidable necessity. With a slouched hat — slovenly shoes and stockings — and a long, loose great coat wrapped round him, he sits upon a bar in front of the carriage and urges on his horses by repeated applications of the whip, accompanied with the most singular speeches, and varied by an involuntary burst of his musical talent, whistling a tune adapted to the melancholy pace of the fatigued animals, as he walks slowly beside them up the ascent of every hill.

'Did you give the horses a feed of oats at the village where we stopped to sketch?' inquired one of my fellow-travellers of the driver, who for the last three or four miles had with much exertion urged on the jaded hacks.

'I did not, your honour,' was his reply, 'but sure and they know I promised them a good one at Limerick.' . . .

To such as can bear with composure and indifference lesser and temporary misfortunes, those attendant on an Irish tour become objects of merriment; the very essence of the innate ingenuity and wit of the people is called out by such evils; and the customary benediction muttered by the peasant on meeting a traveller, is changed into the whimsical remark or shrewd reply that mock anticipation.

Of late, jingles, as they are termed, have been established between the principal towns. These are carriages on easy springs, calculated to contain six or eight persons. The roof is supported by a slight iron frame capable of being unfixed in fine weather, and the curtains, which may be opened and closed at will, afford complete protection from sun and rain; their rate of travelling is nearly the same as that of the stage-coach, and they are both a cheaper and more agreeable conveyance. . . .

The road leading from Limerick towards Cork is for some miles flat and un-interesting, though the horizon is abounded by mountains with an agreeable outline. The cabins of the peasantry are most deplorable; and the state of filth in which the owners live, inconceivable to an Englishman who has not travelled in Ireland. Twenty of these hovels sometimes succeed each other without a chimney; and invariably a stagnant black puddle is seen close to the door, appointed receiver-general of all kinds of filth, streams from which issue in every direction, one generally entering at the cabin door and trickling down over its mud floor: — 'Such inhabitations', to use the words of Sir Richard Hoare, 'teeming with a numerous population of children, pigs and poultry, present a truly deplorable and affecting sight to every man of feeling and humanity.'

About nine miles distant from Limerick, not far from the road, lies Lough Gur, formerly a place of consideration. . . . Two miles farther brought us to Bruff, or Brough, a wretched village, with the ruins of an old castle, mentioned in the Pacata Hibernia. Continuing our route we arrived at Kilmallock, sixteen miles from Limerick, and entered the town, under a dark and massive gateway, late in the evening. The gloom which partially obscured every object, as we drove along a street composed of mean cabins, mingled with the ancient stateliness of towers and embattled walls, produced rather a mournful impression on the mind not unfavourable to useful thought, but it was soon dispelled by the prospect of miserable accommodations and the consequential officiousness of our landlady. . . .

Kilmallock seems to have been gradually sinking into decay since the time of Cromwell, when it was dismantled and received much injury from the parliamentary army. Two (of the four) gateways still exist, and have a solid heavy effect, with a strong resemblance to Spanish or Moorish architecture. But it is from the main street that a just idea of its ancient consequence may be formed; on each side are the remains of houses built of hewn stone, which seem to have been constructed on a uniform plan; and so excellent is the workmanship, the walls of many of them are now in perfect preservation, only wanting roofs and floors to make them as complete as when inhabited. These houses are three storeys high, ornamented with an embattlement and a tasteful stone moulding on the outside. . . . The square window frames and large fire-places are well carved, in a bold and massive style; and such is the durability of the limestone, though exposed to the weather and casual injuries, that it retains the sharpness of the chisel as if only yesterday from the hands of the sculptor. . . .

Little attention is paid by its present inhabitants to the preservation of the remains of its former importance. On the contrary they are daily destroyed. Whenever a hovel is required to be built, the materials are procured by breaking down part of these once splendid mansions, some of which have been lowered and fitted up in accordance with the neglect and desertion of the place, and the interior of others is occupied by sheds for cattle, or more loathsome pigsties.

The town walls, still retaining in some places their original height, may be traced uninterruptedly from the gate on the Charleville side to that on the Limerick, which I am inclined to consider a fourth part of their former extent.

A stream, named the Cummogue, runs close to the town, and falls into the river Maig; on its opposite banks are the ruins of two abbeys, which complete the vestiges of ancient Kilmallock. That on the same side with the town contains monuments to members of the Fitzgerald, Verdon, Blakeney, and Haly families, erected during the seventeenth century, and it is difficult to imagine more barbarous or grotesque pieces of sculpture than some of them exhibit; indeed it is surprising, after beholding the beautiful masonry of that time so conspicuous in the town, to find tombs of the same date, on which much labour has been bestowed — such unskilful productions. The bas reliefs copied from the Verdon tomb, bearing the years 1614 and 1626, may serve as an illustration; yet Ferrar, in his *History of Limerick*, says: 'This monument was of excellent workmanship, and esteemed one of the best in Munster'; and speaking of the uncouth figures I have sketched, says, they are 'done in a masterly style in alto relievo'. Were it not for the coincidence of name and dates I should doubt the identity of the monument. The singularity of a Fitzgerald tomb (equally rude with the Verdon) perhaps requires mention. A figure of Death is conspicuously engraven on it, with the hexameter verse —

'Non fugiam! prius experiar — Non Mors mihi terror.'

The chancel of this abbey has been fitted up and is used as a church. The ruined abbey on the other side of the water is of greater extent, but has too lonely and stern an appearance to be picturesque, circumstances which render it more sublime. The architecture, though solid, is graceful, and the great altar window, a fine specimen of the chaste lightness of the pure Gothic style. In the centre of its chancel stands the family tomb of the White Knight, a title assumed by a branch of the Fitzgeralds, or, as they are frequently called, Geraldines, and according to Camden, originating from the grey hairs of the founder of that line. In the pedigree of the Fitzgerald family, the titles of some of the branches settled in the south of Ireland are so romantic that they carry us completely back to the days of chivalry, as we find, beside the White Knight, the Knight of Glen, sometimes called the Knight of the Valley, the Black Knight, and the Knight of Kerry; appellations that continue to be bestowed on the lineal representative at the present day. . . .

The charges at inferior towns and villages are extravagant in an inverse proportion to the indifference of their accommodation, and generally exceed those of the first hotels in the metropolis. Our bill at Kilmallock was anything but moderate, and yet the house, though the best the town afforded, appeared to be one where carmen were oftener lodged than gentry. The landlady stood at the door, and with a low curtsey and a good-humoured smile welcomed us to 'the ancient city of Kilmallock'; in the same breath informed us that she was a gentlewoman born and bred, and that she had a son, 'as fine an officer as ever you could set eyes on in a day's walk, who was a *patriarch* (a patriot) in South America'; then leading us up a dark and narrow staircase to the apartment we were to occupy, wished to know our names and business, whence we came and where we were going; but left the room on our inquiring, in the first place, what we could have to eat. After waiting a reasonable time, our demands were attended to by a barefooted female, who to our anxiety respecting what we could have for supper, replied with perfect confidence, 'Just any thing you like, sure!'

'Have you any thing in the house?'

'Indeed and we have not, but it's likely I might be able to get an egg for ye.'

An examination of the bedrooms will not prove more satisfactory; a glass or soap are luxuries seldom found. Sometimes one coarse and very small towel is provided; at Kilmallock the measurement of mine was half a yard in length and a quarter in breadth; its complexion, too, evinced that it had assisted in the partial ablutions of many unfastidious persons. Mr Arthur Young's constant ejaculation when he lighted on such quarters in Ireland usually occurred to my mind, 'Preserve me, Fate, from such another!' and I have no doubt he would agree with me that two very essential requisites in an Irish tour are, a stock of linen, and a tolerable partiality for bacon. But travellers, any more than beggars, cannot always be choosers, and those who will not submit with patience to the accidents and inconveniences of a journey must sit at home and read the road that others travel.

From *Researches in the South of Ireland*, John Murray, 1824

A Tour of Duty
William Cobbett

Castle Comfort, Abington, Co. Limerick
25 October 1834

In one street in the outskirts of the city of Limerick (which is made a fine city by the trade of sending away meat and butter and corn out of Ireland), I saw more misery than any man could have believed existed in the whole world. Men sleeping in the same wisp of straw, or weeds, with their mothers, sisters, and aunts; and compelled to do this, or perish: two or three families in one room, that is to say, a miserable hole 10 feet by 8 or 9; and husbands, wives, sons, daughters, all huddled together, paying 6d. or 8d. or 10d. a week for the room; and the rent paid to a 'nobleman' in England. Here I saw one woman with a baby in her arms, both nearly naked. The poor mother's body was naked from the middle of her thighs downwards; and to hide her bosom, she caught up a dirty piece of old sack; she hung down her face (naturally very pretty); when she lifted it up, the tears were streaming down her cheeks. Her husband, who had just got better after illness, was out of work. She had two other children quite naked, and covered up in some dirty hay, in one corner of the room! At a place in the country, I went to the dwelling of a widower, who is 60 years of age, and who has five children, all very nearly stark naked. The eldest girl, who is 15 years of age, had on a sort of apron to hide the middle part of her body before; and that was all she had. She hid herself well as she could, behind, or at the end of an old broken cupboard; and she held up her two arms and hands to hide her breasts! This man pays 30s. rent for an acre of the poorest land!

From *Weekly Political Register*, 1 November 1834

Dysert*
Thomas MacGreevy

> Grayer than the tide below, the tower;
> The day is gray above;
> About the walls
> A curlew flies, calls;
> Rain threatens, west;
> This hour,
> Driving,
> I thought how this land, so desolate,
> Long, long ago, was rich in living,
> More reckless, consciously, in strife,
> More conscious daring-delicate
> In love.
>
> And then the tower veered
> Grayly to me,
> Passed . . .
> I meditated,
> Feared
> The thought experience sent,
> That the gold years
> Of Limerick life
> Might be but consecrated
> Lie,

Heroic lives
So often merely meant
The brave stupidity of soldiers,
The proud stupidity of soldiers' wives.

* Dysert Castle, Askeaton

From *The Criterion* IV, 1 January 1926

Freewheeling into Limerick
William Bulfin

I tarried for half an hour on the bridge, and watched the shadows lengthen on the water, and on the sunny slopes over the town. The evening gold was deepening along the crests of the hills of Clare as I came within earshot of the rapids of Castleconnell. The Shannon is in playful mood at this point, and for three or four hundred yards its course leaps and tumbles and breaks into cataracts, and churns itself into foam as white as the bark of the birch trees which look down upon the romping current. And as if the salmon were infected with the boisterous mood of the river, they put their tails in their mouths and leap from the foamy pools underneath the falls into the smooth water above. There is another salmon leap at Meelick, above Lough Derg, and even a better one than at Castleconnell. There is a certain fascination in watching the big fish take the leap and make it. Sometimes a fish will fail once or twice. But another and a stronger effort whirls it like a huge half-moon of golden green through the sunshine over the point where the glassy current breaks into a foamy torrent, and throws itself roaring down the fall. . . .

The red sun was sinking behind the mountains as I took to the wheel again. A few more miles now in the rosy afterglow, a hill or two, a long shaded downward gradient, then a spin along the level. I was on the sidewalk now running smoothly, and wondering if I would reach my journey's end before dark. I did it. A turn in the road brought me within view of the suburbs, and in the dew-laden gloaming I rode into Limerick. The cyclometer registered seventy miles, and I would not sell the tamest of them for a free pass on a railway.

After a hungry cyclist's supper at one of the hotels — and Limerick has some good hotels — I strolled through the city by lamplight. Next morning I was astir early and had made a tour of the principal streets before breakfast. I made several other tours during the day, and found much that was interesting at every other turn and crossing. It would have been the same if I had stayed for a week. Limerick is packed with great memories. It breathes history. Even its very stone-heaps are eloquent. I crossed the river over and over again, strolled through Garryowen, and throughout the streets where the great Munster fair is held, out to the reservoir. I prowled around the old parts of the city, and throughout the more modern streets, visited all that is left of the walls, saw where the fighting was hottest, sat on the wharves of the river, rested beside the Treaty Stone, lounged on the bridges, stood at shop doors and at street corners looking at the faces of the passers-by, and when the time came for me to leave I was sorry. I arrived there prejudiced in its favour. Consequently I liked it to some extent before I saw it. I like the imperfect view I got of it as I entered it in the gloaming. I liked it ten times better when I saw it in the light of day. I liked it better than ever when I was leaving it, not because I was parting from it, for I have told you I was sorry to go, but just because it had grown upon me.

And yet, as far as appearances go, Limerick is not a show place. It is a quiet old town, a good deal dilapidated here and there, not by any means tidy or methodical, not by any means over-clean, even in the most central streets, grim and grimy and sombre-looking, but very lovable. I saw a youth of nineteen or twenty summers working mightily on the quays discharging cargo from a steamer. He was poorly clad; shirts and pants were quilted with patches; yet vigour was in his cheeks and laughter in his eyes; and he seemed ready for the worst that fortune might send him. He struck me as being, in a certain sense, the incarnation of the spirit of his native city. For Limerick, too, works hard, is careless of appearance, is apparently devil-may-care in many things, and defiant of fate. Its defiance is not strident or theatrical. There is nothing blatant or melodramatic about Limerick at all. It seems to regard destiny with genial mockery, flinging a challenge from out its battered walls amidst a peal of musical laughter.

When you analyse your impressions of places you have seen, you often find them associated with some particular colour — white or brown, or black, or sky-blue, or yellow or red. Grey is the colour that rises before me when I think of Limerick — dark grey, steel grey, pearly grey, bluish-grey. Its walls and roofs and streets are grey. The morning sky over it was grey. The wide river was thinly veiled with greyish mist. There were grey hazes on the Thomond fields and in the southern distances. But this greyness is not the fading of age. I cannot think of Limerick as being stricken in years. You meet occasionally a man in the world who is independent of circum-stances, who is superior to every depressing and depreciating prank of adversity, who is independent in thought, untamed in soul, in spite of everything, who is out-at-elbows but unashamed — a weather-beaten, healthy, lovable heroic kind of tatterdemalion. Well, as with men, so with cities. Each has an individuality. The individuality of Limerick is that of the man I have described. At least that is my impression of it. Another man may go thither and find it a dudish, perfumed, fastidious, starched, and hot-ironed individuality. I did not.

From *Rambles in Éirinn*, Roberts Wholesale Books; first published 1907

Waterways
Robert Lloyd Praeger

Lough Gur, Limerick's only lake, is a place of much and varied interest. It lies three miles north of Bruff, among limestone hills. . . . The lowering of the water years ago also exposed some lake-dwellings, while all around is a wealth of monuments of earlier periods — many stone circles, stone alignments, dolmens, gallauns, raths. The finest circle, fifty-six yards across, is peculiar in that it is erected on the inside slope of a great earthen vallum of ring-fort appearance. Numbers of weapons of stone and bronze have been found in the vicinity, and it is clear that the place was one of great importance in early days. Botanically, also, Lough Gur is interesting. One of its abundant plants is the Golden Dock, now almost extinct in Ireland; and in its waters the Hornwort and other uncommon species flourish. Close by is a bog which has yielded many antlers of the Great Deer or 'Irish Elk'. . . .

Adare (*Ath dara*, the ford of the oak), on the river Maigue, while never a place of civil importance, was a notable ecclesiastical centre, with three friaries grouped near the great fourteenth-century castle of the Fitzgeralds. . . . The Franciscan friary, much the most beautiful of the three, has, like the others, had the advantage of being under the care of the Earls of Dunraven, whose seat, Adare Manor, close by, is one of the handsomest residences in Ireland. Adare is indeed an architectural museum, and has besides attractions for the naturalist in its river and rich woods: and the presence of an excellent inn make it an interesting and pleasant place in which to sojourn.

Limerick city was a Danish foundation, like so many of the Irish seaports. . . . There is a large rise and fall of tide here, and flood, with its deep water extending the length of the town, is very different from ebb, when much of the bed of the Shannon is exposed, and the river rushes swiftly through the banks of gravel and reefs of rock. Muddy gravels here are the home of at least one very rare plant. This is the Three-angled Bullrush, unknown elsewhere in Ireland, and in Great Britain confined to a few river-estuaries in southern England. At Limerick, between the bridges, it forms tall dark groves, much resembling those of the Common Bullrush. The estuarine habitat which it affects in Britain and Ireland affords a good illustration of the law that towards the limit of its range a plant often becomes very faddy — if one may use the term — as to the kind of place in which it will grow. On the continent, where the species is frequent, it is found not only in brackish water around the coasts, but in Central Europe, along the edges of rivers and lakes; whereas in these western islands its few stations are in estuaries only. But if you follow the old canal from Limerick to where it strikes the Shannon a mile away, you will see the plant growing again, quite dwarfed, it is true, in the swiftly flowing river well above the point to which even the spring tides rise. . . .

Below Limerick the Shannon assumes at once estuarine form, with muddy foreshores fringed with tall reeds (among which the Three-angled Bullrush mentioned above is conspicuous); seven miles down it begins to widen, and ten miles further on the broad Fergus estuary, choked with islands and mud-banks, opens on the north. Opposite to this, on the Limerick side, a narrow tidal creek leads up to Askeaton. This is an attractive place. There are the remains of a noble Franciscan abbey, and of a great castle built in 1199. The wide area of bare limestone, throughout which the River Deel has cut a deep trench, recalls the remarkable similar tracts in Clare and eastern Galway: and it is, indeed, a southward extension of this driftless, soilless country. But the peculiar vegetation which makes the naked limestones of such unusual interest further north dies out southward. About Ennis some of the characteristic plants, such as the Spring Gentian, still persist; but at Askeaton the only representative of the rarer species is the Salzburg Eyebright. This, along with plenty of Madder, Squinancywort, Scale Fern, etc. growing in the crevices of the limestone, recall the wonderful flora of Burren: but it is only an insipid make-believe, not the genuine thing.

A little further west, at Foynes and Newcastle, the limestone passes under shales of Upper Carboniferous age, which inland rise into bare heathery uplands running down into Kerry; and the incoming of sporadic patches of Giant Butterwort and Irish Spurge show that we have finally left the flora of the Central Plain for the fascinating vegetation of the south-west.

From *The way that I went: an Irishman in Ireland*, Allen Figgis, 1980; first published 1937

Sailing Down the Shannon
Sean O'Faolain

I got out of the train again at Newcastle West and began to walk. Here, to me, is holy ground, my mother's country, along the banks of the little river Deel. I put it all into a novel once, *A Nest of Simple Folk*, and I have no more to say about it. It is, to the traveller who travels only with his eyes, one of the most uninteresting regions in the whole of Ireland. It is flat, monotonous, colourless, shaggy, half-asleep, but to me. . . . O *Splendeur et magnificence des pays plats!* I fall silent when I think of it. Childhood — boyhood — youth — nostalgia. I passed the old farm where my mother grew, with ten sisters, her father dead, no brother, only my old grandmother Mag Power to run the place, twenty-five poor acres of it and bogland on the Deel. I sat by the well at Ballyallinan, and watched, as I used to do thirty years ago, it might have been the same water-spider crawling across the cold water from out of his cold cavern. It is a Holy Well. Rags and medals and bits of indecipherable clothing hang from the tree over it, an alder mingled with a thorn. There is not a sound. The limestone plain is on all sides, unbroken — except off there behind Newcastle where I see a pretence at a hill, a bit of the old red rock unwashed away, a faint heathery slope good for rabbit-catching. It is the only sport the boys have on Sundays; a barking dog; distant voices hallooing. . . . It is a vantage point from which to see the lighthouse on the Shannon blinking on a clear night. . . . I see a line of cows pass along the road below the worn path to the well. It is all a fairy-tale, a child's song, a cradle memory. . . .

They talk about the slavery of the senses. These are as nothing compared with the slavery of the heart. All Ireland, for me, is in and about Rathkeale: a dead, lousy, flea-bitten, snoring pig of a town that I cannot think of without going as soft as a woman.

But we are not bits of logic, and I wallowed in the sty of my melancholy pleasure. Then I skirted the little town, and sat again as the evening grew cold over the lakes of the Commons, and smelled the old turf-tang that is like a kick in the stomach to a homeless man, an exile, or a man dreaming of his past. My aunt lives in Rathkeale but I refused to visit her. That would be as bad as singing 'Come Back to Erin'. Finally, after a few satisfactory, womanish tears, which I have no business confessing, I caught a fortunate train at Ballingrane for Limerick city. The Marx Brothers at the Savoy restored sanity. The one night I had planned to stay with relatives stretched into a lovely lazy week. On the strength of it I strongly advise the traveller to spend a day, at least, at Adare ('O sweet Adare, O lovely vale!') and at Killaloe at the foot of Lough Derg.

O Limerick is beautiful as everybody knows . . .

So the song says . . .

There is dignity in Limerick, a place bearing the vestiges of history, marchings and counter-marchings, worn smooth by being in the track of the history of Europe for its little space. The Williamite Wars in Ireland ended here. The bad century began here. Kinsale was the virtual end of the Gaelic order. The Siege of Limerick shot the bolt home. After that there was the hundred years night. Anglo-Ireland walked in.

Observe the history of Ireland in the layout of Limerick. Irishtown is down at the end of the main street, where the old walls of Limerick may be found embedded in commerce and penury. Compare these cabins of Irishtown at one end, and the graceful Georgian houses at the other. Modern times have added their equally appropriate mark. The hydroelectric scheme behind Irishtown. Suburbia beyond that gracious Crescent. How right, too, that the monument to Dan O'Connell should stand in the Crescent, at the top of George's Street, with the red-brick Georgian houses to his right and left. How right that we find to his west the Dominican church, and to his east the church of St Joseph — the power that made him and broke him, freed the Irishtowns and then sat on them, took over from Anglo-Ireland, and blessed the villas out to Mungret. Up here it is all planned and regular, pleasant and reasonable, as befitted the age of reason: Cecil Street, Glentworth Street, Hartstonge Street, Pery Square, Military Road. The sun warms the ruby faces of the houses, ruddy as the port no longer in the cellars, or where there is a patch of the yellow brick, gold as the vanished madeira and the biscuits. Lovely houses, from whose backs one looks down on the Shannon and can peep at the hills of Clare. Down there, behind the market, it is a network of streets and lanes, and because the Longstone quarries make excellent paving-sets (which have superseded those once imported from Wales and Arklow, once exclusively used in Limerick), the carts rumble and there always seems to be a drove of pigs going to the bacon-factory, and there is a general smell of corn-stores, hay, hucksters' shops, diaries, and petrol from the garages. The names accord — Pennywell, Whitewine, Gerald Griffin, Ellen, Michael, Garryowen, and the Spital. And then comes the canal, and on a half-island is Englishtown about the castle that you find in all the old prints of Limerick. This is the oldest Limerick, this and Irishtown, which between them were once the fortified city. Here you find what is left of the old walls, includ-ing the Ramparts which the women of Limerick defended with bricks and bottles — a buttress twelve yards thick.

Limerick has dignity, and Limerick has charm — the river for water always soothes a town — a sense of age, and a resignation, and contentment; but Limerick has not a bit of grandeur about it; except in the colloquial sense, slightly derisive of upstart vainglory. . . .

It is not too big to hold, nor so small as to be over-simplified. It has mobility — it is not a stagnant town, far from it, and even in my short memory it has improved and is improving by leaps and bounds. Twenty years ago it was drab and dirty. Now the streets are first-class. It was inhospitable to the stranger. I have bitter recollections of hours spent shivering in the railway station while waiting for a train to the west or the south, having no earthly place to go. Now there are cinemas, a cheerful restaurant or two, and there are the beginnings of a picture-gallery. The Public Library has much improved. One can now get a few periodicals to read. It looks far more like a little city than when (was it?) Robert Graves took from it only an impression of red-coated soldiers marching, and a donkey rolling in the middle of the main street.

For most people in Ireland the outstanding thing about Limerick is its piety. It is always boasting that it has the biggest Men's Confraternity in the country. It is the only city outside Dublin, except Galway, where there is a Jesuit community; but the SJs do not seem to add much to the culture of Limerick; why I do not know. There are also Redemptorists and Dominicans. Redemptorists are the great popular Hell-Fire-and-Damnation preachers, much in demand for Retreats and Missions, where they employ the genius of their Order first to put the fear of God across the toughest souls, and then win their confidence by a pitying benevolence. They are really in the old tradition of the priest with the blackthorn. I must say that, in my experience, they are, as men, the most gentle and lovable men in the Irish priest-hood; but as priests and preachers I have too often found their methods not in the best of taste; and I am certain that these methods are slowly becoming anachron-istic in modern Ireland. . . .

I sailed down the Shannon to Foynes in an old boat laden with Guinness and coal. The traveller should try hard to do this, or to reverse the journey, as I have also done on another occasion. On land one is, to some extent, always entangled in the geography. On river there is a sense of quiet possession. It is as if one possessed a human body by a perfect knowledge of the line of every artery. It is a grand river for a long quiet sail. It soothes like milk. The shores are wide and low. There is an amalgam of all the sweet river smells that ever were — fresh water, salt water, the pleasant smell of wrack, the intangible smell of the tiny water-mint mingled with and buried under leaves and mud. At the slow bends a faint down of golden reeds will adventure into the stream. Beyond, and sometimes below, the banks and levees there is — or was this August day — the sharp tang of mown hay and sedge. My main impression of that journey is composed of pictures of soft reeds and low meadow-lands, all giving the general idea of *spread* — especially the reeds which, muddied at the base by the tides, soften the outline and give additional seeming width to the water.

The fine residences look across from either side, and old castles bless. Rocks appear as one comes to the width of the estuary. The entry of the wide Fergus changes the river into an islanded lake. On the Limerick side of the bare and flat Aughinish Island the Deel invites one to Askeaton, a village that is well worth a visit, a place so old that one takes away a dread that at one's heels there may come a rumbling rattle of destruction. The castle is nobly placed, on a hillock over the tiny harbour on the river, and at low tide it returns with the declining water and the disclosed mud to its own centuries. There is a sense of history everywhere. Once I was walking through Askeaton with a local antiquary and he suddenly gripped my arm and pointed to a tiny hole-in-the-wall of a pub, over it on the faded facia-board the name Perrott.

'You remember?' he said, excitedly. 'The Desmond Rebellions? Sir John Perrott — the Lord Deputy? How he chased Desmond's light troops all over Munster with his cumbersome army?'

I gazed at the dusty facia-board with something of the astonishment of old Durbeyfield, in Hardy's novel, *Tess of the d'Urbervilles*, when he was told his magnificent line of descent. Sir John Perrott was the reputed natural son of Henry VIII.

From *An Irish Journey*, Longmans, Green and Co., 1940

Frank O'Connor: 'Spying' in the Rain
James Matthews

Michael (Frank O'Connor) was scheduled to give a broadcast talk in Dublin at the end of May (1940). The week before the broadcast he and Evelyn boarded the train with their bicycles at Kingsbridge station, bound for Limerick. From Limerick each day they cycled out in all directions, returning to the city before dark. They visited the church in Mungret, the friary at Askeaton, and Manister Abbey near Shanagolden. On the advice of Stan Stewart they also took a loop trip through Patrickswell and Adare to Rathkeale, circling back into Limerick by way of Croom. There they turned off the main road in search of a Cistercian abbey they had been told was thereabouts. Soon a car approached, and as they edged to the side of the road Michael tumbled from his bike. He started to curse the driver, but Evelyn cautioned that it was a Garda car. A little while later the same automobile came up behind them again, slowed down, and went by. Eventually, they got to Monasteranenagh and walked about the place admiring what was left of the cloisters and refectory. Poking around the ruins of the belfry, they came face to face with the men they had seen in the car. It suddenly struck them that they were being followed, because police weren't normally to be found inspecting ruined churches.

In the hotel that evening over drinks with Stan Stewart they talked about what had happened. The owner of the hotel, knowing Stan and figuring that if they were his friends they must be respectable folks, told them that the moment they had left that morning two gardaí had been in to search their bags. Apparently, they were suspected of being German spies. Parachute incidents during May south of Dublin and in Clare had made the police especially concerned about espionage activity. And why would a man and a woman be out cycling around the countryside in foul weather looking at deserted ruins? . . .

Toward the middle of June, Michael and Evelyn embarked on their western tour. . . .

All the miles and all the ruins had by this time exacted a great toll on Evelyn. Michael must have had more than enough of scenic wonder and wet roads because he consented without resistance to her suggestion that they board the train to Limerick, where they were to meet Stan Stewart for the Tipperary portion of their adventure. . . .

Stan Stewart's house on Shelbourne Road in Limerick proved to be a much-needed place of recovery. Stan took great delight in fussing over the expectant mother, who was content to stay in while her excitable husband roamed the town. Two days in Limerick, a city Michael considered the 'pleasantest in Ireland,' were refreshing enough to put them all on the road in search of Romanesque architecture once again. Stan's idea of cycling, however, ran more to pub stops and gentlemanly conversation than to feverish athletic peddling.

From *Voices: A Life of Frank O'Connor*, Gill & Macmillan, 1983

A Town Called Foynes
From: A Town
Knute Skinner

I was too busy looking at the Shannon
to catch the name of this town.
It's a river port — look at that ship docked there.
It's passing a quiet enough holiday
waiting to be loaded or unloaded.
And here's a row of attached buildings,
all done in cut stone,
one a closed but imposing
Bank of Ireland.

No one's in sight; everyone's at the dinner
or stepping along paths by the riverbank.
Oh, I think I'll remember this town
till the day I die,
but what will I call it?
Are they keeping its name secret, or is there some sign
on the road out?
Slow down here, please, and let me twist my neck.
Ah, it's called Foynes.

From *Learning to Spell Zucchini*, Salmon Publishing, 1988

Journey to the Maigue
Benedict Kiely

From the Maigue river in the County Limerick to Glangevlin in Cavan and then
to Moville and Carrigart in Donegal is not a long journey: a lot less than the little
length of Ireland. But to the best of my knowledge that's as far as my father's father
ever travelled. Nor might he ever have left the Maigue, with all its memories of
Gaelic poets, if he had not joined the Royal Irish Constabulary. In which force a
knowledge of Gaelic poetry was not compulsory. The members of the force, though,
had many other sterling qualities now belatedly acknowledged, sometimes and by
some people.

My grandfather's father had made an even shorter journey from Lisvernane in the slumberous Glen of Aherlow, in Tipperary, to the Maigue, to settle on the land near the small town of Bruff, around which is written one of the loveliest songs of the many songs of the poets of that tuneful river: 'Binnlisín Aerach an Bhrogha: The Sweet Little Airy Fort of Bruff'.

> The birds carolled songs of delight
> And the flowers bloomed bright on my path,
> As I stood all alone on the height
> Where rises Bruff's old fairy rath.
> Before me, unstirred by the wind,
> That beautiful lake lay outspread,
> Whose waters give sight to the blind
> And would almost awaken the dead.

In the aisling or visionary poem the poet walks out and finds the fair lady lamenting the sorrows of the Gael. On one great and memorable day in my life, Mannix Joyce, the historian of the Maigue, led myself and two learned friends along that river: from sweet Adare, oh lovely vale, oh soft retreat of sylvan splendour, then by Croom, and by Brurce where de Valera spent his boyhood, and on to Kilmallock and, beyond Kilmallock, to the high place of Ardpatrick where Domhnall Cam Ó Suilleabháin camped for a night on his marathon northward march at the end of the Elizabethan wars. And to the enchanted waters of Lough Gur, and to the sweet little airy fort of Bruff on the top of which Mannix produced a tape-machine and the voice of Mícheál Ó Ceallacháin sang the song out over the sleepy little town.

A most moving moment.

The poet walked out and we walked with him. And gazed on the silvery stream so loved by the heroes of old. And saw, as if in a dream, a maiden with tresses of gold. And asked her who she was and from whom descended. Was she the demi-goddess, Aoibhill, come to sadden our spirits with gloom? Or the woman who brought the legions to Troy? Or Deirdre, doomed to destroy?

Somewhere down there the ghost of my grandfather might, with ill-concealed impatience, have been listening to all that. If, that is, a ghost can be allowed to be anything but eternally patient. The ghost would know, as well as would you or I or the poet, that the lady was not Helen nor Deirdre nor Aoibhill, nor Aurora nor the goddess Flora, nor Artemidora nor Venus bright. But a spirit of faery, mourning the fate of the Gael and waiting in vain for succour from the Stuart over the sea.

But my grandfather left the faery lady to mourn by the Maigue and headed north and as far as he could get without falling into the ocean, meeting on his journey that woman by the name of McGovern. One of his sons, my father, had a much longer journey to make before destiny overtook him in the village of Drumquin. And on the morning of a Holy Thursday when he was seeking to praise the Lord in a chalice of brandy and burgundy.

From *Drink to the Bird: A Memoir*, Methuen, 1991

'Change at the Junction'
Kevin O'Connor

Now that the Dublin-Limerick train runs 'on-the-hour', give-or-take-twenty-minutes or so, a whole world of fluttery aunts and men with bags of meal slung over their shoulders gazing the length of the long, cold platform at Limerick Junction is gone forever.

The fluttering aunts and the men with the sacks of meal hardly had much in common, except an innate respect for each other's lives — and the train at Limerick Junction. And to understand how the two met you would need to know a little about the workings of the railway south of Portlaoise. In order to get from Dublin to Limerick by rail you boarded a train at what used to be Kingsbridge station and, after a series of stops, there would be a long stop at what appeared to be a railway platform a mile long in the middle of nowhere. This is Limerick Junction, situated in County Tipperary, and so called because in order to get to Limerick you disembarked there and waited for the train which had come out specially from Limerick 'to meet' the Dublin train to bear you on to Limerick. But if you were hoping to get to Limerick, you had to be alert approaching the long platform. Although you would have to wait once you got off there, the Cork train didn't hang about too long at the Junction.

When the train for Limerick came in and the porter with the brown trousers and pullover inside a black jacket started shouting 'Limerick train, Limerick train' through his railwayman's cap with the shiny peak, the lady of refinement and the man with the sack over his shoulder would move together towards a carriage. Moreover, they moved with the certainty of a couple going on a journey together. They would often sit on opposite seats and look sideways past each other's gaze as the train trundled towards Limerick, the essence of polite tolerance. I don't see many such aunts or mealbag men today, with seven trains running daily between Dublin and Limerick. I mull over how travel and things generally have changed. Time was not so long ago when a man could make a whole day's journey out of getting from Charleville to Limerick. With a stop at the Junction to change trains. . . .

From *The Old Limerick Journal*, No. 3, 1980

Mountcollins
From: Pilgrims
Bernard O'Donoghue

We're never only driving to the sea,
But also on the watch for dippers,
Red-berried holly, bagged turf
Or logs to burn, though we rarely
Find what we are looking for.
The most familiar roadsigns are to places
We've never been: 'O'Grady's Hold';
'The Earl of Desmond's Monument';
'The Boathouse at Laugharne'.

On childhood trips to Ballybunion
We always bypassed 'Mountcollins a quarter'.
But recently, thinking I'd time to spare,
I did turn for Mountcollins, finding it
A hilly village of narrow bridges
Over a stony river where you might well
See dippers: a place that in Italy
Would have been made picturesque
With hanging baskets and umber rooftiles.

I noted trailers there with outsize,
Mud-caked tyres: also powerlines sagging
Over the road. And then I drove on,
As though pursuing love and knowledge like
Some medieval pilgrim who, not resting
At the long-imagined shrine, obdures
In curiosity, wanting wonders:
The great Khan or Prester John or Juggernaut.
But what I found when I left Mountcollins was

That the sick friend I should have been hurrying
To visit, had left already
To winter on the coastline further north.

From *Gunpowder*, Chatto & Windus, 1995

On the Road to Abbeyfeale
Christopher Somerville

At the top of the sleepy main street of Ardagh village I found the green ramparts of Reerasta ring fort. On another September day, back in 1868, a local man by the name of Quinn had gone to Reerasta fort to dig potatoes. What he unearthed there turned out to be one of Ireland's finest hoards of buried treasure. Quinn's spade first brought up the pin of a brooch, then four complete brooches, a wooden cross, a bronze cup (he inadvertently broke this with an over-vigorous thrust) and, the cream of the hoard, a two-handled vessel of gold, silver and bronze seven inches tall, superbly worked and decorated with amber, crystal and enamel. It was a Communion chalice from the eighth century, the most beautiful example ever found in Ireland.

Quinn was more than satisfied with the bargain he struck when he sold his discoveries to Dr Hanlon of Rathkeale town for £50. But the better-informed doctor realised the true worth of what had been lying under Quinn's potatoes. So, belatedly and after her husband had died, did the widow Quinn. After numerous squabbles over ownership and proper compensation, the treasure ended up in 1874 in the National Museum in Dublin. Four years later the Bishop of Limerick received £100 in recognition of his stewardship of the land where the hoard had been found, and confirmed his reputation for fair dealing by giving half his windfall to the widow Quinn.

Strangely enough, it was the humble wooden cross that provided the answer as to how the chalice and the rest of the hoard had come to be buried in the old fort. Quinn made a present of the cross to his parish priest, and on examination the numbers '727' were found inscribed on the back. They probably stood for the date 1727, which suggested that that was when the cross had been made. Local history quickly pieced the rest of the story together.

In 1736 the parish priest, Father Christopher Bermingham, had been at loggerheads with the local landlord, Oliver Stephenson. Stephenson had a reputation as a 'ramping, stamping, tearing, swearing' squire. He had tried to exercise his *droit de seigneur* by attempting to seduce a bride as she and her brand-new husband were on the way home from their marriage service, but Father Bermingham had intervened to save the woman from her fate worse than death. Knowing full well the likely consequences of crossing the hot-blooded squire, the priest had then fled to Limerick. The chances were that he had taken time before his flight to conceal the treasure, which he must have felt lay under his protection, where neither Oliver Stephenson nor anyone else would have a chance of getting hold of it. There, in the seldom-disturbed sanctity of the fort, doubly protected by the fear local people had of the fairies they knew to frequent such places, it stayed hidden until revealed by the spade of the unsuspecting Quinn.

On the third morning out of Limerick I left Newcastle West as the early Mass bell was ringing. Cold trails of mist were swirling through the streets of the little town, refusing to be sucked up by the sun. Westward lay the outlying hills of the Mullaghareirk mountains, through which County Limerick slips over into County Kerry, and after the long miles through flat pasturelands I had been looking forward to exhilarating views from their tops. But for all the prospect that the enveloping mist allowed, I might as well have been walking in my own back garden.

Ancient and decrepit cars held together by bands of rust came clattering out of the murk to swerve past me on the road, carrying 'mountainy men' and their families from farms up in the hills to Mass in the town. The drivers raised their index fingers off their steering wheels, whether in greeting or admonition I couldn't be sure. I waved back anyway, and trudged on up side lanes where spiders' webs hung in pearly nets across the hedges. I never saw the top of the hill I was climbing. There were signs in what I could make out near at hand, however, to tell me of height being slowly gained — the appearance of bracken in the hedgebanks, tufts of purple heather beginning to show in the ground on each side, a deterioration in the sur face of the lane and a growth of grass in a green strip along its centre. The barking of dogs in farmyards far below became hollower and fainter the further I climbed. The mist chilled and thickened, blanking off the crests of Knockanimpaha and Sugar Hill at eleven hundred feet. I came to a junction where six unmarked roads met, and pulled up, soaked in mist and sweat, straining to decipher the minute, spidery lines on the map. . . .

I walked on across the crest of the hills in a wasteland of bog and heather where plantations of Sitka spruce shook their blue needles in a breeze that was springing up. The mist began to shred away and a wan disc of sun looked through the clouds, striking lines of silver out of the hillsides where the narrow bog roads curled. The spruce plantations steamed and glowed blue and green. I shook off my lethargy and walked fast over the high ground, looking down into the valley of the Oolagh river that ran parallel with the road a couple of hundred feet below. . . .

Next morning, wincing out of Abbeyfeale with a head as sore as my feet, I passed the statue of Father William Casey in the square. Father Casey had come to Abbeyfeale as a curate in 1869, taking on the duties of parish priest from 1883 until his death in 1907. The town had always had a reputation as a troublesome place; there were enough cattle-rustlers, robbers and outlaws in the surrounding hills to make Abbeyfeale notorious even before the mysterious and well-marshalled rebels known as the 'Rockites' gave the British soldiers a hard time in the early 1820s. The Rockites, a tough and determined group of insurgents, gained their nickname from the 'Captain Rock' signature on their anti-British proclamations. They were eventually crushed, but the rebellious spirit of Abbeyfeale remained. Father Casey was an ardent supporter of his flock in the land wars of the 1870s when the Irish tenants were struggling to break the power of their landlords and free themselves from the threats of eviction, excessive rent demands and other evils of living on land owned mostly by absentee English and Irish men. They gained partial redress in 1881 with the introduction of the Land Act, which allowed rents to be assessed impartially and guaranteed security of tenure to the tenants. (Charles Stewart Parnell had made his name and fame in backing these measures and forcing the Westminster parliament to accept them.) In 1903 the British Government gave the Irish peasantry the right to buy out their holdings from the landlords, and the bad old system was swept away with a rush. In Abbeyfeale Father William Casey is still well remembered and respected for his part in the early moves towards free ownership of land. 'He found his people struggling in the toils of landlordism', read the inscription on the plinth under the verdigrised statue in the square. 'He left them owners of the soil and freemen.'

Father Casey fought hard for the rights of his parishioners a century ago, but this morning he seemed to have espoused a new and international cause. His right hand was raised over the sleeping town, apparently clad in a black leather glove, with every appearance of giving a forceful Black Power salute. Closer inspection showed the glove to be a wrapping of shiny masking tape. From his gleaming black fingers dangled a blue-and-white football supporter's flag. Knotted round his shoulders by the sleeves was a blue-and-white football jersey. He stared across the square at a sagging banner stretched across the street, with 'Good Luck Fr Casey's' lettered in blue along its white strip. The smallest of smiles lay on Father Casey's green bronze lips.

I crossed the bridge on the outskirts of Abbeyfeale and was in Kerry. Almost immediately, it seemed, the landscape hardened, roughened and steepened.

From *The Road to Roaringwater: A Walk Down the West of Ireland*, HarperCollins Publishers, 1993

I Can Go Home Again
Frank McCourt

The best way to return to Limerick is to write a best-selling memoir, *Angela's Ashes*, and have its Irish launch in O'Mahony's Book Shop on O'Connell Street. . . .

The book was first launched on 5 September 1996 at Ireland House in New York. My brothers were there with their wives: Malachy and Alphie from New York, Michael from San Francisco. Down the years we've had our brotherly disputes; one might not talk to the other three; two might not talk to the other two. We grumbled and gossiped and complained about each other and there were times when we seemed to have nothing in common. But it was this book, set in Limerick, which brought us together and, I think, helped heal our wounds.

When I told them I'd be going to Limerick for the launch at O'Mahony's, Malachy said he'd like to go. Michael and Alphie said they could never manage it and what did it matter anyway? Later, Alphie changed his mind: he wanted to come. He called Michael who resisted — but not for long.

We hadn't been together in Limerick since I left in 1949. Longer and longer in the tooth, we were ready for another reunion. . . .

And why is it that after the success of *Angela's Ashes* in various countries on both sides of the Atlantic, the one place that mattered to me was Ireland, and Limerick in particular . . . the place I grew up economically miserable and spiritually terrified?

Interviewers asked me repeatedly: 'Do you consider yourself Irish or American?' And I answered: 'Neither. I'm a New Yorker.' That's what I said before I returned to Limerick. Now I'm not so sure. For years I had struggled with the writing of *Angela's Ashes*. I had assumed the mantle of victim and blamed Limerick and everyone in it for my troubles. Twenty-five years ago the book would have been an indictment, an essay in savage indignation. Then the news began to filter across the ocean: all was not well in the city by the river. You'd tell people from other parts of Ireland you were from Limerick and they'd give you a pitying look. Americans, fresh from Dublin, would say how they passed through Limerick on the way to Shannon and they'd quote from a travel guide that 'the best view of Limerick is through the rear-view mirror' and, for some reason, you'd find yourself bristling. You'd want to say, 'Hold on, hold on. It isn't that bad.'. . . You'd want to tell the world, 'No, no. Dublin is worse.'

While all this is going on you're wondering, 'What the hell do I care in the first place? I live in New York.'

No, I don't understand that mysterious thing called sense of place. I don't understand why I trek all the way up to 42nd Street to buy the *Limerick Leader*. I don't understand why my brothers and I are so 'Limerick' when we get together, why we laugh and use a down and dirty Limerick accent. . . .

Why does my heart break when the Limerick hurlers lose to Offaly and Wexford in the final minutes, and when I read about the glorious deeds of the Young Munster, Garryowen and Shannon rugby teams? Why do I want to run into the streets and pubs of New York with the good news? . . .

By the time I arrived in Dublin with my wife, Ellen, *Angela's Ashes* had already climbed into the *New York Times* best-seller list. . . .

And then I think of the journey to Limerick

Uneasy lies the head that wears a crown. . . .

Limerick. I drive in on the Dublin Road and all the green fields I knew when I delivered telegrams are gone. There's a university which everyone says has changed the life and energy of the city. There is traffic as thick as anything around New York.

I'm here now with my three brothers, the first time since 1949, and I know, like me, they can hardly catch their breath with the surge of feeling, that tears are ready to roll. My brother, Michael, *lets* them roll.

There's a reception in the City Hall and Mayor O'Hanlon makes a presentation, tells us how proud Limerick is to welcome us back, how the success of *Angela's Ashes* has, once again, placed Limerick in the limelight. I respond that this is the high point of my brief career as an author, that I'm honoured beyond words.

Until that night, that is.

I sign books and try to have a few seconds with people talking about the old days in the lanes, the school, the churches, the Archconfraternity of the Holy Family. I want to stop and tell everyone to stay so that I can talk to them. . . . I want to talk to the flesh and blood of the Horrigans, the Campbells, the Harolds, the Clohessys. . . . They've brought pictures of my mother, my brothers, St Joseph's troop of the Catholic Boy Scouts, outings to Kilkee, picnics to Cratloe.

I won't have this night again. I won't have hundreds of people from the old lanes smiling at me, welcoming me. This is beyond my wildest dreams and I wish I could stop signing books for a minute and go out for a pint with everyone.

I think of all the years I came here from New York with a chip on my shoulder. Now the chip is melted and I'm home. The next morning I meet my brothers for breakfast at the Royal George Hotel. They're going to the airport and when it's time to leave we embrace. . . .

All I did was write a book about a miserable childhood in Limerick and this is my reward.

Oh, Limerick . . .

From *The Irish Times*, 24 December 1996

TWELVE

FICTION

A City of Old Women
Mervyn Wall

Fursey proceeded hurriedly: 'It would be an exaggeration to say that you can't move around Clonmacnoise without tripping over piles of gold and other valuables; but gold is there, nevertheless, in great quantities. The monastery is situated in the interior on the River Shannon, and the religious settlements on the coast have for many years past sent their treasures inland to Clonmacnoise for safety.'

'Describe the exact location of the monastery,' commanded Sigurd.

'It's situated many miles inland from the sea and above the Danish city of Limerick,' replied Fursey, 'but it lies on the Shannon, a great river, readily navigable by ships of shallow draught such as yours.'

Sigurd motioned a warrior to step forward. He was a tall, spare man of most uninviting aspect, with only one eye, which was a large, melancholy one. Fursey noticed that he had only two teeth, big, yellow fangs, which dwelt apart.

'Snorro,' Sigurd addressed him, 'you've heard what the stranger says. Is it true?'

'Yes,' replied Snorro. 'It is even as he says. I've been in the Danish settlement called Limerick.' . . .

Even though it was still only early afternoon, the night life of Ballybunion was already under way, and one could hear the wicked hum of the settlement, the barking of depraved dogs, the incessant rattling of dice boxes and the indignant howls of drunkards being ejected from taverns because they had no more money. But the dragonship soon left this modern Babylon behind and crept up the estuary of the River Shannon.

It was almost dusk when they arrived at Limerick and, rowing some hundred yards beyond the settlement, anchored in mid-stream. There was much whispering among the crew, and at length a boat was lowered, into which Sigurd and Snorro scrambled.

'Come on,' said Snorro to Fursey, 'but leave your weapons and helmet behind.'

The surprised Fursey climbed into the boat and Snorro quickly rowed ashore. There Sigurd gave his final instructions to Snorro in undertones, and strode away by himself into the town.

Fursey glanced around him and saw that the city consisted of an irregular patch of grass, around which were dotted at intervals some fifty or sixty circular cabins, built of wickerwork and thatched with straw. Beyond the houses he could see in the gathering dusk fields of tillage and pasture stretching away to the outskirts of the forest. The inhabitants, who were mostly Danes, wore multicoloured cloaks chequered with spots and stripes. An occasional Irishman was to be seen clad in a loose-sleeved mantle of frieze. On the quay beside Fursey a local saint was solemnly shaking hands with his friends before setting out on a perilous journey into the wilds of north Kerry, where he was to make his fourth attempt to convert the robber lord of that territory, known far and wide as the Wolf of Ballybunion. In the centre of the green an idle crowd was listening to a street preacher, clad in a kilt of severe and uncompromising cut, who was urging them to burn something or other of which he didn't approve.

'Come, and I'll show you the city,' said Snorro, touching Fursey's arm.

'Why have the others not landed?' asked Fursey as they set out.

'Sigurd is afraid that they'll start drinking in some Mariners' Rest and betray the fact that we're not traders. So he has confined them on board ship until we start upstream before dawn.'

'And where has he gone himself?'

'He has gone to the King's house to fix things. That's it over there, the building with the three skeletons hanging from the tree outside the door.'

'What do you mean by "fix things"?'

'Well,' explained Snorro, 'when we sack Clonmacnoise and pass by here again tomorrow evening the King will expect a percentage in return for keeping his mouth shut and not impeding our passage. After all, he's a Christian, and would normally be expected to oppose a raid on a monastery.'

'It's all very bewildering,' said Fursey. 'I always understood that although this is a Norse settlement it had been converted to Christianity and was notable for its piety.'

'It is rather in process of conversion. The King is a Christian, but most of his subjects still cling to the older faith. He does not persecute them on that account, being a liberal and enlightened man. Most of the public institutions are still what you people call pagan. And certainly it is the case that Limerick has always been noted for its many religious institutions. There, for instance,' said Snorro, pointing to a cluster of huts within a palisade, 'is the Sick and Indigent Sea Rovers' Institution.'

Fursey peered over the palisade and saw half a dozen ancients doddering round the enclosure.

'All hardy Vikings once,' declared Snorro. 'Now all they're any good for is eating porridge and yapping about their battles with their toes to the fire. Over there is the Broken-Down Norsemen's Institute. It's necessary to have lost a minimum of two limbs to secure admittance.' . . .

Fursey was very pensive as they walked back through the town. Although it was now quite dark, most of the inhabitants seemed to be out of doors, leaning against the walls of the houses gazing into nothingness.

'What do you think of Limerick?' asked Snorro.

'It seems to be a city of bewhiskered old women,' replied Fursey.

'It is,' replied Snorro, 'both male and female.'

They had come to a low, rambling building in the centre of the town.

'This is where we stay for the night,' said Snorro, and he read for Fursey the inscription over the doorway. 'Night shelter for Unemployed Vikings, under the patronage of Thor the Thunderer. That's Thor,' he added, pointing to where there stood over the doorway an immense statue of a very formidable character waving a hammer. They had to take their place in a queue of Norse down-and-outs in sordid and base attire. It was hard to believe of most of them that they had once ridden the seas in search of adventure, for they were in general low and obscure fellows with squalid beards and dangling hair. They all appeared to be suffering from malnutrition, and those that weren't either lame or halt had broken backs or lacked their full complement of eyes, ears and arms. When the queue moved forward sufficiently to bring Snorro and himself within the doorway, Fursey saw a broad-shouldered warrior seated behind a table in the entrance. He had a battleaxe swinging from his wrist by a leathern thong, and he was entering each man's name in a sheepskin register. . . .

Fursey and Snorro passed into the dormitory. About thirty inmates were huddled over a spark in the fireplace at the far end of the room. The hall was long and narrow, and a long bench ran its entire length. About three feet higher than the bench a rope also ran the length of the room. One slept sitting on the bench with one's hands on the rope. You then rested your chin on your hands like a dog resting its chin on its paws. At sunrise the superintendent, after a warning shout, cut the rope with his battleaxe and all the late sleepers fell on to the floor. These things were explained to Fursey by a thin, white-faced creature who sat down beside him. . . .

When questioned he answered in deep, sepulchral tones. 'Oh, yes, this is a very religious institution. Only last week there was an atheist in here, and he hid in the washroom while the rest of us were committing our well-being to Thor. The superintendent dragged him out and nearly hacked him to pieces before throwing him out. Oh, the superintendent is a very pious man.' . . .

From *The Return of Fursey*, Pilot Press, 1948; *The Complete Fursey*, Wolfhound Press, 1985

'The Whole Country was like a Puddle'
Laurence Sterne

The description of the siege of Jericho itself, could not have engaged the attention of my uncle Toby more powerfully than the last chapter; — his eyes were fixed upon my father throughout it; — he never mentioned radical heat and radical moisture, but my uncle Toby took his pipe out of his mouth, and shook his head; and as soon as the chapter was finished, he beckoned to the corporal to come close to his chair, to ask him a question. . . . It was at the siege of Limerick, an' please your honour, replied the corporal, making a bow.

The poor fellow and I, quoth my uncle Toby addressing himself to my father, were scarce able to crawl out of our tents, at the time the siege of Limerick was raised, upon the very account you mention. — Now what can have got into that precious noddle of thine, my dear brother Toby? cried my father, mentally. — By Heaven! continued he, communing still with himself, it would puzzle an Oedipus to bring it in point.—

I believe, an' please your honour, quoth the corporal, that if it had not been for the quantity of brandy we set fire to every night, and the claret and cinnamon with which I plied your honour off; — And the geneva, Trim, added my uncle Toby, which did us more good than all — I verily believe, continued the corporal, we had both, an' please your honour, left our lives in the trenches, and been buried in them too. — The noblest grave, corporal! cried my uncle Toby, his eyes sparkling as he spoke, that a soldier could wish to lie down in. — But a pitiful death for him! an' please your honour, replied the corporal.

All this was as much Arabic to my father, as the rites of the Colchi and Troglodites had been before to my uncle Toby; my father could not determine whether he was to frown or to smile. —

My uncle Toby, turning to Yorick, resumed the case at Limerick, more intelligently than he had begun it, — and so settled the point for my father at once.

It was undoubtedly, said my uncle Toby, a great happiness for myself and the corporal, that we had all along a burning fever, attended with a most raging thirst, during the whole five-and-twenty days the flux was upon us in the camp; otherwise what my brother calls the radical moisture, must, as I conceive it, inevitably have got the better. — My father drew in his lungs top-full of air, and looking up, blew it forth again, as slowly as he possibly could. —

— It was Heaven's mercy to us, continued my uncle Toby, which put it into the corporal's head to maintain that due contention betwixt the radical heat and the radical moisture, by reinforcing the fever, as he did all along, with hot wine and spices; whereby the corporal kept up (as it were) a continual firing, so that the radical heat stood its ground from the beginning to the end, and was a fair match for the moisture, terrible as it was. — Upon my honour, added my uncle Toby, you might have heard the contention within our bodies, brother Shandy, twenty toises. — If there was no firing, said Yorick.

Well — said my father, with a full aspiration, and pausing a while after the word — Was I a judge, and the laws of the country which made me one permitted it, I would condemn some of the worst malefactors, provided they had had their clergy — Yorick, foreseeing the sentence was likely to end with no sort of mercy, laid his hand upon my father's breast, and begged he would respite it for a few minutes, till he asked the corporal a question. — Prithee, Trim, said Yorick, without staying for my father's leave, — tell us honestly — what is thy opinion concerning this self-same radical heat and radical moisture?

With humble submission to his honour's better judgment, quoth the corporal, making a bow to my uncle Toby — Speak thy opinion freely, corporal, said my uncle Toby. — The poor fellow is my servant, — not my slave, — added my uncle Toby, turning to my father. —

The corporal put his hat under his left arm, and with his stick hanging upon the wrist of it, by a black thong split into a tassel about the knot, he marched up to the ground where he had performed his catechism; then touching his under-jaw with the thumb and fingers of his right hand before he opened his mouth, — he delivered his notion thus.

The corporal made a bow to his old friend, Dr Slop, and then delivered his opinion concerning heat and radical moisture in the following words.

The city of Limerick, the siege of which was begun under his majesty King William himself, the year after I went into the army — lies, an' please your honours, in the middle of a devilish wet, swampy country. — 'Tis quite surrounded, said my uncle Toby, with the Shannon, and is, by its situation, one of the strongest fortified places in Ireland.

I think this is a new fashion, quoth Dr Slop, of beginning a medical lecture. — 'Tis all true, answered Trim. — Then I wish the faculty would follow the cut of it, said Yorick. — 'Tis all cut through, an' please your reverence, said the corporal, with drains and bogs; and besides, there was such a quantity of rain fell during the siege, the whole country was like a puddle, — 'twas that, and nothing else, which brought on the flux, and which had like to have killed both his honour and myself; now there was no such thing, after the first ten days, continued the corporal, for a soldier to lie dry in his tent, without cutting a ditch round it, to draw off the water; — nor was that enough, for those who could afford it, as his honour could, without setting fire every night to a pewter dish full of brandy, which took off the damp of the air, and made the inside of the tent as warm as a stove. —

And what conclusion dost thou draw, corporal Trim, cried my father, from all these premises?

I infer, an' please your worship, replied Trim, that the radical moisture is nothing in the world but ditch-water — and that the radical heat, of those who can go to the expense of it, is burnt brandy, — the radical heat and moisture of a private man, an' please your honour, is nothing but ditch-water — and a dram of geneva — and give us but enough of it, with a pipe of tobacco, to give us spirits, and drive away the vapours — we know not what it is to fear death.

I am at a loss, Captain Shandy, quoth Dr Slop, to determine in which branch of learning your servant shines most, whether in physiology or divinity. — Slop had not forgot Trim's comment upon the sermon. —

It is but an hour ago, replied Yorick, since the corporal was examined in the latter, and passed muster with great honour. —

The radical heat and moisture, quoth Dr Slop, turning to my father, you must know, is the basis and foundation of our being — as the root of a tree is the source and principle of its vegetation. — It is inherent in the seeds of all animals, and may be preserved sundry ways, but principally in my opinion by consubstantials, impriments, and occludents. — Now this poor fellow, continued Dr Slop, pointing to the corporal, has had the misfortune to have heard some superficial empiric discourse upon this nice point. — That he has, — said my father. — Very likely, said my uncle. — I'm sure of it — quoth Yorick. — . . .

For my own part, quoth my uncle Toby, I have given it up. — The Danes, an' please your honour, quoth the corporal, who were on the left at the siege of Limerick, were all auxiliaries. — And very good ones, said my uncle Toby. — But the auxiliaries, Trim, my brother is talking about, — I conceive to be different things. —

— You do? Said my father, rising up.

From *Tristram Shandy and A Sentimental Journey through France and Italy*, The Modern Library, New York, n.d.

Sylvester O'Halloran
Ronan Sheehan

Scurvy broke out among the children of St Francis's Abbey, the filthiest and most impoverished district of the city. Round black spots discoloured the soles of the children's feet and they generally died three or four days afterwards. Six children presented themselves at Sylvester O'Halloran's rooms for treatment. He advised them to bathe their feet in warm water in the morning and afternoon and in the lees of wine at night. They said that they could not come by wine because they had no money. So they must die, it seemed, like their friends before them. Sylvester promised to get what they needed from a cousin who owned a tavern on condition that they kept his gift a secret. He said they must drink sage tea or barley water made slightly acid with elixir of vitriol. He would furnish them with a supply of this also, upon the same condition. 'Thank you,' said the eldest of the group, 'I'm sure our lives will be saved.' In the event four of the six survived. But these four returned in summer with sores behind their ears. He prescribed a similar course of treatment which saved two. The following March these last two were among the many who perished through spontaneous gushings of blood from the arteries and veins of the head.

It was all of it due to lack of proper food. The children had died of poverty despite the fact that their native city was surrounded by some of the best farming land in Europe. He remarked upon the irony of this state of affairs to August Schweiss, the wigmaker, at whose premises he stopped *en route* to the funeral of one of the children. Schweiss said he could tell a man's rank in society simply by touching his hair. The hair of the very rich was stiffest and most firm whereas the hair of indigent people was weak and thin. He had learned to identify the various intervening grades from close inspection of the scalps that had been offered for sale to him over the years. The wig Sylvester had ordered, why it was composed of a mixture, a labourer's son and a farmer's wife. The point he wished to make was that if diet affected people's hair in this way it was no wonder that their constitutions were similarly affected.

'Parents,' he said, 'are generally willing to sell the hair of a declining child since the price they get affords the opportunity of saving the lives of other children. It's a sign of the times. In my grandfather's day the Irish were very proud of their long hair and would not sell it for love or money. Nowadays they can't afford to be so particular. I believe anatomists like yourself experience a similar situation. The wretches are forthcoming with the carcasses of their dead for the sake of a few shillings. Am I right or wrong?'

There must be an infirmary for Limerick, he decided, where the poor would get proper treatment, as they did at the Hôtel Dieu. Máire was sceptical. She said that the poor were going to be miserable and die one way or another and that he should take good care to spend whatever proportion was necessary of the sum raised for the infirmary upon surgical equipment with which he could develop his expertise. In this way he might attend to ailments which, unlike poverty, a surgeon could hope to cure, while benefiting himself at the same time. She teased him when he protested at the suggestion of self-interest, saying that he wasn't as innocent as he used to be and that she could see this idea at the back of his mind.

He joined forces with a colleague and took a lease of four houses in the Little Island which were quickly adapted to their purposes. They paid the rent themselves and raised other sums through subscriptions, charity plays and the like. The rich paid for treatment while the poor got it for nothing. There were few enough beds to begin with and the rich were anxious to try out the hospital, if only for the sake of the novelty, so that often the poor were turned away because no bed was free. The poor did not complain. They were astounded that they had any claim at all upon the place. Then the infirmary was completely occupied by people suffering from injuries inflicted by the Whiteboys, whose violence had broken out in reaction to the enclosures of commonage by landlords and the increasingly merciless exactions of the tithe proctors. The injuries did not often call for major surgery but were nevertheless serious. Victims were dragged from bed and left buried to their chins in graves filled with furze or thorns, their ears having been cut off. They were beaten, tied and placed on horses with a hedgehog's skin for a saddle. They were branded with irons and thrown in ditches. A Member of Parliament reported that a friend of his, while travelling along a country road, had come upon a pair of ears and a cheek nailed to a post. Soon he overtook a clergyman, his head muffled in a great cloak, to whom they belonged.

'If those children had had possession of their great grandfathers' lands,' Sylvester said, 'they would not have died from want of food. If the landlords had not enclosed the commonage, or the rectors been so greedy, I would not be treating injuries caused by the Whiteboys. These illnesses spring from injustice, do they not? Should I not issue a prescription to the government, advising that they return the land to Catholics?'

'That,' said Máire, 'is a prescription for losing your practice.'

'Seán Clárach,' said Sylvester, 'went blind because he preferred not to have to look at what was there. I'm blind if I refuse to see, for the sake of my practice or any other reason.'

Máire replied that it was the same for everyone. Doctors thrived on illness, lawyers on injustice. The army did not defend the people but oppressed it. The Protestant clergy were only interested in milking cash from their parishes. The laws against Catholic bishops were usually enforced at the instigation of priests whom they had censured or full-time hunters who were themselves Catholics as often as not. You couldn't get away from the fact that people were twisted. She told him secrets that women friends of both religions had confided to her, revealing unimagined distortions beneath the outward appearance of marriages he was familiar with. She told him how she had helped some of these women who, in return, had hurt and betrayed her out of resentment for the fact of having needed her help. What would he prescribe for that illness? The restoration of lands to Catholics? A hat with a large crown and a wide brim?

When after a few years the Whiteboy violence subsided the infirmary attracted cases which afforded him an opportunity of developing his new method of amputation. A man from Abbeyfeale had an extraordinary growth upon his back which Sylvester removed by painstaking and protracted surgery. Máire passed the details of this operation to *The Limerick Chronicle* which subsequently described the excrescence as a variety of cartilaginous teats which spread like the foliage of trees from a bleeding trunk which measured fourteen inches in circumference. The hospital was putting this object on display 'for the inspection of the curious'. Next Sylvester removed a cancerous breast from a local woman and then he amputated a series of arms and legs. The bone and half the stump of John Linnane's thigh were covered by a firm cushion of flesh ten days after his operation. *The Limerick Chronicle* invited the public to view this phenomenon on the ground that it was a matter of great consequence, not only for the public but for the military, whose medical men were already applying to Mr O'Halloran, by whom the new method of amputation had been developed in Limerick. The method was already being used in England and France, the article said. Irishmen should regard this success as a matter of national pride.

The publicity attracted patients from all classes to Sylvester's rooms, making his the most lucrative practice in the city. The new influx included members of the German colony, called the Palatinate, who had been given grants of land on very favourable terms in the neighbourhood of Adare.

From *Boy With An Injured Eye*, Brandon Book Publishers Ltd, 1983

In the Jury Room
Gerald Griffin

It was during the assize week of an important city in the South of Ireland, that a grave-looking gentleman dressed in a sober suit of brown and petersham topcoat, was observed riding with a somewhat inquisitive air through the dense crowds who thronged the open space before the city and county court-house. Everything in his appearance announced a person of good sense and prudence. His dress was neither too good for the road nor too mean for the wearer's rank as indicated by his demeanour; his hat was decent, but evidently not his best; a small spotted shawl folded cravat-wise, protected his throat and ears from the rather moist and chilly air of an early Irish spring. A pair of doeskin caps or overalls, buttoned on the knees, defended those essential hinges of the lower man from the danger of contracting any rheumatic rust in the open air; while gloves of the same material, and toe-boots neatly *foxed*, evinced in the extremities of the wearer's person the same union of economy and just sufficient attention to appearances which was observable in all the rest of his attire.

The countenance likewise was one which at the first glance attracted the respect and confidence of the beholder. It was marked by a certain air of goodwill and probity of character, with a due consciousness of the owner's position in life, and an expression which seemed to intimate that he would not be willingly deficient in what was due to others, nor readily forfeit any portion of what was fairly owing to himself.

As is usually the case when a stranger makes his appearance amid an idle crowd, all eyes were fixed upon him as he leisurely walked his horse toward a small hotel which stood a little distance from the court-house. Giving the bridle to the hostler, with the easy air of one who seldom hurries about anything, and of the two feels less satisfaction in motion than in rest, he alighted, and after desiring, in what seemed an English accent, that the horse should not be fed until he had leisure, himself, to visit the animal in the stall, he drew off his gloves, looked up and down the street, then up at the sky, where the clouds seemed just deliberating whether they would rain or no, took off his hat, inspected it all over, thrust his gloves into the pocket of his greatcoat, and finally entered the coffee-room. It may seem trifling to mention all those motions of the traveller with as much precision, but not one of them was lost upon the intelligent observers in the street, who doubtless would not have employed a thing so valuable as time in watching the movements of an entire stranger, if there were not something very important, though still a mystery to them, in every turn he took.

The coffee-room was at this instant the scene of a very animated discussion. . . .

Stimulated rather by a general feeling of curiosity than moved by any particular interest in the suit at issue, the stranger . . . put on his hat and walked out in the direction of the court-house. There was something in his appearance which opened a way for him through the crowd, and the police and bailiffs were seen to push aside all the country people with the butts of their carbines, and hold the little iron gateways open as he drew nigh. After listening for some time to the counsel and witnesses, who seemed bent up to harangue and swear their best in honour of the occasion, our traveller began to feel as if he had heard enough of it, and returning to the inward flagged hall, cast his eyes about, and seemed desirous to inspect the remainder of the building. Passing along a somewhat lengthy hall which divided the civil from the criminal court, he ascended a short circular flight of stairs, which brought him to a landing place on which he could perceive several doors, leading in different directions. One of those by some unaccountable neglect stood ajar at the present moment. It would appear that if the grave-looking stranger had a foible it was that for which the tender-hearted wife of Bluebeard was so near forfeiting her life. The silence of the place, the mystery of so many closed doors at a moment of so much bustle and confusion, and the tempting air of that which stood invitingly half open, provoked his curiosity with a degree of force which he had not firmness to resist. He pushed in the door. All was silent inside. The room had a bare and scantily furnished appearance. A painted deal table stood in the centre, on which were scattered some paper, pens, and ink. Near it, irregularly placed, stood one or two wooden forms and a few chairs. On the side of the chamber opposite to the door by which he had entered, was a window dim with dust, which looked out upon the narrow and ill-paved back street of the city. A neglected though still tolerable fire burned in the capacious grate. In one corner was a large press or double cupboard inserted into the wall, the upper portion of which was locked. Not so the lower, in which the inquisitive stranger only observed a few acts of parliament in stitched covers, barony books, and some torn law papers. Near this stood an enormous basket filled with turf for the purpose of replenishing the fire.

It needed not now the aid of a conjuror to tell our traveller into what chamber of the building he had penetrated. It was the Jury Room. Struck by the natural reflections, which the place was calculated to excite in any mind, but more especially in one of a thoughtful and generous turn, such as that of the grave stranger, it was some time before he recollected the awkwardness of his own situation in the absorbing reverie which seized upon him. The many fellow-beings on which the *fiat* of life or death had been passed within that room, the families who had been consigned to misery, the many occasions on which passion and interest had there taken the place of justice, to the condemnation perhaps of the innocent, or the absolution of the guilty, all those and other circumstances furnished matter which detained him in the mood of thought for a considerable time. Insensibly he passed to the institution of the much valued system, thence to the manifold schemes by which the 'wisdom of ages' has sought at various times to defend the pure administration of justice from the intermeddling of human passion, and thence again, ascending higher in abstraction as he continued his musing, to the corruption of society in general, and the misery of man, whom not even a device so beautiful as this great boast of the British constitution could protect against the evil of his own perverse and fallen nature.

By this time the night had already begun to close. The din of the city was hushed into a low murmur in which might be distinguished the call of the watchman in the street, the occasional rattle of a passing vehicle, and the ringing of some of the chapel bells summoning the people to the evening prayers, usual in the time of Lent. The same evening silence had fallen within the circuit of the place of justice, and the voice of the presiding judge was heard distinctly, though faintly, in the act of delivering his concluding charge. Even this sound ceased at length, and nothing was heard except that general murmur which arises in a crowd when something occurs to relax the absorbing attention in which all have been enchained for a considerable time before.

'And wretches hang, that jurymen may dine!'

exclaimed the stranger, awaking from his reverie, when he was startled by an alarming sound, which first brought to his mind the critical position in which he had placed himself. A door was heard to open and shut, and presently the clattering of a bailiff's halberd and the tramp of many feet was heard upon the little flight of steps by which he had ascended. The jury were coming!

From *Tales From the Jury Room*, James Duffy and Co. Ltd

The Vale of Honey
Kate O'Brien

The light of the October day was dropping from afternoon clarity to softness when Anthony Considine led his limping horse round the last curve of the Gap of Storm and halted there to behold the Vale of Honey.

The Vale of Honey is a wide plain of fertile pastures and deep woods, watered by many streams and ringed about by mountains. Westward the Bearnagh hills, through whose Gap of Storm the traveller had just tramped, shelter it from the Atlantic-salted wind, and at the foot of these hills a great river sweeps about the western valley, zigzagging passionately westward and southward and westward again in its search for the sea.

A few miles below him on this river's banks the traveller saw the grey blur of a town.

'That must be Mellick', he said to hearten himself and his horse.

In the south two remote green hills had wrapped their heads in cloud; eastward the stonier, bluer peaks wore caps of snow already. To the north the mountains of St Phelim were bronzed and warmly wooded.

Villages lay untidily about the plain; smoke floated from the chimneys of parked mansions and the broken thatch of cowmen's huts; green, blue, brown, in all their shades of dark and brightness, lay folded together across the stretching acres in a colour-tranquillity as absolute as sleep, and which neither the breaking glint of lake and stream nor the seasonal flame of woodtops could disquiet. Lark songs, the thin sibilance of dried leaves, and the crying of milk-heavy cows were all the sounds that came up to the man who stood in the Gap of Storm and scanned the drowsed and age-saddened vista out of eyes that were neither drowsed nor sad.

Bright, self-confident eyes they were indeed, deep-set and brilliantly blue, seeming all the bluer because of the too black, too thick bar of eyebrow that brooded quarrelsomely above them. In spite of these savage eyebrows the eyes and face of the man were gay and his whole body had a coarse beauty. He was tall, and black-haired, with white skin, white teeth, ruddy cheeks, and heavy shoulders. His thick hands supported the indication of pugnacity in his brows, but they were nimble too, the hands of a horseman. One of them, playing lightly now on the neck of his strawberry roan mare, seemed to have hypnotised her restive weariness into peace. His hair was wild and his ragged clothes were stained with sweat and dirt. But he wore his rags and the three days' beard on his chin with as much ease as he carried his strength, all these things being natural to him.

They were a contrast, this horse and man who seemed so much in harmony. His was the beauty of a peasant, something flung up accidentally by life. A root his bodily fineness might be called, but the horse he caressed was a flower. He was nature's heedless work, but she, taking her inbred and high-bred quality from generations of great blood stock, was a work of art. The breeders of Rose Red had brought beauty, through her, to the threshold of degeneracy. She was superb, she was the end of beauty in her kind.

Anthony Considine looked tenderly at her now and dropped his hand from her neck to caress her injured fetlock, laughing contentedly to think of the clever way he had stolen her.

She had a stud-book name, this strawberry roan, a noble name, which revealed her great descent, and was written above her loose box in the aristocratic stable she would never see again. But Anthony Considine, the first time he laid his thief's hand on her neck, murmured 'Rose Red' to her, and named her for himself for ever, as a lover names his mistress.

Now he had ridden her and led her seventy-two hours' journey and more from her aristocratic stable, and the Bearnagh hills were a shelter at their backs. The tramp and his stolen love were tolerably safe, so long as they did not return to the treeless, lovely west. If they were to stay together they must descend into the Vale of Honey that was strange to them, and see what chances there were of free stable and bed in that grey smudge of a town called Mellick.

The man tossed back his curly, greasy hair.

'The Vale of Honey!' he said softly. 'I've often heard 'tis a grand, rich, easy-going place. It's like a saucer, upon my word, the shape of it, or like a dish, the way the little hills come up all round it. Faith, if it's a dish, I hope it's got our supper on it, Rose Red!'

He stood up and drew the bridle through his arm.

'Can you do it for me, asthore?' he asked the horse. 'Can you limp five or six more miles along with me, God help you?'

Dusk was past and it was already full starlight when the horse-thief led his lovely roan past the crumbling gates of Mellick and along a well-paved and lighted street, which was called 'Kilmoney Street' on its cleanly painted name-board, and which had a lively and a prosperous air.

From *Without My Cloak*, William Heinemann Ltd, 1931

The Chaplain's Concert
Kate O'Brien

One of the anomalies about the annual Chaplain's Concert was that whereas, listening to Mother Mary Andrew's threats at rehearsal, and appraising the tension in all performers, one might think that a hitch was a major offence, deserving a mark for conduct perhaps — yet, on the night, it was almost *de rigueur* that a few things should go wrong, and any girl who broke down in a song, knocked a wig askew, or got outright hysterics during a big scene, became at once a heroine with high entertainment value, raising a most gratifying laugh from a rather nervous audience, breaking the ice, and as a rule even being let off Mother Mary Andrew's wrath at the end of the day.

Anna Murphy noticed this every year, but it did not prevent her from getting as nervously excited as everyone else a day or two before the concert.

This always took place at the end of the autumn term, about three days before the Christmas break-up. In November, for Foundress's Day, the concert had its first, and very formal, try-out. The audience then was the community and a large number of 'old girls', many of whom returned to stay in the house for the reunion. And although this might have been an informal celebration, somehow by tradition it was not, but, on the contrary was a full-dress parade of '*la pudeur et la politesse*'. Everything had to go smoothly for Foundress's Concert, and therefore somehow, by hook or by crook, comedy and disaster were kept to the wings, and the result was that, the first anxieties allayed, everyone was a little bored — the school sitting very decorously, in white silk dresses and scratchy white silk gloves; the old girls, watchful and shy of each other, in carefully chosen dinner-gowns; even the benevolent lay-sisters, amused on their perilous perch on desks at the back and willing to enjoy anything, were unable to escape some boredom, at Foundress's Concert.

Indeed, Reverend Mother, seated in a very grand chair in the front row, and with the more loyal and important of the married 'old girls' to left and right of her, marvelled often at the self-control of the children, ranged along the walls of the *salle* to left and right, and could only conclude that youth was illimitably interested in its own events — even in such a programme as the traditional one of *Sainte Famille* — a bit of everything, in every language, or on every musical instrument which was taught in the school; and affording chances of self-expression to all, from Senior to Second Preparatory. Also she thought gently that youth, on the whole, is patient and well-mannered. For herself, she knew with compunction that her chief interest in Foundress's Concert was in observation of the social comedy of the 'old girls' — which often indeed touched and saddened more than it amused her. But there was — to make a saint smile, she pleaded for herself — the perennial tussle for precedence between Lady de la Pole, a punctilious 'old girl' who loved this yearly chance to show her contemporaries where she had got to, and Madame O'Hea, who, daughter of a Lord Chief Justice and wife of The O'Hea, was more arrogant with, in her own view, incomparably more right. But Lady de la Pole, although never quite sure of herself, could not see why the wife of a fifth baronet should have to concede social importance to the wife of anything so absurd as a 'The' — and calling herself Madame too — for all the world like a dressmaker! Reverend Mother sometimes wondered why the fires of antagonism, blazing across her chair from these two poised and smiling ladies, did not scorch her.

However, none of this grown-up, bitter comedy infected Chaplain's Concert.

Only priests were invited to it — usually about twenty-five or thirty priests. The chaplain, of course, and the parish priest and senior curate of the village; parish priests and curates from neighbouring villages; Jesuits and Cistercians from nearby colleges, one or two Franciscans, and any ex-chaplains who were within driving distance of the convent. It was probable that at least to the younger of the priests the function was alarming and even unattractive — but most of the invited came, sheepish and friendly. And whether or not they enjoyed the evening, it is certain that the young ladies of *Saint Famille* did so.

However, the preparations for it were as uneasy as for an *auto da fé*.

The concert took place in the *salle*. This was an awkward arrangement, but the tradition of *Saint Famille* was to keep theatrical effort as amateur as possible, so that no young lady should be encouraged to think of herself as a gifted actress. No platform was erected and there was no drop-curtain. Performers took their stand on a red carpet in the middle of the *salle* and did what they could with the roles assigned to them. They made their exits and entrances upstage, through the barrier of three pianos arranged as a kind of wall. The concert was begun and concluded by the execution of a piece of music by six young ladies, seated at the three pianos. Music was not well taught at *Sainte Famille*, as the six-handed performance of 'Dichter und Bauer' or 'Si j'étais Roi' gave proof. If any girl played a musical instrument well, or played any composition worth listening to, that was entirely accidental. However, the three pianos made 'wings' for the actors, and covered their exits from the *salle* to extempore dressing-rooms.

The morning of Concert Day was mad and stormy in the *salle*.

Lay-sisters were laying the red drugget; Mother Bonaventure, seated at one of the three pianos, was rehearsing Madge Willis in a song; people were moving desks and tramping about with pots of flowering plants. And almost all the girls, falling over each other and delighting in the nervy confusion, which, for its sheer stimulation, they sought to increase, muttered or chanted unexpected words, often in foreign languages — their parts for tonight. Some of them carried pots of hydrangeas in one hand and a tattered manuscript of *Wallensteins Tod* in the other. For the Seniors, coached deliriously by Mère Martine, were to entertain their guests with scenes from the fifth act of that tragedy.

Mother Mary Andrew, riding the whirlwind, also rehearsed Una Madden in her Irish recitation. This was a rendering into Gaelic, by Mother Mary Andrew herself, of 'Who Fears to Speak of Ninety-Eight?' In 1912 a great many of the rich *bourgeoisie* did fear, or dislike, to speak of it — but mentioned in Irish it would not make much impression, and in any case, this timidity was not true of the younger priests. Though whether their linguistic appreciation of Una Madden's performance would equal their emotional no one might hastily gauge. However, study of the Irish language, though not compulsory, was a living part of the *Sainte Famille* curriculum now, thanks to the brains and energy of Mother Mary Andrew, and in tonight's programme Gaelic studies would be represented by Una Madden's recitation, an 'action song' called 'An *Maidrin Ruadh*' by the little ones, an eight-hand Irish reel, and, to conclude the concert, a three-part choral rendering by the whole school of 'Faith of Our Fathers' in Irish — 'A *Creidh-eamh Athara*.' It could not so glibly be said now that *Saint Famille* trained its girls to be the wives of British majors and colonial governors; for at least there was a choice of cultures offered to them. But ignoring the jibes and exaggerations launched by partisans alike of old and new ideas, and approving the theory, if not the execution so far, of the optional revival of the Irish language in Irish education — Reverend Mother still regarded that as a local incident, and not as the mission of her Order. She still held out as strongly as ever for the European and polite tradition initiated 150 years ago at Rouen — indifferent alike to the future needs of Gaelic Leaguer or British officer. She still thought it necessary to train girls, for their own sakes and for the glory of God, to be Christians and to be civilised.

Anna Murphy and Norrie O'Dowd, captaining some little ones, were decorating gaseliers with the silk flags and garlands of tradition. . . .

Anna was 14 now, would be 15 in four months. The long years she had spent under school discipline and the accidental training given to her naturally good memory by the years of learning 'Reverend Mother's poems' still gave her an advantage at her lessons which exasperated girls who knew themselves to be as intelligent as she but were less well adjusted to the *Saint Famille* system of teaching.

Having had to spend three years grinding over the First Preparatory course before she was allowed to take the examination, her boredom with it had seemed insolent to those who came to it fresh each year; and this boredom drove her into bouts of fevered reading, which made her even more exasperating. Moreover the bitter lesson taught her when she was 8 by Mother Mary Andrew and the verb *finir* made her into a careful, alert examinee who was not going to fall twice into such a trap. Now in Honours Junior, and second time round, she enjoyed her lessons, and, although she worried over recurrent charges of 'conceit' and 'cockiness,' she tried to make a point of seeming to ignore them. She did not know that this defence increased the impression of vanity. When her Rec. played Stool of Repentance sometimes at night, it hurt very much to have to hear when she sat on the stool that somebody said she thought she was Julius Caesar, or that somebody said '*Saint Famille, c'est moi*', or that somebody said she was 'intoxicated with the exuberance of her verbosity'. But she accepted that it was a cruel game, and always played cruelly at *Sainte Famille*; so she learnt not to weep as her attackers wanted her to, and in her turn she endeavoured to give as good as she got.

But the trouble really lay in her continued detachment from the personalities of school. She was genuinely more interested in books and her own thoughts than in people. She underwent, as it happened, none of the emotional phases common to those around her; she could discover as yet no stimulus at all in the other sex or in jokes about it; and she could only look on in mystification at the storms of *Schwärmerei* for nuns or senior girls which swept the school like epidemics. She simply did not feel these things. Sometimes those who disliked her called her 'Reverend Mother's pet', and addressed her humorously as 'my dear child' in what they conceived to be an English accent; but this immovable general idea puzzled her. She did not like Reverend Mother very much; she thought her stiff and old-fashioned, and she always felt nervous when she was around. She did not see why, just because she had been in the school since she was 6, she should be made into such a fool as 'Reverend Mother's pet'. Good Lord, it seemed to her that you might as well call her Mother Mary Andrew's pet — and Heaven knew she wasn't that! . . .

She did not notice the chaplain's gentle smile. Father Quinn was his name and he sat in the chair of honour with Reverend Mother on the left hand, and the Abbot of Mohervin on his right.

Father Quinn was fat and small, and made up of nervous mannerisms which were the delight of the watchful, mimicking school. He hiccuped; he tapped his nose violently when in thought; he even cleared his throat so loudly and suddenly sometimes, even during Mass, that the noise threw the whole school into exquisite agonies of giggling. He was the perfect butt, and Colette Bermingham and numerous rivals worked very hard at polishing and improving their imitations of him. . . .

The school always thought that, to a girl, they were made to look ridiculous on occasions of festivity; and it is true that the massed white silk dresses of Foundress's Day and Prize Day were unbecoming in general and particular result. There was something countrified in their effect which always depressed Reverend Mother. But for Chaplain's Concert the white silk dresses were not worn. Instead the girls wore their Sunday black dresses, their prettiest white collars, white gloves — and curious final touch, wide sashes, tied in great bows at the back, stiff silk sashes, uniformly of brilliant salmon pink.

They were a tradition — and no one knew why they were salmon-pink. There was a general feeling that they were diabolically ugly, and they were donned by the girls in a mood of hilarious ribaldry. But in truth their effect was miraculous. In the warmly lighted *salle*, with its dark red curtains and dark green potted palms, against the black garb of nuns and priests, and worn on black, these flashing swishing sashes were urbane and gay. They made graceful girls into sylphs; they made the little ones look merry and surprised with themselves; and they lent a mild sophistication even to the plain and the large.

They were accidentally lovely in effect.

From *The Land of Spices*, William Heinemann Ltd, 1941

Faith, Hope and Charity
Michael M. McNamara

On Thursday afternoon, my mother, Sadie, and I drove to the lawyer's office in Pery Square. Kevin would meet us there, as he had dole cards to turn in at the labour exchange. We stood outside the tall Georgian doorway with its brass plate. Mr Patrick J. Rundon, Solicitor. Impressive. Impassive, too. My mother and sister showed signs of nervousness as though they were about to enter into the presence of some supreme person. I banged on the door. 'Oh, my god, Thady, not so loud,' my mother said.

'It's just a lawyer's office.'

'Come on now, love. Don't be showing off. Not today.'

'Jesus, will all of you be under everyone's and anyone's thumb for the rest of your lives? You pay him. He is your servant. Not . . .'

The door opened. A young country girl ushered us into the hall. She seemed capable only of indifference. She called to some friends of hers who were picking their hair inside a glass sliding window. Quinlan. Yes. Mr Rundon was to see these people. Oh, he's not in yet. My mother made some apology and said that we would be glad to wait. I tried to interrupt, but she waved me aside. She found a seat and left me in the centre of the hall feeling foolish. When I reached her and Sadie, I whispered, 'What did you do that for? We had an appointment. Are you just going to sit there and be insulted?'

'Thady, sit down,' my mother commanded. 'You can't make any fuss in places like this or they'll ignore you. These people are very learned, and they come and go as they please. Just look over there in that other room. There are people waiting longer than ourselves. Have some respect.'

'Some respect? He's the one without respect. My position is equal to his, any day.'

'These people are different to us. They're educated and have high appointments. We're not the same as . . .'

'I'm not educated? I'm just a tramp who came in off the street?'

'Hush!'

At that moment the hall door opened and Kevin entered. He came over to the seat and asked if we had seen the solicitor yet. When told the story, he just shook his head and said, 'Jesus!' He went outside again.

I sat back against the hard seat. Inside the glass, girls were taking their tea break. Their loud laughter circled the room, falling on the cowed heads of the old men and uneasy women waiting all about. A man in a raincoat shook his head in annoyance when I caught his eye. He shifted his position against the wall and turned away. I heard others complain and tell yarns of how they had waited several hours on previous days only to find that the lawyer had decided not to come at all because of the rain. Some predicted that he was at the seaside and might not come at all today. The phone rang several times, but no one answered. It was tea break. Their world had stopped.

I got up and opened the door. Kevin was sitting on the steps smoking. I sat beside him. His look of disgust told me that we were of a mind. 'It's disgraceful, isn't it?' he said.

'I thought that it was only at the dispensary, long ago, that they were able to get away with that?'

'It's everywhere. You'd want to knock every one of them on their arse to wake them up. But then they'd put you in jail. They have you every way.'

In his mad way he was right. I thought of the long lines at the dispensary, as a child, waiting for the free medicine. The smell of piss. The sauntering of the doctors past, as people fell aside like feudal serfs. The shouting of surnames at the collection window as though they were obscenities. No wonder the Irish exaggerated. If they didn't, the world would completely ignore them; but, more importantly, even their own would forget their existence.

I got up. Kevin looked frightenedly in my direction. Through the door. I ignored my mother and sister and made straight for the window. The tea break was finishing. A girl was answering the phone. Yaas. Noo. He's not in yet. Yaas. Noo. I banged on the window. The girl on the phone came towards me, stopping to pick up her cup on the way. The slide opened.

'Yaas?' she intoned in her affected accent.

'When will Mr Rundon be in?'

We're not sure. Wait over . . .'

'Wait, hell! My name is Mr Thaddeus Quinlan. I had an appointment with your solicitor this afternoon. . . .'

'I can't help . . .'

'You'll help it, by God, when I take our family account out of this dirty stable. I want to see your office manager immediately.'

'What?'

'The man in charge when your errant employer is not around.'

'You mean Mr Tidings?'

'Get him now. I have never in my life witnessed such inefficiency. Or such a conglomeration of asinine peasants gathered together in one place.'

It worked. More than the fury, the bite of the words took hold. Glares arose from the desks, but heads went back to their keyboards. An amazing rhythm of typing began to replace the careless chatter. I heard doors slam. People behind me began to cough delightedly. My mother was talking furiously to the man who had nodded before. But he was laughing in her face. 'Oh, Jesus,' I heard her say.

More doors shutting. The glass partition behind the busy typists quivered. First the girl came through the quaking door, her face resentful. She was followed by an elderly man in a grey striped suit. He came immediately to the kiosk window.

'Mr Quinlan?'

'Mr Tomkins?'

'Tidings. May I help you, sir? There seems to have been some misunderstanding.'

'Only in the matter of an appointment which your Mr Rundon seems to have forgotten.'

'Ah, yes. My apologies.' His voice lowered, in confidence. 'You see, our Mr Rundon is not the most punctual, you might say. It seems that we are in the midst of the horse showing in Dooradoyle. And, being an equestrian, he cannot resist the temptation to skip off between the courthouse and here to see some of his old friends who are in town for the occasion.'

'Horses?'

'Heavens, no, Mr Quinlan. You do have the Irish sense of humour.'

'Ha.'

'Well, in the meantime, here we are. If you wouldn't mind, Mr Quinlan, I can read your late father's will in Mr Rundon's place.'

'Will?'

'Yes. Your father did not die intestate.'

What could this mean? 'Very well, then. If you would read the will. The quicker the better.'

My mother heard his words. She said nothing. We followed the grey gentleman into a large dark office which was bordered by shelves laden in rolled brown scrolls, piled carelessly upon each other. In the corner, a heap of the same documents gathered dust on the floor. Never in my life had I witnessed such disarray. The desk, too, was cluttered in ledgers, scraps of paper, and electrical wiring which ran in every direction. I thought of my lawyer's office in Nebraska. The clean mahogany desk. The pert, almost too efficient secretaries. No nonsense.

Mr Tidings, having seated my mother in a soft chair and Sadie across from her on the sofa, beckoned to Kevin and me. 'You may both sit on the couch, if you care to,' he said. 'However, it won't take very long. You may stand if you wish. Times were when these matters were so very formal. Progress. Progress.'

'Yes,' I said. 'We'll stand.'

Mr Tidings did not look up from his desk again for several minutes. First he pored over some ledgers, and I saw him mouth the name Quinlan and the date 1940. That date was perhaps the time of my father's first business with the firm. From the books he took some correspondence which directed him to a sheaf of pages within his desk. He glanced over these, shuffling and reshuffling until a torn document was fished out. This he placed to his right. He rose from his desk without a word and stepped in the direction of the pile of manila envelopes in the corner. One after another of the folders was opened, examined, and replaced in the chaotic mound. Kevin cursed under his breath. Sadie made a tight face. My mother alone was calm and patient.

After a longer search, he suddenly exclaimed, 'Ah, here it is. I knew I put it back just yesterday. Now we can get started.'

He looked solemnly at all of us. His eyes assumed the cold stare of the solicitor he was not. He said very seriously as he tore open the seal, 'Shall I proceed, with your permission?'

'Yes. By all means, do,' I said.

'Yes, sir,' my mother cried, turning a scowl in my direction.

He reared back like an eagle assuming full stature. The tiny pince-nez perched right on the point of his nose. I thought of a Dickensian character. A name suitable to the profession. Tidings. Of great joy. Which seldom are, in these premises. He began.

'The late Mr Quinlan's affairs are uncomplicated. The will provides for yourself, Mrs Quinlan, and for each of your children.' He paused to adjust his collar. 'To be brief, the property at 3 Higher Brazil Street, which has no liens and is free and clear, goes to Mrs Quinlan. And a sum of one hundred pounds each to Thaddeus, Patrick, Madeline, Sarah, and Kevin Quinlan. These sums are at present in Mr Quinlan's account at the Munster Provincial.'

He removed his pince-nez.

'That's all?' I said.

'Quite,' Tidings replied. 'You realise, of course, that had the deceased died intestate, the inheritance would have, under the Succession Act, approximated its present terms.'

'When was this will drawn?'

'Over two months ago.'

'Was this the total of my father's estate — five hundred pounds and the house property?'

'No, Mr Quinlan. The estate was closer to several thousand pounds. However, the deceased, several months before his death, liquidated the greater amount of his assets.'

'Where, then, are the monies?'

'I regret to say this, but they went to several Catholic charities. I am not a Catholic myself, but I believe that Masses and such took a great part of the sum.'

'You mean that my father in his sane mind gave practically everything he owned to the Church?'

'The question of sanity, Mr Quinlan, is a matter of opinion. The deceased was, at the time he issued those cheques, extremely upset and distraught. I believe that, a day or so before, he had come to realise how little time he had to live.'

'He knew exactly?'

'He did.'

'Jesus Christ!'

My mother was the first to break the silence. She moaned, 'Oh, Jesus, save us!' Sadie went to her side. Kevin was nervously scratching his back. Mr Tidings asked if he could get us some tea, and, when no one accepted, offered us his office for as long as we wished, to gain our composure. If we needed him, all we had to do was touch the bell on his desk. We thanked him and he left.

The game was over at last. The final caper revealed. The great joke, a sad one for the player and all of the played, except myself. Through the thunder and flashing of antlers my father had come down to nothing but a frightened man. All the songs and words and fires were mere illusions. All the bravado as empty as a spoiled sepulchre. But the pain and death of compassion were very real to my mother and sister. I watched them console each other. They had been cheated of that which we had come to regard as a natural right. But more than the myth of self-to-family-to-race-to-humanity, they saw now the only vital bond discarded and sneered at. The bond of friendship. Their obligation to him had ended years before, when, instead of being the giant of all he surveyed, he had become an old toothless dog whose snarls are tolerated. They could judge him now but wouldn't, because their ways forbade it. But I, who owed him nothing except the very severance that set me free, could see his guilt, and yet, being so like him myself, would have to beg off on any judgment. I tried to imagine my father making his awful decision in our kitchen with my mother preparing his food and Sadie washing his clothes. Could he have taken a pen right there and cut himself off from human feeling? I doubted if he could have done that. Rather had he contrived to disinherit by feigning this paltry inheritance. He had come to this stranger's office and commissioned this impartial lackey to arrange the proper but artificial words of deceit. Not his own words, but staid and blunt terms used by both high and low alike in their common dealings.

What galled me more than anything else was that for this final abandonment to self he would be spoken of as a giant by his cronies and priests alike. What sort of human society is it that sneers at the plight of other living things and calls selfishness and indulgence true virtue? A man of the Church, they would say. A firebrand! A terrible man! And it all utter nonsense. The reality of the tormented man without hope would never be known. The human soul tortured by memories of drudgery and goaded by medieval threats of eternal damnation would never be discussed for fear that the bravado would die and with it the fantasy that, though the world rejected them, the Irish were indeed the children of God. They would never face up to life, if they lived a thousand years. Inside their souls was the land of Faery. Outside was dire peasant ignorance and poverty. There never had been and never would be a middle ground of hope. For one man alone, Bernard Mary Quinlan, I would see to it that the myth died with the man, that the normal antics of heart and head were kept at an even keel and never allowed to abscess into fantasy.

I went across to my mother. She had stopped crying at this point and was staring straight ahead. Sadie showed concern and did not betray her own disappointment.

'Let's go,' I said. 'Let's get out of here.'

From *The Vision of Thady Quinlan*, Crown Publishers, Inc., 1974

Paddy Carmody's Pub
Leo Simpson

The emigrant did not return with bits of glory sticking to him, nor amid whispers of rumoured feats like John Wayne in *The Quiet Man*; rather, he slipped through the back door of Paddy Carmody's place, because it was close to his house, to buy a bottle of whiskey. He was bulky and alien in a Canadian overcoat too heavy for the mild Irish autumn, and this was how he truly first came home. (The other brushes had been nothing of substance — idle, polite meetings, mildly embarrassing for those unlucky enough to be involved.) Now his shifting eyes met the stares, sensing the attitudes that caused nightmares, and here and there he saw a grotesque, a child's eyes peering from under a balding head, or a known smile almost encased in fat.

Joe McMahon put a hand on my shoulder first. I didn't know it was Joe, of course, until later, and for the moment I used no names except Declan and Harry, who were impossible not to remember and recognise. In fact, the nightmarish thing for me was that they were impossible to forget. They stood a little apart, smiling and slightly questioning, confident in their relationship to me. When the wrapped whiskey came I had my nose in a pint of porter, wishing I had chosen another pub, and I left the bottle behind the counter. One might expect that they would have something to say to such a stranger, but they paid me the compliment of supposing — or letting me suppose — that my words would be more important than theirs, and I choked on hesitant commonplaces until I was rescued by a few hearty questions, and the failure of interest of those on the fringes, who drifted away to livelier conversations. It was like a gang of children temporarily held by an untoward event.

'Where are you now?' Declan said, and the effort to seem interested itself betrayed him. Here was a veteran of too many returned emigrants and their overblown tales. When I said Canada, it meant only as much as London or Manchester. There was in them the distance and pride of a defended integrity, and they concealed it poorly.

Paddy Carmody's was a house before it became a pub. It had an entrance hallway, and the kitchen had been converted into the dispensing section of the bar. The counter was small, since it served only as a serving-hatch, made durably of rough painted wood. Two barrels of porter were on tap beneath the counter; the reserve barrels and the empties were used as seats by the patrons of the front room — those wishing only a quick one, and stray drinkers from other districts. The back room, the main room of the house, was much longer, furnished with chairs and a wide bench along the wall. A piled turf fire burned in that room. The accordion player and the fiddler sat near the fire. They were talking quietly and drinking when the emigrant was brought in, their instruments nowhere visible, and they continued unheeding. No lengthy ceremonial of a medieval court was as formal as the behaviour of these musicians, who played before the turf fire of Paddy Carmody's every night, and whose surprise at being requested to play was as great each night as the night before. . . .

The modesty of those who came to sing, which was everybody in Paddy Carmody's, men and women, was so ritualised that a leader was necessary to encourage them, ensuring that no individual was missed or over-used. Harry had this part. . . .

New songs were rarely sung in the house. Usually Harry specified the song when he called the singer. The most popular were the patriotic ballads, and, of course, the love-songs. The love-songs were of lost love, most with a still mood of resignment, and not need: just recollection of the beauty in the gift, untainted by self-pity and self. During a recitation — some recitations were as worn and appreciated as the songs — the emigrant felt a tug on his sleeve and turned to find a small tubby man in a cap grinning at him. 'Terry McNamara,' the man said, sensibly identifying himself. 'How are you? How are you at all? God, it must be ages. Where are you now?'

'Terry, nice to see you,' I said, wondering dismally who Terry McNamara could have been. 'Are you drinking there?' He was noticeably drunk. . . .

'Terry, where's your drink. Let me get you a pint there.'

'Well, I won't say no, for old times.'

Although they had had little enough to say to each other in the old times, since dreams were always private. The emigrant listened to the singer when he had brought the pint, and thought that there was no other place in the world where a hollowed old man could sing with drunken sentiment of young love to an attentive audience. The faces continued to appear, recalling their earlier selves for him, and occasionally a new pint would be put in his hand. They smiled and joked, but he entertained no illusion about his importance to them. Paddy Carmody's was a permanent institution, and he was a Wednesday night phenomenon, an emigrant briefly home, a confirmer of green memories for the close friends and a curiosity for the rest. The matter of being among them was urgent only to himself. He couldn't ask their forgiveness for leaving, yet he needed the pardon and wasn't even sure how they could grant it. He understood why many returned emigrants boasted, praising the wealth and excellence of the new country, pointing to Ireland's backwardness, desperately seeking the absolution of a compliment to their wisdom in leaving home. All the emigrants lived in Tír na nÓg, bringing back predictable magic now and then, but the substance stayed behind, with the pain. No man could be successful enough in fairy places to become more than an emigrant to his friends. For me, for my homecoming, they were gathered together in one room, like a jury.

From *The Lady and the Travelling Salesman. Stories of Leo Simpson*, edited by Henry Imbleau, The University of Ottawa Press, 1976

No Apostates at Sexton Street
Michael M. McNamara

On Friday afternoon, William Street was more crowded and congested than I had remembered it to be years before. With no small difficulty, I found a parking space near the Rialto Theatre where as schoolboys we often hid from the keen eyes of the parading Brothers in the primary school yard across the street. The theatre was closed now, but the same strips of black tape covered the breasts and crotches of the actresses lounging in their sun-filled bills. Once we had opened the glass cases and removed the tapes. It was all a game to lure us on — the ladies were decently dressed underneath. I stood now and surveyed the old school. The grey dark walls gave no indication of life within. Occasionally a black Brother drifted out of a door, but just as suddenly disappeared. I felt the same apprehension that I had felt on cold winter mornings, standing shivering outside the railings in my short and worn trousers, without a morsel in my stomach.

I walked through the outer yard. Along the sides, flower gardens had been planted, and the early plants brightened the drabness of the grounds. Through the small stile and into the secondary's compound. To the left the jakes were still gushing their cleansing fluid. Two boys were urinating and carrying on a lively conversation. I remembered all the cigarette breaks taken down there. The jokes told. The girls seduced, in word only. I walked into the centre yard and faced the monastery house.

The door buzzer rang through what seemed a hollow shell. I waited for a response. At first, nothing. Then the closing of a door inside. Another, louder sound. The door within the glass vestibule opened, revealing a dark mahogany hall. A pert country maid undid the latch and smiled. I said that I had an appointment with Brother Cleary, the headmaster. She seemed to know all about it and said that I should make myself comfortable in the parlour. She took my coat. I was ushered into a spacious room off the main hall. Then she was gone.

I sat in a black leather chair close to the fireplace. The room, despite its vaultlike appearance, was quite cosy. On the walls hung portraits of past superiors of the monastery, their solemn faces seeming to pry into the darkest corners of the room. Above the mantel was a painting of Edmund Tracey, the founder of the Saint Joseph Brothers. He was smiling at some distant mission on the painted horizon. I had always liked his kind face. I liked this room, too, and could visualise long chats by the hearth on winter nights.

Through the house I could hear the velvet bells calling various Brothers to their prayers and duties. *One bell, Brother John. Two bells, Brother Stephen.* Secret names, since their Order used only surnames to the outside world. *Brother Thadde . . .* The door opened, breaking my reverie. A tall, robust man came towards me and grabbed my hand. 'How are you, Thady?' he said. 'It's a pleasure, indeed, to meet you.'

'Thank you, Brother. My pleasure, too.' . . .

'None of that *Brother* stuff. You're not over in the dusty halls anymore. Seán Cleary is me name and fame. Call me Seán.'

'Seán, then.'

'Grand. Can I get you a little brandy? I'm going to have one myself.'

'Well, if you're going to, Brother. I mean Seán.' . . .

He settled himself into his chair. I knew that he was going to discuss the position. I placed my brandy on the fireside table.

'Thady,' he said. 'I don't have to tell you that your credentials are in order. And how you got them is important, too. It's not as if you sat on your duff and let your parents or a benevolent government hand-feed you, as we say. No. There's no problem there. However, and I feel ashamed to have to say this, there are some things that present a stumbling block. Mind you, they don't hinder the educational possibilities, but they do hinder such chances *in Ireland.* And that's a cat of a different colour.'

'How do you mean?'

'Well, Thady, take the least first. You haven't a dog's notion of Irish, do you? I mean of the language, or the legends? Not so much that you don't have a notion, really, but that you would not be able to teach Irish. Would you now?'

'I wouldn't.'

'There you are, and I'll admit it's a small thing, but it's there in black and white. You must have a speaking and writing knowledge of the language. And a certificate to prove it.'

'But the children are versed in English. I would be teaching English, wouldn't I?'

'You would. But you'd still have to have that certificate.'

'Could I work toward one and teach in the interim?'

'Not here. In Dublin, yes. But it would take a full course of a teacher's college.'

'How long would that take?'

'A year, at least, but . . .'

'That's a tall order, but I have a little money. I should . . .'

'There's more, Thady, I'm sorry to say.'

'What?'

'You see, you didn't have to tell me this afternoon about your marriage. I knew. The superior here had a full report. I argued your side, but he's a country man, and God bless him, he has never been out of Ireland in his life. He thinks that there's only one way. And that's the old one. He wouldn't hear of your appointment, Thady. I'm sorry.'

'Where did he get this information?'

'From some wagging tongue. There are many of those around.'

'Probably one of my own, more than likely.'

'I wouldn't doubt it.'

'By the way then, what of this Englishman who's on your staff? Isn't he an outsider? And a Protestant? What does he think of him?'

'I brought that up in your defence. His words were very hard.'

'Yes?'

'He said that heretics were one thing, but apostates were quite another story.'

'An apostate?'

'Yes, Thady, if you take Saint Paul's narrow mind for your basis. But that includes all of us who went off the beaten track. I'm dreadfully sorry. I can never act as judge. I'm always weighing the possibilities. I'll make a poor superior when my day comes around.'

'I don't think so.'

These words that described my spiritual condition were terrifying. It was being declared officially an outcast. Made alone by the edict of some anointed one. Cast out from the fold. Cursed. Branded. Pronounced dead by Divine Godhead. . . . I thanked Brother Cleary for his kindness. . . .

I crossed the yard quickly. As I unlatched the outer gate, I turned and looked back. He was standing in the archway where I had left him. He waved. But I did not wave back.

From *The Vision of Thady Quinlan*, Crown Publishers, Inc., 1974

Hometown
David Hanly

Mulligan read the note for a fifth time, sitting on the edge of his bed in the Pery Grand Hotel in Limerick, the receiver cradled under his chin. He looked miserably out of the bedroom window.

The weather, so benign through Connemara and Clare, had grown dark and angry on the road in from Ennis, and within a few miles from Limerick city the rain was a steady downpour, washing the fields and trees. It was no surprise to Haslam. 'Every time I come back to this poxy kip it's pissing', he said, but with resignation. Limerick was his hometown and he always spoke of it with an exalted dislike whose very intensity seemed to belie the feeling expressed.

The city did, indeed, have the sullen heartbroken air of a town forgotten, its few Georgian buildings augmented by patchy glass and concrete blocks, but with great holes everywhere, where untenable buildings had been razed without heed of replacement. The inhabitants were in tune with their surroundings, exuding a glum and philistine provincialism.

'It's the Redemptorists', Haslam had insisted, while the minibus halted outside Cranmore Castle, a few miles from the city, to drop off the camera team for an hour while they set up the scene for that evening. 'They've had their thick evangelists' brogues on the necks of these people for too long. There hasn't been a man who thought for himself in this city for half a century.' And the city, when they reached it, threw back his gloom, myopically indifferent to the rest of the country, the rest of the world. . . .

The day had started late.

Haslam could not be awoken in the Pery Grand in Limerick, and Ellen was not in her room. The rest of the party walked around the hotel, bumping into each other all over the place and pointedly saying nothing about the reason for the delay. Towards midday, Haslam and Ellen had come into the hotel together, Ellen calmly telling a diffident Ober that departure time on her schedule was twelve o'clock. 'And here I am.' She was beaming.

In fact Ellen had risen early, awakened by Haslam's telephone call.

'I'm sorry for waking you, but I can't sleep and I was wondering if you would care to ramble with me through my hometown?'

'I'd love to.' She did not need to force any enthusiasm in her acceptance of his invitation. . . .

They breakfasted alone in the empty dining room and sallied forth on to Sarsfield Bridge, where they paused for a while, looking down on the swift Shannon River.

Haslam pointed to the greensward on the bank.

'That used to be called the poor man's Kilkee. Every summer Saturday and Sunday it was full of old men and women, too poor to give themselves a seaside holiday. But they'd get the sun there and the river flowed past them, and they could use their imaginations. . . .

They crossed the road to the other side of the bridge and he pointed up the river to Thomond Bridge and the Treaty Stone. 'Limerick is called the city of the broken treaty. But God knows every city in Ireland could be so called. There's King John's Castle down there on your right. A noble remnant. But you'll notice that the local Corporation has built public housing in it. That's the respect these people have for the past.' He turned around and pointed downriver to a green-and-white concrete office block. 'And that's the respect they have for the future. Worse than Dublin. But not much.' . . .

He took her into Tom Collins's cosy snug in Cecil Street, remarking the painting hanging on the wall. 'How many publicans' sons become artists, do you think?'

From *In Guilt and in Glory*, Hutchinson, 1979

No Place Like Plassey
Michael M. McNamara

We decided to take the Annacotty road to Plassey. It was completely asphalted and would eliminate any scratching of the car or walking through the fields and swamps surrounding the road's end of the other route. Of course, in the other direction there was always the delicious reward for the trouble, as one staggered, torn and hot, into Jack Noonan's pub, there to sit under the cool trees and sip shandies, brought foaming by Jack to your table. This could wait, though. Perhaps another day. Sunday or Monday of next week. Plassey, like a magic crystal, brought to itself a new image by reason of every route taken to its core of sand islands and ruined castles. The paths along the canal banks wound their ways through reeds and tall grass and gave the notion of a perilous journey through devouring undergrowth to that place of light and placidity. The Corbally road tunnelled under the trees of Blackwater, deep into the black thorn core of darkness and fright, only to bound in whorls of windfall brightness on to the even altar fields below Castle Bridge. Our way by Annacotty was not without its romance either. The road turned beyond the small village into lanes of thick briar and furze bushes. At a sharp corner in the bohreen, the hedgerow separated to reveal a tiny stretch of scoured field where bicycles could be parked or cars set under the heavy chestnut foliage, safe from the sun. We had often taken that road as children and walked in terror past Mount Shannon House, scarred and blackened by the fires of the Troubles, long before our times. But all that was long ago. Perhaps Plassey and the roads to it had changed. I would see very soon.

We turned beyond Groody river. . . .

We were past Annacotty now . . . as we bumped over the ruts and holes of the disjointed road and out under the heavy trees and spots of fleeting sunshine. The opening to the bohreen seemed no different than before except that a small gate had been strung across its mouth. But it was a latch affair and had no lock. The spring rains had left the road in a soft bog of green and black mud. I drove fast at first, hoping to be out of the swamp as soon as possible, but several lurches of the car convinced me that my impatience, if I wasn't careful, could become expensive. Softened by my sudden failure to control, I set the stick in high gear and we ambled awkwardly but safely through the mud. Soon we were on to dry tar, leaving the tracks of our experience behind us. . . .

I parked in the same area where I had so often in the past ditched my rusty bicycle. The smoothness of the ground seemed different, worn down to the fine hardened clay. Through the trees the turrets and gables of Mount Shannon House were outlined against the bright cumulus. I felt a slight shudder run through me. Was it the old fear from childhood or the memory of the many legends spun about this place? We had often skirted hedges in one jump, when someone swore to seeing dark figures fleet through the courts or peer from the upper windows of the house, gazing eternally at the stables where it was said that the children and horses burned, their flesh, or what remained of it, becoming one in the terrible heat. . . .

Once past the mansion, we made our way through the first woods, finding the paths clearly marked and worn. Small bridges had been built across the various streams. There were new cabins here and there, but not enough to change the fine austerity of the thick green places. In one section the branches of chestnut had been broken, though ever so carefully, so that the splintering light could fall on the rise of a small hillock clearing. We stood in the warmth. Down below lay the second woods. . . . It wasn't far to the real Plassey. There was no need to cheat ourselves of the best.

The second woods were untouched except for a small pump-house. But that had always been there. We had often thrown stones against it and listened to the echoes drift across the river. Soon the grass and undergrowth became thickly interwoven. . . . The reward would be worth all the pain . . . the density was only temporary. We were approaching the light again in a matter of minutes. I could hear the sounds of the main river. The rush of water over stones and against the leafy islands. We were in a dark trench for several seconds, then up a thorny rise and into the brightness.

Instantly we were in that world stolen away by the necessity of separation but always bright and glistening in the mind's eye. It was as though the years, despite the constant reviewing of each detail, had dulled and numbed the vision ever so slightly. And now the trees, the rushes, the falls, and the white sand burst into my consciousness, brighter than they had ever been before, each thing in itself a vital part of that mosaic clutched by me in the throng of all the dissuasions. There was no other place like this.

From *The Vision of Thady Quinlan*, Crown Publishers, Inc., 1974

Up and Down O'Connell Street
Michael Curtin

He lurched down O'Connell Street to meet Cyril in the Wimpy. The Wimpy had replaced the Café Capri where he had used to sit catching the crumbs from the Higgins cubicle. He passed a queue of stragglers at the Kentucky Chicken shop; looking younger than Dorian Gray, Colonel Sanders was on genial advertising duty, beaming from his placard outside the door for all the world like a man who would not dream of organising a nigger-shoot. He passed Burton's, where once an august T.A. Dufficy in striped trousers and black coat and tape measure around the neck had used to encourage: but it's a beautiful piece of cloth, madam, and where now Italian suits at one fifty a week and no deposit peered out the window. He turned to enter Cruise's Hotel, a great haunt of nighthawks in search of free urination but the management, he now discovered, had executed the legerdemain of moving the dance box office in front of the toilets and converted free urination into the price of the dance. He could not complain; he himself gave away free milk at racecourses. He relieved himself down a lane around the corner from the Capri and was grateful to the alert management of Cruise's Hotel — it was unnatural to piss elsewhere than down a lane. Put that into the book — toilets out. Colonel Sanders was definitely in. John Harnett and his wife, the former Anna Roche-Reilly, had objected; indeed afterwards T.A. Dufficy wondered out loud what was coming over Whelan. But Whelan was adamant; any man who sold pigeons in batter and called them Kentucky Chicken deserved the palm.

From *The Self-Made Men*, André Deutsch Limited, 1980

Novena Succour
Maeve Kelly

In June, Adrian was in Limerick buying equipment for his home-made wines and found himself caught in a queue of cars in one of the narrow side streets. He could move neither forwards nor backwards. The source of the delay was soon apparent — a procession of people moving down the main street. Among them a group carrying banners sang hymns. On one of the banners was an image of Christ's mother painted in the style of a Russian icon. Another bore the words 'Novena in Honour of Our Lady of Perpetual Succour'. Of course. It was the time of year for the nine days' prayer. He knew that in Limerick it reached particular fervour. An order of priests who had the imagination to employ a PR man ran the event with the aplomb of a highly efficient multinational company. Each day of the Novena thousands flocked to the church to pray and sing hymns and listen to sermons. Out of curiosity and perhaps a touch of nostalgia he decided to participate. He followed the surge of traffic behind the procession, parked the car dutifully where he was directed and, self-consciously sheep-like, pushed with the crowd into the church.

It was a building of Gothic design with huge marble pillars and a high domed sanctuary. Splendidly triumphant, it reeked of majesty and authority. How was it, Adrian reflected as he was ushered into a seat by an official, that Hugh never considered the great churches and cathedrals as expressing whatever it was he felt should be expressed? Far removed from the little beehive huts of the ancient Irish monks and the pleasant functional monasteries of the early Christians, this was surely a magnificent monument, a flamboyant celebration of the humble life of Christ, as proud and challenging as the pagan tomb of Bru na Bóinne. Built at a time of poverty and near starvation, such a building could be seen either as a justification for the people's suffering or a further symbol of exploitation. Adrian didn't care which it was. He sat back in his seat and wallowed in memories.

As a boy he had scarcely been aware of this church's architecture. He knew only that it was a place of quietness and peace where the faint smell of polish mingled with the scents of burning candles and incense. At night the glow from the sanctuary lamps outshone the flickering candles before the side altars, with their special dedications to special saints. When he accompanied his mother on her evening visits for prayer and meditation they shared a magic world of dreams and shadows. It seemed now, as he looked back in memory, that the warm glow of sanctuary lamps and candles pervaded his childhood. The religious certainty of that time was a happy taste of paradise. It was good to be able to reach out and touch it with his thought.

Each evening he and his mother waited for the lay brother to extinguish, one by one, the altar lights and the candles until the soft dimness was overcome by the velvety smoothness of the dark. The single light in front of the tabernacle would never be extinguished. That was the light of the world. If that went out, evil captured men's hearts. As he left, he always turned to look again at the lamp while the lay brother stood patiently, rattling his keys to encourage their departure. Up at five o'clock each morning to practise the virtues of chastity and obedience, without any of the recognition given his priestly superiors, he must have thought their last reluctant walk was yet another cross for him to bear. Adrian used to watch him fearfully as he scurried out but there was never any response. His mother would murmur, 'Goodnight, Brother', and the pale long face would dip in acknowledgment. At home by their own fireside, his mother sighed for the lonely, cold life of all lay brothers, as they made their way through stone corridors to their bleak cells. His father would laugh and shock her by saying they were all probably rushing to tipple at the altar wine.

As he sat packed with a thousand others in neat organised rows, the suppressed excitement of the audience was almost palpable. In the gallery above, the organ tuned up. The altar was vivid with flowers and, even in the bright sunlight shafting through the windows, hundreds of candles added their pale light to its magnificence. The light of Christendom battled with the light of the natural world. The organ pealed out a triumphant Ave and the congregation rose to greet the priest, who made his way quietly to the pulpit, wearing his long black soutane. The perform-ance began.

Adrian was not interested in the words the priest used, or in the message they conveyed, but only in their great rolling sound. They echoed through the church, bouncing off the pillars, swooping in great curves to penetrate the hearts of the hearers. They filled every crevice in the arched ceiling, each corner of the side altars, so that the whole building became nothing more than a gigantic receptacle for the words of this one man. Adrian was overawed by the power invested in the preacher and every now and again he glanced furtively at his neighbours for evidence of inattention or even incredulity. There was none. Their attention was unbroken. They were admonished and exhorted and they took it with the utmost equanimity. The Mother of God was described in the glowing terms of rhetoric but the preacher never exceeded himself, never ventured too far into his flights of fancy.

His sudden swoops down to earth came with reminders of the practical favours granted by God's mother to her earth-bound children. Examples were read out of exams passed, illnesses survived, even the grace of a happy death. The congregation was urged to pray for the safe return of some fishermen who had been missing off the coast for several days. Adrian, feeling that such pleading must be heard, silently added his own prayers to theirs. Willingly, he was swallowed up in the fellowship of common prayer, became part of the one great spirit, and abandoned without a qualm his individual need. . . .

Adrian's hands trembled. If he had cried no one would have noticed or cared. Around him noses sniffed. Handkerchiefs were everywhere. He was moved to love and being so moved wished to weep out loud. Memories of his mother taking him by the hand up to the altar, lighting the candles, encouraging him to insert the pennies in the slot, telling him about the love of Jesus in the tabernacle, overwhelmed him.

From *Necessary Treasons*, Michael Joseph Ltd, 1985; The Blackstaff Press, 1991

Stood Up At Todd's
Michael Curtin

The block-long shelter that abutted from Todd's first storey was a contributory factor in the store's possession of a hallowed name as a trysting spot for those of a certain class — the carless. He would have preferred to haul up in the van and take

Breda for a drive out the country where they might stop in a quiet bohreen where somehow it might happen that he would end up with his arm around her and get a court. But in the matter of transport he was a realist on his first date. He joined the throng respectably distanced from each other and assumed an interest in the window displays. It was five minutes to eight. He was wearing the blue suit in which he had been dressed on his return from London and at eight o'clock he had a red face to go with it. At five past eight, as his fellow suitors were picked up, linked and had umbrellas thrust at them and were forced to walk on the outside, Whelan had the feeling that he was being watched and that those who watched him thought: stood up. At ten past eight he suspected agonisingly that he was indeed stood up. He walked to the next window which was now without a vigil. The female dummies were naked. Whelan crossed the road and slunk into the doorway of Burton's where the dummies wore modest executive suits. His own suit began to feel tight under the armpits and his shirt tight at the neck, a drop of sweat fell from his forehead. He extended the fingers of both hands and was not at all surprised to see them tremble. He began to prepare every kind of vengeance in the event of her not showing up. Go out there on Christmas night with ice cream. He would be set upon. Find out where she worked, send a young fella in there with chips at ten in the morning. It was twenty past eight. He crossed back to Todd's where he was now the lone sentry and where, at twenty-five minutes past eight, he decided he could not stomach further humiliation and thought of her with old-fashioned hatred as he departed.

From *The Self-Made Men*, André Deutsch Ltd, 1980

Old Tribal Jealousies
Maeve Kelly

Adrian drove through the main street and turned at St Mary's Cathedral. A little further on was the Protestant graveyard where his grandmother was buried. He had promised his father that he would maintain an annual commemoration there.

'The Church,' his father had said, 'separated in death those whom they could not divide in life.'

So in a little green oasis, practically in the heart of the old town, with a chieftain's view of the river, his grandmother lay with her Protestant cousins, while the man she married, loved and bore children for lay at the other side of the city with his Catholic family. His grandmother had the best view of Limerick. There were moments, after all, when the city was quite lovely. Adrian admired the glimpses of the towers built to support huge cannon reaching down to the river's edge. The stone balustrades of the principal bridge were imposing too. Where the river flowed high and deep to become the long curving estuary, the effect was of elegance tinged with hints of a noble past. A famous actor had once described it in his melancholy tones as a lonely and beautiful widow. Perhaps, thought Adrian, he wasn't so far off the mark. There was something bereft about it, as if it could never quite understand its loss. The aged cathedral with its Romanesque arches hugged the remains of the city walls. Here and there other fragments of the old walls straggled behind back streets, buttressed to withstand the attacks which had destroyed the city and the spirit within it. Of all the places in Ireland, Limerick, and indeed the whole of Thomond — which in the old days stretched back to Hugh's house on the Shannon mouth, embracing virtually all of Clare — suffered as much from dissension within as from attacks from without. In a way Limerick epitomised that lack of unity and ability to compromise which had brought about the final destruction of Gaelic Ireland. Hugh, of course, would say that the same spirit still lived on in Limerick and in Ireland. Adrian had to agree that his native city had turned in on itself, become ever more insular and incestuous, lived and died licking its wounds. Other towns throughout the world had arisen again after worse defeats. Why should this one have lost its soul? Old tribal jealousies, resistance to change, all played their part. But was it more than that? Had the taste of defeat been so bitter that the people had lost the stomach for fight? The broken Treaty of Limerick and the ensuing penal laws left an indelible mark on each new generation. Bad government, poverty and famine compounded despair. Long memories and ancient history were impossible burdens. After all the fighting and the little uprisings, the wish for peace and a quiet life might very well have led to stagnation and apathy. Adrian sometimes fancifully compared the destruction of the spirit of the city (though in his more realistic moments he asked himself if such a spirit had ever come truly alive) with the death of the Inca civilisation. Limerick was the last frontier of Gaelic Ireland. There was no hope of recovering that Ireland yet tantalising reminders were still there, in the language, in stone carvings, even in the faces of the population, who might have been the living models of those round-eyed, thin-mouthed images immortalised on abbey and church walls and on Celtic crosses. At times it seemed to Adrian that he walked through a doomed city, peopled by ghosts who had managed to acquire the outward habits and clothing of a modern age but who fretted constantly while they searched for their lost souls.

He was always glad when he left Limerick, and he rushed back to his tower with as much speed as possible, although his conscience pricked him because he used the city as a large warehouse, a place to purchase material goods. He had no feeling of affection for it. The clouds billowing up the estuary blocked out sunlight, excluding signs of the immense universe around. Nothing much happened in Limerick. No one was doing anything important or going anywhere in particular. But then, he thought, where in Ireland could you go? Ireland was the place you came back to, to die.

You could not enjoy a vital, purposeful existence here. Hemmed in by the implacable sea, you pondered on the meaning of life and became a poet or a priest. What country could afford such luxury? Too many poets, too many priests.

From *Necessary Treasons*, Michael Joseph Ltd, 1985; The Blackstaff Press, 1991

Kick Ahead!
Michael Curtin

It was hard on a child but it did not stop there with Bateman. He was a tough young fellow then. Not a bully but able to look after himself. Frankie Timmons had suggested that he was good enough to shove into the three-quarters on the under-15s and Frankie Timmons was not a mentor easily pleased. Percy Bateman at 13 was tough and hard. . . . He began to study his father. He saw that his father held an elitest position in the house. The pillow covers on his own bed and sometimes the sheets, the shorts he wore playing for Young Thomond were all made by his mother on her sewing machine out of Rank's flour bags. When his shoes were out he had to sit in while his father repaired them with leather bought in a hardware shop. Someone in the road had an anvil that was used by so many families that it was communal so there was nothing unusual in his having to sit in watching the tacks between his father's teeth. But Percy Bateman began to compare everything that happened to him not with what happened to other children but with his father's privileges. His father's shoes were mended at the shoemaker's. His father did not wear anything made out of a flour bag. His father's bad teeth were pulled immediately by a dentist while he had to wait three weeks for an appointment at the clinic, the throbbing palliated by a concoction called Mrs Cullen's Powders.

Percy Bateman began to hate his father.

He could hardly look at his father, the man he had so loved, the man who had stood him on the kitchen table and taught him to sing:

> Beautiful, beautiful, Thomond,
> Star of my life fade away.
> I sigh when I think of Young Thomond,
> For whom I played many a day.

When his father Johnny Bateman was dressed to go to London . . . the neighbours came into the kitchen and walked around him and were satisfied that he would not let anybody down. And the club sent Frankie Timmons along to mind him. Frankie

Timmons was famous. He had played for the Province against the All Blacks and lost the use of his left ear after going down on the ball.

For five years . . . Percy Bateman was buried in books as was everybody else his age who was not pulled out to be a messenger boy or join the army. It was the only way up at that time — there was not an electronics industry to absorb those who kept their heads empty. Bateman flew through school and won a scholarship to University College, Cork, and as an undergraduate he thought that the way Bateman senior was the centre of his own life was something that he could now outgrow. But it caught up with him again when he was 20.

During the Easter recess Percy Bateman was chosen as full-back for Young Thomond against Garryowen in the under-20s cup. Young Thomond men were made in the under-20s cup, especially against Garryowen; they went on to the full Young Thomond team like Johnny Bateman had and all Percy's uncles. But young Percy had begun to change at 13 when he was done out of his suit. He did get the suit at Christmas out of the diddly club but that meant that it was a poor Christmas all round. His father gave him a florin to hansel the suit and ruined the gesture by reminding his son how he had kept his promise. Percy started to hate not alone his father, but everything with which his father was associated particularly Young Thomond and, more seriously, the Young Thomond ethos. He managed to avoid the youth team by affecting to have to study hard to get the Leaving Certificate Honours that would render him eligible for a college scholarship. His father understood. Johnny Bateman put it to Frankie Timmons that a good job was important too and Percy would not go stale, he would be fresh coming back to the game and it was about time that they all came into their own, Percy would be the first Young Thomond man with a degree.

At UCC Percy had to play for the college but despite the skull and crossbones on the jersey it was college rugby, a different style to Young Thomond rugby, a club whose motto was: *Non Manus Vincere Sed Pes*. But that Easter he could not avoid togging off with Young Thomond particularly that year when it was Johnny Bateman's turn to have charge of the goat. The goat dated back to the occupation when Young Thomond won a famous match against the garrison of Welsh Fusiliers and captured the soldiers' goat, their mascot, and which ever after was Young Thomond's mascot. The goat was togged out in the red and white colours — the blood and bandage — of Young Thomond. And Johnny Bateman wore his Savile Row suit even though the day was a Saturday.

As befitted a college boy Bateman had an excellent positional sense. With twenty minutes play remaining and the sides scoreless Young Thomond were attacking on the Garryowen twenty-five. The Young Thomond three-quarters were stretched diagonally across the field in classic attacking formation — a superfluous echelon since Young Thomond, true to its motto, had never run the ball in its history in a cup game. The heel from the scrum was ragged. Garryowen wheeled, won the ball and initiated a foot rush. Bateman immediately retreated towards his own goal, supposedly to cover, actually to avoid the foot rush. But when he turned he saw that he was the last man between Garryowen and a certain score. He ran out to the ball and fly-kicked. The ball sliced off his boot and up in the air. The Garryowen pack arrived. His jaw was dislocated, he was knocked unconscious and a try was scored under the posts.

His father refused to visit him in hospital. On the way home from the game Johnny Bateman threw the goat over Sarsfield Bridge into the Shannon where the unfortunate animal perished in the spring tide. Percy's mother tried to console him in the hospital by saying that it could happen to anyone, that he was to try and forget it, his father would get over it in time, and he would yet prove himself. On the day of his discharge Percy Bateman waited stubbornly at the tea table until his father came home from work. Johnny Bateman hung up his coat and washed his hands and sat down and asked.

'How is that face?'

'It's all right.'

Johnny Bateman did not speak again until on his third cup, which he poured for the purpose: 'I've been thinking all day at work.' He did not look at anyone, only straight ahead. 'They say charity begins at home so it may as well do it here. Everyone, including Percy, is entitled to one wrong turning so what we'll do is we'll never mention what happened again in this house.'

Percy's mother nodded: 'Good, Johnny.'

From *The League Against Christmas*, André Deutsch Ltd, 1989

Those Shoestring Years
Emma Cooke

I scraped everything into the bin, dressed myself up and left the house looking for something or someone. My walk up to the racecourse brought me past the gate of Rosepark House. The main wall of the largest wing had been painted but the roof still sagged. Twenty years ago that roof used to worry Clive and me. On windy nights every creak and rattle convinced us that it was about to cave in and bury us alive.

It was the first house that we lived in when we came to Limerick. We could eventually have bought it for peanuts but it was too ungainly, too dilapidated, too ugly with its yard walls flush with the road. A back-to-front house, its imposing entrance porch facing out over grassy hummocks towards the racecourse.

Today I peeped through the bars of the small gates as the side entrance which leads to our old hall-door. There are highly coloured flower-beds where I'd had only weeds and a long clothes-line. Clive moaned about the clothes-line, asking me to remove the nappies at sundown to make the place less of an eyesore on a summer's evening. . . .

'I suppose you'd like me to dig the garden too, while you sit around like Lord Muck,' I'd shout.

When we moved into Rosepark House Clive swore that it would just be for a month or two. We ended up living there for five years. My stomach muscles clenched with an old ache as I gazed in at the display of hollyhocks and dahlias. Whoever owns that garden now has more spare time than I had. I wished them luck.

Clive once slapped me in that house and I went for him like a fishwife. Clive was more frightened by the incident than I was. He hates violence. (Maybe he's always been afraid to broach the subject of our splitting up in case I try to kill him.) Even at the time I didn't blame him for the slap. I had provoked him beyond endurance in revenge against a miserable house-bound day of cranky children and unending rain. I was sick of a draughty house with broken floor boards and inadequate plumbing. All the children had tummy aches.

'Next time I'm walking out,' I warned, though I had nowhere to go except back to my ageing parents.

I remembered how hot and dry his hand felt as he reached out to me in apology. I remembered pushing him away.

'This is the end of the road, Clive,' I'd said and we stared at each other in mute desperation.

'What the hell are we going to do?' asked Clive softly.

But next day things had changed. It was as if our confrontation had acted as a catharsis. In the morning a phone call confirmed Clive's first big assignment. We were saved. We need never look back.

I moved away from Rosepark's gate and those shoestring years. Our problems are of a different nature now. At least in Rosepark House we were, willy-nilly, totally involved in getting by. There was no need to look for outside excitement. A glance at our overdraft was enough to get our hearts racing, our hands to grab at each other for support.

And on good days the sun streamed through the front door and the children played long involved games on the front step. And there were minor triumphs; like Christmas dinner cooked in the poky kitchenette, and a woman who arrived on horseback for afternoon tea. There were flagons of cider shared with Clive in the woodworm-riddled sitting-room.

When I got into the showgrounds I could see the house facing me across the racetrack. It made me smile. It's such a cheat of a house with its bare rump exposed to the public road instead of its pretty facade. I stared at the window of what was once our bedroom and had an unexpectedly vivid recollection of Clive and I fumbling for each other through layers of flannelette as we burrowed for comfort in our freezing bed under a dangerously sagging ceiling. And a mouse that ran across our blankets as the city church bells rang in a frosty New Year. Our startled laughter. The kids with measles and myself pinning old sheets across the windows because we hadn't money for curtains. Was that happiness or was it just being young?

From *Wedlocked*, Poolbeg, 1994

Campanology
Michael Curtin

The Society of Bellringers attached to the Redemptorist church has served the community in its own way without ever impinging on my humble bailiwick of instruction. Good luck to the Redemptorists — and for that matter the Christian Brothers — but their constituency thrives on a less subtle brand of indoctrination that I am comfortable with at the Jesuits. I accept the mob's hunger for rough theology and doff my hat to those who answer the call to provide the beads of solace to the lower orders. But what has baffled me as long as I can remember is Dr John Cagney's decision to sacrifice Donat to the leper colony of rope pullers — as their needs must be drawn from the area for whom they peal and represented as they are by Halvey, the campanologist. True, Jack Molyneaux, the undertaker, was also a member of the tower, but perhaps there must have been a different element there in his early days. Then again in Molyneaux's profession one is obliged to act the democrat more than one would wish — a coffin is indiscriminate in its choice of corpse. Halvey, young Donat and Jack Molyneaux were the only ringers I had heard of — one could only surmise in what circles the rest of them mixed. So I was shocked that from out of that belfry came a climactic thunderbolt in the person of Tim Harding.

Harding — I now know — was a couple of years younger than Cecelia Sloan and was brought to the tower as a protégé of Donat Cagney. He and another ringer, Brown, began to frequent the Drapers' Club — as a guest of Halvey. I am as good a judge of appearances as the next man and Harding did not quite seem to me to have the colour of a Halvey disciple, viz. a Wank Mitchell or a Johnny Skaw. Indeed Brown too looked respectable. Yet apart from the Drapers' Club I had also seen both of them patronise the Statue of Liberty as regulars. I thought of Sir Thomas's funeral: it may have been that Halvey's belief that he could mix with kings and princes and still have the common touch was so strong that he communicated his credo to his victims. I questioned Simpson.

'Tell me, Simpson. Those two with Halvey . . .'

'They're in the bells with him, Mr Yendall.'

'. . . just so. But don't they seem to you a cut above him — not that that would take much effort.'

Simpson smiled at me. 'Charlie has depths, Mr Yendall, that not many people know of.'

'Depths, Simpson, yes. I agree with you there.'

The draw for our Annual Handicap always ensures a full house. Simpson alone of his ilk entered. He pleaded with them to put down their names. Sitting in the bay window I listened to him. He offered to stake them to the fiver a head entrance fee. No. The money was no deterrent to a lifelong newsboy. Wally Kirwan was self-sufficient again thanks to his job in the electronics factory. Phil Thompson showed his age and his philosophical vocabulary: 'No point pissin' against the breeze, is there?' They accepted that they were simply not good enough to put up a show. Not so Halvey and his friends from the tower. Harding was as good as any of the young fellows I had seen playing. Snooker to Halvey was just another aspect of his jack-of-all-trades, follow-the-band motley: he would as quickly have put his name down for bowls. And not Simpson. He joked to me later: 'Mr Yendall, I believe the boys have lost their — their bottle, Mr Yendall.' I did not find that funny. There is no more need to lower oneself in speech than there is to grow sideburns. Simpson thought he was amusing, though his were the only antennae alert to the music of the young. I don't care for the pathetic accommodation of a language's massacre.

A few days before the draw for our handicap Halvey hit the headlines again. His photograph appeared in the paper, not as a singing cowboy, not as a French tonsorial artist, and not in his capacity as mine host of the knocking shop. No. This time Halvey was the recipient of a medal from the Pope. One pinched oneself. That pontiffs and potentates live lives remote from the rest of us has long gone unchallenged, yet how a pope through his hierarchy could convey such an honour on Halvey makes one wonder if there is any institution uninfected with ineptitude. Halvey's medal was for his long service of thirty years ringing bells. Did nobody think of giving him a medal for his thirty years standing on the pavement shouting obscenities? Or of giving me or Mr Sloan a medal for having to listen to him? And, I wondered, would His Holiness have been gratified to learn through the ecclesiastical grapevine that Halvey — before the novelty wore off — took to wearing his medal while he wielded his cue against his fellow ringer, Harding, addressing him — out of his depths — with the affectionate: 'You black English Protestant, you've fuckall chance tonight against me medal. Rome rules OK.' As I have long observed: as we sow, so shall we reap.

From *The Plastic Tomato Cutter*, Fourth Estate Ltd, 1991

In Search of Inga
Clairr O'Connor

The drive to Limerick has a few scary moments but I make it OK, park the car and register in the George. I take a shower. It's still very warm. There's a lazy feeling in the early evening and I lie down for a short nap before dinner. I wake to darkness. It's twelve o'clock. I had no idea I was that tired. . . .

Much later I ring room service for coffee and a sandwich. When it comes I realise I'm not hungry and can't eat it but I gulp down the coffee thirstily. I sit up the rest of the night and study the book of photographs I found in dad's study. . . . It is a small book with a few photos in black and white. . . . There is no writing apart from the title on the book, 'Pictures from Hungary'.

I tell the same story at the three local newspapers. I am researching an article on the Hungarian Revolution in 1956. I am interested in the refugees who came to Limerick from Hungary at the time. I want to find out where some of them went after Limerick. The article is spanning thirty-three years, 1956–1989. Hungary is changing so quickly, almost each week, I gush. It will be published in America, I assure them. Yes, of course I'll send copies. I am presented with the yellowed news-papers of winter 1956 and spring 1957. The headlines are both pathetic and exciting.

I head for the camp at Knocklasheelin. An army camp. A refugee camp. Temporary dwellings then. Only one long low prefabricated building now. But it's not muddy or cold as it was in the newspaper accounts that December and the following spring. Unreal heat cracks the paint and reveals its life of wear and tear. I peer through windows. Part of the building seems to be used as an office. My newspaper research in Limerick matches dad's cuttings in the copybook.

'Inga, Inga, Inga.' I shout her name to sky and trees.

The entry in dad's journal reads:

> Inga is both foolish and courageous. She has lied about her age. Told them she was 21 instead of 15. Poor child! She thinks 21 is a wise age. I worry about her and this hunger strike business. The refugees are on hunger strike because they say there is no work or future for them in Limerick. They want to go to America or Canada. Days now and she had not eaten. She has a small statue of St Gertrude. She keeps it in the pocket of her skirt.
>
> She will call the child Gertrude if it is a girl, Janos, after its father if a boy. The nuns have appealed to her to eat for the sake of the child. She is stubborn. The bishop visits the camp and brings assurances of passports for Canada and America. The strike is over.

I think of Inga, child-mother, my mother, walking over Sarsfield Bridge in Limerick, listening to seagulls squawk, holding me tight to her heart, thinking that

21 was wise. To go on hunger strike is an act of will. Asserting one's will through denial of food. To go on hunger strike when you are pregnant is both foolhardy and courageous. To have such will in a foreign country, remote from everything you have known, is heroic. I applaud Inga. I think of Simone Weill in Middlesex Hospital refusing food, not to take more than the rations of her compatriots in wartime France. Refusing food in England, then refusing to eat anything at all. Going out on an act of will. Becoming absolutely herself in spite of everyone around her. Inga, Simone, Simone, Inga. I have found a mother indeed. Not mam, the pale invalid. On the prayer list for the sick all my life. Pulling me to her heart by anxious threads. But Inga who knew what she wanted and took what she could.

Inga Kadar went to Canada in May 1957. It says so on the list, the list in the newspaper office. She went to Toronto. There is no other Inga on the list. She came from Budapest. That's what it says. Inga Kadar from Budapest, refugee, stayed in Knocklasheelin Camp from December 1956 to May 1957. I will not follow her there. She did not intend that. But I will set my eyes towards Budapest.

From *Belonging*, Attic Press, 1991

Mediocrity Loves Misery
Michael Collins

Ambrose boarded the midday train to Limerick. . . . He found an empty seat, curled up and slept until he reached Limerick three hours later.

A neighbour who worked at the station spotted Ambrose when he arrived and took him to his car. 'You're doing OK are you?' the neighbour said, eyeing Ambrose suspiciously. . . .

Ambrose nodded and shuffled along, his body lost in his coat, his hair dishevelled from sleep. Sounds echoed in the station, pigeons cooing overhead in the rafters, the place splattered with droppings. . . .

The narrow street intersected lanes that dated back beyond the Famine. Limerick's labyrinth of shadows and doorways, the musty smell of sawdust sprinkled outside doorways, the city within the city, the lanes dipping down slants where the water rushed during heavy downpours. Things were bartered for other things in the lanes. There were people in there who had not come out in years, occupying the domains of small pubs and little shops tucked into the sides of walls. They had no interest in coming out into the city. Ambrose liked the feeling of enclosure, the murky window fronts hiding those inside, commerce carried on in secrecy. . . .

Proto-Limerick types, small little men with pinched weasel faces and small teeth, hands behind their backs, and others big and cumbersome, heavy drinkers moved around chatting with one another, tipping their caps on their heads, saluting the women in slippers and aprons with scarves on their heads, coming and going from shops. . . .

The men got work done despite themselves. It was a constant effort to appear as though you had nothing to do, but they pulled it off.

Each return to Limerick made the place seem more antiquated. The three months in Dublin had been like an eternity. The old walls of the city were in desperate shape. They would have called Limerick a case study in pervasive and contented apathy up in the institution, a semi-conscious fatalism lived with a smile. . . .

The crowds were now pouring into the streets. It pleased Ambrose, allowed him to recatalogue his life in an easy manner. The providence of routine had its numbing effect. The provincialism he'd loved as a boy still prevailed. He could hide away in this city for the rest of his life. He would never leave his home again, never let himself go back to Dublin. The three months he'd spent in the institution in Dublin would be his last. There was peace here in Limerick with his mother and father. This was where he was born, and where he'd die in his own self-conscious anguish and be just like all the rest of them. He'd reached the point where he knew he would do nothing in this world of any significance. Now the challenge was to ally himself with mediocrity, which, no matter how easy it looked, took a certain talent. But he was willing to learn, to start again with no expectations. . . .

Ambrose didn't feel like conceding these brief moments of re-experiencing the city. He continued to look silently out the small windshield at the people moving around, the same old characters as always. The place would never reach that point where a mass of people could preserve their own anonymity while dealing with one another. Limerick was too small. Everyone knew everyone else. . . . From an economic standpoint, they were all one step above hunters and gatherers, coming to market, bartering and buying bits of this and that, dealing in live animals killed on the spot. Limerick was the slaughter capital of Ireland, every word and action driven by a solid meal of animal meat. Limerick: the meat and potatoes dynasty of the world. In Limerick you could not buy something from someone without knowing that person somewhat. . . .

The echo of metal hooves against the concrete brought peace to Ambrose. And then a man about his father's age slipped in through a gap between two cars, his handlebars balanced with two plastic bags of something, and Ambrose smiled to himself again. All the ways man was trying to define life, just so he could live it. . . . Here it was, this enigma, life, the thing he couldn't cope with, going on in Limerick, acted out by seasoned veterans, the old and the young, the old man on the bicycle, a small boy selling the newspaper with a sing-song Limerick accent on a corner, his neighbour driving his car, playing the system, knowing when the train came in. They had all learned to live in Limerick. . . .

This coldness added to the general malignancy. If it had been colder, an Arctic winter with snow, then something would have been done. People would have built proper houses and dressed warmly. But in Limerick the coldness only nagged. It was treated with irksome familiarity, the troublesome child, people standing around and complaining about it in doorways. 'Oh, the weather', the women would say under their breaths as the sky moved overhead, how a shower soaked the clothes on the line, how the holiday was wrecked. The city was full of men hunched on bicycles, wavering as they pedalled into rain and wind, men who walked around with damp clothes on their backs that smelt of rain and sweat. There was no sense of conquering, only living with what the weather brought. Half-measures sufficed, an old coat or heavy jumper, a hot-water bottle for the feet, a cup of tea before bedtime. Once you were born into this way of thinking, this mystifying benign way, on the verge of recognition, with a mulling disposition, but in the realm of indecision, there was no hope for you. Ambrose knew this only too well. Mediocrity loves misery.

From *The Life and Times of a Teaboy*, Phoenix House, 1994

The Launch of the Sunday Poets' Broadsheet
Michael Curtin

I have worked hard in the interest of my craft at nurturing a catholic taste and now in the mellow years shun only golf, basketball, tennis, classical music, painting, fine art, symphony concerts, opera, sculpture and poetry. This launch of the Sunday Poets' Broadsheet was held in the Pinky Downey Art Gallery, where an exhibition of visual art was yet showing. There were a few enamel buckets hanging from ropes. A Coca-Cola bottle was embedded at the base in a mound of sand. On my way in I had to skirt a sculpture of two holes joined together that the uninitiated might identify as a figure of eight but had, I have no doubt, a much more profound significance. There was nothing Sunday about the paintings. A squiggle of spaghetti or maybe intestines was titled *Labyrinth of the Soul*. I was about to study a self-portrait of Cyclopean angst when I spotted the saddle of a bicycle swanning on a ledge and beside it the most exotic exhibit in the whole hall, Maxie McManus. He was almost hidden by the broadsheet that he held open with his right hand on top and his left at the bottom. The Sunday Poets did not skimp. The broadsheet was an imperial twenty-two by thirty inches. I went straight to Maxie for comfort, to establish our mutual philistinic bona fides.

I said, 'Did you get lost?'

'Junior Nash. How are you?'

I pointed to the saddle of the bicycle. 'What are we supposed to make of that?'

'What?'

'That. That there.'

'That's mine. To keep in shape. I've a three hundred quid bike chained to the railings, why make it comfortable for the fucking thieves.'

'What are you doing here anyway?'

'I'm reading.'

'You are? Whose?'

'The young fella there selling the things. Are you buying one? Let me bring you over, make me look good.'

The poet selling the broadsheets — at a fiver a go — wore a fedora hat to shade his beard. Maxie introduced me, just my name. It didn't mean anything to the lad. Maxie said, 'He's unwaged.' So I got the broadsheet for three quid. Maxie asked him, 'How do you pronounce your man's name again?' I opened my broadsheet to read where Maxie had put his finger. 'O Euripides, lib of long ago . . .'

I chose the white wine because that's the colour Maxie was drinking. The Sunday Poets suffer from an attack of collective modesty. They do not read their own work. The tradition is that each poet has his or her offering read by a celebrity. Like Maxie McManus is a celebrity. Our town is not London. Or New York. Or Japan. . . .

There was a tape going someplace in the background, something I'd heard before, sure of it. . . .

I held the broadsheet under my arm and the wine and fag in my other hand. I was looking for someplace other than the floor to put the glass down and see what bilge I had been doomed to deliver. But Maxie pushed me on towards the next knot of luminaries, which included Charlie Anka and Pinky Downey himself, Maxie saying, 'Slyboots, you didn't tell me you were reading. What chance have I with a professional like you?'

Pinky Downey was dressed as an art gallery proprietor should be. Like a queer. He wore a frilled Scaramouche shirt and a cummerbund. But he had the flabby handshake of the heterosexual. 'Welcome,' Pinky said to me. 'My gallery is honoured.' Since I had wallowed in fifteen years of anonymity in my home town, I could only deduce that Pinky was saying any reader of Charlie's I'll lick his arse too, because Charlie has big bucks. To go with his ponytail Charlie had one of those jackets that motor-rally groupies wear, with a logo of his agency. What else goes with a ponytail? A Paisley cravat, obviously, lumberjack shirt, blue jeans with a belt with a big buckle and cowboy boots. As if I wasn't dwarfed enough as it was. . . .

Tinkling a pound coin against the side of his wine glass, Pinky Downey shushed the throng. He welcomed us all to the monthly launch of the Sunday Poets' Broadsheet. It was perfunctory stuff. I looked around the gallery to try and identify my fellow surrogates. Francis Coleman was the only one who stood out as having any stature and he had been dropped in my favour. After all, where would the Sunday Poets go to find victims? The first poet up introduced his poem. It was a simple landscape, he claimed. He got the inspiration in this very art gallery, for which he owed a debt of gratitude to Pinky Downey himself, just looking at a painting of the Falls of Doonass — it was so vivid that he knew he must capture it in words. And without further ado he would now call on Miss Mitchell, who taught him at infant school, taught him his first poems, the ball is in the hall, the cat is on the mat. A big hand please, for Miss Mitchell.

The poor old dear unfolded the monstrous broadsheet and began:

Incessant drops of spectrum wonder . . .

Why didn't I faint? Or clutch my chest and gasp for air? Or something? Because I didn't think of it. I watched the landscape poet listening hard to his old teacher to make sure she caught every nuance of his brushstrokes. She did read well. And it was her pupil the poet who led the applause, proclaiming with every loud clap that he was content with the background and would ever acknowledge Miss Mitchell as the true fount of his talents.

Maxie was up next. It is one of the great pleasures of life to watch someone make a bollix of himself. Maxie was brutal. 'O Euripides, lib of long ago,' Maxie began, saying the first two words as though he was writing to a mate of his. He ran one line into another where that was unintended by the poet with the fedora hat, the beard and the mother who might fall for a conservatory. Maxie paused only for breath and the odds were against a station being where the train stopped. For Maxie confidence equalled speed and his ordeal was over so fast that he was lucky not to include the first line of the next poem. I joined in the big hand but noticed that the poet did not contribute. Yet he looked happy. I realised after a few more readings that some poets applauded and others didn't. Apparently the protocol of the Sunday Poets' Broadsheet Launch was à la carte. . . .

I forget what the next two offerings were because I felt entitled to unfold the broadsheet to prepare for my own stage entrance and divined that I was third next. Reading the shite that would have to come out of my own mouth, I asked God to forgive my gloating over Maxie and to help me get through and I would never sin again.

It seemed that a second passed and Charlie Anka was at the rostrum introducing his 'Nihil'. Asked us all to bear with him. New to this business. Consider it an honour if the well-known writer Mr Junior Nash could convey some sense — or should he say senses? — of what he was aiming for, put it all straight down without thinking, thinking one night, couldn't sleep, where would we all be without God, if there was no one up there? Without further ado, ladies and gentlemen, Mr Junior Nash.

I folded the broadsheet as tenderly as I could so as not to put a crease in the parchment and I was distracted by Charlie's car logo at the bottom where he was prominently thanked as the sole sponsor. The delay, I fancied, might have been interpreted by the gallery as my indulgence in osmosis to ensure I did justice to the work, as might reasonably have been expected from someone in the business, from one whose alley it was right up.

'"Nihil",' I began, 'by Charles Anka.'

In my delivery I paused after every line or word, whichever was the longer. Or shorter.

> Nihil
> To know
> Knowing
> That
> In the knowing
> There
> Is
> No
> Knowing.

I looked up from the broadsheet and around the room at the attentive faces and I knew. I knew what was going to happen. I knew it in an instant. I knew it would happen in an instant. I had read so far brilliantly. Where there had been the odd uncontainable polite cough during the earlier readings, now all was so quiet I could hear Charlie Anka's heart beat. I could certainly hear it from the look on his face.

I ploughed on.

> To feel
> Feeling
> That
> In the feeling
> There
> Is
> No
> Feeling.

I felt. I felt a tear plop out of my eye. And I knew. I knew it was going to happen any second. It took only a second for me to tell myself that it was going to happen any second. . . . The tear was not for the shite as the mob surmised. It was for myself. Nobody had the right to tell me what was right up my alley. What was right up my alley was me down in a basement, writing. I owed it to myself now to defend my alley.

I tried to go on.

> To love
> Knowing
> That
> In
> The
> Loving
> There is the taste
> Of touch.

I owed it to Brother Chuckey, who beat *The Golden Treasury* into me. I owed it to the world.

>Not to hate
>Loving
>In the not hating.

And there I stopped. Cannily fingering the tear to buy time. The time to be seemingly overcome and roll up the broadsheet and carry it, walking slowly, through the attendance . . . until I turned and had my back to the near exit and positioned the broadsheet before my toe and executed a drop-kick that was successful in its soar and I roared, 'Fuck this shite', and added, because I had the floor, 'and Fuck the Banks.' Then I ran.

Before I reached the pub I, too, had been so infected that I composed:

>Sportsmen all
>They kept their eye on the ball
>As I ducked out the hall.

From *The Cove Shivering Club*, Fourth Estate Ltd, 1996

Acknowledgments

For permission to reproduce copyright material, grateful acknowledgment is made to the following:

Souvenir Press for an extract (pp 67–9) from *Collecting Irish Silver 1637–1900* by Douglas Bennett

Elsa Franklin for an extract (pp 110–13) from *The Last Spike* by Pierre Berton

Jeremy Sandford for extracts (pp 72, 76–9 & 106–7) from *The Farm by Lough Gur* by Mary Carbery

Oxford University Press for an extract (pp 221–3) from *The Irish Stage in the County Towns 1720 to 1800* by William Smith Clark

The O'Brien Press for extracts (pp 290–92 & 295–6) by Kathleen Clarke in *Revolutionary Woman: My Fight for Irish Freedom, Kathleen Clarke 1878–1972*

The Orion Publishing Group for an extract (pp 374–6) from *The Life and Times of a Teaboy* by Michael Collins

Poolbeg Group Services for an extract (pp 369–71) from *Wedlocked* by Emma Cooke

Poolbeg Group Services for extracts (pp 183–4 & 186–7) from *The Irish Lions 1896–1983* by Barry Coughlan

Fourth Estate Ltd for an extract (pp 371–2) from *The Plastic Tomato Cutter* © 1991 Michael Curtin; and an extract (pp 376–80) from *The Cove Shivering Club* © 1996 by Michael Curtin

The Newcastle West Historical Society and the estate of Robert J. Cussen deceased for an extract (pp 115–18) from *The Annual Observer* by Robert J. Cussen

Anvil Books for an extract (pp 307–8) from *True History of the Colleen Bawn* by Richard Fitzgerald

Cork University Press for an extract (pp 286–8) from *The Plan of Campaign 1886–1891* by Laurence M. Geary

Little, Brown for an extract (p. 42) from *The Fool's Pardon* by Kenneth Griffith

The Gallery Press for extracts (pp 34–5, 36, 88–9, 97–9 & 169) from *Collected Poems* and *Ó Bruadair: Translations from the Irish* by Michael Hartnett

Salmon Publishing for an extract (pp 292–5) from *The Betrayal* by Michael D. Higgins

David & Charles for an extract (pp 173–4) from *The Great Hunts* by Alastair Jackson

Maeve Kelly for extracts (pp 362–4 & 365–6) from *Necessary Treasons*

Poolbeg Group Services for extracts (pp 89–90 & 167–9) from *The People Who Drank Water from the River* by James Kennedy

Brendan Kennelly for his translation of 'The Shannon' (p. xviii)

Tralee VEC for an extract (pp 134–6) by Benedict Kiely in *Asylum*, Winter 1996

Salmon Publishing for an extract by James Liddy (pp 63–4) in *On the Counterscarp*

Anvil Books for an extract (pp 58–63) by Patrick Lynch from *Limerick's Fighting Story*

Blackwater Press for extracts (pp 95–7 & 130–32) from *Brief Lives of Irish Doctors* by J.B. Lyons

The Kerryman Ltd for an extract (pp 56–7) from *War by the Irish* by John McCann

HarperCollins Publishers for extracts (pp 260–62 & 263–4) from *Angela's Ashes* by Frank McCourt

Mainstream Publishing for extracts (181–2 & 183) from *The Complete Who's Who of Irish International Football, 1945–1996* by Stephen McGarrigle

Colin Smythe for an extract (p. 178) from *A Man May Fish* by T.C. Kingsmill Moore

Roger Moran for an extract (p. 86) from *The Wildfowler*

John O'Brien for extracts (pp 26–9, 31–3, 118–20, 232 & 345–9) from *Presentation Parlour, My Ireland* and *The Land of Spices* by Kate O'Brien

Colm O'Callaghan for an extract (pp 241–2) from *The Sunday Tribune*

Attic Press for an extract (pp 373–4) from *Belonging* by Clairr O'Connor

The Messenger for an extract (pp 274–5) by Cormac O'Connor

Cork University for an extract (pp 83–4) from *Syndicalism in Ireland 1917–1923* by Emmet O'Connor

Mercier Press for an extract (pp 87–8) from *The Days of the Servant Boy* by Liam O'Donnell

The Dedalus Press for an extract (p. 273–4) from *The Poet and His Shadow* by Ciaran O'Driscoll

Desmond O'Grady for extracts (pp 84–5, 122–4 & 137–8) from *The Dark Edge of Europe* and *A Memoir*

Críostóir Ó Floinn for extracts (pp 184–5 & 246–8) from *Centenary* and *The Bard of Thomond*

Poolbeg Group Services for an extract (p. 180) from *Over the Bar* by Breandán Ó hEithir

Mainchín Seoighe for extracts (pp 3–4 & 212–13) in *The Pope in Limerick* and *Castle Poets*

Ronan Sheehan for an extract (pp 338–40) from *Boy With An Injured Eye*

University of Ottawa Press for an extract (pp 354–6) by Leo Simpson in *The Lady and the Travelling Salesman* © University of Ottawa Press, 1976

Mercier Press for an extract (pp 236–7) from *John B: The Real Keane* by Gus Smith and Des Hickey

HarperCollins Publishers for extracts (pp 272–3 & 326–8) from *The Road to Roaringwater* by Christopher Somerville

Poolbeg Group Services for an extract (pp 233–6) from *Stage by Stage* by Carolyn Swift

Mark Tierney for an extract (pp 45–6) from *Glenstal Abbey: A Historical Guide*

Wolfhound Press for an extract (pp 333–5) from *The Return of Fursey* by Mervyn Wall

The publishers have used their best efforts to trace all copyright holders. They will, however, make the usual and appropriate arrangements with any who may have inadvertently been overlooked and who contact them.